STRATEGIC
SURVEY
1998/99

Published by
OXFORD
UNIVERSITY PRESS

for
**International Institute
for Strategic Studies**
23 Tavistock Street
London WC2E 7NQ

Strategic Survey 1998/99

Published by
OXFORD
UNIVERSITY PRESS

for
**International Institute
for Strategic Studies**
23 Tavistock Street,
London WC2E 7NQ

Director	Dr John Chipman
Editor	Sidney Bearman

Assistant Editor:
Maps	Dr Mats R. Berdal
Managing Editor	Susan Bevan
Research Assistant	Ellen Peacock

Design and Production ..... Mark Taylor

This publication has been prepared by the Director of the Institute and his Staff, who accept full responsibility for its contents, which describe and analyse events up to 26 March 1999. These do not, and indeed cannot, represent a consensus of views among the worldwide membership of the Institute as a whole.

First published .... May 1999

ISBN 0-19-922380-7
ISSN 0459-7230

Strategic Survey (ISSN 0459-7230) is published annually by Oxford University Press.

The 1999 annual subscription rate is: UK £29.00; overseas US$48.00.

Payment is required with all orders and subscriptions. Prices include air-speeded delivery to Australia, Canada, India, Japan, New Zealand and the USA. Delivery elsewhere is by surface mail. Air-mail rates are available on request. Payment may be made by cheque or Eurocheque (payable to Oxford University Press), National Girobank (account 500 1056), credit card (Access, Mastercard, Visa, American Express, Diner's Club), direct debit (please send for details) or UNESCO coupons. Bankers: Barclays Bank plc. PO Box 333, Oxford, UK, code 20-65-18, account 00715654.

Claims for non-receipt must be made within four months of dispatch/order (whichever is later).

Please send subscription orders to the Journals Subscription Department, Oxford University Press, Great Clarendon Street, Oxford, OX2 6DP, UK. *Tel* +44 (0) 1865 267907. *Fax* +44 (0) 1865 267485. *e-mail* jnlorders@oup.co.uk

Strategic Survey is distributed by M.A.I.L. America, 2323 Randolph Avenue, Avenel, NJ 07001, USA. Periodical postage paid at Newark, New Jersey, USA and additional entry points.

US POSTMASTER: Send address corrections to *Strategic Survey*, c/o M.A.I.L. America, 2323 Randolph Avenue, Avenel, NJ 07001, USA.

PRINTED IN THE UK by Bell & Bain Ltd, Glasgow.

Contents

List of Tables, Figures and Maps

Perspectives

After ten years of the unambitiously named 'post-Cold War' world, it appeared in 1998 that a new era might be defined around the first global crisis of capitalism. In the event, the buffers of the international economic system worked, and the essential political and economic realities of the pre-crisis order were, if anything, enhanced. While there were some local political effects of the economic crisis in Asia, there was no generalised international security drama. Little, if any, of the military conflict that took place in 1998–99 owed its origins to the economic and financial disturbances.

Links between economics and security notwithstanding, all the important challenges to security emanating from Iraq, the Balkans, Africa, South Asia or the Korean peninsula continued according to their own logic and along their own routes. Despite talk of the economic crisis spreading, there was no global collapse, even if there were regional tremors, of the edifice of capitalism. Against the experience of 1998–99 two pre-existing trends were solidly confirmed: with only one great power, regional conflict will remain regional, and its intensity will remain configured by the presence or absence of an American will to intervene. Similarly, global capitalism remains a robust force that cannot be easily shaken by a regional crisis. Of course, it did not always look that way.

Crisis, What Crisis?

It was, according to US President Bill Clinton, the most serious challenge to face the international financial system for 50 years. In a rare moment of unambiguous exasperation, Alan Greenspan, Chairman of the American Federal Reserve, confessed he had never seen anything like it. Phrases such as 'global meltdown' were muttered by securities and currency traders frozen in front of bewildering computer screens. 'Deflationary spirals' swirled out of East Asia; comparisons were drawn with the late 1920s and the Great Depression that followed; the entire edifice of the postwar economic order, and its multilateral cornerstones, the World Bank and the International Monetary Fund (IMF), was, by common consent, outdated and in need of rebuilding; a new buzz-phrase entered the communiqués of international summitry: 'reform of the global financial architecture'.

That, in any event, was how it all looked for a few weeks in autumn 1998, following Russia's default on some of its sovereign debts in August, and the market panic caused when a prestigious hedge-fund was forced, the next month, to be rescued by some of its creditors. By the next spring, however, it was almost as if this had never happened. The American economy, much the world's largest, had by then entered its longest peacetime expansion – 96 consecutive months of growth in gross domestic product (GDP), including an astonishing 6.1% growth in the final quarter of 1998. It was striking for a record; with just another few months of growth, it would overtake even the Vietnam War-era boom of the 1960s.

The big American and European banks, whose health was thought to be vulnerable to the mayhem, reported, by and large, slower growth in their profits than their shareholders might have liked. But, despite a wave of bank mergers (usually more as a long-planned response to competitive pressures than a panicky huddling together for safety), no major financial institution collapsed. The American stock market, and some markets in Europe, were flirting with the record highs set in summer 1998. The greatest international monetary experiment ever undertaken – the launch of the euro – had been smoother than many feared. Brazil, the world's eighth- or ninth-largest economy (depending on the measure), had come close to collapse, but had failed to rattle the apparently serene confidence of investors elsewhere. True, much of the world, including Europe, was, at best, locked into a period of slower growth; at worst, into a wrenching recession, as in Japan and much of East Asia. But even there optimists saw signs of recovery.

So was President Clinton simply over-reacting to the hysterical fears of a few Wall Street financiers and the man some see as their representative in Washington, Robert Rubin, the Treasury Secretary? Was it as misguided an assessment as his characterisation, a year earlier, of Asia's financial troubles as 'a few glitches in the road'? Or, alternatively, have the few months following his warning been those of a phoney war – a lull before the financial carnage feared last year breaks out again in earnest?

These questions have a bearing not just on the perception of the economic risks facing the world; self-evidently, one would also expect them to have political and security implications. The threat of global depression is not one that can be taken lightly. The Great Depression did not only cause economic misery in some of the richest countries in the world, as the economy of the United States shrank 30% from 1930 to 1933. It also nurtured fascism and communism in Europe and Asia; isolationism and nationalism; and, ultimately, the Second World War. Even the gloomiest forecasters now do not anticipate either such complete economic devastation, or such drastic political outcomes. In fact, the economic upheaval that began with the forced devaluation of the Thai *baht* in July 1997, has had only the most marginal impact on the security map, even of the countries and regions worst affected: notably East Asia and Russia.

Before, however, considering the security implications of these seemingly uncontrollable economic and financial forces, it is important to consider the nature of the 'crisis' that provoked such alarm and the competing diagnoses of what caused it; the ideas, or lack of them, about how to fix it and prevent it happening again; and the perceptible fault-lines that might yet cause all those gloomy prognostications to come true.

Diagnoses and Cures

'Crisis' – in the strict sense of the term, a decisive moment or turning-point – has long been a misnomer for the financial markets' behaviour since mid-1997. Rather, this has been a series of financial crises, which have broken out like aftershocks from an earthquake, ever further from their original epicentre. Each individual crisis has taken the form of a few days of drama on the foreign exchanges and stock markets, each of which has had some global repercussions. It has then been succeeded by a period of relative calm. But in every country affected (with the exception of the US), it has left economic destruction which may take years to clear up.

Whether or not the last of this spate of 'crises' has settled, few doubt that another will occur at some point in the future – it is seen as inherent in the current architecture of the world economy. This widely held belief marks a considerable shift from the conventional wisdom of summer 1997. Then, there were, broadly speaking, two prevalent explanations for the calamity that had hit East Asia. The dominant belief in the financial capitals of the Western world, and even in the region itself, was that the affected countries – at the time, Thailand, the Philippines, Indonesia and Malaysia – were facing a painful but necessary period of adjustment that they had brought upon themselves. They had borrowed too much, invested the money unwisely, and could not cope with the consequences of an inevitable slowdown in the hectic rates of economic growth they had enjoyed for a decade.

The second, minority view – articulated most ferociously by Malaysia's Prime Minister Mahathir Mohamad – saw the trouble as the fault not of the countries themselves but of the international financial system, which placed too much power in the hands of unaccountable and mysterious money-managers. At best, the sheer volume of capital whizzing across borders was a source of instability. At worst, there was a conspiracy by the rich powers to keep a resurgent Asia (and especially China) in its impoverished place.

Mahathir's outbursts – coloured by a post-colonial grudge that at times seemed to encompass xenophobia and even anti-Semitism – seemed easy to dismiss as the sour grapes of a cranky financial illiterate. But the 'crisis' was not, as some confidently predicted at the time 'over by Christmas'. Rather, after starting in Thailand, and spreading quickly to its South-east Asian neighbours, it engulfed South Korea in November and December. Thailand's Prime Minister Chuan Leekpai, remarked, rather touchingly, that the vulnerability of such a large economy (the eleventh biggest in the world) showed the trouble could not be all Thailand's fault.

In January 1998, currencies, which had seemed to have reached a ledge in their precipitous descent, came under pressure again, as political worries led to the collapse of the Indonesian *rupiah*. As the year progressed, the Hong Kong dollar came under repeated attack, and that economy too plunged into recession. China avoided a sharp slowdown in its own economy (though perhaps not by as much as its official statistics, which recorded a GDP growth rate of nearly 8% in 1998, might suggest); but there were recurrent fears that it might be forced to devalue its currency, the *yuan*, triggering a new round of competitive devaluations. Contagion was felt in Eastern Europe and Latin America, prompting, by November, a huge 'preventive' rescue package from the IMF to shore up Brazil's finances. In August, Russia had defaulted on its government debt, with drastic effects on credit and currency markets around the world. Within a three-day period in October, the market trading the Japanese *yen* against the US dollar – arguably the world's most liquid – moved an astonishing 20%. Some of the world's most important financial markets were barely functioning.

As a result, what was at first diagnosed as a sickness suffered by some countries in Asia which had been pursuing dangerous lifestyles, became interpreted more broadly, as a crisis of global capitalism. Asia's troubles were no longer the disease itself, which carrier countries had transmitted to their neighbours and beyond through a process of epidemic contagion. Rather, they were no more than a symptom of a more fundamental malaise. The Asian countries seemed less villains than victims; condemned to years of economic misery because of their misplaced faith in the virtues of capital mobility, free markets and the global economy. Though few in the West would acknowledge it, there was a tacit, grudging admission contained in this interpretation that, while Mahathir may have gone over the top, he did have a point. Figures as improbable and diverse as the new German Chancellor Gerhard Schröder, and the hedge-fund operator George Soros (the money manager who had been the target of Mahathir's wrath) echoed his views that unbridled capital flows demanded some form of regulatory change.

Whereas, at the outset, most thinkers in the West were content to blame the region's troubles on mistaken economic policies, and, increasingly, on the flawed and corrupt social and political systems which produced them, the minority view gained ground: that Asia's troubles showed up a more fundamental deficiency in global economic management. Yet the cocksure analysis spouted at the beginning of the crisis was not born out of stupidity. In Thailand, at least, the financial markets saw it coming. The surprise was only in the extent of the disaster, and the speed of contagion elsewhere. But even when the Asian countries were widely seen as guilty of bringing their own houses down, there were two distinct strands to the conventional wisdom about why. At first, analysis concentrated on macro-economic problems and misguided policies in the countries affected – current account deficits, manufacturing overcapacity, uncompetitive export industries, property bubbles and so on. The second phase, however, stressed the business and political cultures of these countries – usefully summed up in the slogan of the protest movement, first against former President Suharto in Indonesia and, more recently, against Mahathir in Malaysia – corruption, collusion and nepotism. In short, these countries' economies had collapsed because they had pursued the wrong policies; and they had pursued the wrong policies because, basically, everybody in the most powerful decision-making positions was on the take.

It is worth remembering now, that, back where it all began, in Thailand, events did seem perfectly explicable in domestic terms at first. By the beginning of 1996, there were already worries about a property bubble in Bangkok and a related bad-debt problem in the Thai banking system. The sharp strengthening in the US dollar (whose value the *baht*, like other currencies in the region, tracked) had dented the competitive edge of regional exports, and so widened current account deficits – especially in Thailand and Malaysia. Meanwhile, high interest rates needed to protect the Thai currency, and relatively liberal rules introduced in 1993 allowing local banks to borrow in US dollars and lend in *baht*, encouraged reckless foreign borrowing. Something had to give. It was the abrupt and violent way in which the exchange rate snapped and the speed with which other countries were forced to follow suit that was surprising.

One could still make a strong case for the macro-economic explanation of all this: indeed, Professor Paul Krugman, an American economist, had, as early as 1994, famously warned that economic growth in the region was fuelled by massive increases in inputs of labour and capital – which were not sustainable – rather than of productivity – which might be. This arrangement could not withstand external shocks: notably the strength of the dollar. But even Krugman admits that he was no more than a little bit right: he foresaw a slowdown, not a screeching lunge into reverse.

Soon, however, outsiders – and many nations in the region – were stressing another, domestic, reason for the disaster: the corrupt links between business and politics. It was in Indonesia that the political consequences of economic collapse were most drastic. This was partly because that economy suffered more than any other. But also because Indonesia's political system was the most rigid, and the most obviously bound up with the causes of economic ruin, due to the commercial dominance of the family and friends of the president.

But if Indonesia was the most acute case, it was by no means alone. In all of South-east Asia, with the exception of Singapore, corruption was deeply embedded. President Suharto's efforts to sabotage reform, thereby further undermining confidence in Indonesia's economy, were the most egregious. But they could also be seen even in Thailand, which, almost by default, became cast as the IMF's model prisoner. Thailand's parliament, for example, has long stalled in passing a foreclosure law, which had become identified as a key test of sincerity in pursuing reform. At the end of March 1999, any creditor seeking to get his hands on the collateral backing a defaulted loan had to wait five years. If, after four years and eleven months, the defaulter made a token payment, the clock started ticking again. Why the delay in improving such bad legislation? Perhaps because many of those sitting in parliament were at risk of foreclosure themselves.

Certainly, corruption and all that goes with it were big factors in what went wrong in Asia. So too were defects in regulation, supervision and the law. As is often noted, capitalism without bankruptcy is like Christianity without Hell. But these problems had always been there. If anything, they were getting smaller, not bigger. (Indonesia may have been the exception. There, with the death of their mother in 1996, President Suharto's children seemed to lose all sense, if not of decency – they may never have had any – then at least of how the public regarded their greed.) But nothing fundamental had changed that would provide a plausible explanation for the sudden economic shock. No international investor who knew the region woke up one morning, opened his newspaper, suddenly learnt to his horror that some Asians were corrupt, and took his money out.

Everybody's Problem

But take it out they did – portfolio investors, bankers, hedge funds. An inflow of capital to the region of $95 billion in 1996 turned into a net outflow in the next two years. To some extent, all 'emerging markets' suffered from the loss of confidence. There was a 'flight to safety' – seen as lying in the much larger markets of the West. Although those markets did at times suffer sudden downward lurches in response to the steady flow of grim news out of Asia – most notably in October 1997 – they usually were quick to recover their poise. It was only in autumn 1998, when those markets too began to seem on the brink of collapse, that the 'crisis' came to be seen as truly global.

The central event of this stage was the near-collapse, in September, of an American hedge fund – Long-Term Capital Management (LTCM). That, in turn, was in part a consequence of Russia's default on its debts the previous month. Although Russia's economy is not large, the exposure to it of a number of international financial institutions led to a scramble to unwind positions in a number of markets. LTCM, although it will be remembered as a fund almost crazily exposed to risk, was in many ways a conservative institution. It took huge bets, to be sure, but they would generally have been regarded as safe ones (for example, that, in the run-up to European monetary union, the yields paid on bonds in different euro-zone countries would converge). For that reason, the profit in such positions was not enormous – unless, through borrowing, LTCM's investment of capital in them was multiplied several times. That was the fund's problem, and, when the bets went wrong, LTCM found itself unable to borrow more to pay back its debts. The traditional herd instincts of lenders and investors had driven many of them to take the same positions in the same markets. When things went wrong, there was nobody on the other side to sell to. In small markets, like those in South-east Asia, this has the effect of magnifying the impact of a change in market perceptions to unbearable levels. Even in rich-world credit markets it had the effect of pushing up borrowing costs to what would have seemed, just a few months earlier, absurd levels.

LTCM was run by the 'rocket scientists' of international capital. Two Nobel Prize-winning economists and perhaps the most famous bond-trader Wall Street has produced had gathered around them the best and brightest of the computer-driven world of high finance. Yet they got it – spectacularly – wrong. The American authorities were sufficiently worried about the potential impact this might have on other institutions, to organise a rescue. The episode had revealed a ghastly secret: that, in conditions of extreme market volatility, the 'value-at-risk' models, which banks and others use to calculate their exposure to risky and sophisticated instruments like some financial derivatives, simply did not work. Unsurprisingly, a whole range of markets more or less dried up for a few weeks. American regulators found themselves in the bizarre position of encouraging banks to take more risks, even though they acknowledged that the ways they measured risk were fundamentally deficient.

This might seem to be an entirely different set of – largely technical – problems from the macro-economic, cultural and political factors identified as having tipped some Asian countries off the cliff. Some senior figures in the financial markets, however, saw it as part of the same phenomenon. Not only were markets everywhere vulnerable to upsets, even in relatively small corners of the financial world, because of the complex interlinking of global asset allocation; they were all prone to the same folly – the 'mispricing of risk'. The long period of economic expansion had forced down the cost of capital, not just for roaring Asian tigers, but for American corporations, financial institutions, and those taking arcane risks in complex financial derivative products. Money had become too cheap to protect the financial system against the risks it was taking. Yet to make money more expensive – most importantly, by an increase in interest rates from the American Federal Reserve – might itself precipitate financial meltdown. Liquidity in important markets – notably in bonds – dried up alarmingly for a few weeks in autumn 1998. To tighten monetary policy would have been disastrous. But to loosen it, as the Federal Reserve did repeatedly, meant the risk of adding fuel to a dangerous fire.

The Fire Brigade

If, by the end of 1998, it was clear that 'something must be done', there was no consensus about what, or by whom, or who should decide. The topic dominated the agendas of international conclaves like the G7 group of rich countries; the somewhat larger G10 gatherings of central-bank governors and finance ministers; the G22, which includes some developing countries; the IMF's policy-making 'interim committee'; the Asia Pacific Economic Cooperation forum; the Basel Committee of financial overlords; and so on.

Change was made difficult by the broad membership of the 'Bretton Woods' institutions, the IMF and the World Bank. To amend their charters would require the consent of all members (and, often, of their parliaments). More important, there was disagreement about what, if any, new powers these institutions should enjoy. After all, the World Bank and the IMF could not agree with each other about the approach to the 'crisis' so far. In December 1998, the World Bank's *Global Economic Prospects*, was, implicitly, highly critical of the IMF's policies during the Asian crisis. The next month, the IMF's own internal evaluation of its role did admit some mistakes – but largely in not having been rigorous enough in enforcing some of its more controversial precepts (especially the raising of domestic interest rates to protect the value of a rapidly depreciating currency).

The most fundamental proposed change was to transform the IMF into a more formal 'lender of last resort' for the world. But the difficulties in such an arrangement are legion.

- The IMF does not have the supervisory and regulatory powers wielded by national central banks, and few countries would be prepared to cede them.

- Some degree of conditionality would have to attach to IMF lending, or the 'moral hazard', already identified as a serious impediment to prudent borrowing (and, more importantly, lending) would be much greater.

- So it would demand far greater 'transparency' from countries 'pre-qualifying' for an IMF bail-out (though transparency itself might cause as many panics as it averted).

- At a time when the IMF has faced brickbats from both conservative congressmen, incensed at the perceived bailing-out of corrupt and incompetent foreign regimes, and liberals, angered at the hardship IMF policies have caused, anyone proposing further large increases in IMF resources would face a hard time in the legislature of its largest single shareholder – the United States.

Certainly, the IMF's first effort at a new way of handling financial crises was hardly an outstanding success. The package of $41.5bn in rescue funds (including $18.1bn from the Fund itself), announced for Brazil in November 1998, differed from earlier rescues in that it was designed to be pre-emptive. The Brazilian currency, the *real*, was perceived to be vulnerable to speculative attack from abroad and domestic capital flight. Its value was determined by a 'crawling peg' to the US dollar (rather as Indonesia's had been), allowing a steady devaluation. Nevertheless, it was thought to be overvalued, partly because of structural economic problems in the country's finances – notably the government's huge fiscal deficit.

The IMF's programme nevertheless backed the defence of the peg, which was seen as important to confidence in Brazil, and hence to the economies of the continent it dominates. Two months later, Brazil was forced to abandon the peg anyway. Within weeks, the *real* lost 40% of its value. IMF and American officials could point out that, when this happened, there was no global panic, whereas, in the far more nervous climate of a few weeks earlier, the international repercussions might have been disastrous. But to proffer so much money and credibility in merely staving-off the inevitable is hardly an advertisement for the new approach.

Some, more modest, steps towards architectural reform were taken. In particular, there was a proliferation of meetings considering global financial regulation – issues such as the minimum levels of capital that banks should retain against the risks they take on; the provisions for rescheduling private-sector lending; the monitoring of bank exposure to risk-taking institutions such as hedge funds; the quicker reporting of national foreign-debt volumes. All of this fell far short of the demands of those, like Mahathir, who had called for global regulation of capital flows, or those who backed the idea of a tax (named after one proponent, the economist James Tobin) on foreign-exchange dealings. It was less a grand redesign of the architecture; more a fiddly plumbing job. But, by spring 1999, as a calmer mood prevailed, it seemed that maybe this was all that was required.

Living with Fragility

Or maybe not. The global economy had not recovered its poise, and the period of stability seemed frangible. Yet the risks now are very different from those that seemed to threaten at the onset of the Asian crisis. Indeed, South-east Asia itself rarely features in the list of the most pressing issues facing international economic policymakers. It is no longer seen as the core of the problem, or even as its cause; rather it has become an early casualty in a struggle between much bigger and more important financial imbalances. The containment of the Brazilian devaluation marked a new stage in the crisis-series: where the focus of concern has shifted from the impact of events in 'peripheral' countries, such as Thailand or Russia, on bigger markets, to the health of the world's largest economies themselves. There are four major geographical concerns.

The United States

The strength of the US economy has been a wonder to behold. It has constantly confounded the expectations of both sceptical foreigners, and its own, cautious, central bankers at the Federal Reserve. Yet it still seemed unlikely, in early 1999, that it could defy gravity forever. Two aspects caused particular concern: a mounting current-account deficit, which may reach $300bn in 1999; and what appears to many observers to be a dangerously over-valued stock market.

The external deficit is the flip-side of a domestic phenomenon: Americans' refusal to save. Both individuals and the private sector as a whole (that is, including companies) have become net borrowers. It is their spending – primarily on consumption, but also on investment – that accounts for most of the remarkable growth rate. As with all borrowing binges, it seems improbable that this one can last forever.

One reason for Americans' high-spending ways is that many of them feel wealthy from the long boom in the stock market. In early 1999, this stood near historic highs both in terms of share-prices' relationship to corporate profits, and in the ratio of total stock market capitalisation to GDP (over 150%). The easing of monetary policy in late 1998 had succeeded in stopping the slide in share values that accompanied the Russian and LTCM crises. But even Alan Greenspan fretted, repeatedly, that they were now too high. Shares in Internet companies, in particular, were at valuations that had no relationship at all to profits (which, often, did not exist). Optimists argued that this was a normal reaction to a technological revolution. Pessimists countered that the very nature of this revolution meant that success by one company would be easily duplicated by another, and that the mania for Internet shares had all the characteristics of a bubble.

Japan

While worries about the US focus on the possible bursting of a bubble, in Japan they centre on the difficulty of putting the economy back together after the deflation of a bubble a decade ago. In 1998, the Japanese economy shrank by about 2.6% – the largest single-year contraction experienced by a G7 country since the Second World War. There was some hope that the Japanese government had finally responded to pressure to take the drastic steps necessary to reverse the decline: massive injections of public money into public works and the banking system; the restructuring of bankrupt financial institutions and their insolvent borrowers; and an easing of monetary policies.

The problem is the mirror image of America's: whereas Americans will not save, Japanese will not spend. Rising unemployment, a demographic bulge in those approaching retirement-age, and growing expectations of falling prices, all militate against the success of the measures demanded of the government. So does the reluctance of the Japanese central bank to print money to finance the ballooning national debt. It fears, with some justification, that such a policy, while it might put paid to concern about deflation, would do so at the expense of uncontrollable inflation and a plunging *yen*. And that, in turn, would exacerbate the tensions caused by Japan's huge trade surplus with the US.

In early 1999, there were some signs that the fiscal stimulus of the previous year was beginning to work its way through the system, and that the recession might be halted, or at least slowed down. However, the struc-tural problems of the banking sector, and the chronic overcapacity of manufacturing industry have not been solved. The hope that Japan will, in the next few years, become the locomotive of regional recovery, seems forlorn.

China

Beijing's refusal to devalue its currency in the face of the Asian crisis was not, as it is often presented, an altruistic gesture towards the global financial system. Success in bringing down inflation, and, since early 1998, quite sharply falling prices, have mitigated the loss of competitiveness of China's exports. Tax rebates to exporters amounted to another, covert, form of devaluation. And when, in late 1998, the bankruptcy of the Guangdong International Trust and Investment Corporation (GITIC), highlighted the difficulties of a number of such provincial-level international borrowers, there was another reason to maintain the value of the *yuan*. Devaluation would increase the cost of foreign debts in *yuan* terms.

But, even from the murky evidence of Chinese statistics, it is clear that the economy is slowing. This is likely to impede efforts to reform state-owned industry, much of which is loss-making, and kept afloat only at the expense of a terrifying level of non-performing loans in the banking system. Should mounting unemployment lead to social unrest on a significant scale, the leadership might be forced to contemplate drastic measures to boost the economy, including devaluation.

Europe

The launch of the euro went so smoothly that within two months opinion polls in Britain, that most euro-sceptic (in all senses) of nations, were moving towards a majority in favour of signing up to the common currency. But in the same period, some of the predictable tensions caused by the sharing of a single currency across 11 countries had already appeared. The most important were between the differing economic requirements of individual countries themselves, and between their governments as a group and the requirement of the European Central Bank (ECB), which, under the Maastricht treaty, they had given almost unique independence, to be guided solely by an inflation target in setting euro-zone monetary policy.

Tensions between the countries were inevitable in the early years of the euro. There was a marked difference between the economic growth rates of some smaller countries, such as Ireland, which were booming, and the larger core countries, such as Germany, which were close to recession. The troubles with the Central Bank, on the other hand, reflected design faults in the currency itself. While the ECB has the freedom to set interest rates unfettered by political constraints, a 'stability pact' also restricts the amounts governments can borrow and the fiscal deficits they can run (to avoid profligate national administrations undermining the common currency). So governments which might previously have been expected to provide a fiscal boost to their economies to prevent too sharp a slowdown, find themselves hamstrung. Inevitably, they have resorted to appealing to the ECB to ease monetary policy, and to start managing the value of the currency, at times, by reference to 'target zones' against the dollar and the *yen*. These are more than just the unavoidable teething troubles of the euro's early years. They are inbuilt structural tensions, which may well be manageable if a deep recession is avoided, but which otherwise may become fierce

But might trouble in any of these economies lead to another Great Depression? It seems unlikely, though there is evidence of two of the dangers that afflicted the world in the 1930s. The first is deflation. By the end of 1998, prices were falling in Japan, China and much of South-east Asia, despite sharp devaluations and hence rising import costs. Even in much of Europe and some of Latin America, inflation had disappeared if measured month by month. In the US, the long boom failed to provide the expected inflationary pressures, although real wages rose at their highest rate for 26 years, and the unemployment rate was at its lowest level for 28 years. Commodity prices were, in real terms, at their lowest levels in more than 150 years.

This is not, in itself, a bad thing. It is perverse, after lamenting for so long the damage wrought by the long post-war inflation, to start hand-wringing about deflationary dangers the moment it seems to be ending. Some of the downward pressure on prices comes from technological advance and reduced barriers to trade, which, presumably, are to be welcomed. But in some places – particularly Japan – there are less benign forces at work: chronic industrial overcapacity; a slump in demand; a mounting burden of debt as repayments cost more in real terms; and a self-reinforcing spiral of falling prices and lower output.

The second danger is protectionist trade policies, which exacerbated the slump in the 1930s. Superficially, similar policy mistakes seem improbable now. Much of the world is bound into the liberalising agenda of the World Trade Organisation, and both the US and Europe support a new 'millennium' round of trade talks. But there are signs that protectionist forces are gathering strength in response to the flood of cheap imports from Asia. They are seen in the proliferation of anti-dumping suits brought by not just the big developed economies but by a growing number of emerging markets too. In his State of the Union speech in January 1999, President Clinton's promise of a new trade round was greeted with polite silence. Applause was reserved for his promise to take action against an influx of steel imports.

The Dogs of War that Did Not Bark

Given the turmoil in the global economy, and the fashionable talk of globalisation, one would have expected a wide range of military implications from economic unrest. In the event, not much has happened that is not explicable by trends already well underway before the crises in emerging markets began.

The most significant area where economic crisis might have been expected to lead to major security risks was Russia. Indeed, it was just such worries that led Western governments and international institutions to continue to prop up the Russian economy well beyond the point of economic rationality. But the balance of argument in favour of bail outs for Russia shifted with some speed as the crises in East Asia demonstrated that the success of economic reform needed to be linked to political reform. The mismanagement, profligacy and corruption demonstrated by the Russian élite have exceeded anything seen in South-east Asia. Unlike even Suharto's Indonesia, the country has defaulted on its debts, and risks becoming a financial outcast. Its rulers seem to have taken to heart the message of those who dubbed the country 'Indonesia with nukes' – that it was too important and too dangerous to be allowed to fail. Now that it, in effect, has failed, there are divided views on whether this makes it a more or less frightening member of the international community.

On the negative side are the implications of empty government coffers for the maintenance of a large nuclear arsenal. In early 1999, American experts were in Russia to help fix 'millennium bug' problems in Russian military computers. But Americans and Europeans had been helping Russia sustain its military scientists for nearly a decade – ever since it was recognised that there could be a major strategic problem if Russian expertise in weapons of mass destruction were sold to the highest bidder around the world. Hundreds of millions of dollars have been spent to keep Russian scientists at home, and it was hoped that collaboration in space exploration would give Russians renewed pride in their technological prowess. The economic crisis makes all these endeavours both harder and more necessary, but remedial efforts are already well underway. Having allowed Russia to fail, it has been a pleasant surprise, so far, that there has been no sudden outflow of 'loose nukes' and 'loose scientists'.

In fact, the economic crisis has had some beneficial effects on Western attitudes towards Russia as a security threat. Financial constraints have clearly impeded the modernisation of Russia's military capabilities. Apart from the introduction of the *Topol* M intercontinental ballistic missile system, the Russian armed forces have not deployed any new major weapons systems for several years. Even before the 1998 implosion, the number of naval ships was halved during 1990–95. According to estimates by the US Central Intelligence Agency, even the 1997 military budget authorised expenditure of only $18bn, roughly 7% of that allowed the American forces. Russia may even have to reduce its strategic arsenal below the ceiling imposed by the Strategic Arms Reduction Treaty (START) II, whether or not it decides to ratify the treaty. It is hard to see a Russia that cannot impose its will on Chechnya as a major threat to countries that lie between its borders and NATO states. The result is a real peace dividend for Europeans and indeed for nearly all of Russia's neighbours.

The biggest danger, however, is less strategic than political – that economic hardship fosters the popularity of xenophobic nationalist politicians, prone to foreign-policy obstructionism But even this nightmare scenario seems to be remote. The favoured successor to President Boris Yeltsin, at least according to public opinion polls, seems to be the current Prime Minister Yevgeny Primakov who is something close to an avatar of the old, bureaucratic/communist order.

Those who worry about the collapse of big countries move quickly from Russia to China and claim to see signs that the economic crisis is leading to dangerous tendencies in Beijing's empire. But, once again, the truth is far more complex. China's economy is clearly approaching crisis, but it is caused only in part by the economic tribulations of its neighbours. The loss of export markets has hit one of the most dynamic sectors of the Chinese economy, but the root causes of China's economic crisis lie much deeper, in its persistent failure to move to the next, and tougher stages of reform. Stagnation in reform of the bankrupt banking system, and reluctance to extend the reforms to the state-owned enterprises are the real causes of China's weakness.

In such difficult times, the government may be tempted to rally support around a nationalist cause. It has one ready to hand: the unresolved status of Taiwan. In early 1999, American sources revealed that China planned a large build up in its missile deployments close to the island. Given the ambiguous position of the US towards the defence of the island, the issue remains one of the biggest threats to world peace. But the Taiwan problem long predated the economic crisis, and the most serious threat in Asia this generation – the missile crisis of 1996 – came more than a year before the economic collapse. Thus, while economic woes can exaggerate security worries, so far, the basic realities of security have not changed.

This pattern is even more striking in the rest of East Asia and particularly in Indonesia. Given the depths of the economic crisis, one might have anticipated mass riots, civil disorder and ethnic violence. What has been remarkable is how quiet the streets have been in most of the region. No red flags fly, no communist guerrillas head to the hills and, for the most part, minority populations have not been made scapegoats. East Asians have been astoundingly mature in blaming their own autocrats for the problems and, where possible (in Thailand and South Korea), turfing out the culprits.

The exception that more than proves the rule is Indonesia. Here there were major riots and attacks on ethnic Chinese, Christians and other minorities. But the result was not a descent into complete chaos, and certainly nothing like the violence of 1965, when almost a million were slaughtered in the aftermath of the coup that overthrew former President Sukarno. In fact, the present dictator was ousted through a version of 'people power' and, even though the succession to a more reformist regime is far from certain, the trend is certainly in the right direction. Signs of reformist thinking are even evident on issues like East Timor, holding out the prospect of reduced tension in an area of long-standing concern. What has been happening, in fact, seems to reinforce an old Chinese cliché: crisis is best seen as a mixture of danger and opportunity.

If the impact of the economic crisis on security is not evident in specific regions, what is the risk that it could shift the broad balance of power? There is little doubt that financial-market turmoil has already led to greater resentment of the role played by the world's only remaining military and economic superpower. Indeed, the economic crisis, by diminishing both Russia and China, has even enhanced the American profile, making it a more obvious target for sniping from lesser powers. Anti-American attitudes are already evident in, for example, the IMF-bashing rhetoric of opposition politicians in Thailand, as well as in Malaysia's decision to impose capital controls in September 1998. Similarly, the moratorium imposed by State Governor Itamar Franco of Minas Gerais in Brazil, and some other state governments, on debt payments to the federal authorities, played on a populist suspicion of IMF motives and the US, which is seen as its paymaster. Even in the developed world, something of the same feeling emerged: certainly in Japan, worn down by perpetual complaints about its economic policy from an overbearing American partner; and even in Europe, faced by American criticism for its failure to bear enough of the 'burden' of reviving world growth through increasing imports.

Some ill-will towards such a successful global leader is perhaps inevitable, but its impact on the balance of power and global strategic manoeuvres is still hard to find. For all their complaints about the US, Asians have mainly blamed their own people for their problems. As recovery seems slowly to emerge, there is grudging understanding that, if the US had not led the IMF and other institutions in a recovery plan, however tardy or riddled with inconsistencies, recovery might have been even more distant. It may be merely a vignette, but the fact that Shanghai and Hong Kong are competing to be the site for the new regional Disney theme park suggests that even the icon of American capitalism is still very welcome.

A potentially more significant area of competition with US power comes from Europe, but with only the smallest connection to the economic crisis. The creation of a single European currency clearly has the potential to create a major shift of economic and political power to the European Union. But in the short term, the creation of the euro has merely highlighted why even Europe is not a rival to the US in anything except trade disputes. The absence of a coherent common European foreign and security policy is glaring. Even in economic terms, the combination of an independent European Central Bank and constraints on deficit spending in individual countries is creating major asymmetric shocks to the European economy and its single currency. With Germany hobbled by slower growth because of structural rigidities in its economy, the EU is in no position to lead, let alone be a rival to the US. To the extent that the structural weaknesses of the German economy make it more susceptible to the effects of the crises in emerging markets, one could even argue that the economic crisis has strengthened the unipolarity of the unipolar power.

And yet it may just be a 'unipolar moment', with the long-term trend being the emergence of competition between different varieties of capitalism. As with its political ideology, the US tends to believe that its economic model (confusingly called 'anglo-saxon') is of universal applicability. This model, in ideal terms, favours unrestricted market competition as the best route to economic efficiency and universal prosperity. But in Japan, parts of continental Europe and much of the developing world, it is still rejected. Rightly or wrongly, it is seen as leading to increased inequality within and between nations, unacceptable levels of lawlessness, an unacceptable level of job insecurity, and inadequate 'social safety nets' for those who lose out.

It Could Have Been Worse

The Asian currency turmoil of 1997–98 was identified as one of the first crises of globalisation because it drew attention to the inter-relatedness of financial markets, the global nature of financial asset allocation, and the sheer speed with which rootless money rushes around the world. The Asian countries had been among the advertisements for globalisation – securing unheard-of rates of wealth-creation by plugging themselves into the international system. With the partial exception of Malaysia, none has responded to the crisis by unplugging itself. Among political élites, at least, there is recognition that the process of internationalisation is irreversible.

Of course there will be a debate about the extent to which globalisation entails globally uniform economic, social and political frameworks, if only because the emergence and success of global capitalism has depended on constant debate and refinement through competition that is often destructive. But the crisis or, more properly, what turned out to be a series of mini-crises, actually demonstrates just how well the current, post-Cold War, order works. The buffers in the system absorbed serious shocks and economic leadership was, for the most part, wise.

In terms of the balance of power, the realities seem much as they have been for nearly a decade – a peerless United States, a rapidly rusting Russia, and a still inchoate Europe. Uncertainties surround China – the only country with the long-term potential to compete with the US on equal terms. But as 1998 ended, it seemed clear that, even though China was a non-status quo power opposed to many US strategic interests, the gap between Chinese and American power was widening, not closing. Just as global economic collapse no longer seemed threatened by probable continuing regional economic difficulties, the certainty of continuing regional conflicts did not threaten to overwhelm global security.

●

Strategic Policy Issues

Transatlantic Defence Industry: Fortresses or Integration?

As militaries shrink and most defence budgets decline, one of the central challenges facing Europe and the US is the future of the industries that provide technology and equipment to the forces of the Atlantic Alliance and to the world market. Defence industries on both sides of the Atlantic were simply too large at the end of the 1980s for the reduced demand for their products. Moreover, as the new decade opened, industries supporting defence were changing in two key ways: they were becoming more global and more commercial in nature.

For much of the 1990s, the defence industries on both sides of the Atlantic have been consolidating. The headlines have been dominated by the moves made by the large defence suppliers in the United States. In 1993, a dinner (which has become known as 'the Last Supper') was attended by US defence officials and industry executives. US industry leaders took away from this event the clear signal from the Defense Department that mergers would be welcomed. Between 1993 and 1998, the many became the few – driven almost entirely by industry decisions. Four significantly larger prime contracting firms emerged: Lockheed Martin, Boeing (which swallowed rival McDonnell Douglas), Raytheon (which absorbed Hughes, among others), and Northrop Grumman. Many other firms which had maintained some defence activity, such as General Motors, Chrysler, Texas Instruments and IBM, had sold it, frequently to one of the emerging giants.

While America's consolidation effort made the bigger headlines, a similar wave was striking Europe. Here the moves involved privatisation, as well as consolidation, though the former proved more difficult in some countries. Much of the consolidation between the mid-1980s and 1998 took place at the national level. British firms gradually drew together under British Aerospace (BAe) and GEC–Marconi Aerospace Inc. (GMAI). German, and some Dutch operations, re-emerged as DASA, the defence arm of DaimlerChrysler. Swedish (Saab), Italian (Finmeccanica), and Spanish (CASA) assets were well integrated at the national level, but privatisation moves began to gather strength. The French, too, moved towards consolidation, but more slowly: Aerospatiale, Dassault, Matra,

Thomson–CSF, DCN (ships) and Giat (land equipment) remained state-owned or state-dominated companies, and shrunk only a little as French defence budgets remained above the European average and exports were actively promoted and subsidised by the government.

Moving Closer Together

An unusual level of merger activity made 1998 a watershed year for European defence industry consolidation. At the political level, the decision of six governments in December 1997 to push towards the creation of a single transnational defence entity – the European Aerospace and Defence Company (EADC) – was an important signal to the European industry to consolidate at the transnational level.

The message was further strengthened by both French and UK policy changes. The French government had clearly concluded that the effort to remain fully independent could no longer be afforded, and that closer defence policy cooperation within NATO, but especially with the European allies, was necessary if France was to maintain its military capabilities. Its European partners made clear that the only way France could participate in industry consolidation would be to privatise its defence industry. With this strong impetus behind them, moves once considered virtually impossible took place in 1998, particularly the decisions to privatise Thomson–CSF and to merge Aerospatiale with the private Matra defence activities of Lagardere, creating a partially government-owned firm, Matra Haute Technologie (MHT). While not a move that went as far as France's partners wished, it was clearly a step, and an unexpected one, in the right direction.

British policy changes were equally significant. While the preceding Conservative administration had already stepped back from the industry

Figure 1 Major US Consolidations, 1990–1997

Lockheed Martin	Northrop Grumman	Raytheon
Loral	Westinghouse Electronics	E-Systems
Unisys Defense	Grumman	BAe Corporate Jets
IBM Federal Systems	LTV Aircraft	Texas Instruments
Ford Aerospace		Hughes
LTV Missiles		
GE Aerospace	**Boeing**	**Rolls-Royce**
GD Fort Worth	Rockwell Aerospace	Allison Engines
GD Space Systems	McDonnell Douglas	

consolidation process, Labour Prime Minister Tony Blair's government made two further critical policy moves. It decided to encourage and then participate actively in European discussions about the formation of the EADC, a company that would combine many of the defence assets of the six participating countries. Additionally, as part of a more active European policy, the British decided to join the French in calling for defence cooperation at the European level. This included a proposal for direct links between the European Union and NATO, which would potentially lead to the absorption of the Western European Union (WEU) into the EU, a proposal long put forward by France. This British proposal sent a highly important signal that defence at the European level was under discussion, and an industry that supported a European policy was desirable.

The merger of BAe and the defence arm of GMAI, announced in January 1999, appeared to run counter to government hopes, since it ended for a time the discussions taking place between DASA, BAe and Aero-spatiale on a cross-border merger. Efforts to achieve this trilateral merger had run into difficulties because DASA was demanding greater control over the combined firm than could be justified, while Aerospatiale was part of a group with substantial (43%) government ownership. The initial reaction to the BAe–GMAI deal was sharply negative in Germany, though less so in France, where it seemed to present opportunities for Franco-German cooperation. However, the initial hostility waned as industry stepped back to re-examine how European capabilities could be combined.

Although the headline news was about national-level mergers and only about discussions of transnational integration, there was considerable evidence that many sectors of the European defence industry were already engaged in transnational cooperation and merger at the European level. The Airbus consortium and joint programmes such as *Jaguar*, *Tornado* and *Eurofighter* had already created a legacy of cooperation. In key sectors such as electronics, missiles and space, a variety of combinations existed or emerged in the 1990s that foreshadowed stronger European cooperation, including the formation of Matra–BAe Dynamics, the NewCo space company (the third largest space company in the world), combining Matra–Marconi Space, DASA and Alenia's space activities; and Alenia Marconi Systems created by GEC and Finmeccanica for work on radar, missiles, and command-and-control.

The Nature of Transatlantic Activity

By the end of 1998, consolidation and globalisation in the defence industry were running at full spate. But there was little evidence of a dynamic transatlantic dimension. British companies had already recognised that access to the American market was an important ingredient of success. General US willingness to cast a benign eye on British activity in the US defence market had already allowed Rolls-Royce to buy the Allison engine company, Lucas and Varity to merge and firms such as BAe, GEC and Dowty to establish a presence in the United States. This trend was amplified by GEC's acquisition of Tracor, a US-based electronics firm, in 1998.

However, there was relatively little other evidence of transatlantic mergers. There were also few joint programmes left between the NATO partners, despite more than two decades of encouraging words about common requirements. The British–American *Tracer* land vehicle could be said to be the only such programme still under way, although some progress was being made towards defining a common air-ground surveillance requirement for the Alliance. A decision is due in 1999 on the British ASTOR airborne radar programme, for which three American aerospace companies, each with a British partner, are competing. ASTOR might provide a platform for the European airborne ground surveillance requirement.

The most visible truly collaborative programme between industry and governments across the Atlantic came to an end in 1998. This was research and development of the Medium Extended Air Defence System (MEADS) terminal phase ballistic defence system, which was designed to meet US, German and Italian requirements through cross-border collaboration. But MEADS had limped along for years, like so many cooperative programmes. In 1998, the US government decided the system was not a major requirement for the army, and production costs, estimated at more than $1.5 billion over several years, would not be funded in its out-year budget plans. This effectively killed the MEADS programme. The US proposed substituting collaboratively produced technology based on the *Patriot* Advanced Capability (PAC)-3 missile. The German and Italian governments were to respond to this proposal in 1999, but it presents much less opportunity for a truly joint programme, with substantial technology sharing, than MEADS.

The Transatlantic Crossroad

In Europe, government decisions and corporate merger activity in 1998 began to suggest that a 'fortress Europe' attitude might be emerging and shutting out US firms. Vance Coffman, Lockheed Martin's chief executive officer, traversed Europe in 1998 warning against such a trend. His comments were met with a strong European reaction, pointing to evidence of a 'fortress America', that already inhibited transatlantic cooperation. Restrictions on technology transfer within cross-national firms, tight controls over the export of defence technologies, and constraints on non-American acquisition of defence-related assets in the US all make transatlantic defence business extremely difficult.

The US appeared to recognise this problem. Secretary of Defense William Cohen created three panels in 1998 to review policies with respect to globalisation and commercialisation in the defence industry, and defence officials began to speak frankly about the need for the US to recognise that the industry had changed and policy needed to reflect that change. American politics were likely to frustrate any rapid opening of the US market, however. A Congressional committee, chaired by Congress-man Christopher Cox, issued a largely classified report reviewing trans-actions between US satellite firms Hughes and Loral and the Chinese in the 1990s. The panel concluded that these interactions may well have compromised American military secrets and enhanced Chinese missile launch capabilities. In March, Congress became further aroused by reports that Chinese intelligence had penetrated the US national laboratories responsible for nuclear warhead research. While no definitive public conclusion could yet be drawn, the Cox report and the laboratory issue clearly made the atmosphere for changing American policy more difficult.

Thus by the end of 1998, the European and US governments and industry were facing a crossroads. Fortresses could emerge on either side of the Atlantic. These edifices would ostensibly protect the American industrial base against technology leakage and preserve US defence technology leadership, while providing the Europeans with a strong technology and production base from which a separate defence identity could emerge. At the same time, powerful forces remain at work to enhance transatlantic defence collaboration.

Strategy, Doctrine and Force Planning

The first set of pressures pointing towards transatlantic cooperation derives from the strategy, doctrines and force planning of the major NATO countries. US and European thinking about strategy and military cap-abilities would appear to have diverged with the end of the Cold War. US strategy is globally focused, and concerned not only with traditional security challenges and military responses, but also with emerging new threats, particularly the proliferation of weapons of mass destruction and missile systems and terrorism. European strategic thinking tends to focus on regional security requirements, extended to the non-NATO Balkan fringe. Only the British and the French extend their strategic and security concerns beyond Europe, to the Middle East, Gulf and Africa.

Doctrine tends to match this strategic concern. US doctrine, as captured in the new conceptual framework 'Joint Vision 2010', focuses on developing overwhelming conventional military capabilities, armed with the most modern technology to provide total awareness of the military situation and battlefield dominance. Dominant manoeuvre, precision engagement, focused logistics, full-dimension protection and information superiority would be blended to give US forces full-spectrum dominance in peacetime and the ability to fight and win, if necessary. Smaller, less combat-oriented operations continue to be seen as an added case, not at the core of military planning. Force planning, as a result, seeks large, active duty forces, which are heavily armed, focused on high technology capabilities, and which have the ability to conduct all the aspects of military operations (complete logistics, communications, transportation and information to back up a broad and large force).

European planning diverges from the American model in each country. German doctrine and capabilities continue to focus on heavily armoured conventional capabilities, though the current government is undertaking a defence review that may consider a somewhat larger expeditionary capability. The smaller NATO allies do not maintain forces across the spectrum of capability, but smaller, niche forces that fit with broader NATO planning. Again, only the French and British have a relatively broad military doctrine, including both heavy combat and expeditionary capabilities. Even here, the recent French and British defence reviews do not seek to maintain capabilities across the full spectrum, but rather acknowledge the need for coalition operations and outside (that is, American) support in such areas as logistics, communications and transport. Both countries are working on maintaining an expeditionary capability of some kind that could operate outside the NATO area, and force planning tends to focus on the use of these forces in a regional peacekeeping/peace-enforcement mode. No European country is considering the scale of investment that is being made by the US in the next generation of defence technology.

Despite these clear divergences in strategic vision, doctrine and force planning, there is considerable convergence of military capabilities in practice. NATO is the only international military organisation in the world with a history of common planning and integrated command structures. The most significant uses of Western force in the post-Cold War era have been in the Gulf, where a coalition army was led by two NATO countries, the US and the UK, and NATO operations in the Balkans, where the ability to cooperate has been of major importance. Rhetoric aside, the French and British have both made clear that coalition operations, either at the European or the NATO level, are integral to defence planning. Moreover, the US has shown a clear preference in the Balkans and the Gulf, for operating with allies, rather than 'going it alone', even if this has meant only the British, as it did in the Gulf in 1998 and 1999. As the US advances the state-of-the-art through the Revolution in Military Affairs (RMA), US capabilities become even more important for integrating the military operations of other partners in the Alliance.

Thus, while military thinking and planning appears to diverge across the Atlantic, military operations push very hard in the direction of convergence. Military logic suggests there is good reason for putting greater emphasis on transatlantic industry cooperation, to support actual operations now and in the future.

Resource Constraints in the US and Europe

Greater cooperation is also dictated by resource constraints on both sides of the Atlantic. The US defence budget is roughly $270bn, compared to around $170bn in total for all the European NATO countries. The US research and development (R&D) investment of $36bn is three times that of the Europeans, and the US procurement budget, at nearly $50bn a year, is 50% larger than European investment. Even so, planned US defence investment, including the increases proposed by the administration for the year 2000, barely covers the anticipated costs of the currently projected weapons-acquisition programme. US procurement budgets have shrunk by nearly two-thirds since 1987, nearly twice as much as European acquisition funding. The Defense Department does not buy any military hardware at what could be called efficient rates. The fate of planned shipbuilding and aircraft programmes is still in the balance, given the scarcity of resources.

The Europeans are hardly better off. Procurement budgets have fallen by a third in constant dollars since 1987, and research and development budgets are small. Part of the impetus for industry consolidation and joint European programmes, such as *Eurofighter*, has been the small order base that flows from these smaller national budgets. Even with joint programmes, order books are thin. Moreover, European producers, who have for years depended more heavily than the Americans on overseas sales, are finding markets significantly affected by the South-east Asian financial crisis, the low price of oil and increased American competition. From the perspective of most European governments, the incentive to consolidate across frontiers, and especially across the Atlantic, is growing.

Technology: Divergence or Convergence?

Technology is also lending its weight to convergence across the Atlantic, despite appearances of divergence. The US is making a significant and growing investment in the RMA technologies, which a large R&D budget can sustain. Europeans are making less investment in the RMA. In specific areas, this divergence is clear: the Americans can afford to maintain five different investment programmes in tactical ballistic defence; the Europeans, partly because of a different perception of the threat, scarcely invest in this area, which is critical to future defence against missiles launched from outside Europe.

There is a more subtle process favouring technological convergence, however. The RMA investment, combined with a general commitment to buy commercial off-the-shelf technology, is pushing the US Defense Department towards increased use of commercial technology, and away from defence-dedicated suppliers. As this occurs, Pentagon procurement relies increasingly on a technology base whose nationality is unclear. The principal providers of information, communications and electronics technology are commercial companies. Their markets, suppliers and, increasingly, their ownership are global.

Even the traditionally defence-oriented prime contractors are looking to their role in commercial markets and technologies. Lockheed Martin's Coffman noted in October 1998 that, while the firm had stayed close to core business, it was now expanding its activities in related dual-use and commercial sectors that are growing faster than the economy as a whole. He identified them as space-based commercial telecommunications, information management services and systems engineering. The same phenomenon is occurring, even more broadly, in Europe, where leading edge technologies are largely found in the commercial sector. In such areas as sensors, imaging satellites and circuitry, it is also far from clear that US-based firms are the dominant international technology providers. European firms have much to bring to the military table, given the interest on both sides of the Atlantic in advanced commercial technology.

As the defence market changes, and as the industry both in the US and in Europe moves towards global, commercial operations, there is increasing incentive to view the defence technology marketplace, at least, as being transatlantic, even if it does not encompass the entire northern hemisphere. Convergence appears to be the logic of technology as well.

The Force of Business Decisions

The third set of convergence trends involves decisions being made by the defence industry itself. Events in 1998 demonstrate a pronounced shift in policy by governments, including the French, towards letting market forces guide industry decisions. While governments continue to be the main purchasers, define requirements and set procurement rules, decisions about how to succeed in this market are increasingly industry-defined. This goes a long way to explain why there has been the recent spate of mergers and acquisitions.

The American industry has probably reached the limit of prime-contractor consolidation at the national level, especially given the government's decision in summer 1998 to veto the planned absorption of Northrop Grumman by Lockheed Martin. For the first time, however, American firms are starting to sense the logic of the global marketplace and global technology. The past year has seen the first serious stirring of US prime-contractor interest in finding partners or merger opportunities in Europe. Although there is as yet no clear direction for this interest, the next few years are likely to see a growing trend towards transatlantic investment by US companies, in order to expand market access and ensure they are not cut off from the European market.

The same can be said for the Europeans. While the formation of a European aerospace and defence company is a major goal in some countries, their industries are increasingly concerned about being shut out of the American market. One of the more significant features of the BAe–GMAI merger, for example, is that the combined company will be doing nearly a quarter of its business in the US. Firms in Germany and France have also expressed interest in the US market. Already, European firms sell components and sub-components worth more than $6bn a year to US defence firms.

The industry would clearly move towards convergence given appropriate incentives. Ultimately, the logic of industry-led evolution may point more clearly across the Atlantic than to the creation of a single European company which might be cut off from the US marketplace.

Policy Directions

The challenge to NATO governments in coming years is how to foster a strong European defence capability, while ensuring an increasingly open transatlantic defence market. The goal will be to create a strong industrial and technological base, with an array of transatlantic relationships permitting greater technology transfer, industry efficiency, and competition for the buying agencies of all NATO member governments.

There are big risks in allowing the still significant forces of divergence to prevail. The European market alone may never be big enough to provide efficient production or adequate competition. The US Defense Department will face growing difficulty in funding its acquisition plan in a cost-effective way. Cutting markets off from each other is probably not possible, but seeking to do so (or causing it to happen) could only reinforce the US lead in military technology and reduce the ability of both sides to operate in military coalitions.

There is particular risk of such an outcome in the proposal to create the European Aerospace and Defence Company. Not only might this cut off technological cooperation, it could also lead to closing the European market to outside suppliers. Even at the combined European level, such a market would not lead to particularly efficient levels of production. Moreover, relying on a single supplier would deprive European governments of competition between suppliers.

Steps could be taken at both national and international level to support the emergence of a healthy transatlantic defence relationship. Perhaps the most important is for the NATO governments to agree on a policy of privatisation, which would permit industry to find the right level of response to changing market conditions. The US and the UK have moved almost entirely in this direction, while the British and the Germans are insisting that any European industry combination which includes the

French must involve substantial, if not total, privatisation of the French companies. Swedish (BAe now owns a third of Saab), Italian and Spanish governments are clearly moving towards privatisation. Even French policy is evolving in this direction, but very gradually.

A parallel recommendation would be for government officials to take a relatively benign view on industry decisions. Sharply negative government reactions to mergers such as that of BAe–GMAI do not clarify how a transatlantic market might emerge. They may well, however, have a chilling effect on companies seeking to fulfil the economic logic of consolidation.

Governments on both sides of the Atlantic could consider further steps, that only they could take, that will facilitate a transatlantic outcome. The US carries a heavy responsibility here, given the powerful disincentives to transatlantic programmes, partnerships and mergers in current American policy. US rules that track in detail every risk of technology transfer need to be reviewed. Export controls require similar scrutiny, moving towards NATO-wide rather than country-by-country approvals. The difficult and complex route through which proposed mergers and acquisitions must travel needs simplification and streamlining. The Defense Department suggestion that countries be ranked preferentially for more relaxed imposition of such rules may go too far, however. It may be better to review such arrangements by company and by technology, rather than considering countries as a whole to be acceptable or unacceptable.

Policy reviews under way in the Defense Department could point in these directions, but will require strong political support to survive the negative views and votes of a predominantly dubious Congress. Also, as difficult as it may seem, the Defense Department needs to consider ways to give bidding preference to cross-Atlantic teams or joint ventures for programmes that will ultimately become transatlantic systems. As part of this change in policy, where a better product can be acquired, the Pentagon might even consider buying a key defence system from Europe, such as the new EUROSAM extended air defence system upgrade, a Franco-Italian programme due to be deployed in 2002.

The Europeans also face important decisions about public policy. The process of developing joint requirements needs to move ahead quickly, as well as the harmonisation of joint programme management through *Organisme Conjoint de Cooperation en matière d'Armement* (OCCAR). The European Union partners need to put flesh on the bones of a proposed EU role in the defence arena, not only in defence policy terms, but also in terms of competition policy. European countries also need to pursue vigorously the EU definition of common export rules and security regimes for technology transfer, which will reassure all partners about the security of industry agreements and combinations and enable the Americans to relax their restrictive policies.

There is also a need for concerted attention to this question on a transatlantic basis. NATO efforts have not led to significant convergence in requirements or in defining the ground rules for cooperation or merger. Nor did the NATO summit contribute much on this subject. Concerned NATO countries should consider creating a separate, high-level advisory group of industry representatives. Such a group could consider the harmonisation of technology transfer, export control and acquisition regimes across the Atlantic, outside the NATO bureaucracy.

A meaningful transatlantic dialogue on the defence industry relationship needs to be established so that fundamental decisions can be carefully crafted. The United States and Europe are at a defence industry crossroads. One route could lead to an enhanced ability to conduct coalition operations, increased technology transfer, greater competition in the defence market and a cost-efficient industrial and technology base. The other could lead to two industrial fortresses, hunkering down behind protectionist ramparts and moats. Not only would neither of these independent defence industries be cost effective, but their creation could lead to greater friction over decisions on the engagement of forces at the expense of NATO unity. By underscoring the need for a strategic shift in the transatlantic defence industry relationship, Western governments could lay the domestic economic basis for building joint forces in the years ahead.

●

NATO Celebrates Its Fiftieth Year

The gala party for NATO's fiftieth birthday held in Washington on 23–25 April 1999 provided its leaders with an opportunity for self-scrutiny as well as for self-congratulation. The new Strategic Concept advanced at the meeting replaced the one issued in 1991 and reflected the new activities and functions that NATO had become engaged in over the decade. The Alliance has confounded those critics who confidently argued that NATO was bound to become an irrelevance once it had lost its traditional external enemy. Its role in Bosnia and Kosovo confirmed NATO's supremacy as the principal defence and security actor in Europe, leaving the UN, the Organisation for Security and Cooperation in Europe (OSCE), the European Union and Western European Union (WEU) far behind. NATO has confidently extended its collective defence provisions to three new members from the former Warsaw Pact – Czech Republic, Hungary and Poland – while the EU's enlargement process remains mired in bickering over fundamental issues such as reform of the Common Agricultural Policy.

Yet, the outward projection of NATO's vitality masks significant internal tensions and unresolved dilemmas. The Alliance struggled during the Kosovo crisis to develop a strategy which would immunise it from the traditional Balkan expertise in manipulating external powers to support the parochial ambitions of ethnic groups. The economic and political crisis that blew up in Russia in 1998 has threatened to undermine Moscow's earlier acquiescence to an enlarged and more activist NATO. France's refusal to return to the Military Structure has placed a significant obstacle to further progress on a European defence capability within, rather than outside, NATO. More generally, there was no significant decrease in Europe's security dependence on the United States, while European reluctance to support US strategic priorities continued to fuel transatlantic tensions.

The new Strategic Concept has had to paper-over these internal contradictions and tensions. For the most part, it tends to codify what has already been done rather than move NATO very far into the future. Like most mission statements for large organisations, the result has been a rather anodyne document, which is almost more interesting for what it does not say than for its actual content. Three particularly significant issues in this respect, reflect important internal divisions: the extent to which NATO has the responsibility and authority to act in peace-support, rather than traditional collective defence, operations; the further evolution of the Alliance's projection to the east; and the construction of a more equitable sharing of defence burdens between the US and its European allies.

From Defence to Attack

Both the old and new Strategic Concepts reflect a clear consensus that mutual obligation for collective defence remains at the core of the Alliance. The role of nuclear weapons in underpinning this commitment is also unchanged, despite the half-hearted attempt by the new German Foreign Minister, Joschka Fischer, to open a debate on the 'no-first-use' policy. What proved far more contentious was the question of 'out-of-area' operations which do not fall within Article 5 of the 1949 Washington Treaty, although, in practice, these have been NATO's main activities since the end of the Cold War. These new responsibilities were recognised in 1991, but the Strategic Concept promulgated that year included no reference to peacekeeping, and it was still generally thought that NATO was not the most appropriate body for conducting such operations. NATO's exclusive command of the Implementation Force (IFOR) operation in Bosnia completely changed this view.

The conceptual difficulty of formulating the new Strategic Concept lay in defining the precise relationship between the collective defence and peace-support or collective security functions of the Alliance. In this area, it was agreed that NATO should not evolve into a collective security

Figure 2 Article 5 of the North Atlantic Treaty, 4 April 1949

The Parties agree that an armed attack against one or more of them in Europe or North America shall be considered an attack against them all, and consequently they agree that, if such an armed attack occurs, each of them, in exercise of the right of individual or collective self-defence recognised by Article 51 of the Charter of the United Nations, will assist the Party or Parties so attacked by taking forthwith, individually, and in concert with the other Parties, such action as it deems necessary, including the use of armed force, to restore and maintain the security of the North Atlantic area. Any such armed attack and all measures taken as a result thereof shall immediately be reported to the Security Council. Such measures shall be terminated when the Security Council has taken the measures necessary to restore and maintain international peace and security.

organisation, with all the well-known weaknesses and limitations of such bodies. Instead, the ambition was to transform NATO into an innovative hybrid organisation.

The benefits of collective defence – with the solidarity that this ensures and the well-developed military cooperation that it fosters – were to be preserved so as to permit the Alliance to play an effective role in collective security, with the ability to make credible threats or use force in achieving political objectives. This marriage between the collective defence and collective security functions was reflected in the military structure finalised at the Washington Summit where the concept of the Combined Joint Task Force (CJTF) as the principal headquarters organisation for a rapid force deployment to areas of crisis, was grafted onto a revised military structure, which is still primarily dedicated to collective defence.

Where ultimate authority in this structure should lie bedevilled intra-Alliance negotiations. The US insisted that a seamless web of command, which ultimately leads to the Supreme Allied Commander Europe (SACEUR), should govern all operations, including small-scale non-Article 5 missions. This has been the main source of tension between the US and France, contributing to the French refusal to rejoin the military structure. France had insisted that, for WEU-led operations, the command structure should bypass the NATO military structure, and authority should reside in the WEU. While the US has accepted that a WEU-led CJTF would have a European command structure, there are still disagreements over key issues of liaison and oversight concerning use of NATO/US assets in a European CJTF.

This specific Franco-American dispute is not the only source of trans-atlantic tension over the authorisation issue. As a result of the unhappy US experiences with its United Nations role in Bosnia and Somalia, Washington resolved never again to subordinate NATO or US troops to a UN military command. There were those who felt that the Activation Order for NATO air-strikes on Serbia in October 1998, which did not depend upon a specific UN resolution sanctioning the use of force, represented a significant and useful precedent concerning the UN role. Many Europeans were less enthusiastic than the US about this, fearing that formalising such a precedent would undermine the perceived impartiality and legality of NATO operations, leading to the Alliance appearing an instrument of US policy. Although they recognised that NATO might sometimes have to act without an explicit UN authorisation, particularly if needing to circumvent a Russian or Chinese veto, the Europeans preferred this to be decided on a case-by-case basis.

The US also disconcerted most Europeans in the run-up to the summit by attempting to widen NATO's geographic scope and to extend its functional responsibilities. Secretary of State Madeleine Albright's reported comment that NATO should be 'a force for peace from the Middle East to Central Africa' caused consternation in European capitals. In practice, the US ambition to 'globalise' NATO was much exaggerated in the press. Washington's main goal was to engage the Europeans in a common policy towards the threat of Weapons of Mass Destruction (WMD) and with regard to Persian Gulf security. Furthermore, the US felt that it was wrong to maintain the view that security cooperation within NATO needed to be geographically circumscribed in an age when threats could emanate from so many directions and crises occur in so many places. A more equitable sharing of defence burdens now requires Europeans to help defend common security interests wherever they are challenged. However, European and US perceptions and policies differ on both issues, although with differing emphases. The UK is closest to the US view, followed by Germany, the rest of NATO, and then France at the furthest end of the spectrum. Given this spread of views, it is fair to say that Europeans generally are reluctant to permit NATO to become a potential instrument for enforcing European consent to American strategic objectives in these contentious and sensitive areas.

Those drafting the new Strategic Concept had to find suitably ambiguous compromises to mask these differences of opinion. Such ambiguities reflect the fact that the Alliance consists of separate and independent nation-states with their own specific strategic and political cultures and their distinctive and divergent national interests. This is hardly a revelation. Transatlantic divergences and intra-alliance disputes were equally, if not more, serious during the Cold War. In the midst of the Cold War, however, such internal divisions did not threaten the ultimate cohesion of the Alliance since the threat, upon which the discipline of collective defence rested, was omnipresent. The danger is that, with that threat dissolved, continuing debilitating disputes between the US and its European allies (and between the European allies themselves) might weaken the collective defence foundations which provide the strength and integrity of the Alliance.

The Limits of Enlargement

The Washington Summit has rightly celebrated the fruition of NATO's policy of engagement and enlargement to the countries of central and eastern Europe. In the face of the more sceptical and reluctant attitude of most of its European allies, the US has successfully pursued a strategy which has secured the entry into NATO of Poland, the Czech Republic and Hungary many years before they are likely to be fully embraced by the EU. Against the predictions of critics of this policy, this extension of NATO has not been gained at the expense of Russian cooperation with the West. Instead, the signing of the NATO–Russia Founding Act in May 1997 created the Permanent Joint Council (PJC), a new mechanism of cooperation between Russia and NATO. The continuation and enhancement of the Partnership for Peace (PfP) programme, the creation of the Euro-Atlantic Partnership Council and the NATO–Ukraine Charter reflect an extraordinarily active NATO engagement with the East.

Nevertheless, the Washington Summit could not fully hide the continuing reservations about future extensions of NATO membership. The US administration successfully ensured in Washington that NATO's 'open-door' policy remains intact and that the membership applications from Romania, Slovenia and the Baltic States will be duly considered. Yet there are signs that domestic support among NATO states for adding further members might be weakening.

While the US Senate overwhelmingly ratified accession of the three new members on 30 April 1998, an amendment seeking to prevent any more additions to NATO for three years was only narrowly defeated. The Senate also sent a clear signal that it would be closely monitoring the actual costs of enlargement and that it was not willing to write a blank cheque for endlessly extending US security guarantees to the east. The barrage of phone calls and letters to Senators from 19 US ethnic groups, brought together by the Central and East European Coalition, also offered an unedifying prospect of future battles. As one US Senator noted, 'what we have done with this vote is to create 10 to 15 years of chaos in Europe in terms of arguing who should come in and why they should come in'.

The enlargement issue has also been complicated by the deterioration of the West's relations with Russia. The Russian economic and political crisis in 1998, and Moscow's subsequent inability to pursue a genuine economic reform policy, has weakened the West's economic levers of influence. Russia has not adopted the stridently anti-Western foreign policy that many feared, but Moscow's opposition has noticeably hardened over its perceived marginalisation in relation to European and international security issues. This has resulted in more obstructive behaviour in fora where Russia's voice can be heard, such as the UN, the OSCE and the PJC. As noted above, this has resulted in NATO seeking to consolidate its autonomy of decision making, further alienating Russia.

On one level, NATO and the West can afford to ignore a Russia whose chronic economic weakness and military paralysis means there is a far greater threat of internal civil war than external aggression. But, such a strategy involves significant costs, as Russia, even in its enfeebled state, continues to wield sufficient diplomatic and political levers to make regional conflicts, whether in the Balkans or the Middle East or elsewhere, more difficult to resolve without its support. Similarly, European and international strategic stability, as realised through the Conventional Armed Forces in Europe or Strategic Arms Reduction Talks processes, remain dependent on Russian cooperation. Prime Minister Yevgeny Primakov's government has also made this dilemma more complex by ensuring that Russian policy remains closer to an exercise of Gaullist exceptionalism than full-scale Soviet obstructionism.

Nevertheless, the hardening of Russian attitudes makes it more likely that further NATO enlargement will intensify, rather than weaken, anti-Western tendencies in Moscow. For some, this only strengthens the arguments for a rapid process of enlargement. Other fainter hearts will continue to question whether the process might not itself create the conditions of insecurity which it is supposed to resolve. This dilemma will arise most starkly when, and if, the applications for NATO membership from the Baltic states are seriously considered.

Bridging the Transatlantic Divide

It is an indication of how little, as well as how much, has changed in NATO since the end of the Cold War that the issue of transatlantic burden-sharing remains as contested and unresolved as ever. The carefully articulated option of a WEU-led CJTF, as unveiled in Berlin in June 1996, was supposed to provide a compromise solution to this perennial dispute. It did reflect a genuine movement closer to the Alliance by France, and a US warming to the prospect of European defence autonomy. However, France's refusal to rejoin the new Military Structure, announced in October 1997, only highlighted the substantive divisions which remained unresolved.

In essence, the problem lies in the structural condition of European security dependence on the US and the benefits, as well as the costs, which this provides for both sides of the Atlantic. For the US, while it may rail against European free-riding and lack of support for US initiatives,

Europe's dependence on US-owned assets for any substantial independent military operation gives Washington a *droit de regard* over such European missions. Likewise, though Europe might remain uneasy that its inability to project military force reflects on its economic and political power, the financial benefits of not incurring the costs of building the defence capabilities that the US provides makes such uneasiness bearable. The idea of a WEU-led CJTF could never, on its own, overcome this security dependence. Indeed, as the French realised, it only accentuated it. More generally, there was a real question whether such cumbersome arrangements, however theoretically elegant they might appear to those versed in the theology of European defence, would ever work in practice.

British Prime Minister Tony Blair's initiative in 1998 to reopen the European defence debate was a genuine attempt to grapple with the substance of the problem. Even for the British, always strongly supportive of an Atlanticist position, the inability of the Europeans to do anything in Kosovo without calling on the Americans was a matter of concern. The Franco-British agreement at St Malo on 3 December 1998 was a recognition that a European defence capability had to be led by French and British defence cooperation, since these are the only European countries with the strategic culture, and the force capabilities, for mounting expeditionary operations. Privately, the British suggest that the WEU should be dissolved

---

Figure 3 Summary of the Declaration on European Defence, UK–French summit, St Malo, 3–4 December 1998

France and the UK agree that:
1 Provisions in the Amsterdam Treaty on a Common Foreign and Security Policy (CFSP) should be implemented fully for the EU to play its role on the international stage. The European Council must be able to take decisions on an intergovernmental basis, framing a common defence policy.
2 The EU must have the capacity for autonomous action, backed by credible military force. Europeans will operate within the institutional framework of the EU and in conformity with their various obligations in NATO.
3 There must be structures and sources of intelligence and analysis to enable the EU to take decisions and approve military action where the Alliance as a whole is not engaged. The EU needs access to suitable military means (taking into account existing WEU assets).
4 Europe needs strengthened armed forces supported by a competitive defence industry and technology.
5 Both states are determined to unite efforts to bring about these objectives.

into the EU and NATO in the belief that the WEU remains part of the problem of the lack of a European defence capability.

Nevertheless, the British *démarche* and the Anglo-French *entente* are only the first building blocks of a true European defence identity, which could only emerge over time when European states draw closer on defence aims and expertise. Hence the suggestion mooted in many circles that the EU should develop 'convergence' criteria for defence cooperation. Certainly, other European countries will need to follow the French and British example in reconfiguring their forces away from static territorial defence to developing force projection capabilities, and there is very little prospect of Germany doing that in the near term. The problem of non-NATO EU members and non-EU European NATO members needs to be finessed institutionally. If these hurdles are surmounted, the Europeans and Americans will then need to construct a more genuinely equitable relationship, where the benefits of cooperation through NATO can be preserved, while accommodating divergences in US and European strategic interests and objectives.

In any case, the advent of the euro has only highlighted the anomaly of a structured inequality in transatlantic security relations, with its threat of a European challenge to US hegemony not only in trade, but potentially now also in monetary terms. As such, the traditional trade-off between US provision for European security and European economic concessions may no longer work as well. The benefit for the US of European security dependence has thus sharply diminished.

Losing an Empire But Yet To Find a Role?

There is no reason to dampen the celebrations of the 50-year old Alliance. There were few people who predicted ten years ago that NATO would be in such good health at this auspicious occasion and would be able to define a new set of functions and roles which secure its relevance as it enters the new millennium. NATO will remain an invaluable forum for managing one critical dimension of the transatlantic relationship. It will continue to be the only effective mechanism for engaging cooperation on European defence and security issues, providing mechanisms for the collective provision of military forces which are responsive to the security demands of the post-Cold War environment. In peace-support operations, NATO will have the competitive advantage of being the only multilateral organisation which can back its political and diplomatic objectives with genuine military muscle. The Alliance will also continue to provide an invaluable service in bridging the East–West divide through its extensive outreach programme and by opening its doors to new members from the former Warsaw Pact countries.

But, just as NATO appears to have defined its new role, the limits of that role have also become more apparent. In terms of non-Article 5 operations, it is likely that these will remain limited to Europe's periphery. Wider afield, it will probably remain the case that, with regard to 'out of area' developments, most Europeans and the US will continue to be 'out of sync'. In these more distant settings – *ad hoc* coalitions of the willing will be the norm. Such coalitions might include individual European states and benefit indirectly from the cooperation fostered by NATO, but they will not directly involve the engagement of the Alliance itself. On enlargement, there are questions whether the accession of further members into NATO will be advisable. Although the EU has been rightly criticised for its tardiness in extending eastwards, the parable of the hare and the tortoise might be relevant. As the EU finally makes decisions on new members in the next few years, it is likely to assume a more prominent role and greater responsibility for bridging a continent which is primarily divided by economic and political disparities rather than by military confrontation.

The future of NATO is also critically dependent on Europe and the EU successfully rising to the challenge of assuming the military and security responsibilities that are consonant with Europe's economic and political power and prestige. This was the original vision of the founding fathers of the Washington Treaty in 1949. After the devastation of the Second World War, the US was strongly committed to the reconstruction of Europe as an independent force in international affairs. It was only the exigencies of the Cold War which led to Europe's security dependence and the benign subordination of the Europeans to the US. Many, though not all, in the US recognise that a continued American investment in a stable and secure Europe will return needed political and economic support and cooperation. Ultimately, however, a healthy transatlantic alliance requires an alliance of political equals: this is the principal challenge for NATO as it enters middle age.

New Momentum for Ballistic Missile Defences?

The sight of modified *Scud* missiles from Iraq striking American forces as well as Israeli and Saudi territory during the 1991 Persian Gulf War galvanised support in the US for the development of theatre missile defence (TMD) capabilities. By 1993, the Pentagon had structured a range of TMD programmes at an annual cost of some $2 billion, with the goal of providing far more effective protection against short-to-intermediate range ballistic missile attack than the *Patriot* Advanced Capability (PAC)-2 version of the *Patriot* air-defence system which was used in 1991. With the notable exception of Israel, however, US allies were slow to follow Washington's lead. While Japan and a number of European NATO member states acquired *Patriot* interceptor systems, in the eight years since the Gulf War only Italy and Germany have participated in the development of a new TMD system. In the US itself, the development and deployment of ballistic missile defence (BMD) for the purpose of protecting national territory has remained a controversial political issue.

A number of significant events related to ballistic missile proliferation took place in 1998, giving a new impetus to BMD development. While this advance is evolutionary rather than radical, turning points were reached in US policy on national missile defence (NMD) and Japanese participation in TMD research and development. The threat of missile proliferation is also having a tangible impact on the direction of US TMD programmes. Although European reaction continues to be mainly circumspect, there are signs that some countries may be rethinking their positions.

The Ballistic Missile Threat

The nature of the ballistic missile threat is a function of proliferation trends as well as the political and military utility of these weapons. Both these issues have been the subject of considerable debate. In one sense, ballistic missile proliferation hardly spiralled out of control during the 1990s. Countries with ballistic missile capabilities at the end of the decade are mainly those that already possessed them at the beginning. This slowdown in horizontal missile proliferation over the past decade is not necessarily the good news it appears to be. Rather, it reflects the fact that the widespread diffusion of Soviet-era *Scud* missiles had already taken place during the Cold War.

The worrying trend of the 1990s was the ability of a number of regional powers to develop increasingly sophisticated infrastructures for ballistic missile production. North Korea and Iran are particular causes for concern. India and Pakistan also established capabilities during the 1990s for intermediate-range ballistic missile development and production. Iraq would certainly have developed its capabilities further had it not been for the controls imposed on its armament programmes after the Gulf War. Baghdad could readily reconstitute its long-range ballistic missile programme if these controls were lifted or became ineffective.

On 31 August 1998, North Korea shocked Japan by testing a three-stage *Taepodong*-1 rocket (whose range is 1,500–2,000 kilometres) that overflew North Korea's eastern neighbour and landed in the Pacific Ocean. Pyongyang subsequently claimed it had used the launch to place a satellite into orbit, a claim that US intelligence eventually accepted as plausible. However, the use of the *Taepodong* to launch a satellite (which failed to achieve orbit) did nothing to diminish the strategic importance of the event. This was North Korea's first test of a multi-stage rocket, with all three stages separating successfully. Not only did the successful use of multi-stage technology signal the operational appearance of a new intermediate-range ballistic-missile threat, but it added credibility to the spectre of North Korea developing the 4,000–6,000km-range *Taepodong*-2 missile. While the US intelligence community had anticipated the launch of the *Taepodong*-1 well in advance of the actual event, the use of the rocket as a space launch vehicle as well as its third stage were surprises.

The *Taepodong* launch appeared to validate the conclusions of the Rumsfeld Commission, an expert panel established by the US Congress to evaluate the ballistic missile threat to the United States. The Commission enjoyed widespread credibility in Washington due to its balanced range of views; its members had been nominated on an equal basis by Republican and Democratic congressional leaders. The Commission's report, issued on 16 July 1998, argued that the threat to US national territory from emerging ballistic missile capabilities is 'broader, more mature, and evolving more rapidly' than US intelligence reports had been indicating. This conclusion could also readily apply to the ballistic missile threat against other countries, notably in Europe, that have considered themselves at a relatively safe distance from the mainly short-range missiles possessed by regional proliferators. Just one week after publication of the Rumsfeld Commission report, Iran tested the 1,300km-range *Shahab*-3 ballistic missile, while in April 1998, Pakistan had tested its *Ghauri* missile to a distance of 1,100km.

The Rumsfeld Commission argued that ballistic missile development in proliferating nations is progressing more rapidly and with less warning time than indicated by conventional intelligence analysis. Commission members based this assessment on three considerations.

- Emerging ballistic missile powers are not following US and Soviet patterns of missile development that required a high degree of missile accuracy, reliability and safety, as well as large numbers of missiles.

- New ballistic missile development programmes are obtaining extensive technical assistance from outside sources through access to dual-use technologies, direct assistance from Russia, China and North Korea, and increased cooperation between emerging ballistic missile powers themselves.

- These countries have become much more adept at concealing their ballistic missile development efforts.

The emergence of new powers able to produce increasingly long-range ballistic missiles heightens the possibility of transfers of complete missile systems from one country to another. China, for example, transferred the

3,100km-range CSS-2 missile to Saudi Arabia in the 1980s. If North Korea or Iran were to export an intermediate-range missile system to Libya, which does not possess its own production capabilities, it would create a new category of ballistic missile threat to North Africa, the Middle East, and Europe.

Political and Military Uses

Ballistic missiles armed with conventional high explosives can cause substantial disruption and have a significant political impact if delivered onto an urban area. As the 1988 'war of the cities' between Iraq and Iran showed, this can play a major role in a conflict between regional powers. Even in the 1991 Gulf War, political considerations forced the allied coalition to divert substantial military resources to countering Iraqi missile strikes against Israel and Saudi Arabia. Despite this, the low accuracy of developing country missiles limits the actual damage and casualties that they can inflict with heavy munitions, and it is, above all, the threat of ballistic missile delivery of nuclear, biological and chemical (NBC) weapons that preoccupies defence planners and political leaders.

Almost every country with ballistic missile assets also possesses one or more types of NBC weapon, with biological and chemical ones the most common. While ballistic missiles constitute an ideal delivery vehicle for nuclear weapons, there are significant technical obstacles to the effective delivery of biologically and chemically armed ballistic missile warheads (CBW). They are most lethally dispersed in the form of low-altitude aerosol clouds spread over a wide area, but it is technically difficult to design ballistic missile warheads that can generate aerosols. But, as difficult as it is, the US and the Soviet Union had achieved it by the 1960s. Designing ballistic missile warheads in which chemical and biological agents can survive space travel and atmospheric re-entry is another challenging, but not insurmountable, task.

Even if they are not an ideal means of CBW delivery, ballistic missiles armed with these weapons can have a potentially devastating impact, especially on unprotected civilian populations and military-support personnel. CBW-armed ballistic missile strikes on troops, logistics nodes, air bases and ports can severely disrupt an adversary's military operations, even if they do not cause heavy casualties. The US Office of Technology Assessment estimated in a 1993 report that a *Scud*-like missile, armed with 30 kg of anthrax could kill 30–100,000 people in an urban setting, if delivered on an overcast day or night with moderate wind. These conditions represent neither a best nor worst case for biological weapon (BW) delivery. Other delivery conditions and population densities could result in even greater casualties. Developing countries with advanced ballistic missile infrastructures are already capable of designing warheads to deliver CBW. Iraq's biological weapon arsenal at the time of the 1991

Gulf War included at least 25 ballistic missile warheads, and ballistic missiles were also among the delivery systems for the massive Iraqi chemical weapon stockpile. Until there is a convincing demonstration that new BMD systems will be effective in combat, countries with military ambitions may well continue to view ballistic missiles as a means of NBC delivery with a high chance of reaching its target.

Evolving US Policy: National Missile Defence ...

The threat from ballistic missile proliferation was felt more acutely in the US in 1998 because of the various tests carried out by a number of countries. They tipped the balance within President Bill Clinton's administration toward a belief that there would soon be a ballistic missile threat to US territory, making technological readiness the 'primary remaining criterion', in the words of US Defense Secretary William Cohen, determining whether to deploy a NMD system.

These developments also gave considerable help to maintaining support within the administration for continued funding of the Theater High Altitude Area Defense (THAAD) system, a core US TMD programme that has an unfortunate record of flight test failures. US TMD programmes will nonetheless become more tightly focused, in an effort to concentrate funding and to achieve better progress towards deploying effective systems.

Secretary Cohen's announcement on 20 January 1999 that the US was adding $6.6bn to the Future Years Defense Plan (FYDP) for NMD, all earmarked for actual deployment of a system, marked the third stage of Clinton administration policy on this issue. In 1993, when it first assumed office, the new administration downgraded NMD to a technology development programme. In 1996, under considerable political pressure from Congress, the administration formulated its '3 plus 3' programme, which shifted the status of the NMD programme to one of 'deployment readiness'. This status meant the US was to bring technology to the point where, starting in the year 2000, it could deploy an NMD system within three years of taking the decision to do so. The 20 January announcement committed the administration to making 'a critical decision' in June 2000 on whether to deploy an NMD system.

Cohen's announcement also implicitly indicated that the administration would not allow the Anti-Ballistic Missile (ABM) Treaty to be an obstacle to US deployment of a limited NMD system able to deal with the threat. The Defense Secretary declared that the administration would seek to open negotiations with Russia on amending the treaty if this were needed to allow the US to deploy an NMD system capable of providing a limited defence of all of US territory. He pointedly added that the ABM Treaty provides for 'right of withdrawal with six months notice' if one of the parties views doing so to be in its supreme national interest.

The new policy does not seem to go far beyond the 3 plus 3 programme, which has already projected the possibility of making a deployment decision in the year 2000. Neither the new NMD funding, nor the expectation that a ballistic missile threat to US territory will soon be at hand, nor the commitment to a June 2000 deployment decision are etched in stone. The administration, in fact, remains divided over NMD policy, and is under pressure from the arms control community as well as congressional Democrats not to undermine the ABM Treaty. In the weeks following the 20 January announcement, the White House gave assurances that the ABM Treaty 'remains a cornerstone of strategic stability', and that an NMD deployment decision must take into account the treaty and US strategic arms reduction objectives. Administration officials also stated that the June 2000 deployment decision will need to confirm whether the threat to US territory has developed as rapidly as now expected.

Barring some dramatic development, such as North Korea's peaceful collapse, that could justify a more benign threat assessment, it will in practice probably be difficult to reverse course on NMD. Both the new threat assessment and the movement of the NMD programme onto an acquisition track are large steps forward from previous policy. The potential for eventual US withdrawal from the ABM Treaty is real. It would be politically untenable for any government in Washington to declare the existence of a 'rogue state' ballistic missile threat to US territory, but then allow Russia to exercise a veto over deploying a technical solution that would defend against that threat.

At the same time, the Clinton administration's clear preference, and even that of most congressional Republicans, is to negotiate amendments to the ABM Treaty rather than simply to discard it. They stress that a limited NMD system would not be capable of blunting a Russian missile attack, and would therefore not change the nature of the US–Russian strategic nuclear relationship. Russia's position is so weak that most American observers believe Moscow will not have any choice but to acquiesce to negotiating a treaty amendment allowing Washington to deploy an NMD system capable of providing limited protection of all US territory.

Such an amendment would not necessarily require a radical revision of the ABM Treaty. It currently allows each side to build a single NMD site; the US has one at Grand Forks, North Dakota. The Pentagon is investigating whether a single site located in Alaska could protect all the 50 states.

... and Theater Missile Defense

The US has four major TMD programmes underway: the Army's lower-tier PAC-3 and upper-tier THAAD system; and their sea-based counterparts, the Navy Area Defense (NAD) and the Navy Theater-Wide (NTW) system. *Patriot* and NAD are intended to intercept ballistic missiles in the latter stages of their flight path, and thus protect relatively small areas only several tens of kilometres wide. The systems are designed to destroy ballistic missiles with ranges up to approximately 1,000km, and, importantly, should also be able to intercept air-breathing delivery systems. THAAD and NTW would intercept missiles outside the atmosphere, defending areas several hundred kilometres across. They would also provide enhanced interception capabilities against missiles with ranges of several thousand kilometres. A 'layered' TMD architecture, consisting of both lower- and upper-tier capabilities would allow for multiple-shot opportunities against incoming missiles and thus reduce system 'leakage'. NAD and NTW, which are both based on the existing *Aegis* air defence system, could deploy earlier in a crisis and would protect US forces seeking theatre access against a hostile power, while the ground-based *Patriot* and THAAD would extend defensive coverage further inland. The US has consequently established a military requirement for all of these TMD systems.

The Medium Extended Air Defence System (MEADS), a cooperative programme between the US, Germany, and Italy, was intended to provide a highly mobile lower-tier capability, designed for immediate deployment into a theatre for protection of manoeuvre forces during offensive operations. MEADS would also have a stronger capability than *Patriot* to intercept cruise missiles, including those with enhanced stealth characteristics. The US also has a Boost Phase Intercept (BPI) programme for destroying ballistic missiles immediately after launch. The airborne laser (ABL) is the lead programme for carrying out this task. One of its advantages is that it will cause toxic agents or radioactive fallout from NBC-tipped warheads to rain back down on the launching country.

Defense Secretary Cohen's 20 January announcement highlighted two major decisions affecting these TMD programmes. First, the Pentagon will increase funding for the NTW programme in order to move it from the development to the acquisition phase. Although rumours burgeoned during autumn 1998 that the THAAD programme was to be eliminated, the Department of Defense (DoD) decided to continue THAAD flight testing because of 'the urgency in fielding an upper tier system'. In November 2000, the Pentagon will compare the test results of NTW and THAAD to decide which should become the lead upper-tier TMD system. This will then receive the bulk of the funding available for upper-tier TMD. The goal of this competitive approach is to deploy an upper-tier capability by 2007, rather than 2008 as currently scheduled for THAAD and 2010 for NTW.

The second major TMD announcement was to downgrade MEADS to a technology development programme. The system was expected to enter the design and development stage during 1999. Protection of manoeuvre forces has always been the lowest of the DoD's TMD priorities, since these forces are viewed as less vulnerable to missile attack than fixed targets such as headquarters, logistics nodes, and sea and air bases. The MEADS decision was therefore part of the Pentagon's effort to focus TMD spending on the most urgent requirements. It also had the effect, however, of virtually killing the one transatlantic programme for acquiring TMD capability, adding significantly to Washington's existing reputation for unreliability in the implementation of cooperative weapons development.

Other Countries

Israel had not needed the ballistic missile proliferation developments of 1998 to spur action. It was already going flat out to deploy TMD assets. Israel plans to have initial operational capability of its *Homa* TMD system in 2002, but it has noted that, should it need to do so, it is already prepared to deploy *Arrow* missiles, which are a vital part of the system. *Arrow* operates in the upper atmosphere, above the maximum altitude of the *Patriot*, but below the exo-atmospheric capability of THAAD. Israel has developed the system in cooperation with the US, and with substantial US funding. The costs of *Arrow*-2 are estimated to be in the range of $1.6–1.7bn, and the US is committed to pay two-thirds of the cost.

On the other hand, Japan received a huge jolt from the *Taepodong* firing, which, along with the other ballistic missile tests carried out in 1998, may also influence some European thinking on TMD acquisition. Tokyo initially reacted to North Korea's test by cutting off economic and humanitarian assistance to Pyongyang. They were soon restored (Japan agreed to restart its payments for the North Korean nuclear reactor project on 21 October 1998), but Tokyo's new interest in TMD capability is certain to last longer. The US and Japan had discussed TMD cooperation throughout the 1990s, but these talks had never resulted in any concrete initiative, due to Japanese defence budgetary issues, concern over the reaction elsewhere in Asia, particularly China, and constitutional constraints on the militarisation of space. Less than one month after the *Taepodong* test, however, Tokyo decided to budget $8 million in 1999 for a cooperative research programme with the US on TMD. The initiative could last up to six years, and cost Japan some $250m.

Japan already operates *Patriot* batteries and four *Aegis* destroyers, which together could form the basis for Japanese NMD. Tokyo conducted two studies during the 1990s which concluded that deploying NTW aboard Japan's *Aegis* ships would constitute the best option for acquiring an advanced BMD capability. US officials hope to sign an agreement with Japan on joint TMD research during 1999. Discussion on areas for cooperation have focused on the second generation missile for the NTW.

European defence ministries have approached the TMD issue with considerable caution because of severe budgetary constraints, uncertainties about the severity of the threat, a temptation to let the US resolve the problem, and scepticism about the prospects for successful transatlantic armaments cooperation. Nonetheless, NATO declarations have endorsed extended air defences, including TMD, as among the most important capabilities required to meet the NBC weapons/missile threat to deployed forces as well as to the territory and forces of regional allies. NATO groups are currently examining potential architectures for layered TMD in Europe.

A number of European countries already have, or plan to acquire, lower-tier TMD systems, but at the beginning of 1998 the majority did not. Some Europeans might support deployment of upper-tier TMD to protect national territory, depending on the mix of perceived threat, cost and degree of protection offered. For many, their geographic position was an important determinant of how strongly they judged the threat. Other Europeans, especially the French, are inclined to rely solely on nuclear deterrence for the protection of national territory.

Europeans consequently differ over the need for and the nature of TMD. Germany and the Netherlands already possess the *Patriot* system, conduct annual joint air-defence exercises with the United States, and plan to purchase *Patriot* PAC-3 enhancements, as does Greece. Germany and Italy were also partners with the US in the MEADS programme. Spain decided in 1997 to purchase the *Aegis* air-defence system for its four new F-100 frigates, although for the time being it is without the Standard Missile (SM) 2 Block IVA missile that will equip the NAD system. But the continued reluctance of the UK and France to acquire TMD systems is a significant issue, since those two countries possess the bulk of European force projection capabilities.

France has the option of upgrading its new Surface-to-air Missile Platform/Terrain (SAMP/T) air defence system, based on the *Aster* interceptor, to give it a lower-tier TMD capability. (Italy has partnered France on the *Aster*.) The French government has been re-examining NBC/missile threats during early 1999 in the light of developments over the preceding year. It may well take a decision during 2000 to implement the *Aster* upgrade, which it views as technically feasible and affordable, although not without sacrificing some other aspect of French defence capability. The UK has established a continuing Technology Readiness and Risk Assessment Programme (TRRAP) in order to stay abreast of the evolving missile threat as well as TMD technology developments. UK policy nonetheless appears focused on seeking protection from US TMD systems for British forces deployed in overseas military interventions. The Pentagon plans to acquire sufficient assets to cover all potential TMD needs within a theatre of operations.

Technical Challenges

The US and other countries have been pursuing two types of BMD technology. The first uses a blast fragmentation warhead. Once the interceptor missile nears its target, a proximity fuse detonates the high-explosives contained in the warhead and sprays the target with metal fragments. Current versions of the *Patriot* system, NAD, the *Arrow*, and the *Aster* all use blast fragmentation warheads. An improved version of the *Patriot* used in the Gulf War achieved a successful intercept against a ballistic missile target in early 1997, as did the SM-2 Block IVA. The latest version of the Israeli *Arrow* intercepted a simulated ballistic target in a full system test carried out in September 1998. Previous *Arrow* intercept tests included two successes and one failure. They were, however, carried out with the *Arrow* interceptor chasing its target rather than against the type of head-on, incoming target that would characterise a real attack. Israel plans to conduct an intercept test against a live, head-on missile in July 1999 to establish the *Arrow* system's operational status.

Most new US BMD systems under development use a hit-to-kill (HTK) interception approach that destroys incoming ballistic missiles through a direct collision. These HTK systems include the latest configuration of the *Patriot* PAC-3 system, THAAD, NTW and NMD. HTK interception involves a direct collision, which can release an enormous amount of energy, comparable to that of a small nuclear explosion. This is essential outside the atmosphere, where blast waves travel poorly. At lower altitudes, the great energy release may offer a solution to the very trouble-some problem of how to destroy CBW-armed missiles without dispersing their contents as a result. A 1993 test of the Extended Range Interceptor (ERINT) missile, which will equip the latest configuration of the *Patriot* PAC-3 system, directly hit a target missile carrying 38 canisters of water to simulate chemical weapons. Only nine submunitions survived, and they no longer contained water.

HTK technology has been compared to hitting a bullet with another bullet, and, not surprisingly, is proving extremely difficult to master. Since 1982, the US has attempted some 20 HTK intercepts of ballistic missile targets. Six of these tests were successful, including two with the ERINT missile. The most widely noticed failures have included five tests in a row of the THAAD system. In March 1999, however, *Patriot* PAC-3 achieved a successful HTK intercept against a target missile.

These difficulties led the US Ballistic Missile Defense Organization (BMDO) to establish an expert panel, chaired by retired Air Force General Larry Welch, to assess the flight test programmes of US HTK systems. The panel, which issued its report in February 1998, asserted that both government and contractor programme managers had underestimated HTK's complexity. The report criticised the strong pressures to deploy early capability in the HTK programmes, resulting in test programmes that have been too limited in number and compressed in schedule. The panel characterised the very aggressive development approach taken as constituting a 'rush to failure' caused by 'poor design, test planning, and pre-flight testing deficiencies; poor fabrication; poor management; and lack of rigorous government oversight'.

The failures in the test flight programme have thus stemmed from factors largely unrelated to HTK technology itself, but they have nonetheless prevented BMDO from demonstrating that HTK interception can work reliably. The Welch report concluded that BMDO was still on 'step one' in demonstrating and validating HTK technology. Beyond this critical first step, HTK technology must then demonstrate reliability at a weapon system level as well as against 'likely real-world targets'. The panel recommended that BMDO programmes focus on demonstrating that HTK interception can consistently succeed against simple targets, then on whether the proposed weapon system is reliable, and finally on whether it can overcome a first layer of countermeasures.

Countering Countermeasures

The US Department of Defense has absorbed a number of the Welch Report recommendations. The 20 January announcement on NMD projected that a deployment decision in June 2000 will lead to actual deployment in 2005 rather than 2003, with the earlier date now viewed as presenting too high a degree of technical risk. Much of the debate over the battlefield effectiveness of HTK systems has centred on the issue of countermeasures. Steps that could theoretically be taken to thwart BMD systems include the use of decoys, designing missiles to have low radar cross-sections in order to reduce radar detection range, and using manoeuvring warheads. BMDO has a programme to assess countermeasures that the countries engaged in missile proliferation may realistically be expected to achieve, as well as US counters to those countermeasures. One benefit of layered defence, for example, will be to complicate the use of countermeasures, since those designed to work at lower altitudes may be ineffective outside the atmosphere and vice versa. The countermeasures debate will certainly continue, but there can be no resolution until BMD test programmes begin to succeed.

The ABL system would destroy ballistic missiles before they could deploy any countermeasures. A first flight test is scheduled to take place in 2002, and, under current plans, the system would be operational by 2006. Although the laser system is based on demonstrated technology, critics question whether it will be able to shoot through clouds, turbulence and other atmospheric disturbances. Computer simulations have indicated that the ABL could shoot down ballistic missiles from distances of several hundred kilometres despite platform vibration and turbulence. This is questioned by the Welch Report, however, which observed that it appears the simulations predict a 100% HTK success rate only by underestimating almost all that could go wrong with those systems. In operational terms, it would be necessary to deploy the laser system relatively near an adversary's ballistic missile launch sites. The laser system would also raise issues of ABM Treaty compliance, since it would be equally effective against both strategic and theatre ballistic missiles. The future may be further complicated by adversaries considering the use of cruise missiles as a countermeasure.

Heading for a Collision

US deployment of NMD, upper-tier TMD, and the ABL systems will not be feasible until major technical challenges are overcome. Where lower-tier TMD, which is not as technically daunting, is concerned, there are still key issues to sort out, especially involving lethality against NBC warheads. Even so, the US is certain to deploy *Patriot* PAC-3 and NAD. Moreover, even if technical uncertainties over the battlefield effectiveness of upper-tier TMD are not fully resolved, the US is highly likely to deploy one or more upper-tier TMD systems because of the perception that has developed of a very high level of threat and the impact of that perception on the politics of the issue in Washington. US Deputy Defense Secretary John Hamre told Congress in October 1998 that TMD was 'as close as the Department of Defense can get to a Manhattan Project'. As was the case with the Japanese, the European NATO countries will probably be reluctant to commit to an upper-tier TMD capability until they see an unambiguous threat to national territory.

While much concern has been voiced over Russian reaction to the US NMD decision, the real clash on the BMD may well take place with China. China currently deploys some 20 intercontinental ballistic missiles, and also has a ballistic missile submarine. The capabilities of the envisioned US NMD system might be insufficient to stop an attack from Russia, but it could be enough to halt a Chinese missile attack.

China has expressed bitter opposition both to an American NMD system and to US TMD deployments in Asia for the protection of regional allies and US forces. Were China to conclude as a result that it had to engage in a substantial build-up of strategic nuclear forces, it might also feel that it needed to resume nuclear testing, with severe consequences for the viability of the Nuclear Non-proliferation Treaty. Yet, there can be no doubt that the US would not allow itself to be vulnerable to ballistic missile attack from North Korea, or from other rogue states, if alternatives were available. The head-on collision with China will be difficult to avoid.

Information Technology: Vulnerabilities and Threats

As the end of the second millennium approaches, the press and technology communities are focusing world attention on the vulnerabilities that the Year 2000 computer problem (dubbed the Y2K problem) will bring. Y2K failures, induced by early programmers' use of two digits, rather than four, to represent years, may have many effects, some patent and some subtle. One thing, however, is clear: the deadline. The attention and the deadline have ensured there are resources to address Y2K effects. Some success is likely before the deadline, and eventually the problem will be overcome.

Y2K, however, is only one of many possible threats to the newly developing information infrastructure. Other important vulnerabilities exist in computer networks that control and coordinate everything from electric power delivery to communications, from transportation to water supply. Military command, control, communications and logistics systems are also at risk. These other vulnerabilities are not as well publicised and not as well understood as Y2K, but are potentially much more serious.

In particular, communications systems and computer networks are subject to denial-of-service attacks, where an intruder shuts out all users from a particular system. Remote-control sabotage of computer-co-ordinated infrastructures is more difficult, but within the demonstrated power of well trained specialists. One bold soul, working on a prominent US study claimed he could bring the United States infrastructure to its knees in ninety days with ten carefully selected computer specialists. Somewhat more cautious, Pentagon experts estimated that thirty special-ists could do the job with $10 million. Finding and fixing both patent and subtle vulnerabilities in these control systems will challenge infrastructure owners and operators. Unlike Y2K, these vulnerabilities have no fixed deadlines. To safeguard key infrastructures, potentially targeted nations must begin to set security measures in place now, before malicious individuals, organisations or governments identify the networks to target, obtain full data and carry out an attack.

What is Vulnerable?

Information infrastructures (including telecommunications, computer-based networks and electric power) may be attractive targets to criminals and enemies of any country that depends heavily on networked com-munications. As global diffusion of computing and communications technology accelerates, more nations are increasingly so dependent. By early 1999, over 200 nations were connected to the distributed computing environments that make up the Internet. The value of hosted services and the use of remote control by computerised infrastructure systems continues to explode. Some believe that Internet commerce in Europe and the US will top $5 trillion by 2005.

As information technology becomes increasingly accessible, organisations around the world use it to improve productivity. Increased efficiency permits larger volumes of information to be delivered and permits completion of individual transactions more quickly, but also brings dependency, because communications traffic volume grows to fill the increased capacity. Increasing military dependence in 'wired' nations is illustrated by the fact that the US military routes 95% of its communications through commercial cables, towers and satellite links. In addition, computer-assisted troop deployment and cargo logistics are the norm in US operations, and are increasingly so in other states. The potential economic and strategic loss from infrastructure collapse or compromise increases in direct proportion to the growth in commercial and government dependence on computer-based control and communication systems and in the number and value of on-line transactions.

Attacking telecommunications, electric power and computer networks is all the more enticing because these three infrastructures link, and increasingly coordinate, daily management of other critical infrastructures, such as transportation (trucking, railroads, airports), water supply, banking and finance, emergency services (police, medical, fire), and essential government services. Failures of power, communications or computer-network systems could therefore be expected to cascade into other areas. The internal dependence of the electric power grid upon itself may cause failures to propagate from one geographic area to another – failure in one portion of a national power grid can unbalance and topple the system in areas geographically distant from the initial failure. Trunk line and switch failures increase communications traffic on surviving links, a situation that may overburden remaining lines and switches and deny service to many users.

History has demonstrated that widespread electrical failures caused by nature and human interference can bring most economic activity to a standstill and even change governments. In January 1998, an overwhelming ice storm left up to 7m people without power in eastern Canada. Two weeks later, at least 500,000 were still blacked-out. Power was not fully restored to residences for a month. Some businesses waited longer. The crisis brought the degree of dependence on electricity sharply into focus: for example, according to one estimate, 80% of Quebec residents are entirely dependent on electricity for their power needs. In the end, dozens died and over C$2 billion was lost. A Canadian Security Intelligence Service article commented, 'Nature may have been the culprit this time, but another time it could be an attack from a computer hacker or terrorist group which knocks out the systems controlling the distribution of electricity'. Another historically instructive electrical disruption occurred in May 1974, when the Ulster Workers' Council (UWC) in Northern

Ireland, with the assistance of paramilitary groups, organised a fourteen-day strike by electrical and oil workers. Impairment of the electrical and oil-delivery infrastructures had a catastrophic effect on the commercial economy. In the words of one writer, the reduction (not blackout) of power to 30–60% of its normal level and the restriction of petrol supplies 'brought an intricate modern economy and way of life to a screeching halt, reducing government to impotence in the space of a few days. This is something the Provisional [Irish Republican Army] has never come near achieving in over twenty years of terror, assassination and guerrilla warfare'. The UWC successfully used the electrical and oil delivery infrastructures as strategic tools to topple the Northern Ireland Executive, the government-sanctioned authority in place at that time.

While the power failures described in the preceding paragraph were not the result of computer-assisted attack, it is evident that a week-long failure of today's computer-controlled infrastructures could have similar effects. Even shorter-lasting failures of information infrastructure control systems would result in large commercial losses, and perhaps even loss of life, if a well prepared enemy decided to launch an information attack. Telecommunications service providers in the US report that a five-hour fibre optic ring failure costs as much as $25,000 in direct expense and $15m in lost revenue. Revenue losses from complete failure of a fully loaded transcontinental or transoceanic bundled fibre trunk could run as high as $1m per second, though full loading would be rare, and competing providers would probably have the spare capacity to permit continued communication.

International corporate espionage, conducted by monitoring telecommunications and unauthorised entry into proprietary computer networks, costs commercial entities at least $10bn every year. Moreover, the armed forces of technologically advanced nations increasingly rely on technology. Preparatory or pre-emptive information attacks on military systems may be used to delay or impair action by the forces. Strategic attacks may be timed to coincide with important events, like military strikes, or computationally challenging events, like the turning of the millennium. In February 1998, one well coordinated attack on US Department of Defense computers, by two teenaged intruders from the US and a third from Israel, actually disrupted troop deployments to the Persian Gulf Region. Lt. Gen. Kenneth Minihan, director of the US National Security Agency, characterised the attack as 'moderately disruptive', and noted that 'the vulnerabilities exploited are relatively easily fixed'. Others observe that the most important consideration was not the ease with which the incident could have been prevented but the fact that it was not prevented. The vulnerability in the Solaris operating system exploited by the intruders was known at least eight months before the attack, and system administrators had been told to fix the problem in the preceding December.

The System's Inherent Fragility

Information infrastructures are vulnerable because they are large, diverse, complex, interconnected, fragmented and growing very rapidly. In 1996, there were 32m Internet devices (for example, personal computers, palmtop communication devices and personal digital assistants accessing the Internet), manufactured with different operating systems, for different purposes, under different standards in countries around the world. One US government study projects that there will be 300m such devices by the year 2002. Each device is itself a complex electronic system, executing various independently developed programs with their own sets of instructions. Each network of devices is therefore a system of systems.

Unpredictable behaviour, such as operating-system failure, routinely occurs in such devices individually. Interconnecting devices to create networks amplifies that unpredictability. In ordinary operation, a general purpose computer may enter more than a trillion-trillion discrete states (configurations). It is already impractical to test general-purpose computers and complex software comprehensively. One way in which attackers exploit this inherent unpredictability involves forcing systems to deal with artificial and unusual inputs, with the hope of causing an error, resulting in a 'buffer overflow'. They can then use buffer overflows to gain information about targeted systems. Sophisticated intruders can use overflows to write executable code in ordinarily protected areas of memory in some systems and thereby gain control.

Unless an opponent is searching a target for vulnerabilities in preparation for an attack, the first indication of a well planned assault may come with a wave of system failures. Like well executed physical onslaughts, the most effective information attacks will involve reconnaissance and planning, which would be conducted as unobtrusively as possible. In late 1998, operatives would scan computer systems linked to public networks for vulnerable points of entry using automated tools like SATAN (which is available from numerous World Wide Web sites). They would then attack those vulnerable points with proven methods (also available in tutorial files and automated script files on Web sites).

Although all systems are not equally vulnerable, most systems are at risk because not enough users and administrators take basic precautions. Once inside a targeted system, an intruder could leave behind a computer program called an 'assistant' or 'agent' which is capable of independently carrying out tasks. These programs include 'sniffers' which capture network data (for later analysis) such as passwords, and 'root kits' which enable an intruder to maintain priviledged access to a system and thereby cover traces of unauthorised activity. In this way, well-secured systems might be compromised when a 'password capture' program records the log-on of a legitimate user seeking access. Intruders may also leave viruses in sensitive systems to replicate and propagate, perhaps lying dormant and awaiting a signal, or trigger-event, to damage or manipulate data or interfere with operations. Sophisticated attackers would use 'stealth' viruses, programmed to hide from virus scanners, and 'mutating' viruses, which change their 'spawn' to evade detection.

Automated, user-friendly attack programs are improving and proliferating. Menu-driven virus development programs bring creation of some classes of mutating viruses within reach of relatively unsophisticated computer users. A second-generation SATAN tool, which not only detects vulnerable points of entry, but also automatically tries commonly successful attacks against those vulnerabilities, was developed by the Russians some time before 1993 and became generally available to those in the 'hacking' community in 1995. Numerous, widely available brute-force and artificially intelligent password-cracking tools expose systems to intrusion by preying upon poor password security practices (such as using first names, dates of birth and words in dictionaries as passwords) which are widespread. In late 1998, there were approximately 1,900 hacking Web sites, containing tutorials on intrusion and automated tools or offering a forum to discuss intrusion techniques. Some of them were as professionally designed and maintained as the best commercial Web pages.

Military forces are seeking to reduce such vulnerabilities internally and to capitalise on the vulnerabilities of adversary states. As the forces of technologically advanced nations enter the 'information battlespace', information attack capacity expands and intensifies. For example, the US Joint Chiefs of Staff published a document in February 1996 which provided guidance on influencing, degrading or destroying adversary command and control systems. By October 1998, this was considered insufficiently comprehensive and a new publication was issued on 'Information Operations', containing broader policy-level direction on:

- offensive and defensive information operations;
- planning, coordinating, and integrating information operations;
- intelligence support;
- defence and inter-agency relationships; and
- information operations training, exercises, modelling and simulation.

There are now at least eight nations with cyberwarfare capabilities on a par with US capabilities. Russia, the UK and Sweden have a strong interest in this sort of aggression. Systematic devotion of military resources to planning information attacks will make government-sponsored information operations more likely to succeed in degrading the infrastructures of targeted states and their militaries.

Whenever experienced specialists have looked for vulnerabilities in government and commercial networks, they have found security failings and were able to defeat whatever protections were in place. For example, a team of 35 US intelligence professionals tested American military and commercial security in 1997. That 'red team', as it was known, proved it was capable of shutting down US Pacific Command's command and control system and blacking out large geographic areas by penetrating electric power-grid control systems. Commercial 'red teams' can also be hired to find vulnerabilities in industrial networks. Such teams routinely find more security holes than their clients can afford to fix.

Attacks can be mounted without penetrating network access barriers. Some of the most effective techniques use the impressive connectivity and data-transfer rates of computer networks and telecommunications systems to saturate a target with incoming data and deny that target meaningful access to the network. A 1998 attack by a group supporting the Zapatista rebels in Mexico targeted computers in President Ernesto Zedillo's office, Mexico's Secretariat of National Defence and the US Department of Defense. Participants in the attack, located around the world, sent repeated requests for data every few seconds to targeted computers, which resulted in their generally being unable to service legitimate incoming data requests because their capacity had been consumed by the denial-of-service attack.

Attacks on entire networks to deny all users meaningful access are likewise possible. One common computer network software feature is a 'broadcast ping' or request for reply from all listening computers. A targeted network may have hundreds or thousands of listening computers. Sending rapid-fire repeated broadcast ping requests, forged to appear as if coming from a computer on the targeted network, can saturate that network with millions of reply messages, thus preventing all its users from having a meaningful service. Security conscious network administrators disable the broadcast ping feature, but not all appreciate the vulnerability. Denial-of-service attacks are also possible on some telephone systems. In countries that have crossbar or side-by-side mechanical telephone switches, or electronic telephone switching systems with in-band control signalling, a team of operatives with a knowledge of telephone control signals can 'seize' and 'stack' long-distance trunk lines from inside or outside the country, essentially denying ordinary callers the use of long distance lines.

Who Would Do Such a Thing?

While the more sensational reports about the Y2K problem, and the splash caused by hacker attacks, capture press attention, it is the secret, systematic devotion of resources to information sabotage by states, or significant sub-state actors with an international presence, that poses the primary threat to information operations. Sophisticated, well-organised forces can afford to spend months or years probing and collecting vulnerability intelligence and planting enabling software in vulnerable systems. Shrewd information operators will wait until the opportunity presents itself to get maximum leverage from their months or years of effort by using their access to disrupt economic stability or military function. Strategic objectives include:

- impairing the ability of an enemy to employ forces in physical combat;

- thwarting or delaying air or other military strikes to embarrass an attacker;

- intensifying economic sanctions by interfering with infrastructure within a target country; and

- improving posture on an issue of international importance by distracting a diplomatic opponent with domestic problems.

Preparatory information attacks may pave the way for air, ground and naval operations, while preventative attacks may preclude the need for air strikes, naval bombardment or ground invasion. If attacked with information techniques, governments may wish to retaliate in kind, rather than with physical invasion of sovereign geographical boundaries, especially if the international community grasps the fact that the UN Charter's definition of 'armed attack' does not include information operations. Additionally, governments could exploit information dominance in a coercive fashion, preventing the reconstitution of infrastructures as a step up from economic sanctions but a step down from physical violence. Combining information and physical attacks, simultaneously or in series, may provide the modern equivalent of the German Blitzkrieg, an attack many nations or commercial businesses may not be equipped to meet.

Poorly organised groups and scattered individual hackers are unlikely to be able to penetrate as many systems as state-sponsored assailants and, rather than having long-term strategic objectives, may be aiming to cause immediate harm or embarrassment to an organisation with which they disagree, to achieve some personal gain or simply to get personal satisfaction from their exploit. Nevertheless, a significant threat is posed by disaffected employees who may sabotage systems in anger at an organisation's policies or actions. These, indeed, have so far been the most common attackers of government and commercial operations.

Organised groups, such as terrorists, may consider disabling infrastructures as a way to draw attention to their ideological views. US President Clinton prominently linked cyber-threats with biological and chemical threats in his January 1999 remarks on American security in the twenty-first century. And when former US Secretary of Defense William Perry expressed concern, in February 1998, about the possibility of 'Grand Terrorism' – state-sponsored terrorism aiming to cause extensive loss of life or vast economic damage – he placed infrastructure-attack schemes alongside chemical, biological and nuclear attack scenarios, precisely because the health and welfare of citizens of the US and its allies depend upon infrastructures. Nevertheless, some analysts have argued that effective terrorists rely on the impact of infrequent but shocking events to draw attention to their ideologies and are unlikely to abandon physical bombs for logic bombs because gross physical violence causes public outrage that is more vigorously expressed than the diffuse reaction to a computer stumble.

Security Techniques

Creating better defences against information attacks must begin with existing security techniques, including redundancy, diversity, cryptography, access controls, intrusion tolerance, backups, software audit, and personnel security. These concepts will be employed and developed to improve infrastructure security gradually. Other traditional approaches to enhancing security include: isolation of systems to protect highly sensitive data; security through obscurity by using proprietary operating systems; and separation of control signals from communications content (out-of-band signalling).

Redundancy and diversity generally increase a system's ability to survive failure or compromise of a component or subsystem. Redundancy – having multiple copies of components that perform the same function in a system – decreases the likelihood of complete system failure. Faced with a point failure, the system can compensate by assigning the failed component's function to an operable alternative component. Redundant communications trunk lines routed through different geographic regions, for example, make long-distance telephone blackouts less likely if one of the trunks fails. Geographically distributed redundancy is particularly useful to counter focused physical disruption of information systems.

Diversity, using components or subsystems of various designs in the same system, increases security, especially against malicious computer-assisted attack, because different designs have different vulnerabilities. This technique prevents a single problem from incapacitating every node on a network. Combining diversity and redundancy can be very effective. For example, running an important database application simultaneously on two computers with different operating systems (perhaps in different geographic locations) means an enemy must probe and simultaneously disable both systems to cause complete failure. Of course there is a downside. Diversity and redundancy increase complexity and this makes standards more difficult to develop and maintain. Complexity also increases the likelihood that some vulnerabilities will be overlooked, while diverse components may interact in unexpected ways to create new vulnerabilities.

Modern cryptographic methods are capable not only of encoding a message to prevent unauthorised parties from understanding it, but also of authenticating its originators' identity and verifying that it has not been tampered with *en route*. A communication can be decrypted, authenticated or verified using a key. Since the late 1970s, public key cryptology, examples of which include RSA and the Diffie-Hellman key exchange, permits secure communication over public networks between parties which have not had an opportunity to meet in secret to exchange keys.

These techniques have their dangers. The US has led efforts to develop export-control policies to prevent proliferation of strong encryption (with key lengths in excess of 56 bits or, in some cases, 64 bits) which, it argues, would help criminals to hide their communications. In December 1998, signatories of the Wassenaar Arrangement (including France, Germany, Japan, the Russian Federation and the UK) also indicated some support for such policies, but they are opposed by some other countries. The Indian government, for example, stated publicly that US encryption products are intentionally weakened before export and called upon India's domestic software industry to develop its own. Despite export controls, strong cryptographic algorithms are available through published academic resources, and software implementations are available on the World Wide Web.

Access controls, including user profiles, static and dynamic passwords and firewall software and hardware, are aimed at preventing unauthorised access to computer control systems and data. Firewalls (dedicated computers that apply policy at the perimeter between private networks and public networks) are designed to prevent intrusion into private network computers, but poor password practice and vulnerabilities in complex operating systems and applications programs work against their effectiveness and make it probable that a determined attack will breach access controls.

Intrusion tolerance is a branch of security research which takes as a starting point the assumption that access controls will frequently fail, and concentrates on reducing the negative consequences. Information 'inside the firewall' can be made intrusion-tolerant by encrypting it. Data (or private cryptographic keys) can be broken into parts, alternating character-by-character if necessary, and stored piece-by-piece on two or more computers, so attackers have to work harder to reassemble data. Careful administration of access privileges, so that even legitimate users can only access those parts of the system they need to use, can reduce the adverse consequences of a legitimate user's account being compromised. Comprehensive activity-logs and audit trails, monitored by computer programs designed to detect unusual activity, can warn system administrators of attacks in progress.

Re-establishing service after failure, and replacing corrupt or lost data, can be made possible through emergency operations plans and backup software. US war-powers legislation permits the president to control and oversee reconstitution of telecommunications infrastructure. Establishing organisational operating procedures that include regular backups at network and local level can reduce losses from information attack.

Software audits and personnel security procedures reduce the threat of malicious action by insiders. Activity logs that monitor access to important equipment, and background checks of personnel to be trusted with sensitive information, are used in nuclear power generation and military organisations. Lessons learned in those communities may profit-ably be applied to sensitive positions in information infrastructure organisations. In particular, security of software code databases can be improved by logging all database changes, and archiving information on the operatives who made them, so that malicious code insertion can be investigated.

Focused Action is Needed

People who live in technologically advanced societies have become familiar with the problems that arise when small networks or individual computers fail. At times they cannot get money from their bank cash machine, or the questions they ask of their insurance company cannot be answered because 'the computer is down'. These difficulties are multiplied many times over as the information infrastructure is enlarged, and made more complex and fragile, through interconnection. The innate vulnerabilities of these systems are open to attack, by hackers, terrorists or antagonistic governments. The consequences are serious, and growing, because if the systems are not protected, they offer the opportunity to disrupt military operations, com-munications, electric power service, banking and finance, transportation, water supply, continuity of emergency services and even of government itself.

'Wired' nations – those that have grown to rely on their information systems to increase productivity and control critical infrastructures – are particularly at risk. Disruptions planned over months or years by one state against another, or a powerful sub-state organisation, could disrupt several infrastructures in such wired nations simultaneously, causing, at the least, significant economic damage and, at the worst, a breakdown in essential systems with consequent loss of life. Existing security concepts provide some protection, but nowhere near enough. It will take focused effort by industry and governments, of the kind and size now being directed at known Y2K vulnerabilities, to expand these concepts and create new solutions to thwart the malicious attacks that are certain to be mounted in the future.

●

The New Face of Terrorism?

In the mid-1980s, terrorism appeared to be a growing threat to Western democracies, orchestrated in part by the Soviet Union and its satellites. Less than a decade later, for a few years following the fall of the Berlin Wall, it appeared the menace was on the wane and might even disappear as incidents declined. Today, the threat is once again rising, but instigated by different terrorists to those that dominated the scene earlier. Alongside the still numerous old-style, politically motivated terrorists, there is a serious new threat from terrorists whose motivation is religious, or purely personal. They are more likely to use chemical or biological weapons and to cause destruction on a larger scale than their politically motivated counterparts, and are therefore more dangerous.

Although a new type of terrorist has appeared, a continuity can be discerned in the tactics and weapons used and the targets that have been recently selected. A threat that causes great concern, however, and which would mark a distinct change, is the possibility that these terrorists could acquire nuclear weapons, which they might not hesitate to use. There has already been a sharp increase in violence and bloodshed using the usual combination of bombs and bullets. Efforts at meeting this threat have also not changed much, although the US has tried to adjust by allocating greater resources to counter-terrorism and by constructing new responses to perceived emergent threats.

The Terrorist Threat

During 1998, there were, as usual, terrorist assassinations and attempted assassinations, kidnappings and bombings. Assassination attempts were made on Georgian President Eduard Shevardnadze, Pakistani Prime Minister Nawaz Sharif and Uzbekistan President Islam Karimov. States like Algeria, Colombia and Sri Lanka were mired in insurgencies in which terrorism figured prominently. Deadly bombings in Nairobi, Dar es Salaam and Omagh demonstrated that conventional terrorism directed against Western democracies and their interests continues to thrive.

Terrorists whose main goal was to wreck the fragile peace processes in Northern Ireland and the Middle East used violence with considerable effect during 1998. The Good Friday Agreement on Northern Ireland was finalised in April 1998 in the midst of a series of attacks designed to disrupt it. In August 1998, the 'Real' Irish Republican Army exploded a bomb in a crowded market in Omagh, killing 29 and injuring more than 200. It was the most deadly single incident in the last 30 years of Northern Ireland's sectarian violence, but its effect was the opposite to what was intended, strengthening rather than weakening the peace process. In March 1999, a car bomb attack killed Rosemary Nelson, a nationalist lawyer, as she was driving from her home in Lurgan. The murder, which was seen as a deliberate attempt to derail the peace process, occurred as Northern Ireland's leaders were gathering in the United States for St Patrick's Day celebrations, where they intended to address the weapon-decommissioning problem.

In the Middle East, bomb attacks in Tel Aviv, Jerusalem and elsewhere in 1998 sought to derail the stalled peace process and prevent its renewal. A suicide bombing in a Jerusalem market, by members of the Islamic extremist group *Hamas,* in November 1998 killed two people and injured 22, and briefly resulted in a suspension of the Israeli cabinet's consideration of the US-brokered Wye Accord for settling the Arab–Israeli conflict. Despite the anger and concern that this outrage engendered, the agreement was finally accepted. Further attacks of this kind could, however, have a significant impact on the Israeli election which is set for 17 May 1999, just as similar violence affected the last polls.

The deadliest acts of international terrorism during 1998 were the bombings of US embassies in Kenya and Tanzania on 7 August 1999, killing 257 and injuring thousands. Twelve Americans died in the attacks which were perpetrated by terrorists linked to wealthy Saudi exile Osama bin Laden. In response, on 20 August, US sea-launched *Tomahawk* cruise missiles were used to attack selected targets in Afghanistan and Sudan. In Afghanistan, targets included the Aswa Kali al Batr base south of Kabul, which according to the US had trained 'hundreds if not thousands' of terrorists, along with a support complex and four training camps. The targets in Sudan included the Shifa pharmaceutical plant in Khartoum, which the US claimed was producing chemicals used for VX nerve gas. US President Bill Clinton stated these targets were linked to bin Laden, but there were widely voiced doubts about his connection with the pharmaceutical plant. Although some US allies supported the strikes, intense criticism from around the world was the dominant reaction. The difficulties in making a public case for the US action illustrate the difficult choices involved in responding to terrorism.

Although such acts show the continued threat posed by terrorists using conventional explosives and arms, the US has become increasingly concerned about the threat from nuclear, biological and chemical (NBC) terrorism, and 'cyber-terrorism' directed against critical infrastructures. US initiatives to combat these emerging threats were announced with a flourish on 22 January 1999. Thus far, however, although reports of terrorist interest in NBC and 'cyber-terrorism' are increasing, they largely involve hoaxes, simple expressions of interest and often amateurish attempts to obtain agents or materials.

US white supremacists have shown interest in biological weaponry, including an alleged plot to attack subways in New York City by Larry Wayne Harris, a former member of Aryan Nation. The US Federal Bureau of Investigation (FBI) arrested Harris and his accomplice William Leavit in Henderson, Nevada, in February 1998, following information that their automobile contained what was believed to be anthrax. Although there was no clear indication of how the agent was to be used, speculation focused on an attack on New York's subways. In any event, the two men were charged with felony counts of conspiracy-to-possess and of possessing a biological agent for use as a weapon. The substance turned out to be an innocuous anthrax vaccine for animals rather than anthrax itself. The two men were cleared of biological-weapons charges.

In early February 1999, letters containing a substance labelled 'anthrax' were received at the *Washington Post* and the Old Executive Office Building in Washington DC, an NBC News office in Atlanta and a US post office in Columbus, Georgia. These incidents were part of a series of anthrax scares throughout the US in late 1998 and early 1999, targeted at sites including abortion clinics, office buildings, courthouses and post offices, especially in the greater Los Angeles area. All of them have so far proved to be hoaxes, and are apparently the result of increased public attention to NBC terrorism in fiction, the media and official pronouncements.

Groups and Causes

Old and new international and indigenous terrorists, both professionals and amateurs, with political, religious, and other powerful motivations are operating in the new environment. The patterns of terrorism familiar in previous decades are breaking down and a complex and murky new reality is emerging. Terrorist groups inspired by Marxism–Leninism are in decline in the West, their future prospects dimmed by the collapse of communism in the former Soviet Union and Eastern Europe. For example, in an eight-page communiqué issued in April 1998, the German Red Army Faction, which conducted a savage campaign of bombings and assassinations in the 1970s, announced that it was disbanding and ending its 'urban guerrilla battle'.

However, there are still a number of Marxist or Maoist revolutionaries active in other parts of the world, including Colombia, Nepal, Peru and the Philippines. In Colombia, the National Liberation Army (ELN) and other leftist groups have been attacking oil installations, pipelines and other infrastructure targets. Persistent ELN attacks in recent years have led to repeated production shutdowns by the Colombian National Oil Company,

ECOPETROL. On 30 July 1997, an ELN bomb caused a major oil spill and the suspension of pumping operations for more than a week. In 1998, three oil workers, two British and one American, were seriously injured when a bomb exploded under the office and sleeping quarters of a British Petroleum drilling rig in Colombia. Organised crime and terrorism are increasingly interwoven, particularly when drugs are involved. Violence arising from the narcotics trade is rife in South America and South-east Asia, and there is a significant rise in this form of terrorism in Central Asia. National, ethnic, tribal, and communal violence is raging through Asia, Africa and Europe, and ethnic and national-separatist objectives continue to inspire terrorism. Terrorist campaigns are being waged by Abkhazi separatists in Georgia, Sikhs and Bodo militants in India, Kosovars in Serbia, Chechens in Russia, Basques in Spain, Tamils in Sri Lanka, Kurds in Turkey and other groups seeking independence or autonomy.

The capture in early 1999 of Abdullah Öcalan – the leader of the Kurdistan Workers' Party (PKK), which has conducted a campaign of terrorism in Turkey and elsewhere in pursuit of an independent 'Greater Kurdistan' – focused world attention on Kurdish violence. Following Öcalan's capture, his brother Osman, who remains a senior PKK member, threatened counter-action. A car bomb attack in the central Turkish town of Cankiri in March 1999, which killed three and injured several others, including the regional governor, was believed to have been a reprisal for Öcalan's arrest, albeit not by the PKK. The Kurdish insurgents were believed responsible for a series of explosions in Istanbul and Ankara, including an attack that killed 13 people when bombs were thrown into a department store in Istanbul. Ethnic separatism in Chechnya apparently inspired a bomb explosion in the crowded central marketplace of the Russian city of Vladikavkaz on 20 March 1999, killing 60 and injuring 100. Russian President Boris Yeltsin condemned the bombing, calling it an 'act of terrorism'.

Terrorists of the ideological right have also grown in significance in Europe and the US. Timothy McVeigh and Terry L. Nichols, who were associated with the US Christian white supremacist and militia movements, planted the bomb which destroyed the federal office building in Oklahoma City in April 1995, killing 168 people and wounding hundreds more. Religious terrorism is also rising elsewhere. Islamic fundamentalists are challenging governments in Algeria and Egypt, conducting widespread campaigns of domestic and, in some cases, international terrorism. In Algeria, massacres by both Islamic extremists and government forces are estimated to have resulted in 78,000 deaths since 1992.

Single-issue terrorism, inspired by such issues as environmental degradation, animal rights or abortion, is rising. For example, abortion clinics and doctors have been the targets of terrorism across the US, including a number of anthrax hoaxes in the past year and a bombing in

Asheville, North Carolina, in early 1999. Attacks on tourists are another growth area. In November 1997, the Islamic Group massacred 58 foreign tourists and four Egyptians visiting a temple in Luxor, Egypt. In December 1998 in Yemen, and in February 1999 in Uganda, tourists were kidnapped and killed with no demands made.

Towards Less Restraint

Striking changes in terrorist groups and the emergence of terrorism by single individuals have been accompanied by significant shifts in terrorist behaviour as new patterns are interwoven with old. From the 1960s to the early 1980s, politically-inspired terrorists were generally restrained in their use of violence to pursue ideological or national-separatist goals. Although these old-style terrorists are still operating, they may soon be eclipsed by a new variety, who pose a different threat and challenge entrenched views about terrorism.

The new terrorists are driven by religious or millenarian beliefs, by motives such as revenge and punishment, or by single issues. To the extent that they are religious in orientation, they are clearly less political than their predecessors. But they are not apolitical, as is evident in the political rationales surrounding such atrocities as the bombings in Oklahoma City and of the World Trade Center in New York in 1993. The new terrorists are likely to be more indiscriminate and more lethal than the old. Some are more sophisticated in technological, operational and other terms than earlier terrorists, and more capable of conducting operations at great distances. Yet others, such as the individuals responsible for the World Trade Center bombing, are clearly amateurs.

The new terrorists are less cohesive organisationally than the old. Indeed, the rise of 'loners' and small, loose-knit groups is critical in shaping perceptions of the new terrorism. The 'Unabomber' campaign and the informal terrorist-financing network of bin Laden are cases in point. Theodore Kaczynski, the Unabomber, was active for nearly 20 years, killing three and injuring 23 with a series of bombs sent through the mail. He is at one end of the terrorist spectrum – an individual with a vague cause or agenda (in Kaczynski's case, an anti-technology, environmental crusade), often troubled by inner demons, and wanting to lash out.

Bin Laden, according to the US State Department, is 'one of the most significant sponsors of Islamic extremist activities in the world today'. It is claimed that he uses his wealth to finance a network of terrorists, many of them 'Arab Afghans' who fought against the Soviet Union in Afghanistan. He is alleged to have been involved in the bombings of the World Trade Center, the Khubar Towers US military accommodation in Dhahran, Saudi Arabia, in 1996 and the US embassies in Nairobi and Dar es Salaam in 1998.

All of these indicators of the new terrorism, from increased lethality to the importance of individuals acting on their own, are evolutionary rather revolutionary. Some predate the end of the Cold War; some arose in the 1990s. But they all point to less restraint on the part of the terrorists.

Weapons and Tactics

The weaponry used by terrorists ranges from the improvised and primitive to the highly technical and sophisticated. Nonetheless, despite a wider range of technological possibilities, terrorists today, as they have in the past, favour old fashioned guns and bombs. Bombings are the most common acts of terrorist violence, and, as those in Oklahoma City, Nairobi and Omagh show, they are also the deadliest. What is most serious is that terrorists are using more efficient weapons than at earlier periods. Their bombs have more sophisticated fuses, and use higher-energy explosives that are less easily detectable. The guns now in use include automatic and plastic weapons. Hand-held surface-to-surface and surface-to-air missiles are now in the hands of terrorists.

Operationally, terrorists remain conservative, although some groups have demonstrated a significant ability to adapt their tactics. Since high technology weaponry and complex operations increase the chances of failure, they have not generally appealed to terrorists who prefer controllable effects. Some innovations in weapons may also increase the likelihood of detection. Because more time is needed to obtain equipment and materials, logistics become more complicated and more training and specialist personnel are required.

Although contemporary terrorists continue to prefer simpler weapons and operations, fears that new patterns of terrorism threaten acts of mass destruction and mass disruption are not entirely out of place. All of these trends are serious and highlight the graver dangers that lie ahead. There is no doubt that there is increased likelihood of NBC terrorism, and perhaps also of attacks on critical infrastructures using 'cyber' means, but they are not inevitable, given the obstacles to their use. Prudent planning to counter them should begin now, but hyperbole and panic should be avoided.

Rising Conventional Worries

Terrorists continue to engage, as they have in the past, in attacks for publicity, money (ransom demands and extortion), to exact revenge or to inflict punishment. Their actions have perhaps become even more important to weaker states as a method of challenging the US and the West generally. The advantages derived from Western military technology could, in principle, disappear if forces or civilians were confronted by terrorists willing to take extreme action. In this context, terrorism may be used by states as a means of waging surrogate warfare against powerful adversaries, or to undermine weak regional neighbours while minimising the risks to the sponsoring state. Terrorism may be used not only directly or indirectly against the Western states, but also against their military operations, including regional intervention, by attacking key ports, airfields and communications networks. Such attacks could be designed to degrade military effectiveness or to sap the will for overseas interventions, even where the object is humanitarian or peacekeeping.

There is no doubt that terrorism as surrogate warfare is already occurring. The truck bomb that exploded at the Khubar Towers apartments near Dhahran, Saudi Arabia, in June 1996, resulting in the deaths of 19 US airmen and injuring 500, including 240 American citizens, was clearly part of an attempt to force the US out of the Middle East and the Gulf. Following the attack there were threats against other US facilities in the region. It has been argued that removing the US military presence in Saudi Arabia is a key motive of bin Laden's campaign. Iraq has consistently threatened terrorist action against US targets, and against neighbouring states that provide bases to US and UK aircraft patrolling the northern and southern no-fly zones. Iraqi threats of terrorist attacks, involving chemical and biological weapons, during diplomatic and military crises in 1998 had to be taken seriously because such terrorism is the only plausible instrument available to Baghdad.

Unconventional Prospects

Awareness of NBC terrorist threats to the West has been heightened by the Sarin nerve gas attack in the Tokyo subway system in March 1995 that killed 12 and injured thousands; continuing reports of terrorist interest in chemical and biological agents; reports of nuclear smuggling out of Russia and its neighbours; and the rapid diffusion of technologies. Growing concerns about NBC terrorism have been paralleled by apprehension that there may be 'cyber-terrorism' against critical infrastructures. There has not yet been anything in this sphere comparable to the Tokyo subway attack, but concern about the possibility of something equally devastating has resulted in a US presidential commission, a presidential decision directive and new US programmes.

These threats are clearly worrying, but the full extent of the danger they pose has not yet been demonstrated. NBC and, to a lesser extent, perhaps, 'cyber-terrorism', are seen as low-probability, high-consequence events. Although worst-case scenarios can be constructed, experience so far indicates the value of a different perspective. Events in this area have mainly turned out to be hoaxes, inept efforts to acquire materials and capabilities, or of minor importance. Future incidents are likely to be similarly low-impact.

New Challenges for Counter-terrorism

In response to its perception that a different kind of terrorist threat is on the increase, the US has declared a 'war' on terrorism; strengthened counter-terrorism through programmes to deal with NBC and 'cyber threats', and increased physical security at US embassies and missions. The most dramatic US response so far has been its military strikes against terrorist bases and suspect sites; in particular the US cruise missile strikes on Afghanistan and Sudan in response to the East African embassy bombings. The other high profile counter-terrorist action was the abduction of Öcalan from Kenya by Turkish forces in February 1999. Öcalan had travelled to Kenya after an odyssey through Europe, evading extradition warrants. His requests for political asylum were rejected, but his fate upset Turkey's relations with Greece, Italy, Russia and elsewhere in the month before his capture and in its aftermath. The unorthodox methods used in both counter-terrorist actions have been criticised sharply, and not only by Afghanistan and Sudan, whose territory was attacked from the air, or by the PKK whose leader was abducted. These two controversial events have created an impression of fundamental change taking place in the approach to counter-terrorism. In fact, the US and other nations around the world combat terrorism with much the same tools as in the past.

The traditional responses to terrorism primarily involve law enforcement, diplomacy and international cooperation, and occasionally the threat or use of military force. The effectiveness of these methods is questionable. Reaction to the US airstrikes against bin Laden and the Öcalan incident demonstrate the limits to international cooperation in this area. Those limits are also clear in the waning role played by sanctions. The UN has imposed sanctions on states that have refused to comply with UN resolutions, such as Libya in its refusal to turn over for trial those suspected of the 1988 Lockerbie bombing of a Pan American aircraft. The US has also imposed unilateral sanctions on states supporting terrorism. The role of sanctions in counter-terrorism and other areas is under fire and may unravel in the future. Even when there is an NBC threat, as posed by Iraq, it is difficult to maintain an international consensus for this form of response.

In addition to the difficulties posed by limits on international cooperation, counter-terrorism is increasingly complicated by the way the threat is changing. The emergence of individual terrorists and small groups, including the loose network of stateless terrorists financed by bin Laden, and of information technologies that make 'virtual' organisations possible, have all made terrorists more difficult to target. These new-style terrorists are more difficult to identify, and they have no territory to defend, or to be attacked. Identifying new apocalyptic organisations that could pose NBC threats is difficult. They do not operate in the manner of traditional terrorist organisations, and indicators or signatures of their behaviour may not be evident or comprehensible. Uncertainties about their organisations and operations, in addition to the intrinsically vague ideologies and characteristics of such groups, especially when they claim religious or racial inspirations or millenarian visions, make their behaviour even more difficult to predict than that of traditional terrorists. There are also specific problems with intelligence related to 'cyber-terrorism'. Terrorists that may be interested in 'cyber-terrorism' may be disaffected 'loners', and their attacks may be undertaken against targets anywhere in the world, which increases the difficulty of detecting those responsible.

Although the military aspect of counter-terrorism has been highlighted by the missile attacks on Afghanistan and Sudan, the US has not given up other instruments of counter-terrorism, as the efforts to bring to trial the perpetrators of the embassy bombings in Africa and the Lockerbie bombing suggest. Moreover, one reading of events suggests that the military response came only after diplomacy failed, at least in Afghanistan, and only after highly provocative attacks against embassies, which are symbolic, high-visibility targets. Finally, while these strikes had unique features (they aimed to disrupt or prevent future actions and to destroy a facility alleged to be linked to NBC weapons as well as to terrorists), military actions have been taken before. In 1986, Libya was bombed in response to its involvement in the 1983 La Belle discotheque bombing in West Berlin. In 1993, the US responded with cruise missiles to revelations that Iraq had planned to assassinate former US President George Bush.

The effectiveness of military responses of this kind is very much in doubt. It was widely believed that the airstrike on Libya deterred it from supporting terrorism, and this may have been the case immediately afterwards, but Libya has continued to support terrorism directed against the US and the UK, and the Lockerbie bombing, in which Libyans were implicated, occurred after the 'deterring strike'. Whether or not the US action provoked retaliation, the Libyan example shows clearly that military strikes are not a panacea, and the expectations of what they can achieve should be appropriately limited.

At best, such military strikes can achieve tactical successes, and perhaps have a benefit in signalling to terrorists and their state supporters the resolve of the responding state. This may be the impact of the missile strikes on Afghanistan. The *Taleban* has been unwilling to surrender bin Laden as the US has demanded, but the *Taleban*'s statements following the strikes, and their later apparent efforts to rein in bin Laden's activities in Afghanistan (which may have prompted him to leave the country), suggest that they received the message that the US would not tolerate terrorist activities emanating from, or planned in, Afghanistan.

Military strikes on terrorists are unlikely to be decisive, but this reaction can be expected in the future from the US and other states threatened by terrorists and capable of launching an attack. Any country using military strikes needs to build domestic consensus for the action and, probably, international consensus as well. If this is not carefully done, the strikes could be counterproductive. They are probably best reserved for reaction to a significant NBC or 'cyber attack', which would create an instant consensus for retaliation. In response to conventional, or even unconventional, terrorism, military forces could be used to support law enforcement by providing logistics, equipment and training. This role for the military has been established in some countries and is emerging in others.

A Never-ending Fight

With the exception of successful surrogate warfare or an effective rejectionist campaign against a peace process, conventional terrorist attacks, while deadly and costly, are unlikely to achieve the terrorists' aims. Perhaps their greatest near-term effect is to reduce democratic freedoms by leading to restrictions in many areas of life. Terrorist attacks are fostering the creation of an extensive and expensive new security culture, even when there is only a suspicion of terrorism. This was the case with the increased airport security that followed the explosion on the Trans World Airlines Flight 800 in 1996, which turned out not to have been the result of a terrorist bomb.

The long-term effects of terrorism are even more difficult to assess. Terrorism is unlikely to weaken the strong democracies in the West fundamentally. It could, however, help undermine some of the fragile ones emerging from authoritarianism. Although terrorism cannot be eliminated in democracies, effective counter-terrorism strategies can be undertaken. What is needed most is to shore up the foundations for improved international cooperation, for any serious effort to combat terrorism will require such cooperation if suspected or actual terrorists are to be located and their activities thwarted.

Within a world being refashioned by profound political and technical changes, terrorism will continue to pose a threat, and the West will undoubtedly remain the primary target of terrorists. The emerging threats of terrorist use of NBC weapons or 'cyber attacks' cannot be dismissed out of hand, but the level of danger should be seen in proportion. This will not for some time be as great as that presented by guns and bombs. Nuclear capabilities are difficult to acquire, and chemical and biological weapons are difficult to handle. Terrorists are apt to rely on tried and true conventional bombs which have, over the years, become ever more damaging. Yet, while conventional terrorism continues to exact a deadly toll and to be economically and physically disruptive, the effects of even these tragic attacks should not be exaggerated.

The Americas

The impeachment crisis in the US came to an anticlimactic end when President Bill Clinton's Republican accusers failed to garner a clear majority vote for either of the two charges they had raised. In effect, the effort to punish the president foundered on the public's belief that, while he was indeed a rogue who had carefully skirted the truth about his sexual peccadilloes, he was doing a fine job of leading the country. And the economic picture had rarely looked rosier; a boom that had lasted for so long that it had all but wiped out memories of what a downturn looked like. If the administration's immediate domestic crisis had ended, however, there were an unfortunate number of foreign crises that needed to be dealt with under difficult political conditions.

While it was running its course, the impeachment process did not seriously dent the president's ability to act decisively, if not always wisely, in foreign policy. He will not be immune from forthcoming Republican attacks, however. Frustrated by their inability to paint the domestic scene in their preferred colours – they had lost the impeachment fight, and were also losing the budget, tax and lifestyle fights – Clinton's political opponents were turning their sights to foreign policy. Because of the bunching of presidential primaries in the early part of 2000, the election campaign has, in effect, already begun and the Republicans have chosen foreign policy as their preferred bludgeon. Accusations filled the air: Clinton had mismanaged alleged spying in the US by China; ignored perfidy by North Korea over nuclear and missile developments; mishandled intransigence by Saddam Hussein and the problem of his hold on power in Iraq; and endangered US troops in the Kosovo imbroglio. The administration's record in 1998 was arguably a good one, but, in what is really an election year, rife with partisan passions, that will make little difference.

Clinton made a visit to South America in March 1999, but among all the problems he had to deal with, Latin America was not a high priority. That was unfortunate, for Latin American problems grew worse in 1998, and threatened to engulf some of the fragile democracies that have developed there. The people of this region faced a drop in economic well-being in almost all countries; drug cultures and growing criminal influence in some; corruption and insecurity in many. They reached out to a strongman in hope that he could turn the tide. In some cases, it was to a former military leader, who may have hung up his uniform but not shed his autocratic ways; and in others it was to civilian leaders who searched for constitutional loopholes to allow them to remain in power beyond their

Map I The Americas

IISSmaps

Alaska (US)

N

C A N A D A

Ottawa

U N I T E D
S T A T E S

Washington DC

Gulf of Mexico

Nassau

Havana

BAHAMAS

MEXICO

CUBA

DOMINICAN
REPUBLIC

Mexico
City

HAITI

Santo Domingo

JAMAICA

ANTIGUA AND BARBUDA

Belmopan

Kingston

Port-au-
Prince

BELIZE

GUATEMALA

HONDURAS

Caribbean Sea

BARBADOS

Guatemala City

Tegucigalpa

EL SALVADOR

NICARAGUA

TRINIDAD AND TOBAGO

San Salvador

Managua

Panama
City

COSTA RICA

Caracas

Port of Spain

San José

Georgetown

PANAMA

VENEZUELA

Paramaribo

Bogotá

GUYANA

Cayenne

SURINAM

FRENCH
GUIANA

COLOMBIA

Quito

ECUADOR

B R A Z I L

PERU

Lima

La Paz

Brasília

BOLIVIA

PARAGUAY

Asunción

URUGUAY

Santiago

Buenos Aires

ARGENTINA

Montevideo

A T L A N T I C   O C E A N

P A C I F I C   O C E A N

— international boundary

■ capital city

0   1,000km

0   500 miles

Falkland Islands
(UK)

present mandates. Unless some way can be found to deal with the pressing needs of the people, it will be difficult to keep these nascent democracies from sliding back to authoritarianism.

●

The United States:
Halcyon Days in a Year of Crisis

For the United States, 1998 was the year of high constitutional crisis and low sexual farce. Upon waking in February 1999 from a 13-month impeachment nightmare, Americans could be forgiven for their bewilderment: what, if anything, of significance had transpired? Where some saw a shameful debacle of American leadership – the fruit of their president's reckless dissembling – others decried a political witch hunt from which President Bill Clinton had not only escaped, but had emerged more popular than any second-term president in more than half a century. In opinion polls it was no contest: with Clinton's acquittal by the United States Senate, most Americans felt that common sense had prevailed.

Certainly Clinton's job performance ratings were buoyed by a continuing and vibrant economic boom, and by general satisfaction with his centrist policies. Yet the Clinton trial also revealed much that was unsettled in the United States: the bitter partisan divide; the sense of a Washington political, judicial and media culture mutating into something alien and out of control; and, not least, a president who had been willing to gamble his presidency for a series of trysts with an young intern, and in the White House – and then lie about it publicly. Although it remained difficult to judge the long-term consequences, one thing seemed clear: the comity of American politics would not soon be restored.

America's place in the world was, by contrast, barely unsettled. In a second year of global economic turmoil, US growth helped keep much of the developed world out of recession. Although it was not clear that the resulting American trade deficit was politically sustainable, nor that the stock market bubble could last forever, predictions of an imminent collapse had been made for at least the previous two years. Likewise, the United States demonstrated a forceful foreign policy in places – such as the Balkans and the Persian Gulf – where force or the threat of force was required. The US also played a critical role in keeping peace processes in Northern Ireland and the Middle East alive, if not healthy. Yet 1998 was also the year in which American leaders grew increasingly anxious about how little they could do to counter global threats to the core security interests of the US and its allies – North Korean ballistic missiles (and potentially nuclear missiles), Iraqi weapons of mass destruction (WMD) programmes, and the unremitting anger of a very rich Saudi terrorist.

The (Culture) War at Home

In the last days of 1998, William Jefferson Clinton became the second US President in history, but the first elected president, to be impeached by the United States House of Representatives. The two articles of impeachment – for perjury in grand jury testimony, and for obstruction of justice – grew out of his denials of, and his efforts to cover up, a sexual affair with White House intern Monica Lewinsky.

Throughout the year-long saga, opinion polls indicated that a large majority of Americans held consistently mixed views. They were disgusted by Clinton's misbehaviour and dishonesty, yet they approved of his performance as president. Fed up with the intensive coverage of the scandal, and angered by what they viewed as an unremittingly partisan campaign by special prosecutor Kenneth Starr and the Republican majority in Congress to drive from office the man they had twice elected as their president, they nevertheless avidly watched the on-going soap opera on TV. In Washington by contrast, partisan passions were unalloyed. Indeed, the battle lines were drawn more clearly as the scandal progressed. Republicans joined together in outrage at Clinton's legal evasions. Democrats formed a united front against what many of them viewed as an attempted coup by the Republican majority in Congress.

For Republicans the case against Clinton was simple: the facts showed that he could not be trusted. While his lack of self-control was disturbing enough, the case was not – they insisted – about sex. Rather, it was about his willingness to subvert the course of justice in order to conceal a sexual affair. In their view, he had not only perjured himself in grand jury testimony, but he had directed a conspiracy to obstruct the course of justice. If it cherished the rule of law and the integrity of its judicial process, the Republicans insisted, the United States could not afford a chief executive who lied under oath, suborned others to lie under oath, and got away with it.

Clinton's defenders focused on the nature of the process against him. They called it an inquisition – targeting not only sex, but human weakness itself – for the purpose of undoing a Democratic presidency that conservative Republicans had considered illegitimate from the start. They maintained – as a matter of common sense if not law – that the most serious charges against Clinton grew out of a series of entrapments. With Democrats holding 45 of 100 seats in the US Senate, it had never appeared likely that a Senate trial would produce the two-thirds majority required for the president's conviction and removal from office. In the event, neither article of impeachment mustered even a simple majority: the closest vote – on the perjury charge – was an even 50-50.

The morning after, Republicans found themselves nursing a painful hangover. They had already suffered losses in the November Congressional elections – prompting their firebrand leader, House Speaker Newt Gingrich, to resign. Although the GOP retained a thin majority in both Houses, it was the first time since 1934 that the party that held the White House had actually won Congressional seats in an off-term election.

While some voters – particularly American blacks, who turned out in unusually high numbers – were evidently punishing the president's pursuers, the results also reflected two broader themes. First, the US basked in phenomenal prosperity. By the end of 1998, the period of economic expansion – only a few months short of being the longest since the Second World War – showed no signs of abating, and indeed accelerated with a fourth-quarter burst that raised the year's growth in gross domestic product (GDP) to 3.9% over 1997. While the deeper causes of this prosperity were complex and in some ways mysterious, the president could take some credit for one enabling factor. A second year of federal budget surpluses allowed the Federal Reserve to lower interest rates without any discernible affect on inflation.

This enviable budget surplus, and the question of what to do with it, highlighted another Democratic advantage. It was evident that whatever public enthusiasm for tax cuts had existed had now run its course. President Clinton scored far more favourable ratings with his stated determination to use the surplus to 'save' Social Security, the American retirement pension system projected to become insolvent as the baby-boom generation retires in the first decades of the twenty-first century. In general, public support for Clinton's modest agenda of new federal programmes in such areas as education and health-care reform indicated that running against government itself was no longer a sure vote-winner for Republicans. Adding insult to injury, the president continued to steal the Right's thunder with tough policies on traditional Republican issues such as crime and welfare reform.

Fighting Economic Turmoil Abroad

As the Asian economic crisis spread to Russia and Latin America, with a third of the world economy in recession (affecting considerably more of its population), and Europe's cyclical upswing sluggish, the US economy remained the indispensable locomotive of global recovery. Staying on track required sound policies and adequate fuel – that is, continued consumer spending.

On the policy side, the Federal Reserve Board and US Treasury Department were tested by the spreading contagion, and generally received high marks. In the autumn, following the Russian financial meltdown and the teetering of a major US hedge fund, a full Wall Street panic seemed possible. But market nerves were soothed by the Federal Reserve's ostentatious easing of interest rates (one of three rate cuts since the crisis began) and by the rapid move to organise a commercial bail out for the hedge fund. As a result, financial markets were able to shrug off the Clinton administration's evident judgement that nothing much could be done for Russia itself.

Brazil succumbed to a currency crisis in early 1999, but US Treasury Secretary Robert E. Rubin was able to persuade US banks not to call in Brazilian loans worth billions of dollars. Happily, the US economy had developed a partial immunity to South American troubles; banks had already liquidated much of their credit exposure following the Latin American debt crisis of the 1980s and the Mexican crisis of the early 1990s. This was one reason that a much-feared credit crunch did not materialise in the developed world by early 1999. Finally, a particularly worrying overhang of uncertainty was removed when, in October 1998, the US Congress finally approved $18 billion in new funds to replenish the coffers of the International Monetary Fund (IMF), depleted by the Asian and Russian crashes.

Washington's economic diplomacy towards Tokyo proved less effective. US officials urged Tokyo not to waste time, and create new 'moral hazards', through regional approaches to the crisis such as setting up an 'Asian Monetary Fund'. Instead, Washington pressed the Japanese to concentrate on what US officials deemed the heart of the problem: Japan's failure to fashion demand policies adequate to pull its own economy out of prolonged slump and stimulate growth in the region. Deputy Treasury Secretary Lawrence Summers set the tone in February 1998 when he derided Japan's limited plans for fiscal stimulus as 'virtual policy'. In March, the Clinton administration pressed the Japanese to implement a $67bn package of tax cuts and public-works spending. In the short term, this US bullying arguably paid off; without it Tokyo might not have been able to implement its April programme of regulatory and fiscal measures totalling $133bn, and even bigger packages in late 1998 and early 1999. Prospects improved for very modest Japanese growth in 1999. But many Japanese remained resentful of what they considered American imperial hectoring about a problem that had no obvious solution: since Japan already had its largest fiscal deficit on record, some feared that it had fallen into a 'liquidity trap' in which almost no degree of stimulus could persuade consumers to cut back on savings.

It was easy, and disconcerting, to see how 'Japan bashing' might again become an American habit. Such a relapse could be one early symptom that the US economic engine itself was spluttering. Undeniably robust, the domestic economy nonetheless faced three major risks with worrying implications for the rest of the world. The first concerned economic confidence: any sizeable correction to the soaring stock market might finally convince consumers that they were in fact poorer than they thought;

if the result were a sharp drop in spending, the US might suddenly stop performing as the world's importer of last resort. The second risk concerned a possible political reaction to the ballooning trade and current-account deficits. Most of the world's major economies had so far eschewed protectionism, but there were worrying indications – including a return to the US–European 'banana war' and proposed US legislation to cut off certain steel imports – that forbearance might not last forever. Finally, any steep decline in the dollar exchange-rate – whether tied to the current-account deficit, a stock-market collapse, the advent of the euro, or all three – might reflect both a conscious political and an involuntary economic withdrawal from global economic leadership.

Foreign Policy: Activism and Anxiety

With its echoes of the 1930s, the world economic crisis reinforced the view that there was no medium-term alternative to global leadership from the sole superpower. Much of the international disquiet provoked by the US impeachment drama stemmed from the recognition that so much depended not just on US power, but on the competence and attention span of the US executive branch. The unease was heightened by the conclusion that the conservative Republican Congress, elected in 1994, had proved to be the most parochial and inward-looking since the Second World War. Evidence included the oft-cited anecdote that most House members did not possess passports or, more substantively, the perennial 'anti-abortion riders' that conservatives attached to every UN funding bill – with the result that by the first quarter of 1999, the US still had not paid its arrears which by then totalled $1.29bn (when the current year's dues become payable in June 1999 it will rise to $1.7bn).

There is no strong evidence, however, that the impeachment process itself seriously distracted, much less paralysed, US foreign policy in 1998. The notion that the president had forfeited international respect was vividly refuted by the standing ovation Clinton received from world leaders at the September opening of the UN General Assembly, just after admitting to the Starr Grand Jury his 'improper' relationship with Lewinsky. Nor can the facts sustain accusations that US military actions – against alleged terrorist facilities in Afghanistan and Sudan in August, and Iraq in December – were motivated by the president's personal predicament rather than the national interest. In general, the US conducted an active diplomacy in the Middle East, Northern Ireland, the Balkans and China. Nowhere could that diplomacy be described as an unmitigated success, and critics faulted the administration for lacking a clear strategy to underpin many of the initiatives. But it was impossible to deny that Clinton and his aides devoted energy and attention to these issues.

Yet even if the United States seemed adequately engaged in many of the places where it was needed, there was a new element of resistance – or, more precisely, a stiffening of the resistance long inherent to the situation of unrivalled US leadership, or 'hegemony'. The resistance came from former enemies such as the Russians and Chinese, and from old allies such as the French and Israelis. Most disconcerting, perhaps, because most unfamiliar, for the first time in more than a decade Americans became seriously worried that resistance to US designs might entail a threat to the American homeland: terrorists or 'rogue states' wielding weapons of mass destruction and even ballistic missiles to deliver them.

In the face of this resistance, US foreign policy became increasingly embarrassed by a gap between forceful rhetoric and limited results. Fairly or unfairly, Secretary of State Madeleine Albright seemed to personify this disconnect. Albright prided herself on the ability to articulate US interests, values and power vigorously. Too often, however, rhetoric became bluster – as when she repeatedly demanded that Libya finally hand over for trial two men suspected in the 1988 Lockerbie bombing of a US jetliner. Such threats and deadlines were often ignored. In the Libyan case, South African President Nelson Mandela managed to extract a promise from Libya's leader Moammar Gadaffi in March 1999 that he would hand over the men.

Iraq remained the most troubling example. Efforts to maintain pressure and formulate credible threats against Saddam Hussein were undermined by the difficulty of holding together the eroding coalition formed against him during the Gulf War. This difficulty was underscored by allegations from former inspector Scott Ritter that Albright had intervened with UNSCOM Chief Inspector Richard Butler to block some critical surprise inspections during the first half of the year. For many critics, such news confirmed their already low expectations about the Clinton administration's real determination to keep up the pressure. The administration's defenders, on the other hand, maintained that it would have been tactically unwise to force a confrontation at a time when the anti-Saddam coalition looked wobbly. It would be more effective to wait, they argued, until Saddam overplayed his hand. That coalition did indeed appear to solidify in the second half of the year, after Iraq officially suspended its cooperation with UNSCOM. This diplomatic re-conver-gence, rare since the early 1990s, explains why most of Clinton's top foreign-policy advisers urged him to go ahead with air strikes in Novem-ber, even in the face of Baghdad's eleventh-hour promise to comply with UN demands. They suspected, correctly, a tactical feint on the part of Saddam. But Clinton decided he could not ignore Iraq's 'surrender', given Pentagon estimates that the planned attack could kill 10,000 Iraqis. Thus in December, once it became clear that non-compliance continued, the president had no choice but to approve the air strikes that he had cancelled the previous month.

Washington faced a similar problem of credibility over Kosovo and its efforts to confront the Belgrade regime of Slobodan Milosevic. Determined not to repeat the mistakes of Bosnia, the US did not hesitate to declare an important American interest in stopping the war. And this time, Washington found considerable support among its European allies for confronting Serbia. Warnings of imminent NATO military action were not sufficient, however, to stop Belgrade's summer-long scorched-earth campaign. NATO preparations for air strikes did provide US envoy Richard Holbrooke with enough clout to wrest an October cease-fire agreement from Milosevic, but the agreement was soon violated. At a February 1999 conference in France, Albright put her own prestige on the line by leading the attempt, in effect, to impose a peace plan on both sides, but with only limited success. The Albanian delegation signed up to the US plan, but Milsovic not only refused to do so, but sent troops into Kosovo in a new offensive. The US and NATO felt there was no choice left but to carry out the repeated threats against the Serbs. The Allies struck Serbian military targets on the evening of 24 March 1999.

Allies could also be troublesome, as was shown during a year in which US relations with Israel descended into unusual, if not unprecedented, bitterness. In the spring, an angry Albright threatened a 're-examination' of the US approach to Israel, unless the government of Binyamin Netanyahu agreed to proceed with the Oslo Accords by handing over another 13% of the West Bank to the Palestinian Authority. The threat, however vague, suggested that the administration was ready to emulate the tough tactics of the Bush administration, which had reacted to the intransigence of an earlier Israeli government by cancelling housing-loan guarantees. However, when Albright's deadline came and passed with the Netanyahu government refusing to budge, it became clear that the administration was not quite ready to brave the domestic political consequences of actually carrying out its threat.

Although Netanyahu, under personal pressure from President Clinton himself, finally did accept a 13% solution at talks with Yasser Arafat in October at the Wye Plantation in Maryland, the road to implementation remained rocky. When Clinton travelled to Israel in December, he delighted the Palestinians and angered many Israelis by spending half his time in the territories controlled by the Palestinian Authority. Not surprisingly, the Palestinians treated it as a kind of state visit, implying tacit US recognition of movements towards a Palestinian state. The inherent tension capped an abrasive year in the personal relations between the US and Israeli leaders. Clinton had snubbed the prime minister, finding no time to see him during a trip to the US. Netanyahu more than reciprocated by using that trip to meet the right-wing Christian leader Jerry Falwell, an unabashed Clinton-hater who has promoted videos accusing the president of numerous murders. And Netanyahu outraged almost the entire US foreign-policy establishment by seeking to tie his signature of the Wye accords to the release from US prison of the convicted Israeli spy, Jonathan Pollard.

Resistance to US designs also affected the symbolic centre-piece of America's European policies: the fiftieth anniversary of NATO, celebrated at a lavish Washington summit in April. Well before this event it became clear that US officials would be frustrated in their efforts to write a new strategic concept expressing a substantially broader definition of Alliance purposes. Early in the process, Secretary of State Albright had to concede that there was no question of NATO going 'global'. Yet, European allies even resisted language promising a common defence of 'common interests'. For its part, the US firmly and successfully resisted language requiring a UN mandate for all NATO interventions out of area. Meanwhile, after the admission of Poland, Hungary and the Czech Republic, America's own diffidence about further enlargements was evident. In spring 1998, as the Senate moved to ratify the extension of the Alliance treaty to these new members, the administration was able to head off the strong sentiment from senators such as Daniel Patrick Moynihan and John Warner for a mandated 'pause' in further enlargements. In effect, however, 'pause' became US policy anyway. In official terms, the 'door remained open'. But with Russian relations deteriorating, neuralgic sensitivity to the looming problem of applications from the Baltic former Soviet Republics, and limited Congressional patience for new commitments, there was no hurry in Washington to see anyone walk through the door.

US diplomacy toward former adversaries brought only meagre results in 1998. In its relations with Moscow, Washington for a time was able to manage the complex issue of Kosovo by finding a clever formula to keep the Russians on board for a 'Contact Group' ultimatum to Belgrade. Moscow could pretend not to notice the simultaneous – and critical – threat of military action that accompanied the ultimatum. But when NATO attacked Serb military targets on 24 March 1999, the US was unable to stop the further unravelling of its once-vaunted 'strategic partnership' with post-Soviet Russia. In China, Washington saw another highly vaunted relationship sour quickly. President Clinton's nine-day visit in June and July had appeared to establish the ascendancy of 'engagement', based on robust commercial relations, over the administration's earlier emphasis on human rights. Clinton seemed delighted by his rapport with Chinese leaders, and was no doubt relieved by the improvement in mood since the 1996 confrontation over Taiwan. The president made the substantial gesture of reiterating on Chinese soil the American 'one-China' policy.

However, a new phase of stormy debate at home focused on two new issues: high technology and campaign finance. First came allegations that the transfer of satellite-launch technology by Loral Space Communications and Hughes Electronics Corporation had improved China's ability to target intercontinental ballistic missiles against the United States. Then there were charges of Chinese nuclear espionage having capitalised, in the mid-1980s, on lax security at New Mexico's Los Alamos laboratories, resulting in China acquiring advanced Multiple, Independently Targetable Re-entry Vehicle (MIRV) warhead technology for nuclear weapons that might be aimed at the US. This was the more annoying, since while China was increasing its missile capabilities against US and Asian targets, it was arguing that the US should not deploy any form of missile defence.

A House committee chaired by Republican Christopher Cox had been conducting an investigation into the extent of technology transfer through much of 1998. Parts of its 1,100-page bipartisan report – though initially classified top secret – began to leak in January 1999 when it appeared that the administration was reluctant to make it public. Republicans in Congress seized on this as an indication that the administration was responding slowly to the spying allegations for fear of offending China. The administration countered by pointing out that the technology transfer had started in former President Ronald Reagan's administration, and insisted that they were moving with all speed. In March 1999 the Department of Energy announced that the alleged spy, against whom the FBI could not develop enough evidence to bring to court, was fired from his job.

Despite the often partisan level of the debate in Washington, it seemed clear that there was sufficient evidence to conclude that the Chinese had pulled off a major intelligence coup. What effect this would have in assuring that a meaningful debate could be mounted on the extent of China's real long-term challenge to the United States was moot.

Defence Policy

In January 1999, President Clinton proposed to reverse a decade-long decline that had reduced defence spending by almost a third in real terms since the Cold War. The proposals, likely to be increased by Congress, included $12bn in additional spending – a 4.2% increase to $296bn for fiscal year 2000 – as the first stage in a $112bn total increase over the next six budget years.

The increases, which Republicans immediately called inadequate, represented the White House response to Pentagon and Congressional criticism that new missions – such as Bosnia, Haiti and air patrols over Iraq – together with declining budgets, had meant deteriorating readiness, recruitment and morale, and problems budgeting for future hardware. Accordingly, the Clinton budget included sizeable increases in pay and retirement benefits, and new hardware funds.

The overall budget included $53bn for weapons procurement, rising to $69.2bn in 2004 and $75.1bn in 2005. This included funds for 30 additional F-16 combat aircraft, plus additional C-17 airlift aircraft. However, most major programmes were unchanged: including the F/A-18 E/F Super Hornet Tactical Fighter, the Air Force's F-22 Advanced Tactical Fighter, and the planned joint strike fighter.

Besides funding for missions abroad, the administration also unveiled very public responses to two classes of threat to the American homeland. First, the president agreed, at least in part, to the Republican clamour for national missile defence. Republicans had never quite given up on Reagan's Strategic Defense Initiative (SDI) programme – although the vision had changed from its original form of an impermeable 'shield' to protect against a massive Soviet attack. Now advocates wanted a more limited system to protect against the proliferating missile programmes of smaller hostile powers. There was no end to the question of whether a workable missile-defence system could actually be built, even on this more modest scale.

What did change in 1998 was the politics of threat perception – a change driven above all by developments in North Korea. Much was involved besides the missile threat: the North's economy continued to implode; the Agreed Framework looked shaky because of suspicions of a second clandestine nuclear-weapons site; and, with Congress threatening to bury the whole arrangement, Clinton asked former Defense Secretary William Perry to conduct a review of US policy. In the midst of these developments came the North's test of a three-stage ballistic missile over Japan – demonstrating a trajectory and capabilities far beyond most expectations. Earlier in the year, Indian nuclear tests had dramatised concerns that the US intelligence community was underestimating the pace of both missile and nuclear-weapons proliferation. This was certainly the message conveyed in a report of the bipartisan 'Commission to Assess the Ballistic Threat to the United States', chaired by former Defense Secretary Donald Rumsfeld. Members of Congress seized on the Commission's suggestion that both North Korea and Iran could develop, in much less than the 10 years estimated by US intelligence agencies, missiles capable of striking US territory.

In response, the Clinton administration committed some $7bn over six years for a limited missile defence system. Although a firm decision on deployment was deferred, the programme already had the effect of further complicating relations with China and Russia. Beijing was furious at suggestions that a theatre anti-ballistic system might be deployed against its missiles aimed at Taiwan; during a March visit Secretary Albright attempted to calm the furore by noting that the issue remained 'hypothetical'. Politicians in Moscow were angered by Defense Secretary William Cohen's suggestion that system deployment could require renegotiation – or US withdrawal – from the Anti-Ballistic Missile (ABM) treaty.

The second source of threat was seared into the American public con-sciousness by terrorist bombings of US embassies in Kenya and Tanzania on 7 August, with more than 250 deaths. Two weeks later the US retaliated with nearly 100 cruise-missile strikes against terrorist camps in Afghanis-tan and a factory in Sudan producing, according to US officials, precursors for chemical weapons. The targeted facilities in both countries were linked to Osama bin Laden, a Saudi businessman-turned-terrorist who directed his operations from the protective fold of *Taleban*-controlled territory in Afghanistan. Although evidence about the Sudan factory was controversial, there was no question that bin Laden had declared a murderous war against Americans everywhere: citing the 'defilement' of the US presence in Saudi Arabia, he vowed to drive US forces from the Persian Gulf. In return, such US officials as Madeleine Albright couched, and justified, the missile strikes in terms of a 'long-term battle against terrorists who have declared war on the United States'. Some critics saw here a problematic concept, akin to oft-declared, but only erratically prosecuted, American 'wars' on poverty and drugs.

In the broad community of US security policy-makers and analysts, however, it is fair to say that 1998 became a year of heightened alert to the threat of terrorism – especially WMD terrorism. CIA Director George Tenet identified the bin Laden network as 'just one of a dozen terrorist groups that have expressed an interest in or have sought chemical, biological, radiological or nuclear weapons'. President Clinton gave two major speeches on the subject. The White House said that on top of $11bn earmarked for counter-terrorism in general, the budget for fiscal year 2000 would seek an additional $2.8bn to counter chemical, biological and 'cyber terrorism'. One proposal was dropped by the Clinton administration, however: the setting up of a 'Homeland Defense Command' of senior military officers directing a joint-forces response to catastrophic terrorist acts. The idea had run into fierce opposition from civil libertarians, who regarded it as over-reaction, and from the military which was reluctant to extend its domestic role in this way.

Assured American Engagement?

For all the drama at home, 1998 was a year of continuity in US policies abroad. Fears that US leadership might collapse were replaced by astonishment that President Clinton had emerged politically strengthened from the crisis, while his Republican opponents were in disarray.

Some historians suggested, however, that the long-term effect might still be a weakening of the Oval Office. They noted that the only other presidential impeachment – of Abraham Lincoln's successor, Andrew Johnson, also acquitted by the Senate – was followed by many decades of ineffective and lack-lustre presidents. Yet surely the larger point is that after the consolidating effects of the American civil war, a new balance between president and Congress had to be found. This suggests a somewhat different parallel. Clinton, America's first post-Cold War president, is nearing the end of his second and last term. The scandals surrounding him did little to enhance the prestige of the presidency, but the office and its relationship with Congress were bound to change anyway after the 'imperial presidency' forged in the emergency conditions of the Second World War and the subsequent Cold War.

In the nearer term, two patterns which emerged in 1998 can be expected to continue into the next few years. First, the bitter partisanship will hardly evaporate; nor will the making of foreign policy be immune to its toxic effects. For all practical purposes, the 2000 election campaign will have started at least by summer 1999. Republican leaders certainly will not be diffident, for example, about accusing the administration of having compromised US national security in its China policies. Second, the US issued solemn warnings and assumed fundamental commitments in a number of areas, including an enlarged NATO, an unsettled Kosovo and the lonely job of policing a post-UNSCOM regime of containment against Iraq. It would be amazing if not even one of these challenges confounded American state-craft.

Overall, therefore, for friends and allies of the US, the lesson of 1998 is a mixed one. Continued American engagement in the affairs of the world can be assumed. But the quality and consistency of that engagement will continue to reflect the bewildering storms of American domestic politics.

Latin America: Voting for the Strongman

The parade of former military men galloping into the arena continued to dominate democratic politics in Latin America during 1998. Most strikingly, in Venezuela, former Lieutenant Colonel Hugo Chavez, leader of a 1992 coup-attempt, won an overwhelming victory in that country's presidential elections in December. In Paraguay, presidential elections were commanded by a jailed general, Lino César Oviedo, who was the front-runner until the nation's Supreme Court annulled his candidacy. Forced to withdraw, his vice-presidential candidate, Raúl Cubas Grau, went on to victory, employing the slogan, 'Cubas to the Presidency, Oviedo to Power'. Since his election, Paraguayan politics have centred around the legal and political status of Oviedo, who was soon amnestied by the new president.

In Bolivia, former general and president Hugo Banzer, once a military strongman, is now in his second year of power following his election in June 1997. He has spent much of his first 18 months in office attempting to undo many of the political and economic reforms of his predecessor. In Chile, former military dictator Augusto Pinochet turned in his uniform for a lifetime Senate seat last year, under rules set out in the 1980 Constitution written under his authority. Pinochet had assumed that he would personally supervise the maintenance of the institutional structure that he had created from his new position in Congress. However, Pinochet's plans were undermined when, during a visit to London in October, British authorities arrested him on a Spanish request for extradition on charges of murder and torture. The Spanish action and British arrest immediately reopened wounds in the Chilean body politic, and have created new fissures in Chilean politics.

Not all the military men turned politicians were successful. In Colombia, a country long-hostile to direct military rule, former army chief Harold Bedoya threw his hat into the ring after being dismissed from his post by then President Ernesto Samper. At first, his hardline position against the guerrillas attracted much favourable attention. By election day in May 1998, however, his support had waned, and politicians advocating a negotiated settlement to the country's long-standing guerrilla war emerged in the top two positions.

Elsewhere in the region, civilians are also taking a firmer – and extended – grip on the rudder of the ship of state. Re-election, once expressly prohibited in almost all Latin American charters – with the exception of the Dominican Republic – has also made steady progress. Beginning with President Alberto Fujimori in Peru and Carlos Menem in Argentina, other Latin American presidents have been reforming constitutions permitting their own re-election. By 1998, re-election fever had spread to Brazil, where President Fernando Henriqué Cardoso also amended the country's charter to permit a second term. In Panama, however, President Ernesto Perez Balladares was less successful; a referendum endorsing re-election was soundly defeated, thus firmly closing the door on his plans to remain in office.

A key aspect of this new form of presidential politics in the region appears to be a desire for political stability and/or the yearning for competent leadership amid the insecurity of the global economy. The lesson seems to be that economic stability – including lower inflation and macro-economic growth – can win broad electoral support even in a time of austerity and hardship. Nevertheless, there has also emerged a parallel trend embracing the 'man on horseback', promising relief, an end to corruption, more welfare and more jobs. This helps to explain the return of Banzer, the clamour for Oviedo and, of course, Chavez's surprising victory.

As such, democracy is spreading its roots with a distinct regional imprimatur. In the face of global economic crisis, continued poverty and rising unemployment, and even the effects of *el Niño* and other forms of climatic and environmental change, key sectors within the electorate are increasingly turning to civilian and military strongmen, regardless of their ideologies or past commitments to democratic governance.

Former Military Men In Politics

The Venezuelans finally buried their traditional parties – at least at the presidential level – in the December 1998 elections. Despite frantic efforts to thwart Chavez's victory, the traditional parties – Democratic Action (AD) and the Independent Political Electoral Organization Committee (COPEI) – could not turn back the tide of support for the former coup-maker. Although the traditional parties still maintain a majority in Congress, Chavez wasted no time in announcing his plans for a new constitution and vowing to disband the existing legislature. Moving quickly, he began to lay the groundwork for a Constituent Assembly. He also went to Havana to meet Cuban President Fidel Castro, and offered to help mediate the end of the insurgency in neighbouring Colombia. Acting on his plans, Chavez hosted talks between the Colombian government and the rebel National Liberation Army (ELN) in February 1999, while entering into his own talks with the ELN to end their military incursions into Venezuelan territory.

Chavez's spectacular rise underscores the voters' tremendous disillusion with the country's principal parties, which have presided over an oil boom that has left most of the population impoverished and feeling unrepresented. Chavez came to the country's attention when he led an uprising against former President Carlos Andrés Pérez in 1992. Pérez, a social democrat turned neo-liberal, had instituted harsh and unpopular austerity measures to stem the growing economic crisis. During riots in Caracas, Pérez called in the army to restore order.

Chavez says that he launched his first coup because he could not support a president who deployed the military against his own people. One of the conditions for his surrender was that he be permitted to give an address to the nation on television. Many credit that speech as being the opening of the campaign which brought Chavez to the presidency almost seven years later. From prison, Chavez launched a second coup attempt in 1994. Although both failed, the uprisings were wildly popular. They contributed to the charges of corruption subsequently levelled against Pérez and to his house arrest, although he returned to public office as a senator in the newly elected Congress.

Chavez does not shy away from discussing his failed uprisings. He rejects the notion that he is 'anti-democratic' or that his coup attempts were against democratic rule. In fact, they proved to be a turning point in Venezuelan politics. Since 1958, when the traditional parties had entered into a governance pact, they had dominated the political arena. By the 1990s, however, their support had eroded and new political forces and parties were emerging at the regional and local levels. Chavez argues that his election signals the end of the old political bosses and the inauguration of a more democratic and representative era of politics. Yet, at this early date, it is still not clear what kind of policies he will pursue, or how he plans to revive the economy, alleviate poverty and redistribute wealth more equitably. As many coup-makers have learned before him, reaching power is the easy part.

In Paraguay, too, democracy appears to be haunted by the spectre of the military in politics. In April 1996, Oviedo openly defied President Juan Carlos Wasmosy's order to resign, precipitating a constitutional crisis which soon drew in the nation's regional trading partners – Brazil, Argentina and Uruguay – the Organization of American States and the US.

At the time of the incident, reports indicated that the people took to the streets to defend their newly created democracy. Moreover, a self-satisfied international community drew praise for its resolution and its commitment to preserving Paraguay's democratic experiment following 35 years of strongman rule by General Alfredo Stroessner. Oviedo was arrested and sentenced to ten years in prison. But the story did not end there. He soon announced that he was running for president from his jail cell, and quickly became the front-runner.

Both Wasmosy and Oviedo are members of the ruling Colorado Party, which was also the party of Stroessner. In this sense, elections have been about continuity, not change. The dispute thus represented a great division within the party. To prevent an Oviedo victory, Wasmosy tried unsuccessfully to postpone the election but, with only a month to go before the June 1998 poll, Paraguay's Supreme Court confirmed Oviedo's sentence, which in effect barred him from elective office. Oviedo then declared that his running mate, Raúl Cubas Grau would stand in his place, and Cubas announced that his first act in office would be to pardon Oviedo.

The widening divisions inside the Colorado Party appeared to open up the race to a victory by the opposition Democratic Alliance candidate, Domingo Laino. But when the polls were cast, Cubas emerged victorious. Six days after taking office in August, the new president replaced the highest military court, commuted Oviedo's sentence to time-served, and restored all of Oviedo's civil and political rights. Many called it a 'constitutional coup' because the Congress – controlled by the anti-Oviedo faction of the Colorado Party – had passed a bill limiting presidential pardons to prisoners who had completed half of their sentences. But Cubas quickly found the loophole maintaining his right to commute sentences. Congress, in turn, cried 'foul' and began impeachment proceedings. By September, the Supreme Court declared the members of Cubas' military tribunal to be in contempt of court for refusing to hand over relevant documents related to their ruling. Cubas remained defiant, however, declaring that he would not comply with the high court's rulings.

Throughout autumn 1998, the Supreme Court continued to issue challenges to the president's decrees releasing Oviedo. In December, the Supreme Court finally ruled that Cubas' presidential decree of 18 August commuting Oviedo's sentence was unconstitutional and ordered Oviedo back to jail. Since then, the institutional and political crisis has escalated. Oviedo, fanning his own popularity, organised a rally in front of the Congress. With the threat of a massive demonstration on their doorstep, and with fears about their own safety, an intimidated Congress postponed its session to debate the Oviedo case.

At the rally, the crowd cheered when Oviedo called for the removal of the Supreme Court justices who had ruled against him. Yet Oviedo's actions have overshadowed Cubas and have left him as a weak stand-in for the cashiered general. Oviedo appears to be following the same electoral formula that worked so well for Chavez in Venezuela: use a failed coup attempt to establish a direct line of communication with the people, by-passing the established political institutions. Some have called this new form of politics, as practiced by Chavez, Oviedo, and even Fujimori, a variation on an old Latin American theme. They call it 'neopopulism.'

Chile, too, has not been able to break free of its recent authoritarian past. In October, former dictator Pinochet was detained in London on an extradition request from Spain. The arrest of Pinochet, who was protected from prosecution in Chile by a 1979 amnesty law promulgated by his own government, and who continues to enjoy immunity from prosecution as a senator, immediately opened up the old conflicts and cleavages of Chilean politics. The two main parties in the ruling coalition, President Eduardo Frei's Christian Democrats and the Socialist Party, found themselves at loggerheads – with the Christian Democrats denouncing the arrest and extradition request, while Socialist Party leader and presidential candidate Ricardo Lagos voiced support. A January 1999 poll showed that 43% of the population agreed with Frei, declaring that the Spanish extradition request and Pinochet's arrest represented violations of Chile's sovereignty, while 43% believe that the international legal action was legitimate.

The incident could split apart the governing coalition, the Concertación, and lead to the separate candidacies of Lagos, the Socialist, against a Christian Democrat, Andrés Zaldívar. Polls during the past year show Lagos leading all of the other candidates, raising the interesting prospect of a transition from a Christian Democrat-led government to a Socialist one. The same pattern occurred in 1970 with the election of Salvador Allende, leading to Pinochet's coup in 1973. Today's Socialists, however, have little in common with Allende's party. Now it is a centre-left party that has been a junior partner in the governing coalition since the return to democracy in 1989.

As for Pinochet, human-rights activists around the world are celebrating his detention and possible extradition. If Pinochet were to stand trial in Spain, a formidable precedent would be set establishing that even national amnesties cannot overrule or block the reach of international law. Yet what so cheers the international human-rights community is precisely what worries the Frei government and many Chileans. They argue that Chile's move to democracy was made possible through a pact that allowed the transition to civilian rule to go forward in exchange for upholding the military's amnesty legislation and respecting the constitutional arrangements guaranteeing Pinochet and the armed forces a continued voice in national affairs. Undermining this pact, they argue, would derail Chile's democratic transition. Others, however, argue that this can never be complete without a full accounting of past atrocities, and without restoring a sense of justice for these crimes. These people believe that the actions in London and in Spain will strengthen Chile's democracy. With the country split, it is still too early to assess the full impact of Pinochet's arrest on Chilean democracy and on the future role of the military in Chile's domestic politics.

How To Get Re-elected

Several of Latin America's democratically-elected presidents have been catching the re-election bug. The first was Alberto Fujimori in Peru. After closing Congress in April 1992, Fujimori, under intense international scrutiny and pressure to restore constitutional authority, convened a Constituent Assembly to re-write the nation's Constitution. A central plank in the new Constitution permitted two consecutive terms. Now Fujimori has his eye on the upcoming election in 2000, arguing that his first term was not covered by the new rules. To this end, he pushed a bill through Congress which made this 'authentic interpretation' a law in 1996. The Supreme Court, stacked with Fujimori supporters, upheld the law. The three dissenters on the high court were then summarily dismissed by the legislature, evidently at the behest of Fujimori.

Such impolitic politics have not been viewed kindly by the public. The president's notable tendency to bypass and even trample on democratic institutions – as when he closed down the Congress in 1992 – have been supported when seen as actions taken for the good of the nation. As the sure-footed president appeared to attack a corrupt, venal and ineffective political class that thwarted decisive action, he was handed a decisive victory in the 1995 election. The victory rewarded Fujimori for defeating a seemingly unstoppable guerrilla movement, Shining Path, and for turning around the economy and producing record rates of growth. In 1995, Peru's economy grew by 13%, faster than in any other country.

However, the machinations for a third term seem more for the benefit and self-aggrandisement of the individual, than for the good of the nation. Now that the insurgent threat has waned, the public is looking for the government to make a frontal assault on the extraordinarily high rates of unemployment, under-employment and poverty that make up Peru's desperate social conditions.

Fujimori may indeed run, but his victory is not assured. His popularity has edged downward during 1998. By the close of the year, his support stood at a relatively low 38%; with 55% saying they disapproved of his performance. The main reason for dissent was his failure to create jobs. Battered by the effects of the Asian financial crisis, as well as the floods and droughts caused by *el Niño* in different regions of the country, Fujimori now seems intent on creating the kind of crisis mentality that led him to past glory in the fight against Shining Path and a failed economy. Then, as now, democracy was not a priority. Fujimori now says that he will focus on social issues, but that he needs a clear mandate and a free hand to do so.

As part of the politics of freeing his hands, Fujimori announced in April 1998 that the national intelligence service, headed by his shadowy intelligence chief, Victor Montesinos, would be put in charge of the fight against crime. The government would now use the same harsh methods of summary and faceless justice that successfully defeated Shining Path guerrillas against criminal gangs that have turned Lima into a lawless and crime-ridden city. Later in the year, the Peruvian president announced that he intended to begin a spending programme designed to alleviate the country's enduring poverty. Many viewed these measures as simply 'neopopulist policies', geared principally to building support for his second re-election. Yet none of this may be enough to ensure a third term.

However, the opposition remains weak and supine. The strongest opponent appears to be the Mayor of Lima, Alberto Andrade, who himself won a resounding re-election victory on 11 October 1998, defeating Fujimori's handpicked candidate. However, Andrade's Party, *Somos Peru*, fared less well outside the capital, winning only three important provincial cities, raising serious questions about Andrade's viability as a national candidate. Moreover, he seems to be cut from the same, neo-liberal, neo-popular mould as Fujimori. What is even more surprising is that the traditional parties, the Revolutionary Popular Alliance of the Americas (APRA) and Popular Action (AP), fared even worse. Together they received less than 8% of the vote in Lima and did not do much better nationally. With a year to go before the next presidential election in April 2000, a viable alternative to Fujimori has still not emerged.

President Carlos Menem in Argentina has apparently been less successful in promoting his second re-election. Like Fujimori, Menem altered the Constitution to permit his re-election in 1994, and was able to take credit for combating inflation and turning the economy around. He spent much of 1998 trying to find a way to stand for election again. Taking a leaf from Fujimori's book, Menem has proposed that the Argentine Supreme Court rule on the constitutionality of the re-election ban, particularly as it applies to himself. Again like Fujimori, Menem was first elected before the ban went into place. Having increased the court's members from four to nine early in his first term, thus creating a majority with his own appointments, Menem believed that he would receive a favourable ruling. However, this would be a tremendous blow to constitutional order and the rule of law, and Menem may not be willing to play this card. In addition to the court option, he has also proposed a national referendum to decide the issue.

By July 1998, Menem's Justicialist Party (founded by populist leader Juan Domingo Perón) declared an all out effort to remove the ban using either or both of Menem's proposed options. However, resistance quickly surfaced. Popular Buenos Aires State Governor Eduardo Duhalde – also of the Justicialist Party – openly opposed Menem's re-election, and his backers stayed away from the convention. Shortly thereafter, in the face of strong opposition and plummeting popular support – a rating of only about 18% at the time of the convention – Menem declared that he would not seek re-election. Duhalde wholeheartedly welcomed and endorsed the decision, as did Menem's hand-picked successor, Ramón 'Palito' Ortega.

Yet, in February 1999, Ortega unexpectedly cut a deal with his rival Duhalde and agreed to join the ticket as his vice presidential candidate. Agile as ever, Menem announced that he would remain head of the Justicialist Party after stepping down from office, and that he probably would run again in 2004. Throughout, Menem continued to drop hints that he was still interested in a more immediate re-election. By spring 1999, buttons were appearing around Buenos Aires calling for his return to office and a removal of the constitutional ban.

The Perónist candidate can expect tough competition in the presidential race, scheduled for October 1999, from Fernando de la Rua, currently mayor of the City of Buenos Aires and candidate of an alliance between the centrist Radical Civic Union (UCR) and the leftist Front for a Country in Solidarity (FREPASO). The opposition alliance is running on an anti-corruption platform, which, despite Menem's success in ending inflation, privatising state industry and spurring economic growth, has multiplied during Menem's years in office.

The political debate now is between those who want Menemism (with or without Menem), continuing market-oriented economic reforms and maintaining a healthy distrust of state intervention in the economy, and those who would like a return to a more closed economy with greater state intervention. Duhalde represents the latter group, with strong support from labour – the classical Perónist base. In between these camps, are the moderate critics of Menemism who would maintain the reforms but would also pursue a social agenda to improve living conditions, wages and benefits. De la Rua carries this banner; six months before the election, he was leading in the polls.

Menem's intentions remain a question mark. He will either be a candidate in 1999, through some form of last minute political manoeuvring, or he will attempt to stand as a candidate in 2004. To a great extent, his supporters in the business community hold the decisive votes; they have benefited from Menem's policies, but may ultimately decide that for Menemism to endure, Menem must step down.

In Brazil, President Cardoso also pushed through a constitutional amendment in 1998 that cleared the way for his re-election. He was rewarded for his efforts when he won a straight, first-round victory on 4 October. His closest challenger was Luiz Ignacio Lula da Silva of the Workers' Party, who tried to make the case that 'monetary stability brought only social instability'. But with continued support for Cardoso's economic plan, known as the *Plan Real*, which had reduced the psychologically and financially destabilising environment of high and hyper-inflation, Cardoso was able to win. Inflation was at 1.5% in mid-1998, an unthinkable figure during the past 30 years.

Nevertheless, the year was a difficult one, with growth projected at zero. In late 1997, Cardoso had to struggle to reduce the effects of the Asian crisis. By summer 1998, Russia's turmoil noisily intruded and again undermined the nation's financial stability. On 10 September stock prices plummeted more than 15% on the São Paulo and Rio de Janeiro exchanges. In a matter of hours, the government responded with a massive interest rate hike to avoid mass capital flight, raising the base rate from 29.7% to 49.5%. Throughout, despite his leftist past and social democratic present, Cardoso insisted that financial stabilisation would be a priority over unemployment and this stemmed the anticipated capital outflows. While $2bn did leave the country on the first day of the crisis, by 11 September the outflow had slowed to $1.7bn. The International Monetary Fund (IMF) and the World Bank responded by offering a $30bn safety net to avoid a Russian-style currency and stock-market crisis.

With tough measures inevitable, Cardoso was forced to admit that another round of austerity measures and tax rises would be necessary to stem the crisis, just as his rival Lula had been warning throughout the campaign. But rather than wait until after the election, Cardoso clearly felt confident enough to lay out the future direction of his programmes. His confidence was boosted by public-opinion polls showing that 77% of all Brazilians believed he was the most capable politician to confront the crisis. The announcements, indeed, only weakened Lula.

In the election Cardoso polled 51.6% of the votes; Lula finished a distant second with 33.5%. The victory was a remarkable achievement for a man presiding over an economic crisis, sclerotic growth, a collapsing stock market, high unemployment and a new round of 'belt-tightening' measures. But neither he nor Brazil emerged unscathed. Cardoso's own Brazilian Democratic Movement Party (PMDB) lost six seats in the lower house of Congress, although it expanded its control of governorships from three to seven. If the governorships won by the five other parties in the coalition are included, the coalition's total rose from 12 to 21 states. It also maintained an overwhelming majority in Congress, although these numbers would not translate into automatic support for the government's fiscal adjustments.

Indeed, both the austerity programme and the defections soon followed the elections. By late October, Cardoso announced his 'Fiscal Stability Program', proposing spending cuts of $7.2bn and new taxes totalling $11.1bn. Not all coalition allies applauded. Former President Itamar Franco, newly elected governor of the state of Minas Gerais, announced, on 6 January 1999, a 90-day moratorium on his state's debt payments to the central government. Minas Gerais owes approximately $15bn to the central government, part of a $100bn debt owed by 24 states. Again the stock market plummeted 5.13%, with the rest of Latin America's exchanges following in Brazil's wake. Franco's moratorium also raised questions about his intention to pay the state's international debts. Cardoso's finance minister, Pedro Sampaio Malan, rushed to assure international markets that the government would meet all debt obligations, even those of the state. But Franco quickly retorted that the federal government did not have the authority to intervene in a contract between a state government and a private bank.

A week later, Brazil's exchange-rate policy collapsed, following four years of stable and gradual adjustments. First the government abruptly devalued the *real* by widening the band in which the currency could float against the dollar. Then, market pressure forced the government to let the *real* float freely.

During his re-election campaign, Cardoso stated that he would like to back away from his neo-liberal policies and pursue more of a social democratic agenda, related to his party's origins. Yet, from the outset of his second term, the international turmoil and domestic consequences have limited any new directions in public policy. With sluggish world demand for Brazilian products, the country's economic outlook may not improve soon. Even bumper coffee crops in 1998 are being offset by low international prices. With one eye on history, Cardoso, the once prominent left-wing sociologist, seems to be aware that he may be better remembered for his conservative economic measures than for his social policies.

Re-election fever also infected Panama. President Ernesto Perez Balladares of the Revolutionary Democratic Party (PRD) – founded by strongman Omar Torrijos and later headed by convicted drug-trafficker Manuel Noriega – also sought to alter his country's constitution to permit re-election. This required approval in two consecutive legislative sessions and then a national referendum. Balladares easily cleared the legislative hurdles and opinion polls suggested that he had gained public support for constitutional reform.

Nevertheless, the 'no' vote won by a 2:1 margin in the August 1998 plebiscite, with about one-third of the electorate abstaining. With the president's re-election bid rebuffed, Torrijos' party turned to the former general's son, Martin Torrijos Espinoso, a lawyer and economist who had led the PRD's youth wing. The rejection of the re-election bid does not signal strong opposition to the PRD, or necessarily of the privatisation programmes instituted during the past four years.

The crucial political issue is the impending turnover of the Panama Canal at midnight on 31 December 1999. If the PRD wins the May 1999 election, the US may well hand over the keys to the canal to the son of the man who signed the Panama Canal treaties with former US President Jimmy Carter in 1977.

One issue will not be on the agenda: after several years of discussion on converting Howard Air Force Base, one of the soon to be unoccupied US military bases, into a multilateral anti-drug centre, talks definitively broke down in June 1998. The US had wanted to continue to station troops at the base and to permit them to engage in tasks beyond anti-narcotic activities. However, Balladares and the Panamanian Foreign Ministry shut the door in June to an extended American presence. The US has since abandoned the idea and is now searching for other sites for a forward anti-narcotics base.

Since former US President Theodore Roosevelt fostered the breakaway of the Colombian province of Panama, with the idea of constructing an inter-oceanic canal in 1903 – through the Carter–Torrijos treaties of 1977, the subsequent end of US sovereignty in the Panama Canal Zone and the 1989 invasion to depose and bring Noriega to trial – the US has maintained a substantial and permanent presence in the country. When the US flag is lowered at the last American facility on 31 December 1999, an historic chapter spanning almost the entire twentieth century will come to a close.

Mexico: The End of Presidential Choice

Slowly, Mexico is moving beyond the one-party state. The monopoly of the ruling Institutional Revolutionary Party (PRI) cracked in 1997 when, for the first time in 68 years, the party lost control of the lower house of Congress. Since then, the PRI has lost the mayorship of Mexico City and has faced strong competition in several gubernatorial elections. With presidential polls scheduled for 2000, there is the real possibility that an opposition party could take power.

This surprising groundswell in favour of democratic polling has affected how the ruling party chooses its presidential candidate. At one time he was simply chosen by the sitting president through a practice called the 'dedazo' (the big finger). The colloquial term indicated the president's ability to choose his successor by simply 'pointing his finger'. The nominee would then go through the routine of running a campaign and travelling around the country in anticipation of his victory on election day. The PRI was not above turning to fraud if the electoral outcome was questioned, as many are certain it did in 1988, when a dissident PRI leader, Cuahtemoc Cárdenas, broke away from the party and founded the Party of the Democratic Revolution (PRD). Since then, however, Mexico has agreed to international election monitors and has allowed opposition victories to stand at the congressional, state and local levels. Cárdenas himself is now mayor of Mexico City, the second most important position in the country.

President Ernesto Zedillo has declared that he will not use the *'dedazo'* method, even joking that he will have his index finger surgically removed. In its place, he has proposed a presidential primary system similar to that of the US. Although the details have yet to be worked out or agreed upon, the PRI has experimented with local primaries to choose candidates in some states and these may provide a model. Such a primary would substantively alter the nature of presidential power – channelling the succession process into a more structured and institutional framework. To be sure, the president will still have a strong voice and will not be without overt and covert influence.

Mexico has already moved beyond the politics of a one-party state. With the lower house in opposition hands, the government no longer has a free ride. Zedillo has been challenged on human rights, the handling of the Zapatista insurgency in the state of Chiapas, the budget, the drug war and on a controversial bail-out of the nation's banks. Yet the PRI is adapting. It still controls the Senate, and it is capable of breaking the opposition PRD–National Action Party (PAN) alliance on certain issues, particularly the budget. Both in 1997 and 1998, the PRI has managed to ally itself with the rightist PAN party to pass a budget, leaving the leftist PRD and a few minor parties alone in opposition. A similar government–PAN alliance occurred with the bank bail-out legislation. They also teamed up to block an initiative that would have raised Mexico City's spending authority by increasing its borrowing ceiling. The move was a blow to Cárdenas and the PRD. But on other issues, the PAN and PRD share a common interest in weakening the PRI and are able to impose a degree of transparency, accountability and independent initiative which has not been seen in Mexico during the PRI's seven-decade reign.

The presidential race is shaping up to be the most competitive in Mexican history, one that the PRI could legitimately win or lose. And, like its neighbours to the south, Mexico is fighting the impact of the Asian crisis, compounded by the severe contraction in government revenue caused by the sharp decline in petroleum income – down to $9.50 a barrel by the end of 1998. However, the move by the Organisation of Petroleum Exporting Countries (OPEC) to restrict supply in late March 1999 boosted the price to over $13 a barrel, suggesting that this constraint might ease. In the Mexican case, the fallout from the Asian crisis could cut either way: it could bolster the incumbent party's hold on power as it argues for continuity in the face of crisis, or it could strengthen the hand of a challenger, from either the left or the right, arguing that 70 years is long enough and it is time for a change.

The country also faces a major armed challenge from a few guerrilla groups in the southern states of Chiapas, Oaxaca and Guerrero, and has drawn substantial international criticism for its human-rights violations in its counter-insurgency, counter-narcotics and crime fighting programmes. Each of the parties will bring a different approach to these problems. The run-up to the elections promises to produce a major national debate, potentially bringing the Mexican voter into the process as an active participant – in many cases for the first time – beyond the traditional role of passive vote-giver and spectator.

Asian and Russian Flues

Latin America braced itself with relative success for the aftershocks of the Asian financial crisis. In the increasingly globalised economy, Latin America feared trouble on three fronts: the fall in commodity prices resulting from lower Asian and world demand; competition from Asian-produced goods made more competitive by the region's devalued currencies; and the 'contagion effect' of foreign speculators investing and withdrawing capital without an institutional framework to regulate these flows.

With the exception of Brazil, Peru and Venezuela, regional growth rates remained relatively unaffected during the first half of 1998. However, in the second half of the year, particularly following the Russian crisis, growth rates turned downwards, in some cases precipitously, and the region as a whole teetered on the edge of recession.

The effects were distributed unevenly. Venezuela was badly hit. Before the crisis, economic growth had been estimated at 5%, but during the second half of 1998 there was a fall of 5%, due mainly to the erosion of oil prices. The sharp decline contributed to the political uncertainty and accelerated the trend toward the electoral rebellion that led to the election of Chavez. Mexico's economy also severely contracted in the second half of the year, due to declining prices for oil and other commodities. And the countries of the Southern Cone suffered fiscal current-account deficits as a result of the decline in their exports.

Despite years of economic reform and diversification of the region's economic base, most countries in the region still fell victim to a long familiar problem: their economic health continues to be tied to the fluctuating prices of one or two commodity exports. A century of economic change – from commodity export-led growth in the early twentieth century, through import substitution, industrialisation and nationalisation at mid-century, to free markets and privatisation policies during the past two decades – has still not altered this basic fact.

However, the world has changed. The one country that stood to lose the most from this 'brave new world' was Brazil, which had to withstand the greatest onslaught against its currency by foreign speculators and other international investors. Cardoso made several attempts to intervene in the currency markets, but by early 1999 had to settle for a free-floating currency. He was also forced to make appeals for international assistance to avert a major financial disaster. The case of Brazil, and to a lesser extent other Latin American countries, underscores the volatility of world financial markets. Because of the international pressures on its currency, Brazil was forced to take measures that should have been unnecessary given the underlying strength of its economy. As the United Nations Economic Commission for Latin America and the Caribbean (ECLAC) put it: 'The situation does not reflect the fundamental economic variables of countries in the region.'

The global instability has shaken up the region's nascent democracies: in Brazil, the electorate turned to a tried and tested leader, their president. In Venezuela, they voted for the proverbial 'man on horseback'. In Mexico, the longstanding economic difficulties may prove to be the final undoing of the PRI.

Hope Mingled with Concern

Latin America is still struggling to find some stability within the whirlpool unleashed at the end of the Cold War. Democracy has brought greater respect for human rights in most countries and has involved more citizens in the political process. Many elected leaders have demonstrated that they can deliver on their promises: Fujimori in Peru, Menem in Argentina and Cardoso in Brazil have each been rewarded with second terms because of their competent handling of economic and political crises. Yet undemocratic practices, such as Fujimori's self-coup in 1992, have not only been tolerated, they have been feted. This same disregard for democratic institutions has benefited, and rewarded, some opposition politicians, most notably in the recent Venezuelan presidential election.

Developments during 1998–99 give cause for both hope and concern as Latin American politics and economic systems continue to evolve. The hope is that, in many countries, institutions are working, and electorates are demanding greater accountability. There is also limited tolerance for the old-fashioned military coup. Today, if a general or a colonel wants to enter politics, the new path is to shed his uniform and enter the democratic arena, in the manner of Banzer in Bolivia, Oviedo in Paraguay, Chavez in Venezuela, Bedoya in Colombia and even Pinochet in Chile. Yet, the fact that this path is becoming so well trodden is a cause for major concern.

Another worry is that after more than a decade of democracy and economic liberalisation, the region's economies and political systems have still failed to address the needs of the majority of citizens who remain mired in poverty, unemployment and under-employment. Moreover, after a decade of economic liberalisation and restructuring, it has become clear that globalisation may open some doors of opportunity with one hand, and then slam them shut with the other. These failures at the national and international levels are contributing to a new form of politics, characterised by the emergence of more 'men on horseback' and more former generals and colonels, shedding their uniforms but not their authoritarian inclinations, and presenting themselves to the public in politicians' clothing.

Europe

It was a momentous year for Western Europe. Against all the odds 11 members of the European Union adopted the euro, a single currency, on 1 January 1999. If this unprecedented financial experiment succeeds, it will take the EU a long way down the road to political union. Before that, much institutional and policy reform will be required. Reform may be induced by the shocking decision of the entire European Commission to resign rather than wait for the European Parliament to act on a report unearthing large-scale fraud and mismanagement by some Commission members. At the least, it will ensure the appointment of a stronger Commission President than might have been expected earlier.

While things were looking brighter for Western Europe, the opposite was true for Russia. President Boris Yeltsin, weakened by illness, has lost his political grip. The economy has continued to sink and there is little sign that the leaders, in the administration or in the parliament, have any real idea of how to improve the situation. Peoples' lives are grim; crime is rife; policing is rudimentary; many who are not paid in cash must depend on barter to fulfil their basic needs. In these circumstances there is a real danger that the voters will reach out to a fiercely nationalist 'strongman' at the presidential election that must be held in 2000.

Slobodan Milosevic fits the stereotype of such a strongman, but no rational people would embrace his style of rule voluntarily. His insistence on forcibly asserting Serbian rule over the Kosovar Albanians has brought the wrath of NATO air strikes on his country. Although the flames of war, which have swept through the Balkans for so much of the past century, engulfed part of the area again, the much larger part had made remarkably positive advances. The Balkans need no longer be considered a diseased area that is best quarantined. The rest of Europe does not appear to believe that its troubled southern fringe is yet ripe to be brought in from the periphery, but its deeper involvement in the region can be expected.

●

Western Europe: A Momentous Year

Taking a giant step towards more political unity, 11 member countries of the European Union adopted a single currency on 1 January 1999, launching an unprecedented monetary experiment and heralding a potential future competitor to the US dollar. Ignoring warnings from many economists about the difficulties of merging European currencies into one, and refusing to listen to their own citizens' antipathy to the concept, leaders of most European countries exercised an act of sheer political will to bring the euro into being in the advertised time-frame. While their arguments were couched in terms of the economic benefits to be derived from a single currency, there was little question but that most viewed this as a necessary, and powerful, tool in the quest for further political integration.

Enlargement, the next big challenge facing the EU, is being held hostage to disagreements over much-needed institutional and policy reform, most notably the overhaul of the EU's budget – the member states have been squabbling over who pays how much and who benefits the most. In the midst of this argument, the EU was rocked on 16 March by the enforced mass resignation of the 20 members of the European Commission. An independent panel, appointed by the European Parliament had been investigating alleged fraud, mismanagement and nepotism. The report that it issued on these matters was so damning that there was little for President Jacques Santer and his colleagues to do but to resign.

Although the startling denouement has temporarily weakened the EU, it will force a review of the relationship between the Commission and the Parliament. Reform of the governing structure, and the relationship of individual governments to it, has been needed for some time. At the least it should lead to the appointment of a proven political manager, who can be expected to keep a tighter rein on the activities of his colleagues than the easy-going Santer did. Germany, in its role as president of the EU Council of Ministers for the six-month period from 1 January 1999, was pushing for an early choice, and backed, along with Britain, France and Italy, former Italian Prime Minister Romano Prodi.

The End of the Kohl Era in Germany

In elections on 27 September 1998, Germans threw out Helmut Kohl's Christian Democrat government. The Social Democrats (SPD) and the Greens garnered a majority of 21 in the Bundestag, ushering in a Red–Green coalition rather than the 'grand' one of Social Democrats and Christian Democrats that many had thought the most likely outcome. Kohl's 16-year record as Chancellor, the longest since the end of the Second World War, came to an end, and Gerhard Schröder, a telegenic, business-friendly, 'modernising' Social Democrat, assumed the Chancellorship on 27 October.

Kohl, the Chancellor of German unification and of Euro-enthusiasm, had been a dominating figure on the European scene, but by the end of his term he was already fading. The German electorate opted for new faces, rather than a clear alternative programme, as the Social Democrats offered

Map 2 Europe

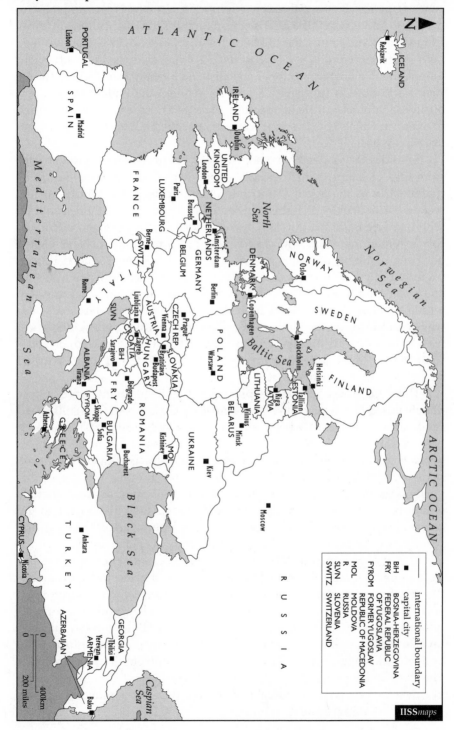

only a confusing set of centrist and traditional leftist promises with few concrete policy details. Schröder, whose appeal to the voters appealed to his party, had wrested the SPD's nomination for the Chancellorship away from Oskar Lafontaine, the SPD chairman, in March 1998. The two men hold quite different views: Schröder is more centrist than left-wing; Lafontaine is a fairly traditional socialist. As a result, the SPD pursued a twin-track election campaign: Schröder soothed the middle classes and business; Lafontaine instead appealed to the SPD's core voters by pledging to overturn Kohl's cuts in social welfare, raise the incomes of the poor, and tax energy use.

Schröder may indeed have hoped that a grand coalition would emerge from the elections, which would have kept the left-wing in check (particularly as the Social Democrats already control the Bundesrat, the second parliamentary chamber). Instead, he had to put together a coalition with the Greens, which put the Greens' leader, Joschka Fischer, into a key role as foreign minister. But Schröder's larger, more immediate, challenge has been handling divisions within the SPD. Lafontaine, who had been promised any job he wanted in the government, chose finance minister, and proceeded to incorporate departments from the economics ministry within his own. He also clearly indicated his own policy preferences (raise wages and lower taxes for the less well-off to boost domestic demand), tried to pressure the Bundesbank to lower interest rates, and advocated – to the horror of the British government – harmonising European taxes on businesses and interest earnings.

These were not Schröder's preferences and questions were immediately raised as to who controlled Germany's government. The split lasted until early March 1999 when Lafontaine suddenly resigned his leading positions. Whether he did so because he felt he could not accomplish his goals as a cabinet minister, or whether he was forced out by the prime minister, was left unclear, but Schröder wasted no time firming up his position as head of the government. He immediately assured that he would be elected leader of the SDP and moved the government to the centrist position which he had always espoused, but which was in question so long as Lafontaine was making the important economic decisions.

The new government had assumed the six-month presidency of the EU's Council of Ministers on 1 January 1999. Its priorities were to combat the very high European unemployment with a 'pact for jobs and growth', and to resolve outstanding issues regarding policy and institutional reforms so as to clear the way for enlargement. But Schröder did not reverse Kohl's previous insistence that Germany pay less into the EU budget – thus aggravating the already thorny problem of budget reform. The German government has also very strongly supported political union, in which the veto power of member states is reduced to a minimum. This is sure to spark disagreements with the UK.

Curiosity about the strength of the Franco-German partnership mounted with Schröder's election, as Schröder is reportedly an Anglophile and had spoken warmly of the possibility of enlarging the duo to include the UK (although Foreign Minister Fischer is decidedly less enthusiastic about this). Schröder's first visit abroad was nonetheless to France, and given French sensitivity about the creation of a trio, Schröder has become much quieter about it. US–German relations are also under scrutiny, particularly now that Germany has a Green foreign minister. Fischer had caused a stir in November 1998 by calling for NATO to renounce first-use of nuclear weapons – a prospect immediately dismissed by the Americans.

France: Settling in to Cohabitation

For much of 1998, the French right was in disarray – notwithstanding Gaullist President Jacques Chirac's continuing popularity. The right, splintered into numerous parties and movements, has quarrelled over Europe, over economic policy, and, above all, over how to handle the National Front (NF). The outcome of regional elections in March 1998 precipitated a rift. Although the share of votes (15% for the NF; 36% for the centre-right as a whole) was the same as in the 1997 parliamentary elections, the balance of power in many regions swung to the NF. Some right-wing politicians controversially agreed to govern with the NF. In response, three centre-right parties – the Rally for the Republic (RPR), the Union for French Democracy (UDF) and Liberal Democracy – set up The Alliance, which explicitly rejected deals with the NF. But by the end of 1998, things were looking up for the right-wing opposition, as the NF disintegrated into two factions in December, led by Jean Marie Le Pen and Bruno Magret. Magret had led a mini-revolt against Le Pen and was forced out of the party as a result. In the first by-election test since the split, the NF candidate scored less than half the vote he achieved in the last election.

While the NF damaged itself, Chirac's 'cohabitation' with the Socialist-led government was proving remarkably friendly. Prime Minister Lionel Jospin's government did have difficulties from within its ranks, notably because on several occasions the Communist Party refused to vote with the government. The three governing parties, the Greens, Communists and Socialists, were all due to put forward separate lists for upcoming European Parliament elections in June 1999. But Jospin remained popular, having pushed forward a mix of policies from the 35-hour working week to further privatisation.

Concerns about the health of the Franco-German partnership may have induced the rather warm French response to Britain's initiative on European defence. The St Malo declaration in December 1998 was characterised by others as an example of 'British vision meeting French pragmatism' (see p. 106). Still, the French, among others, remain suspicious of Britain's commitment to the EU, and France does not take kindly to the prospect of letting the UK into its cosy relationship with Germany. In mid-December, France denounced British and US strikes against Iraq, and withdrew from the air force patrolling the no-fly zone in southern Iraq. In March 1999, however, French planes took full part in the US-led NATO operation in Yugoslavia.

The UK: A New Euro-Enthusiast?

During 1998, Prime Minister Tony Blair's Labour government moved ahead with some of the reforms the party had promised during the election: in particular with the devolution of power to Scotland and Wales, the creation of mayors for large cities, and the abolition of hereditary peers' voting rights in the House of Lords. Its Strategic Defence Review, which it revealed in July 1998, however, was a surprisingly forward-looking and thorough. The government has played on the UK's traditional military strengths, emphasising its ability to project forces quickly to endangered areas; it has become a model that other European countries are following.

Although cuts are to be made in the number of aircraft and surface ships, and a modest reduction has been achieved in the budget itself, mostly through efficiency savings, the Review promised two new large aircraft carriers and a rapid-reaction force. The UK's existing global defence commitments were not touched, nor were the *Eurofighter* project and *Trident* nuclear missiles, although the number of deployed warheads was reduced. New threats of the post-Cold War world (including terrorism, organised crime, nuclear proliferation, and the collapse of states) were highlighted, but the UK, like other West European governments, had little idea of how best to deal with such problems.

With regard to the enforcement of international human-rights law, however, the British legal system was at the centre of an unprecedented drama. On 16 October, Chilean General Augusto Pinochet (and senator-for-life) was arrested in London at the request of a Spanish magistrate who sought to try the former dictator for crimes against humanity committed while he was Chile's leader. On 28 October, the High Court ruled that Pinochet, as a former head of state, enjoyed immunity from arrest or extradition proceedings – regardless of the crimes attributed to him. When this ruling was appealed to the Law Lords (Britain's highest court) it was heard by a five-member panel that ruled by a three-to-two margin that even former heads of state could not enjoy immunity for crimes of torture, genocide and hostage-taking, and crimes against humanity. Pinochet could therefore be extradited to Spain.

The Law Lords' ruling sparked elation among human-rights activities and Chilean dissidents, and the anger of the Chilean government, which protested vigorously. UK Home Secretary Jack Straw then decided that extradition proceedings could proceed. However, in the meantime,

Pinochet's lawyers successfully argued to a hastily assembled new five-member Law Lord's panel that the earlier decision should be set aside because one of three who had voted against Pinochet had failed to declare his interest in a charity run by Amnesty International, the human-rights pressure group. A new trial, being heard by seven members of the Law Lords, opened in January 1999. On 24 March the Lords handed down their verdict; by a six-to-one margin they ruled that the arrest of Pinochet in England did not contravene British law, but that Pinochet could only be extradited for alleged crimes committed after October 1988. The question of extradition will now go back to Straw for a decision. Should he agree with the Spanish courts request, many years of appeals can be expected. Whatever the final outcome, the Pinochet affair has already emboldened human-rights activists and lawyers in several countries to seek prosecution of other dictators and former dictators, and has strengthened the case for ratifying the July 1997 Convention that would establish an International Criminal Court.

The UK held the presidency of the EU's Council of Ministers during the first half of 1998. While the tone and style of this British presidency was much more positive towards the EU than any previous one (there was much rhetoric about Britain's leading role in Europe), a gap remains between the UK and its EU partners. A number of successes were reached during the UK's presidency, including agreement on a non-binding Code of Conduct on Conventional Arms Exports. Under the Code, member states agreed that they must justify arms exports to countries that have been denied licenses by another member state, and stipulated eight criteria for arms exports, including evaluating the risk of regional instability and of aggravating internal conflicts. But Blair's handling of the row between France and the rest of the EU over the president of the European Central Bank was widely derided.

The distance between Britain and the EU 'core' has been highlighted most clearly by the advent of the euro. In early 1998, Britain's request to join the Euro Eleven Group, an informal committee of finance ministers to discuss matters relating to the euro, was summarily brushed aside. Although the British electorate is still opposed to the euro, some of its antagonism seemed to slackening, and the government has begun to call upon business and government ministries to begin preparations in case a decision is taken to enter the euro zone. No firm decision will be made until the beginning of the next parliament in 2002, but it appears more and more likely that if Labour leads the country after that election it will opt to enter the zone.

These considerations undoubtedly led to the UK's review of the problem of a European defence identity. In 1997, the UK (along with the neutral EU member states) had vetoed the merger of the EU with the Western European Union (WEU). Under the Amsterdam Treaty, the WEU would remain a separate defence arm: the EU could request the WEU to carry out decisions that had military implications, including peacekeeping and humanitarian interventions. In October and November 1998, Blair declared that Europe must have the capacity to carry out military operations without relying on the US and argued for EU involvement in defence matters. Exactly what institutional arrangements the British envisage remain unclear. What they perhaps would prefer – absorbing the WEU into the EU, and reliance on European capabilities within NATO – would not be acceptable to all EU member states.

To pursue the initiative, Blair turned to France, a close military partner particularly in Bosnia, and the only other European state with similar military capabilities. Blair and Chirac met in St Malo on 3–4 December 1998 and issued a declaration on European defence which stated that the EU 'must have the capacity for autonomous action, backed up by credible military forces, the means to decide to use them, and a readiness to do so, in order to respond to international crises'.

The Euro is Launched

On 1 January 1999, 11 EU member states fixed their exchange rates irrevocably and handed over control of interest rates to the European Central Bank (ECB). Eighteen months earlier, hardly anyone would have predicted that 11 countries would qualify for the third stage of Economic and Monetary Union (EMU) as set out in the February 1992 Maastricht Treaty, and there were several voices calling for a delay. Yet, in March 1998, the European Commission recommended that 11 countries join the euro at the start. Only Greece did not meet the Maastricht criteria; Denmark and the UK exercised their formal opt-outs, and Sweden was allowed an informal one. While some eyebrows were raised at the prospect of a euro-zone stretching from Finland to Portugal, the financial markets accepted the judgement with remarkable calm. The 11 were formally chosen at a meeting in May 1998, and their bilateral exchange rates fixed, without much fuss.

That meeting hit the news headlines for quite another matter. As has been the case so often in the past, the selection of a candidate for a top job in Europe – in this case, the president of the ECB – was hotly contested. This row exposed divisions in the Franco-German partnership. Most member states, including Germany, had agreed that Wim Duisenberg, a Dutchman then heading the European Monetary Institute (the body overseeing the transition to the third stage of EMU), should have the post. But in November 1997, France nominated its own candidate, Jean-Claude Trichet, head of the French Central Bank. Due partly to inept handling by the UK during its EU presidency, the row exploded in May. France insisted that Duisenberg could have the job only if he stepped down halfway through his eight-year term in favour of Trichet. This was apparently the compromise reached, although Duisenberg at the end of 1998 was hinting that he might choose to stay for his full term.

The transition to the euro on 1 January went smoothly, although the new euro coins and notes will not replace national currencies in circulation until 2002. Several potential problems could mar the euphoria which accompanied the euro's launch. The euro-zone is not an optimal currency area – labour is not mobile and there are no cross-border fiscal transfers to compensate countries and regions that suffer under anti-inflation policies or are affected differently by external shocks. The loss of control over monetary policy by participating member states has been compounded by the Stability Pact, agreed largely on the insistence of the Kohl government: governments are to be fined for overshooting the 3% limit on budget deficits. This means that even in a recession, governments may not be able to loosen fiscal policy, which could prolong the pain and, ultimately, undermine the mostly passive public support for the euro.

The lack of accountability and democracy in the workings of EMU compound these potential problems. The ECB is the most independent and least accountable central bank in the world. It does not have to publish its minutes, and though its president will appear before the European Parliament, the ECB is to be free of any influences from EU institutions and member states. But the creation of the Euro Eleven Group represents an attempt to exercise some political influence over monetary policy, and there could be tussles between member-state finance ministers and the ECB.

The advent of the euro has solidified a two-speed Europe for the foreseeable future. While those member states currently outside may join the currency in a few years time, the Central and East European countries (due to join the EU in the next decade) will not be in a position to join it in the conceivable future. And the core of euro-participants may proceed with deeper integration. Already the issue of tax harmonisation has been raised and, at some point, the need for centralised fiscal control may be acknowledged.

The euro also has potentially enormous international implications, as it could challenge the primacy of the US dollar. Understandably, the US remains watchful of a development which could not only threaten its leadership in international economic institutions such as the International Monetary fund (IMF) but make it much more difficult to finance its current account deficit. Yet the new currency's strength still has to be tested, and it is not clear how the ECB and/or the Euro Eleven Group will manage the international representation of the currency.

Enlargement Delayed

The other major challenge facing the EU at the turn of the twenty-first century is enlargement. It may turn out to be one challenge too many.

Currently, 11 countries are in the accession queue – ten from Central and Eastern Europe, plus Cyprus. In its *Agenda 2000* report, published in July 1997, the European Commission recommended that membership negotiations be opened with Cyprus, and five of the Central and East European countries: Czech Republic, Estonia, Hungary, Poland and Slovenia. These countries were judged to be closest to meeting the economic, political and legal criteria for membership; the other five countries would have to wait. The Luxembourg European Council, in December 1997, agreed with the Commission's recommendation.

At the end of March 1998, the first stage of membership talks opened with the six front-runners. This stage consisted of a screening process of the applicants' ability to implement EU law (the *acquis communautaire*) and the setting out of their negotiating positions on seven of the 31 chapters of EU law covered in the process. In November, formal negotiations at ministerial level opened with the six countries. Although the talks have proceeded smoothly thus far, the first wave of enlargement will most probably not take place before 2005 – considerably later than the 2002 assumed in *Agenda 2000*. Several contentious areas have yet to be tackled in negotiations, including agricultural policy, the free movement of people and environmental standards. But the biggest obstacles to enlargement now lie on the EU side – the member states have yet to agree on the necessary budgetary, policy and institutional reforms.

EU member states seem decidedly unenthusiastic about the challenge ahead. The need for policy and institutional reform arises at a time when 11 member states are adjusting to life within a euro-zone, and follow two tiring rounds of negotiations on institutional reform which led to the Maastricht and Amsterdam treaties. It is not the most propitious time for the Central and East European countries (CEECs) to try to push their way into the EU.

Agenda 2000 contained proposals for reforming the two EU policies causing the most problems for enlargement: the Common Agricultural Policy (CAP) and the provision of structural funds for poor regions (which together account for two-thirds of the EU's budget). Accession of the poorer and more rural CEECs would clearly break the budget for these two policies. For almost two years, the member states put off hard bargaining on *Agenda 2000*. Initially, discussions were held up until after the German elections, but things became considerably more complicated when Kohl, in an obvious move to gain domestic popularity, called for a reduction in Germany's net contribution to the budget. Schröder, however, has not dropped the demand. Opposition to reforming the CAP is particularly strong in France, but, somewhat paradoxically, also in Germany (as CAP reform would help to reduce the budget). The poor, southern member states are dead-set against losing their structural funds to the Central and East European newcomers. And the UK has steadfastly refused to give up the budgetary rebate won by former Prime Minister Margaret Thatcher back in the early 1980s.

At their Vienna summit in December 1998, the heads of state and government again disagreed over the budget. The northern member states supported a budget freeze, to control expenditure, while the southern member states called for increased spending so that their structural funds would not be cut when the CEECs join. A special European Council was held at the end of March 1999 to settle the matter, but, in effect, finessed the problem to a later date.

Institutional reform also remains high on the agenda, following the disappointing results of the Amsterdam Treaty; a change in Council voting procedures and the re-weighting of votes in the Council are the principal reforms considered necessary before enlargement. Several member states, including Belgium, France and Italy, have declared that enlargement should not go ahead unless reforms are agreed. Yet another intergovernmental conference may be called in late 1999 to try to tackle these issues.

Another complication arose just as the hard negotiations on reforms were to begin: institutional war broke out in Brussels. The European Parliament, disgusted by reports of fraud, mismanagement and cronyism in the European Commission, exercised two of the only real powers it possesses. It refused to discharge the 1998 budget, and then called for a vote of censure on the Commission, which was held on 14 January 1999. A vote by two-thirds of Euro-parliamentarians (MEPs) is needed to throw out the entire Commission (the parliament cannot force individual Commissioners out), and, with pressure from member states not to censure the Commission, the MEPs could, in the end, only force the Commission to adopt reforms. In the event Jacques Santer and the entire Commission were forced to resign in March 1999.

A further, potentially serious problem facing the enlargement process is that of relations with the so-called 'pre-ins' – the five CEECs left out of the first wave of EU enlargement. Accession Partnerships were concluded in March 1998 with each of the CEECs, setting out short-term and long-term priorities for preparing for EU membership, and provided additional aid for that purpose. The pre-ins were promised that if they proceeded quickly in meeting the objectives they might be able to jump into the first wave of enlargement.

While there is little doubt that Bulgaria and Romania need more time to prepare for membership, progress made by the other pre-ins has complicated the EU's strategy. Slovakia's primary problem had been the autocratic government of Vladimir Meciar, but in September 1998, Slovaks elected a much more democratically-inclined government. Latvia and Lithuania have also raced to prepare for membership. Thus nine countries could, in theory, be included in the first wave of enlargement. Add Malta to this – changing governments there have alternately frozen and revived that country's membership application, and it is now active again – and that number rises to ten. Such a large first wave of enlargement, however, would strain the institutions and policies of the EU to breaking point. In its first set of progress reports on the ten countries, released in early November, the Commission maintained that negotiations should not be opened with additional countries. It did admit, however, that Latvia might be let into talks in 1999. If the EU does not open talks with countries that have made impressive progress in meeting its conditions, it could find it difficult to cope with the inevitable disappointment and frustration that would follow.

Europe and Turkey: Still at Loggerheads

Relations between Turkey and Western Europe have hit an all-time low, with problems arising over the treatment of Turkey's EU membership aspirations; the opening of EU membership negotiations with the Republic of Cyprus; and Italy's treatment of the Turkish request for the extradition of Abdullah Öcalan, the leader of the Kurdistan Workers' Party (PKK).

Turkey applied for membership of the European Community in 1987, but has had to settle for a customs union instead – which, after Greek objections were finally withdrawn, and the European Parliament's human-rights concerns mollified, entered into force only in January 1996. Meanwhile, ten CEECs have not only jumped the queue, but have been offered participation in a specially-designed 'accession process', including the conclusion of Accession Partnerships. In December 1997, Turkey took extreme offence that the EU agreed to open negotiations with several CEECs, but placed Turkey in a different category altogether.

The EU attempted to placate Turkey by inviting it to participate in a 'European Conference', in which the leaders of the 15 member states and the applicant states would discuss foreign policy, immigration, the fight against international crime, and other such matters. The first meeting was held in March 1998, just before membership talks opened with the six front-runners. Turkey, however, declined the invitation to attend, as well as a subsequent invitation to a meeting in December. It has insisted that the Union formally grant it 'candidate status' (equal to that of the CEECs) and include it in the accession process. Balked by Greek objections, the EU has only confirmed Turkey's eligibility for membership and declared a separate strategy for Turkey's accession to the Union. In November 1998, the European Commission included Turkey in its progress report on the applicant states (noting serious problems with respect to the rule of law and protection of minorities). None of this has satisfied Turkey, whose relations with the EU remain deadlocked over the issue. Turkey's fear is that the Union will never allow it in – not on economic, political, or even strategic grounds, but on cultural and religious ones. Certainly Kohl's government gave this impression; the new German government may, however, be less hostile to Turkish membership ambitions and could therefore increase the pressure on Greece to be more accommodating.

A further strain arises from the prospect that, if the EU takes in Cyprus, it will only be the Greek part of Cyprus. Initially, the EU's 1994 offer of membership to Cyprus was optimistically viewed as one way of overcoming the impasse between the two communities on the island. But the EU then limited its potential influence by promising to go ahead with negotiations with Greek Cyprus if representatives of the Turkish side refused to take part. The opening of negotiations with the Republic of Cyprus in March 1998 was accompanied by a war of words, in which Turkey threatened to block NATO expansion to Central Europe, and to merge with the Turkish part of Cyprus if EU enlargement to Greek Cyprus went ahead. This led to the inevitable Greek counter-threat that it would block EU expansion to Central and Eastern Europe unless the EU proceeded with talks with Greek Cyprus.

With Greece an EU member state, it was difficult for the EU to act credibly as a mediator, and the seemingly ubiquitous US negotiator Richard Holbrooke stepped in again to try (unsuccessfully) to work out a settlement, with back-up from the UN Secretary-General Kofi Annan. The EU has tried to encourage Turkish Cypriots to participate in the Greek Cypriot delegation, but they have refused to do so. Rauf Denktash, leader of the Turkish Cypriots, has insisted that international recognition of his mini-state must precede negotiations on the status of the island and its relation to the EU. Matters threatened to spin out of control over the delivery of Russian air-defence missiles to the Republic of Cyprus, which Turkey vowed to destroy if they were deployed. In December 1998, Greek Cypriot President Glafkos Clerides agreed, under Western pressure and in the face of intense domestic opposition, that the missiles should be stored on Crete. Yet whether Turkey could respond to the compromise was not certain due to its continuing government crisis. The coalition government lost a vote of confidence in November; a successor was patched together only in January 1999, but elections are to be held in April. Resolution of the Cyprus problem thus went on hold yet again, particularly as the new Turkish prime minister, Bulent Ecevit, had taken a hard stance on Cyprus.

The fall of the Turkish government came in the middle of a diplomatic scuffle with Italy over the Öcalan affair. On 12 November, Öcalan was arrested in Rome, having arrived there from Russia on a false passport. Turkey demanded his extradition, considering him a terrorist. Italy refused, because its constitution forbids extradition to countries which allow the death penalty. Turkey protested, declared a boycott of Italian arms purchases, and threatened a boycott of Italian trade. The European Commission warned against a trade boycott, which would contravene the customs union agreement. Germany, which had previously issued an arrest warrant for Öcalan for the murder of PKK defectors there, declined to request his extradition out of concern about the effects this would have on its Kurdish community. The Italian government suggested that Öcalan be tried by an international court, and tried to use the occasion to launch a peace initiative. A lull in the row was provided only by the collapse of Turkey's ruling coalition. In mid-January 1999, Italy announced, with an almost audible sigh of relief, that Öcalan had left the country for an undisclosed destination. The PKK leader was ultimately captured by Turkish security services in Kenya in February 1999 and was brought home to Turkey for trial.

A European Defence Identity?

The other enlargement process in Europe, that of NATO, has not hit any of the snags that are dogging EU enlargement. Only three countries – Czech Republic, Hungary and Poland – joined in March 1999. In April, NATO's Washington summit – held to commemorate the Alliance's fiftieth anniversary – will reconsider the enlargement process (as well as approve a new strategic doctrine); Slovenia and Romania are particularly keen on joining and were promised special consideration back in June 1997. There have been concerns about the readiness of the first three CEECs to join NATO, the costs of the entire operation, and the effects that NATO enlargement will have on Russia. But with Russia effectively sidelined due to internal turmoil, by the end of 1998, NATO enlargement was no longer so newsworthy.

Nevertheless, NATO enlargement does complicate the issue of a European defence identity, because it signals that the 'tangle of different memberships in European security organisations – 'variable geometry' in the buzz-phrase – will not be unravelled any time soon. This particularly affects the debate about a European security and defence identity centred around the EU, which recently entered a new phase following the British initiative on European defence. But it will be difficult for the EU to assume a defence role if some of its member states are not in NATO, as that would imply a US security guarantee through the back door. Boosting the WEU's role, or incorporating it as the EU's 'fourth pillar', does not solve the problem, as full membership of the WEU still implies full NATO membership. As for the EU taking on more defence decisions, with five European countries (Norway, Iceland, Poland, Hungary and the Czech Republic) members of NATO but not the EU, the complications are great. Furthermore, ironing out the institutional arrangements also does not automatically translate into the political will to use military means – as the recent debate over intervention in Kosovo (or even Iraq) illustrated.

But Is There a Common European Foreign Policy?

The Amsterdam Treaty did not enter into effect in 1998 or early 1999 because several member states still had to ratify it, so Common Foreign and Security Policy (CFSP) reforms, in particular the creation of the Policy Planning and Early Warning Unit and the appointment of a High Representative, were delayed. CFSP had a fairly quiet year, with the Iraqi and Kosovan crises handled in other fora. Nuclear weapon tests in India and Pakistan were condemned, but the EU itself took little action. The EU remained a small player in the search for a resolution of the Middle East conflict, despite, or because, of a British presidency attempt to exercise influence. While on a tour of the Middle East in March 1998, UK Foreign Secretary Robin Cook visited a site on the edge of Arab East Jerusalem where a Jewish settlement is being built and shook hands with a Palestinian member of parliament. The Israeli government reacted furiously, cancelling an official dinner and accusing Cook and the EU of being pro-Palestinian.

One of the factors purportedly motivating the UK's European defence initiative was the EU's failure to act in Kosovo, as Serbian President Slobadan Milosevic launched an offensive against the Kosovo Liberation Army (KLA). Warnings of an explosion there had been sounded for a decade, but when the crisis erupted the West stumbled before agreeing on a limited strategy, and remained wary of using force in Kosovo until finally doing so, in very imperfect style, in late March 1999. The EU initially had trouble even with imposing a ban on flights from Serbia, and once again, the impetus for action was left to the US and to NATO. NATO initially threatened action against Serbia, then backed off when the KLA rejected the West's preferred solution of autonomy and insisted on Kosovan independence. But continuing Serbian military action in Kosovo prompted renewed NATO threats – which temporarily worked. Under a deal negotiated by Richard Holbrooke in October 1998, unarmed observers from the Organisation for Security and Cooperation in Europe (OSCE) would monitor a cease-fire and the withdrawal of Serbian troops from the province. This agreement broke down almost before it was signed and by March 1999 Milosovich was once again using his army to attempt to cleanse northern Kosovo of Albanians. On 24 March 1999, NATO began striking his military assets with cruise missiles and bombers after he had refused to sign the Rambouillet Accords.

Tussles over Transatlantic Trade

In mid-1998, transatlantic trade relations appeared to be on a much friendlier footing than they had been for several years, as the British EU presidency managed to broker a resolution of the dispute over America's Helms-Burton and D'Amato legislation. These laws would impose sanctions on foreign firms doing business with Cuba, Iran or Libya. The EU threatened to take the matter to the World Trade Organisation (WTO), but held off as long as the Clinton Administration waived the application of sanctions on European businesses. In May, the US agreed to make the waivers for Cuba permanent and to waive sanctions on investments in Iran, while the EU promised to deter investment in Cuba that used illegally expropriated assets. This deal made it possible for work to proceed on building a Transatlantic Economic Partnership – a scaled-down version of a more ambitious proposal for a Transatlantic Marketplace which had been opposed primarily by the French and Spanish. The Partnership would provide for free trade in goods, services and investments, but not agricultural products.

But several trade disputes remained and, in early 1999, a transatlantic 'banana war' loomed. The US had won a case at the WTO against the EU's preferential treatment of banana imports from Caribbean countries; when the EU delayed making minimal changes to the regime by January 1999, the US threatened to slap duties of 100% on a long list of EU products (an act which would also be illegal under WTO rules). The banana war seemed superficially silly, but increased protectionism in a time of global economic turbulence was anything but funny.

No Rest for the Weary

Europe could congratulate itself for having successfully brought in the euro as projected many years ago, but there was only a brief moment for savouring the accomplishment. The EU's leaders barely had time to gulp down a congratulatory glass of champagne before they had to turn to meet the challenges of Kosovo, enlargement of the EU, NATO enlargement and establishment of a new strategic doctrine, and economic and trade difficulties. This docket of tough problems will sorely test the untried new German government which finds itself saddled with the presidency of the EU almost before it has settled itself in to deal with Germany's own problems. It will probably be best if it does not set its sights too high. While Europe catches its breath after the euphoria of the establishment of the euro, solid, if incremental, steps forward on most of the remaining problems would be a significant goal to aim for.

The Balkans: Still at a Boil

On the evening of 24 March 1999 NATO launched air attacks against the Federal Republic of Yugoslavia (FRY). The announced aims of the attacks were to demonstrate NATO's resolve; deter the use of force by FRY against Kosovo's Albanian population; and degrade, if necessary, Serbia's military capacity to conduct offensive operations. The decision to attack followed the failure of Ambassador Richard Holbrooke, accompanied by other diplomats from the European Union (EU) and the Organisation for Security and Cooperation in Europe (OSCE), to convince Serbia's President Slobodan Milosevic to sign the political agreement that the Albanian Kosovars had eventually signed. The stated reluctance of NATO to introduce a fighting force on the ground encouraged Milosevic to adopt a hedgehog strategy: taking air strikes in the hope that NATO would not wish to destroy Serbian assets to the extent that the local balance of power would shift entirely to the Kosovo Liberation Army (KLA). As the air strikes took place, a lasting peace in the Balkans appeared as distant in March 1999 as it had at any time in the recent past.

The Balkans have never been amenable to easy solutions imposed from outside. Even at the height of the Cold War, the Soviet Union gradually lost control over Yugoslavia, Albania and Romania, while the West barely contained perennial Greek–Turkish rows, despite the fact that both were NATO members and, at least formally, allies. Compared to the Cold War, the current condition of the Balkans is quite favourable. Although the Yugoslav war has played havoc with the economies of the area, and with the Balkans' aspiration to project an image of stability, the region is now at the top of the European agenda.

Not only has NATO mounted in Yugoslavia the biggest military operation in its history, but every international organisation is now deeply engaged in the area. The EU is financing infrastructure projects designed to connect Romania and Bulgaria to main transport routes. Turkey is seen as one of Europe's key strategic allies in the effort to change the regime in Iraq, and the US is mediating in the Greek–Turkish dispute over Cyprus and islands in the Aegean. More significantly, the promise of full integration into both NATO and the EU has been extended to most of the region's states in return for their good behaviour.

The sincere intentions of Western governments and institutions are not in doubt. Nevertheless, the chances are that, far from heralding the Balkans' integration into Europe, they could still result in little more than the area's isolation from the rest of the continent. At the beginning of the twentieth century, the Balkans were regarded as partly a geographic region, and partly a disease for which effective quarantine measures were the only adequate response. The Balkans may yet end the century in exactly the same situation. The history of the 1990s is not one of mischief or cynicism (although there was plenty of both), but of a persistent lack of vision which could lead to missed opportunities.

Stable But Surly

The multinational peacekeeping operation in Bosnia-Herzegovina appears well established. Almost five years after the agreement reached at Dayton,

Ohio, Bosnia's constitutional bodies are in place, but their election has only contributed to the republic's irrevocable division. Meanwhile, many of the strategies which the West has pursued have basically failed.

The West concentrated on encouraging a division between the Serb leaders in Pale, the capital of the Serb statelet originally controlled by Radovan Karadzic, and another set of Serb leaders led by Biljana Plavsic, based in Banja Luka, the north-western part of Bosnia. The division between the two strands of the Bosnian-Serb community is serious, because it coincides with historical and economic differences. By playing on such distinctions, NATO hoped to divide the Serbs, thereby forcing them to cooperate with Muslims and Croats. The tactic worked until autumn 1998, when presidential, parliamentary and local-authority elections – mandated by the Dayton Accords – complicated Western tactics even further.

The elections took place in late September 1998, and were broadly democratic and peaceful. But their credibility was not helped when the results were delayed for a full two weeks because of 'technical problems'. More importantly, the presidential poll resulted in a triumph for a hard-line Serb nationalist, Nikola Poplasen, who defeated the incumbent Plavsic by 38,000 votes. Plavsic was backed by Western countries because of her support for Dayton.

Western governments put a brave face on the exercise: in an official statement on 26 September 1998, the US hailed the results as 'a step towards a multi-ethnic democracy'. American hopes were not entirely misplaced. Despite Poplasen's victory, the wider results of parliamentary and local-authority elections revealed that support for hard-liners in all of Bosnia's main ethnic groups was waning. Serb hard-liners lost to moderates in both the Bosnian three-member presidency and in the Bosnian Serb assembly. Moderate Serb politician Zivko Radisic won the post of Serbian representative on Bosnia's collective presidency, for instance, while the Muslim wartime leader of the republic and current chairman of the joint presidency, Alija Izetbegovic, won re-election by more than 450,000 votes. But in the race for the Croat seat on the presidency, the Western-backed candidate Kresimir Zubak lost to hard-liner Ante Jelavic, who is close to the president of neighbouring Croatia, Franjo Tudjman.

Carlos Westendorp, the international administrator for Bosnia, originally hoped to benefit from a battle between a more moderate Serb parliament in Bosnia and Poplasen, in which the extremists and the moderates in the Serb community check-mated each other. But the paralysis which resulted from this fight could not continue for long, and, in early March 1999, Westendorp resolved it by dismissing Poplasen from office. The mediator's action was hailed as 'decisive'. Correct, but hardly the end of the story: the reality remains that, although the Serbs are now more divided than ever, they are united in their rejection of any meaningful cooperation with the Muslim-dominated government in Sarajevo. The more the West expresses its preference for a 'tame' Serb leader, the less chance this leader has of winning an election in his or her community.

The strategy of promoting cooperation between Croats and Muslims has also failed. Although Croatia itself has been persuaded to limit its assistance to extremist Croats in Bosnia, no one has succeeded in persuading the Croats to take part in the government in Sarajevo. The Croat-controlled areas of the country maintain their separate administration, and still look to Zagreb – rather than Sarajevo – for ultimate protection. Matters may change when Tudjman disappears (a demise which has often been predicted over the past few years). Tudjman depends on the votes of the ethnic Croats of Bosnia, and on their financial support, none of which his successor is likely to enjoy. But, until he goes, cooperation between Serbs and Croats will remain more formal than real. One of the most difficult issues facing international mediators in Bosnia – the future of the strategically important town of Brcko – reached a decisive moment on 15 January 1999, when the deadline for the submission of rival claims to the town expired. Brcko, which was under international arbitration, is wanted by both the Muslim–Croat Federation and by the Serb Republic. Because the Muslim and Croat majority were driven out during the 1992–95 war, it is now mainly populated by Serbs. There were fears that a decision on the final disposition of the town could lead to renewed violence. In the event, it was left outside the control of both entities, a defeat for the Serbs who controlled the area, but hardly a victory for the government in Sarajevo either. It was a decision postponed, rather than a problem solved. But it showed that the international community was determined to confront the Bosnian Serbs. It also came at the height of a crisis in Kosovo, when Milosevic was hardly in a position to cause too much trouble.

Elsewhere, Westendorp continued to intervene on the ground in order to ensure compliance with the Dayton Accords. He imposed new passports, new currency and a new flag, using special powers granted to him in summer 1997. These measures have, however, failed to create a self-sustaining Bosnia. The country remains a *de facto* Western protectorate, with Westendorp as its viceroy. At the same time, there has been some progress on the arrest and punishment of war criminals. A spectacular operation which resulted in the arrest of Karadzic and other major alleged war criminals is possible, and would undoubtedly boost the credibility of Bosnian peace efforts. But the effects would be short-lived and, apart from restoring faith in international justice, would do nothing to recreate pre-war Bosnia. In many respects, apprehending war criminals – hesitantly begun by American and British forces during 1998 – has allowed a second generation of national leaders to come to the fore, unencumbered by the stigma of their predecessors. Tudjman, for instance, saw no difficulty in handing over some of his own alleged war criminals while continuing to exercise effective control over Croat-populated territory in Bosnia. Milosevic may actually welcome the removal of some Bosnian Serb leaders.

In effect, the division of the Bosnian republic is now an accomplished fact. The one decisive policy which could reverse this division – the return of refugees – will not be attempted by Western forces because it is both risky, and necessitates an even greater military commitment on the ground for an indeterminate period, which no Western government is prepared to contemplate. Furthermore, even the Muslims, who continue to demand the return of refugees mainly because they were the chief victims of 'ethnic cleansing', would not be overly happy if this means the return of Serbs to the housing estates around Sarajevo. Westendorp proclaimed 1998 as 'The Year of Return' for the country's displaced persons, but he now prefers not to be reminded of this slogan.

Nevertheless, the current deadlock, frustrating as it may be, does not mean that Bosnia is certain to be plunged into another war. Muslims may have an interest in regaining some of their lost territory, and they believe that they are in a better strategic position to launch an offensive. Yet they cannot actually both launch and sustain an attack on the Serbs unless they can be sure of Croat encouragement. And the Croats have no interest in renewed warfare.

As history has shown, when it comes to keeping the Bosnian Muslim state under control, Serbs and Croats are potential allies, rather than enemies. For better or worse, therefore, a balance of power (or terror) has been created in Bosnia. This curious stalemate, intolerable in political terms but quite tolerable militarily, has emboldened governments, both in the region and in the West, to reduce their military commitment. In early January 1999, NATO planned to cut its military presence by 10%, or roughly 3,200 military personnel. The reduction, scheduled for March, had to be slightly delayed. But the trend was unmistakable, and it was reinforced by an initiative put forward on 24 February 1999 by the collective Bosnian presidency.

Under the proposal, the two self-governing parts of Bosnia – the Muslim–Croat Federation and the Serb Republic – would cut their military budgets by 30% and would use the money saved for post-war reconstruction. During 1998, the Muslim–Croat Federation alone spent more than $160 million on its armed forces. The offer was conditional on disarmament in both neighbouring Croatia and Yugoslavia, and, predictably, there was no response from either. But, almost regardless of what happens, Bosnia is in many respects yesterday's story: the real challenges in the former Yugoslavia are now elsewhere, particularly in Serbia, Kosovo and the Former Yugoslav Republic of Macedonia.

Milosevic's Disaster ...

Serbia represents the classic example of what can go wrong in the process of transition from a communist-controlled society. The Yugoslav war, for which Milosevic bears heavy responsibility, served only to perpetuate disguised communist rule, and postpone serious decisions about the nature of the Serbian state. Milosevic began the war in the name of Serbian unity and ethnic purity, yet Serbs are still divided, many have been forcefully removed, and Serbia itself still contains the highest number of ethnic minorities of all the republics of the former Yugoslavia. Having been the most integrated Eastern European state before 1989, rump Yugoslavia is now a pariah country.

To complete this cycle of tragedies, the Yugoslavia which Milosevic invented after 1991 remains a rickety affair. Montenegro, Serbia's partner in the federation, looks increasingly unreliable. The institutions of the state are an even greater farce than they were during Tito's communist dictatorship. For a number of years after the demise of the old Yugoslavia, the Yugoslav federal presidency, which was meant to represent both Montenegro and Serbia, remained a cipher designed to obscure Milosevic's effective political control. But, since he was prevented by the constitution from holding a third term of office, he assumed the mantle of the federal presidency in August 1998.

Serbia and, to a lesser extent, Montenegro, have therefore ended up with the worst possible combination: they not only lost the war, but are also the only former Yugoslav republics not to have found a new identity. Serbia's citizens have responded accordingly. Roughly a third support Milosevic's Socialist party, another third have opted for extreme nationalists, while the rest do not vote at all. Milosevic has failed to realise his nationalist dreams, but he appears to have succeeded in destroying his country's civic society. Ten years ago, the Serbs were in the forefront of all communist states, at least in terms of political culture. In early 1999, they were at the bottom of the pile, with no salvation in sight: opposition political parties remained divided, and hardly represented an alternative power base. But Serbia's travails were only beginning, for the crucial issue of Kosovo had still to be addressed.

... And The Kosovo Conundrum

Contrary to common assumptions in the West, Milosevic never had any intention of starting a war in Kosovo, Serbia's southern province and an area overwhelmingly populated by ethnic Albanians. His long-term strategy was to increase the pressure on Kosovo until the Albanians left of their own accord, or until the ethnic balance of the province was reversed. Nothing of the kind happened. The virtual collapse of neighbouring Albania during 1997 may have eased Milosevic's strategic concerns for a while, but it also fuelled an ethnic Albanian guerrilla movement, which benefited from the large quantities of weapons released by the disintegration of the Albanian army.

Milosevic's attempts to populate the region with ethnic Serbs from other areas of the former Yugoslavia – pursued particularly during 1994–95 – also failed. By summer 1998, therefore, the Yugoslav leader was faced with an armed insurrection in Kosovo, one which he probably wanted to avoid, but which he was determined to crush. In September 1998, the bloody scenario of Croatia and Bosnia looked like repeating itself in Kosovo: massacres and burnt villages, which international diplomacy fails to avert.

Some Western governments – particularly the US and the UK – were determined that history would not repeat itself. A resolution demanding an immediate end to hostilities had already been passed (with Russian support) in the UN Security Council at the end of August 1998, and this was used to forge a consensus for a dual-track strategy of imposing a settlement on the ground, while threatening the use of air power against the Yugoslav authorities. September 1998 was spent in almost continuous shuttle diplomacy, while the military preparations for air strikes continued. The consensus for this operation was fragile and superficial, but it was achieved, even with the newly elected Socialist government in Germany.

And yet, at the very last moment, Holbrooke, the architect of the Bosnian accord and the man perceived to have the 'Midas touch' in the Balkans, negotiated a deal with Milosevic which, far from providing a solution, actually complicated matters further. The deal, concluded on 13 October 1998 without consultation with America's allies, demanded concessions from everyone involved in the conflict. Milosevic was forced to admit that Kosovo was no longer a Yugoslav internal matter; it had become an issue that he would have to discuss with other countries. He was forced to withdraw his troops from the province, and to allow the presence of 2,000 foreign personnel to supervise the implementation of the deal. Milosevic also accepted new elections in Kosovo, which, as he knew only too well, could only result in the creation of a local parliament dominated by ethnic Albanian nationalists. There was also the promise of a new federal arrangement within Yugoslavia, and Belgrade's agreement to open the air space above Kosovo to NATO aircraft.

In return, Milosevic prevented for a time a destructive air campaign against his army, and won tacit support for his position that, whatever constitutional arrangements may be provided for Kosovo, the province would remain within Yugoslavia. In turn, the ethnic Albanians were told to moderate their demands for total independence. But they had managed to internationalise the Kosovo conflict – something which they had sought to do for years – and also gained Western protection just as their guerrilla organisation, the Kosovo Liberation Army (KLA), was being destroyed by

Yugoslav forces. Western governments could plausibly claim that it was only their resolute approach which had produced this outcome: diplomacy backed by force, as US President Bill Clinton insisted, had worked. The reality, however, was somewhat different.

The tasks of the 2,000 people introduced into Kosovo, in an operation which became known as the Kosovo Verification Mission (KVM), were never clarified. No one knew whether the KVM was simply passively to collect facts, or whether the observers were able to take an active role in implementing the accord. Western governments were hoping for a mixture of the two: the mission in Kosovo was lightly armed (suggesting that it was not there to impose peace), but enjoyed NATO air protection, indicating that it was expected to perform larger roles than just observing what was happening.

It is easy to understand why Holbrooke adopted this deliberate ambiguity. Yugoslavia would never have agreed to the introduction of troops designed to implement a deal. To Milosevic, this would have meant the loss of Kosovo. But the West did not want to repeat the sad experience of the EU observer mission in Croatia earlier in the Yugoslav wars, when the men and women dressed in white and equipped with little more than pen, paper and a telephone, came to be called 'ice-cream sellers' by the local population. The result was a Kosovo mission which tried to frighten Milosevic in theory, while reassuring him in practice.

Milosevic's response was rather simple. He withdrew his regular forces, but insisted that the Serbian police should continue operating. Paramilitary formations in the ethnic Serb areas of Kosovo were not disbanded, and Milosevic claimed that he had little control over their activities, just as he had done in Croatia and Bosnia. The Albanians of Kosovo promptly demanded, with some justification, special protection for every village to which refugees were expected to return. They also insisted that the local police in Kosovo should include ethnic Albanians, or that the Albanians should be allowed to form their own police force. Both the Serbs and the Albanians accused each other of inflating the number of refugees in order to affect the ethnic balance of the province, and both expected the West to feed them through the winter. Meanwhile, constitutional discussions between the two made no progress.

Milosevic also viewed Holbrooke's decision to entrust the KVM operation to the OSCE, rather than NATO, as a clear indication that the West was not serious about imposing peace in the province, and that the US was not ready to dispatch troops for this purpose. The American decision to contract out its personnel contribution to the KVM to US private security firms reinforced this impression. The very best that can be said about the Holbrooke deal is that it bought some time before the peace negotiations between the Albanians and the Yugoslav authorities started at Rambouillet in France in early February 1999.

The peace conference was always a finely balanced exercise attempting to reconcile the impossible. It sought to promise the ethnic Albanians enough freedom to persuade them to stop fighting, while reassuring the Serbs that the province would remain part of Yugoslavia. None of the sides fighting in the Balkans ever believed in the autonomy plans which France and Britain – the two chairs of the conference – put forward. The people of the Balkans always knew that autonomy was merely a prelude to independence, and that Kosovo was unlikely to be an exception.

The Albanians and Serbs were ultimately compelled to come to the negotiating table by intense international pressure, including from the US and Russia. The clinching factor was the visit of US Secretary of State Madeleine Albright to Moscow in late January 1999. Once the Russians were persuaded to support a peace effort, the Yugoslav authorities had to accept the offer of discussions. But both sides arrived at the conference not to get a deal, but to find out what the international community was prepared to tolerate.

The Albanians demanded a referendum at the end of the three years of autonomy which they were offered as part of the peace deal, knowing full well that this was a nicer way of saying that independence was their ultimate fate. Milosevic – that veteran of so many previous unobserved agreements – was prepared to sign any document provided that the deal was not monitored by Western forces, and he could not be held accountable for what followed. To avoid such dangers, Western nego-tiators demanded from the start that there should be a link between the political and the military agreements: without the presence of NATO troops, no deal was likely to stick. However, after almost three weeks of intense negotiations during February 1999, the political part of the peace – autonomy and elections in Kosovo – and the military side of the deal, which should have provided for the stationing of Western forces, remained separate.

The reasons for this failure were manifold. The US administration hoped to isolate Yugoslavia by persuading the Albanians to accept a deal quickly. The tactic backfired, as the ethnic Albanians held off until mid-March 1999 before accepting. Second, attempts to coordinate policy with Russia failed. Moscow supported the negotiations, but adamantly refused to accept the military protocol attached by the West to the political deal. As a result, Western negotiators were left in the uncomfortable position of demanding acceptance for a deal on which the Contact Group remained divided. Moreover, there were too many threats from the American delegation, which Washington must have known could not be carried out, and which annoyed the French and British.

Milosevic had no intention of accepting a deal that included the introduction of Western forces. He had already realised that he would lose control over Kosovo. His choice was thus either to accept this loss peacefully (through the introduction of peacekeepers and elections resulting in Kosovo's independence) or through violence. Predictably, he chose violence. He refused to sign the agreement which the Albanians had accepted, and instead sent Serbian troops accompanied by tanks and armoured personnel carriers into Kosovo. These troops drove the Albanians from their villages, and then burned their houses behind them. Milosevic's tactic was to 'ethnically cleanse' the northern part of Kosovo, and partition the province. The rump could then either be left for the West to mull over for years to come, or allowed to join Albania. This was a dangerous tactic, for it risked forcing NATO to fulfil its constant threat to bomb his military machine if the troops did not leave Kosovo.

The Yugoslav actions opened the way for the West to put more military pressure on Milosevic. After Holbrooke failed to convince him on 22–23 March to sign the peace accord, NATO had no option but to carry out its threat of air attack, which began on the evening of 24 March. In an angry letter to the co-chairs of the Rambouillet peace conference on the eve of the attack, Milosevic rejected the negotiating process as a sham, claiming that there had never really been a proper agreement that Serbia could consider. As air strikes were launched, it was clear that Milosevic had chosen the line of maximum resistance, betting that he could survive the air strikes, and that, despite the damage that they could do to his military, the West would be unable to ram the autonomy agreement down his throat.

A Changing Macedonia

Only a year ago, received wisdom in the West suggested that fighting in Kosovo would inevitably infect neighbouring Macedonia and ignite a wider war. In fact, almost precisely the opposite happened. A centre-right government came to power in Macedonia following peaceful and democratic elections in November 1998, ending seven years of socialist rule since independence. The change of government was an advantage on three counts. At long last, Macedonia had leaders who were prepared to engage in serious economic reform. The authorities were also determined to resolve the long-standing disputes with their neighbours, and to cooperate with the West in keeping the republic outside the region's conflicts. And, just as important, the new government was also prepared to make peace with its own sizeable ethnic Albanian community.

Theodoros Pangalos, then the Greek Foreign Minister, paid a historic visit to Macedonia on 22 December 1998. Although the question of the name 'Macedonia' (to which Greece objects because it has a region of the same name) remained on hold, the relaxation in the tense relations between the two countries was noticeable. On 22 February 1999, a much more important accommodation was reached with Bulgaria, when the two countries signed a declaration ending a long-running language dispute which went to the heart of the Macedonian ethnic identity.

The declaration, including agreements to promote trade and cultural relations, was signed during a visit to Sofia by the newly elected Macedonian prime minister, Ljubco Georgievski. Bulgaria has long been opposed to recognising Macedonian as a distinct language, insisting that it was only a regional dialect of Bulgarian. Traditionally, the Bulgarian government has been worried that recognising Macedonian as a separate language would prompt Macedonia to make territorial claims on regions in Bulgaria, where a dialect similar to Macedonian is spoken. But the accommodation with Bulgaria went beyond the resolution of the language dispute: seven other deals, mainly traffic and trade agreements, were also signed, and military cooperation was discussed. Bulgaria is to give 150 tanks, along with other artillery equipment, to the Macedonian armed forces, and the two countries pledged to respect current frontiers.

Inside Macedonia, representatives of the ethnic Albanian community were coopted into the government. The threat of ethnic violence, or of the spread of the Albanian rebellion in Kosovo into Macedonia, was instantly reduced. This trend was reinforced by a general amnesty declared by the government in early February 1999. Among the beneficiaries were two ethnic Albanian activists, Rufi Osmani and Alaydin Demiri, mayors of two towns in western Macedonia, who had been jailed following street riots in 1997.

There are, however, at least four important caveats to this generally positive trend. First, the stability of the republic still depends on events in Kosovo. A large stream of ethnic Albanian refugees will impose intolerable burdens and rekindle Macedonian fears about being 'swamped' by other ethnic groups. In October 1998, Macedonian border guards opened fire on Albanian refugees, and the government can be expected to do the same again if the humanitarian crisis in Kosovo worsens. Second, the newly elected authorities are well-meaning, but inexperienced. Little has been done to reform the economy, which still depends on smuggling to embargoed Yugoslavia, and is still dominated by monopolies and shady trading organisations.

The government is also clumsy in the conduct of its international relations. It over-estimates the presence of international troops on its soil (a UN contingent of roughly 1,000, plus a NATO-led force of around 12,000) by assuming that this presence shields the republic from any international responsibility. Macedonia's unexpected decision to establish diplomatic relations with Taiwan created an instant complication, as China vetoed a UN Security Council Resolution on 28 February 1999 renewing the mandate of UN peacekeepers. More importantly, there is a constant tussle between the reformist government and the country's president, Kiro

Gligorov, who belongs to the communist old guard. Gligorov opposed the amnesty given to political prisoners, and criticised his country's foreign policy. Macedonia's brittle coalition therefore faced many challenges, and the delicate political balance in the country could be easily upset.

Not Altogether a Bad Future

At every stage of the Yugoslav war, which has lasted for almost a decade, the West dealt with the immediate crisis, but refused to look at the region as a whole. First it was Slovenia, and nobody dealt with Croatia. Then it was Croatia's turn, while the violence started in Bosnia. And, when every Western government was preoccupied with Bosnia, Milosevic ended the last vestiges of dialogue with Serbia's ethnic Albanians, virtually guaranteeing the disaster in Kosovo. Milosevic, together with the other dictators who have risen from the ashes of Yugoslavia by playing on nationalist feelings and economic frustration, are part of the problem, not a stepping stone to a solution. Any deal concluded with them, and which does not create a system of security for the entire region, is bound to fail.

Despite this confusing pattern of policies, the outcome of the Kosovo episode is clear. Kosovo will become *de facto* independent: it will have its own Albanian-dominated elected institutions, and possibly an ethnic Albanian police force, created out of the nucleus of the KLA. The Yugoslav authorities will keep control of Serb-populated areas, in the hope that, even if they lose the province politically, they will be able to hang on to its strategic assets, such as the main towns, power stations and natural resources. In Macedonia, the presence of Western forces – strengthened to support the operation in Kosovo – will prevent ethnic Albanians from making any new demands for autonomy. In Albania, economic assistance will be predicated on the promise that the Albanian government will not pursue its objective of national unity. Albania will remain legally independent, but with little of the substance of such independence, while Kosovo will be *de facto* independent, while legally still part of the Yugoslav Federation. Given the region's history, Western governments may be tempted to think that such an outcome is not necessarily bad. But it is inherently unstable, and will depend on the continued presence of foreign troops.

The Balkans began this century with the Albanian question; they are ending it with essentially the same problem, still unanswered. But the worst policy which the West could pursue is to treat the rest of the Balkans as a mere appendix of the Yugoslav tragedy. Despite the disaster in the former Yugoslavia, the outlook for the region as a whole is actually bright. Most of the dark predictions so frequently made after the collapse of communism have been confounded. The record of positive developments in the Balkans is impressive:

- Romania's neo-communist regime has been removed from power.

- The widely predicted violence against ethnic Hungarians in Romania has not occurred; Hungary and Romania are now close allies, and representatives of the ethnic Hungarian party serve as members of the ruling coalition.

- Despite all its troubles and many temptations, post-communist Bulgaria has not sought to play off Greeks against Turks in its foreign policy.

- Bulgaria's Socialists returned to power, predictably ruining the country's economy. But they were ultimately removed by a popular mood of revulsion and peaceful, free elections.

- Muslims are active in Bulgaria's national politics, and did not become the subject of nationalist baiting even at the height of the country's political crisis in 1999.

- Nationalist and openly anti-Semitic political formations remained on the peripheries of politics, and gathered fewer votes in the Balkans than their counterparts in, for example, France or Italy.

- With the notable exception of Albania, severe economic downturns did not lead to major violence anywhere.

- The Greeks and the Turks may continue to infuriate everyone, but both instinctively know the limits of their actions. The Greek government has gone out of its way to appear moderate; it behaved responsibly when Albania collapsed, preferring to leave Italy to take the lead in peacekeeping operations, despite a large ethnic Greek community in Albania.

- The Turkish Islamist government of Prime Minister Necmettin Erbakan turned into a farce, and lost power. Turkey's military was active behind the political scenes, but the country's generals knew their limits and did not contemplate a coup.

- Ultimately, all the region's governments knew that they could not afford either war or isolation; they were eager to integrate into European institutions, and were willing to pay any price if such a prospect were realistic.

A great deal can be built on the basis of such developments. But the difficulty is that the West is already committed to a set of policies which, curiously, promise both deeper European involvement in the region, and a longer quarantine for the Balkans.

Both the EU and NATO are suggesting that, while they restructure their societies and reform their economies, the Balkan states should be encouraged to cooperate with each other. Such cooperation makes sense, and should not come at the expense of wider European integration. Correct, but only up to a point. There is a great deal that the region's states can do, especially in coordinating their fight against organised crime and drug smuggling, as well as improving their transport infrastructure overland, on the Danube and across the Black Sea.

Much is already being done, and many of these activities do not require government coordination. Greek investors dominate markets in Serbia and Macedonia, and the remittances of Albanian workers in Greece are Albania's only real source of foreign revenue. Turkish construction and transport firms, as well as bakeries, predominate in Romania. These investors, who are more attuned to local markets and willing to take greater risks, will clearly remain in a better position to exploit regional opportunities.

But there are also limitations to how far this process can go. First, all the region's states suffer from similar problems: relatively large agricultural sectors, redundant industrial capacity, a surplus of labour and a decaying infrastructure. Not only do they have little to offer each other, but they actually compete with each other for the same Western funds.

Second, Greece will always be in a different position from the rest of the region: as an EU member, it is bound by certain tariff restrictions and trade practices which do not apply to others. Furthermore, if the West as a whole proved unable to resolve the Greek–Turkish dispute, the Balkan states cannot be expected to do better. Often, their solution is carefully to skirt around the dispute, in the hope of avoiding new tensions. A meeting of Balkan heads of state in Varna, Bulgaria, in February 1999 – in order to coordinate the fight against organised crime – went ahead only because Greece was not invited.

Ultimately, the obstacle to regional cooperation is psychological. Although everyone assures the Balkan states that they have nothing to fear, the area's leaders instinctively regard regional cooperation as inferior to European integration, and suspect that, the more they succeed in cooperating regionally, the less they will be considered serious candidates for membership of either the EU or NATO. The almost universal opinion in Brussels – that Greece's EU membership was a serious mistake – heightens the Balkan states' fears.

Undoubtedly, many of these fears are exaggerated, and some are used by the region's states to justify failures for which local leaders carry most of the blame. Without democratic societies, market economies and internal stability, the Balkan states do not deserve to become members of wider European institutions. The region's reconstruction must begin from within, by people persuaded that it is in their own interest, rather than by leaders eager to mimic the West's forms, but with little of the substance. Just as important is the impression that, if the countries of the region actually manage this feat, they will be integrated into existing continental institutions. The enlargement of both NATO and the EU has been presented as partly a reward for the performance of the Central Europeans, and partly as a mechanism for consolidating it. By implication, therefore, none of Europe's former-communist countries has actually completed this transformation.

While Central Europeans are deemed acceptable as candidates for membership, the Balkan states are expected to perform the same feats without a serious prospect of becoming full members, either of the EU, or of NATO. Even if local economies are transformed overnight, it is difficult to see how the EU will accept either Romania or Bulgaria before the second decade of the next century. Even if NATO enlargement proceeds smoothly, it is hard to envisage another wave of enlargement in the near future. The Balkan states will soldier on because they have no alternative. But they could become increasingly surly, and handling the region could grow increasingly difficult.

The biggest danger is a revival of a local balance of power, of the kind which already exists in Bosnia, coupled with the creation of satellite states. Muslims, Croats and Serbs in Bosnia are already three satellites, of the international community, Croatia and Serbia respectively. Croatia already behaves as the satellite of Germany and the US, although Tudjman prefers to call it a 'strategic partnership'. Romanians depend on French political support for almost everything they do in Europe, while the Russians are hoping to keep their economic influence in Bulgaria, and to maintain Moscow's influence over Serbia. The Balkans will not be divided into strict zones of influence, nor will they return to their role as Europe's 'powderkeg'. But the region could revert to its traditional role as Europe's periphery, a zone which is theoretically part of the continent, almost ready to integrate but, somehow, still not making it.

The End of the Yeltsin Era

President Boris Yeltsin reported to the Federal Assembly in February 1998 that Russia was entering a period of economic growth. For the first time in more than a decade, Russia's gross domestic product (GDP) had risen in 1997, if only by 0.8%. Yeltsin happily declared that growth would continue over the next few years and would open opportunities for rebuilding Russia's industry and for implementing comprehensive social and military reforms. The optimism among Russia's political élite was supported by the confidence of Western financial institutions, whose heavy investment in Russian securities markets between 1995 and 1998 gave Russia the world's fastest growing stock market.

It should have been evident earlier that this optimism was misplaced, for, by January 1998, there were already signs that Moscow's forecasts were fragile. The Asian economic crisis, combined with the fall in oil prices, sharply reduced Russia's revenues. The exodus of foreign invest-ment from other emerging markets in 1997 hit the Russian market in turn. It began falling in autumn 1997. The country's domestic debts were rising and sky-high interest rates exceeded 60%. By the beginning of 1998, many were aware that between 1999 and 2002 the Russian government would have to pay $15–$17 billion to service its current loans.

Despite these signs, few predicted that the myth of Russia's coming 'economic boom' would collapse as dramatically as it did on 17 August 1998. Practically overnight, Russia's economy was thrown back into the deep trough of the early 1990s, and the reported achievements of Yeltsin's seven-year-long reforms were completely discredited. As the picture of a Russia with increasing stability and economic growth faded away, so did the Yeltsin era in Russia's post-communist transition. Although the president remained in office after 17 August, he had lost the political, moral and physical authority to have an active influence on formulating a strategy to rescue Russia from its new crisis.

The Economic Meltdown

The bombshell that fell on 17 August was the announcement, by then Prime Minister Sergei Kiriyenko, of a 30% devaluation of the *rouble* and a default on all of Russia's domestic and foreign commercial debts for three months. This led to a paralysis of Russia's banking system. Most financial transactions were terminated; personal and corporate accounts were frozen; foreign imports were immediately reduced; and Russia's access to all commercial and institutional loans was cut off. Many major banks were driven into bankruptcy. The Russian economy was in chaos.

By the end of 1998, Russian GDP had declined by 4.6% – the biggest drop in the past four years – while annual inflation had risen from 14% in 1997 to over 90%. Industrial production declined by 5.5%. The Russian stock market lost over 85% of its value in less than a year – the largest decline ever registered anywhere. Foreign trade fell 16% in 1998. Not surprisingly, foreign investors are now reluctant to invest in Russia, leading to government estimates that total foreign direct investment in Russia in 1999 will only be around $1bn. At the same time, domestic investment resources are very limited, and, on top of it all, there continues to be a massive flight of capital abroad; in early March 1999, it was estimated that up to $2bn was flowing out of the country every month.

Russia's most urgent and in many ways most difficult problem is how to repay its outstanding foreign loans. According to independent Russian estimates, state debt before the August crisis was equivalent to 55% of GDP, jumping to 95% after 17 August. (Foreign debt alone amounted to 75% of GDP and domestic debt 20%.) Foreign analysts estimated that Russia's debt to private and public institutions at the end of 1998 was $183–195bn. This was equivalent to over $900 per head compared to annual per capita income of around $1,200.

Russia needs $17.5bn to service its debt in 1999 alone, against the entire state budget for the year of about $20bn. But at the end of March 1999, international lending institutions, such as the International Monetary Fund (IMF), were questioning whether to continue to help Russia finance its loans through new borrowings. The IMF had refused to release any of the $22.6bn package which was negotiated with Kiriyenko's government just a month before the August 1998 crisis. The Fund did not believe that the new Russian government had a realistic economic programme to justify further loans. Moreover, the West was concerned about mounting allegations that a large portion of previous IMF loans was mismanaged or stolen. Yet, at the end of March 1999, the IMF offered a further loan so that Russia could meet its debts. Commercial creditors were, however, less likely to provide Russia with any funds. Their investments in Russian State Treasury Bills were frozen on 17 August and they were offered mere pennies in the dollar on their investments. Unless Russia receives new loans, or its creditors agree to restructure its debts, it will inevitably default on its loans and may even face the prospect of state bankruptcy.

Social Cost of Reforms

Russian living standards dropped sharply again in 1998. Real income declined by 16%. Prices of basic foods doubled. By early 1999, almost one-third of the population had an income below the subsistence level ($22 per month), and the official unemployment rate was over 12%. For the emerging middle class, the crisis meant a sharp decline in real incomes and the loss of many jobs. The crisis had proved devastating to state sector employees, most of whom had not been paid for many months and had few savings to fall back on.

In many Russian regions money is rarely used in the everyday struggle for survival. According to various estimates 50–80% of all transactions are barter. In many regions employees are paid in the goods produced by their employer – coal, tyres, electronic parts, cables, or even bottles of vodka. Often these are goods that the factories cannot sell. They are therefore passing on to their employees the responsibility for selling them, or exchanging them for other goods. To make matters worse, many towns are built around one large plant, all of whose inhabitants are consequently paid in the same goods, which they can neither sell nor exchange locally, and which they cannot afford to take elsewhere. Increasingly people are forced to depend on small garden plots to grow their own food. Those who live in Russia's northern regions where the land is not very fertile are among the most severely affected by the crisis.

All of Russia is engaged in subsistence agriculture, including the military which is given land to grow the food for local regiments that the Ministry of Defence is unable to supply regularly or in an adequate amount. Many Russian regions help the forces based on their territory by providing them with basic necessities, including food. The military is under great pressure to allow conscripts to serve in their own regions where their families can at least help provide them with food and clothing. The situation is further undermining military readiness and leading to the possibility of divisions within the military on a regional basis.

No institution, whether civilian, military or state can afford to pay its utility bills any longer. The government insists that the largely state-owned utilities – such as *Gazprom* and United Energy Systems (EES) – continue to supply energy practically free of charge. Only 10–12% of payments for utilities are made in cash. As a result, *Gazprom* – one of the strongest state monopolies, with over 45% of the world's gas reserves – declared a loss of $2bn in 1998.

Yeltsin's efforts to create a stable post-Soviet economy in Russia have clearly failed. His political successors are faced with implementing painful measures to overcome the current crisis and to save the increasingly fragile Russian state from descending further into chaos. After many years of hardship, however, the Russian people are no longer prepared to rally to new calls for sacrifices in the cause of a stable and prosperous future.

From the Failing President to the Failing State

Since the August crisis, Yeltsin has no longer been involved in the day-to-day management of the country, leaving this task to the new Prime Minister Yevgeny Primakov. Since his appointment on a cross-party political mandate in October 1998, Primakov remains the most popular politician in Russia, despite making little progress in overcoming the economic crisis.

The next presidential election is not due until the summer of 2000, but the fragile state of Yeltsin's health has raised considerable doubts over whether he will survive until then. There are fears that the president's failure to exercise his authority to implement urgently needed economic policies will further weaken Russia, exacerbating the crisis and leading to the federal government losing control throughout Russia's 89 federal entities. The Constitution, however, provides no procedure for a formal transfer of power when the president is unable to fulfil his duties. Even if such a procedure existed, the parliament has limited ability to obtain an objective assessment of Yeltsin's health from his doctors.

The Constitution provides two ways to remove a president from office: resignation and impeachment. The first option has been supported by most of the political parties, but it remains unlikely, given Yeltsin's personal commitment to power, and his close advisers' growing fear that his resignation would be followed by a political campaign to investigate, and then prosecute, members of the current regime for corruption. Impeachment is even more difficult because the drafting of the Constitution is oriented towards protecting the president. The procedure is very complicated and long drawn-out. In early 1999, an impeachment committee, established by the *Duma* the previous year, presented four broad charges against Yeltsin. However they are unlikely to be addressed by the courts because the parliament lacks the necessary evidence about the president's intentions or degree of responsibility.

Given the difficulties of implementing the impeachment process and the unlikelihood of Yeltsin's resignation, early presidential elections in Russia are likely only if Yeltsin dies. Should this happen before the end of his term in 2000, the Constitution authorises the prime minister to assume presidential power temporarily and to announce that a presidential election will take place in three month's time. Some analysts speculate that the prime minister may not have adequate funds for an election, or the political will to hold one during a crisis, and thus may postpone polling. If the three-month period coincides with the gap between the end of the current parliament and new parliamentary elections, the prime minister could have almost unlimited power. But Primakov does not lack political authority now; it is his emphasis on consensus and political stability which has prevented the government from formulating and implementing a meaningful anti-crisis policy.

Political Roots of Russia's Economic Crisis

Primakov was Russia's third prime minister in less than a year. But the way he came to power and his new political role set him apart from his two immediate predecessors – Kiriyenko and Victor Chernomyrdin. They were widely held responsible for Russia's economic meltdown, but Primakov has so far escaped blame and continues to top the opinion polls as the most trusted and popular politician in Russia. This has propelled him to the front rank of candidates for the presidency were an election to be held in 1999.

Primakov clearly learned from the experience of his predecessors, who had failed to create a political and bureaucratic power base independent of the president and were eventually victims of Yeltsin's schizophrenic style of asserting his authority. During Primakov's first six months in office, he managed to consolidate his political power base through close ties with the legislature. He also quickly imitated Yeltsin's strategy; quietly surrounding himself with his own allies – mainly former colleagues from the KGB and other intelligence bodies – and placing them in key media and revenue-generating companies, such as the arms exporter *Rosvooruzhenye*, as well as in the executive branch. As a result, Yeltsin and his close advisers are in no position to treat Primakov as they did past prime ministers.

Despite former Prime Minister Chernomyrdin's loyalty over the previous five years, Yeltsin unexpectedly dismissed him in March 1998 and dissolved his government, firing all the most powerful 'reformers', including Anatoly Chubais and Boris Nemtsov. The real motives behind the decision are still disputed, but the result of Chernomyrdin's dismissal was a period of political instability that was the beginning of the end of Yeltsin's era rather than a boost to his power.

The president then made one of the most unexpected and poorly judged of his personnel decisions, proposing the 35-year-old, inexperienced and politically vulnerable former energy minister, Kiriyenko, to replace Chernomyrdin. Kiriyenko's authority rested entirely on Yeltsin's patronage – which may have been his appeal. He was virtually unknown and had no political support, unlike his predecessor who was popular and well connected. In his favour, Kiriyenko was more competent in economic matters and supported by the West.

Kiriyenko therefore appeared likely to secure additional Western finance for Russia's economy, which was already feeling the impact of the East Asian economic crisis and the fall in world oil prices. He turned to the IMF with the help of sacked reformer Chubais, whom he reinstated in July 1998 as a special government negotiator with international financial institutions. An IMF commitment was obtained for an additional $22.6bn loan, conditional on Russia implementing a set of economic policies backed by appropriate legislation to reform its tax system and increase tax collection. Only a $4bn tranche was released before the 17 August crisis.

Kiriyenko's professional talents and international support, however, quickly proved a disadvantage in Russia's domestic political context. Parliament, hostile to the policy of the 'young reformers', who were strongly supported by the West, had twice refused to confirm Kiriyenko as prime minister. They had only agreed when Yeltsin threatened to dissolve the *Duma* and cut deputies off from their economic benefits. After the vote, the humiliated and angry legislature refused to support Kiriyenko's economic programme and rejected a package of economic measures which were required by the IMF. The Fund refused to release the bulk of the loan, leaving Kiriyenko unable to stem the impact of the approaching economic crisis.

On 23 August, Yeltsin dismissed Kiriyenko and his government and again proposed his old ally Chernomyrdin as prime minister. A frustrated and defiant *Duma*, openly resentful of Yeltsin's attempt to undermine its authority, refused twice to accept Chernomyrdin's return. This time, a politically weakened Yeltsin did not nominate Chernomyrdin for a third time, avoiding an open stand-off with the legislature. Instead he accepted and nominated a candidate proposed by the *Duma*. After almost a month of political vacuum in the midst of looming economic crisis, on 11 September 1998 the parliament overwhelmingly approved former foreign minister Primakov. He was a 'political heavyweight' whom the Russian political élite thought they could trust to find a way out of Russia's economic crisis.

Political Stability Comes at a Price

Primakov was selected partly because of his unprecedented political and public support, and partly because he is viewed as a pragmatic politician who consistently supports Russia's interests abroad. He has also forged strong political alliances at home. These qualities should help him in rebuilding Russia's political stability and maintaining a dialogue with international financial institutions on how to help limit Russia's economic crisis.

Primakov's first task was to consolidate Russia's political élite and obtain necessary support from the Russian parliament. He tackled this by forming Russia's first true coalition government, giving members of parties previously opposed to Yeltsin's reforms, including the communists, key ministerial positions including that of First Deputy Prime Minister in charge of the economy. That Primakov was able to carry through this strategy was another sign that Yeltsin's era in Russian politics was ending. Yeltsin had always been reluctant to allow communists to influence his policy, and at best, he would only allow Communist Party members to occupy marginally important or highly unpopular political positions – for example, Aman Tuleev had a term as the Minister for Commonwealth of Independent States (CIS) Affairs. Yeltsin also preferred to impose his economic policies by decree, and repeatedly vetoed laws the *Duma* had passed. The only significant economic policy-related negotiations between parliament and government during Chernomyrdin's time were conducted over the budget. Even then, the government was free to sequester the budget at any point during the year, or simply to sabotage it by releasing only a fraction of the funds to particular institutions, thus further marginalising legislative power over Yeltsin's economic reforms.

Primakov has rejected Yeltsin's approach and emphasised the importance of the legislative branch in formulating and implementing Russia's domestic reforms. He has made a real effort to make his government politically and publicly accountable and thus to develop a programme which enjoys cross-party parliamentary support. Given the composition of the legislature, which is near the end of its term, Primakov's strategy has forced him to ally himself too closely with the communist-dominated majority, while distancing himself from the new, increasingly powerful, political forces, which are not represented in the current parliament. These include the centre-right coalition led by Moscow

Mayor Yuri Luzhkov. Reliance on parliament has forced Primakov to adopt ideas which were popular at the last election in December 1995, but which no longer reflected mainstream political thinking.

Primakov's main principle has been that, in order to implement economic reform, Russia needed political stability with no confrontation between the different branches of government. At the end of 1998, the Russian public and political élite agreed, hailing the semblance of political stability as the main achievement of Primakov's government. However, in early 1999 the mood started to change. It was apparent that Primakov's search for political stability had narrowed, rather than expanded, his options for formulating and implementing a consistent economic programme.

Primakov's government now finds itself in limbo between two pressing concerns. First, the parliament is demanding the reintroduction of old-style economic policies with stronger state intervention in the economy, and nationalisation of some privatised entities in strategically important sectors. To keep the legislators quiet, Primakov and his key government officials continue to proclaim their intention to implement many such interventionist policies.

But Primakov's ability to fulfil this demand is extremely limited by the lack of financial resources to support a greater state role. The projected budget for 1999 is just over $20bn, and many experts believe that even this figure is based on unrealistic assumptions about the *rouble* exchange rate, inflation and the government's ability to collect tax. It also does not factor in the reality that the government has to pay more than $17bn of interest on Russian debts in 1999. The pressure of these considerations has shifted the government's policies, despite its conservative rhetoric, towards those which will increase the chance of obtaining sufficient new funds from international lending institutions to cover interest payments.

To this end, the government introduced, and got the *Duma* to pass, the toughest budget of the past eight years – one which significantly reduces government spending. Nevertheless, Primakov's search for political stability in Moscow keeps him a hostage of the conservative parliamentary majority which discourages real reforms, and his inability to implement unpopular measures has contributed to a steady drift of power from the federal authority to the local governors.

Regional Solutions to the Crisis

Primakov's tenure as foreign minister and foreign intelligence chief gave him little experience of maintaining the delicate balance in relations between the regions and the federal authorities. By the time he became prime minister there had already been increasing devolution of real power from the centre to the regions, and the new economic crisis resulted in increasingly chaotic relations between the two. Primakov became prime minister after the elections of governors had taken place in all federal entities (the first elections where governors were directly elected by their constituents and not appointed by Moscow), and after a time when the governors had served long enough to have built a strong power base in their regions. This could not be challenged by a Moscow which no longer had important economic leverage.

Until the crisis of August 1998, the final arbiter between centre and regions had been Yeltsin himself, who defused successive confrontations with recalcitrant regional leaders through bilateral treaties and less formal agreements. With Yeltsin no longer actively ruling, the inability of the present federal government to channel increased regional power into productive policy-making is crystal clear. Primakov has tried to build a more structured and rigorous framework. In recognition of the increased political weight of the regions, and as a sign of the government's desire to cooperate with them, he invited the chairmen of the eight inter-regional economic associations to sit on the government's presidium. But he has repeatedly called on regional leaders to end their 'fiefdom mentality' and has proposed legislation that would lead to the removal from office of regional governors who contravened the Constitution (which most routinely do), despite their having been popularly elected.

More radical proposals for restructuring the Federation on rational lines were revived in the wake of the economic crisis. They involved reducing the Federation's 89 component parts to a more manageable number. This is not feasible in the near term, since the regional leaders are too conscious of their individual power to be prepared to share it, and the centre does not have the authority to impose a solution.

If the regional leaders increased their power at the expense of the centre in 1998, their hold on their own bailiwicks became less absolute than their popular mandate (in their own eyes) warranted. Against the prevailing trend of regional legislatures being sidelined, the electorates of Sverdlovsk region in April, and St Petersburg in December returned assemblies capable of challenging the governor. A further challenge is emerging from the mayors of the regions' principal cities, where the revenue raising potential tends to be concentrated. Two mayors (in Smolensk and the Karelian Republic) defeated the incumbent governor in routine elections.

The August crisis sparked a rash of emergency measures by regional leaders anxious to protect their electorates. Many imposed price controls, and agricultural regions banned 'exports' of foodstuffs, but the controls were quietly abandoned as producers evaded them. A relative strengthening of the regions' financial basis may turn out to be a more lasting legacy of the crisis. Regional banks had had little money to invest in State Treasury Bills and therefore escaped relatively lightly from the financial collapse. Those regions which were endowed with gold, or had access to it, began to hoard. Nonetheless, the crisis demonstrated that most regions remain heavily dependent on the centre, and none is self-sufficient. Nor do any of the regions entertain separatist aspirations. A dramatic secessionist announcement by President of Kalmykia Kirsan Ilyumzhinov on 17 November 1998 was little more than a successful stunt to attract Moscow's attention to his republic.

Primakov's attempts to take a tough line with the regions only highlights the limits of his authority. His emphasis on political stability and observance of constitutional norms is in conflict with his proposals to reform Russia's federal structure, or even to abolish the elections of the governors. The budgetary debate was the first illustration of Primakov's dependence on the Federation Council – the upper chamber of parliament which represents the regions. In addition to approving any constitutional changes, it has to approve the federal budget. The government failed to impose a tougher tax distribution policy on 12 economically strong regions and to reduce subsidies to the economically weak majority. As a result, it had to agree to a compromise which deprived the federal budget of much-needed revenue and led to more IMF criticism, further putting into question future release of loans.

The failures of the federal government to convince the governors that it had a strategy for pulling Russia out of the current crisis led the governors to conclude that their local solutions, backed by a larger portion of local taxes, are more likely to guarantee stability in their regions. But many of the regions are unlikely to find regional solutions which work in the long run. They continue to enforce non-market solutions by imposing protectionist measures on exports of goods from the region or by introducing price controls, while at the same time, they will continue to hit economic problems which cannot be resolved locally. According to some estimates, more than half of the regions which received loans or floated Eurobonds will be forced to default on them.

Many parts of Russia are facing elections in 1999, and many incumbents are losing their mandate due to the parlous state of the economy. After the elections there will be many new governors who do not have a strong power base and may therefore be reluctant to antagonise the centre. One example is Krasnoyarsk Governor Alexander Lebed who, until his election last year, was considered a strong presidential candidate. Lebed rapidly lost popularity when it became clear that he was unable to manage a regional economy effectively and he was no longer eager to enter into a public confrontation with the federal government.

Russia's Economic Crisis and Future Elections

Although the majority of Russia's political parties agree that Yeltsin has to resign, no one can confidently predict the outcome of a presidential election held at a time of an economic crisis. In many ways the forthcoming parliamentary elections, due in December 1999, will help test the mood of Russia's volatile and distrustful electorate. Many of the country's most powerful oligarchs are sitting on the ruins of their financial empires, which until recently included powerful press and media resources, leaving many political parties scrambling for the necessary funding for a Russia-wide campaign.

The economic crisis has had myriad effects. It has undermined the chances for reformers, or any leftist 'reformist' parties, to gain much, if any, parliamentary representation. The only pro-reform party which retained its popularity – because of its consistent opposition to Yeltsin's reform policy and refusal to participate in his governments – is *Yabloko* which supports Grigory Yavlinsky for the presidency. While *Yabloko* is likely to receive strong support during parliamentary elections – easily clearing the 5% threshold – its leader has little chance of becoming president.

The crisis has also magnified the voices of ultra-nationalist and extremist parties that espouse nationalist, anti-Semitic and fascist causes. An extreme wing of the Communist Party has reverted to the use of anti-Semitic slogans, exploiting the people's disillusionment with Yeltsin's reforms. Although these extremist forces are unlikely to obtain either official registration for the elections or, if they do, to receive significant votes, they will support populist and nationalist sentiments to be used by other parties which will be seeking to gather their votes.

Another important effect of the crisis was the emergence of centrist political forces with strong regional backing. The most popular of these movements is *Otechestvo* (Fatherland) which supports Moscow Mayor Yuri Luzhkov's presidential bid. Although the movement supports a stronger role for the state in managing Russia's economy, it simultaneously claims a commitment to support small businesses and to seek greater private investment to restructure Russia's industry. Luzhkov is seen as one of the strongest presidential contenders, but his future prospects will be undermined if the crisis hits Moscow even harder, thus tarnishing his image as an able manager who produced the city's 'economic miracle'. His chances for success are also hindered by the fact that, like any Moscow boss, he is not very popular in the regions.

The Communist Party has benefited from the crisis, and Gennady Zyuganov, its leader, is strong in the early opinion polls. But the party's close association with Primakov's government, which has so far failed to do anything to improve the economic climate, may cause a split between its extremist elements and what is increasingly seen as the more moderate wing of the party – which is slowly beginning to look like the party of power. As a result of internal disputes, the communists are unlikely to emerge as winners in the next presidential elections; they are likely, however, to retain a significant number of seats in the next parliament.

The only political actor who had not announced his intention by early 1999 to run for president, but who is widely viewed as the strongest candidate if he does do so, is Primakov. Primakov's popularity is largely due to his image rather than his policies. For many Russians who were severely affected by Yeltsin's reforms and thrown into poverty and uncertainty, Primakov's rhetoric and management style revived nostalgia for the certainties of the Soviet era. At the same time, he is seen as a guarantor that some elements of that era can be re-instituted without new instability or violence. But his position is far from assured. Any escalation of the economic crisis, or any need to implement unpopular reforms, could destroy his popularity and support. Primakov's political vulnerability is even greater because he is following Yeltsin's earlier example of not associating himself with any political party or coalition which is seeking office – he has formed a government of a parliamentary majority without representing any of its parties.

Only one thing is certain. The longer Yeltsin remains in office while the economic crisis runs its course, the less predictable the outcome of Russia's presidential elections will be. This will become clearer as the images of competence which the main contenders are trying to project at the moment begin to give way to the reality that they have no painless solution to the crisis. While this might lead to the appearance of a new demagogue who trumpets the failed policies of the past, it might also be the catalyst that forces Russia to look to the future and bring forth a new generation of political leaders who no longer hide in the shadows of the past.

Northern Ireland's Year of Reckoning

From the partition of Ireland in 1921 until 1972, Northern Ireland's Protestant majority dominated the devolved parliamentary assembly, informally known as 'Stormont' after the grandiose Belfast building in which it was housed. Stormont's marginalisation of Catholics eventually led to civil-rights protests, public disorder, and, starting in 1969, outright terrorism by the Irish Republican Army (IRA) and its pro-British Loyalist adversaries. Since partition, Irish Republicans had rejected the political axiom – known as the 'consent principle' to pro-British Protestants, and the 'Unionist veto' to Republicans – that any change in the constitutional status of Northern Ireland had to be approved by a majority of its people. When the civil-rights protest blossomed, the IRA had the popular momentum required to build its base and reassert its rejection of the consent principle. Thus began 'the troubles'.

In 1972, terrorist violence in Northern Ireland peaked at 472 deaths in one year. Westminster deemed Stormont unable to contain the situation, prorogued the parliament, and assumed direct rule. For nearly 25 years, little lasting headway was made towards political reconciliation. Ritual cross- and intra-community violence persisted, claiming, on average, about 100 deaths per year. During this period, the 'constitutional question' of whether Northern Ireland would remain a part of the UK or unite with the Republic of Ireland has been the overriding issue in Northern Irish politics. The Protestant majority of Northern Ireland's inhabitants have steadfastly insisted that the province stay British. The sizeable (now approximately 40%) Catholic minority strongly favours a united Ireland.

Under direct rule from Westminster, despite occasional excesses by the security forces, the inequities in civil rights, housing, and employment which Stormont had neglected were significantly reduced. The notorious constitutional question became more emotional than substantive. In apparent recognition that the Republican terrorist campaign to bring about a united Ireland was futile, *Sinn Féin*, the IRA's political wing, declared a unilateral cease-fire on 31 August 1994. Six weeks later, on 13 October, the two main Loyalist terrorist groups, the Ulster Freedom Fighters/Ulster Defence Association (UFF/UDA), and the Ulster Volunteer Force (UVF), began cease-fires of their own.

For 17 months, there was almost no cross-community political violence, but little political headway was made. Washington, which had provided *Sinn Féin* President Gerry Adams with an international audience by granting him a visa in February 1994, aggressively pushed for a permanent political settlement, and President Bill Clinton made a state visit to the province in November 1995. The British and Irish governments, impatiently attempting to shepherd Northern Irish politicians to agreement, promulgated the 'framework document' in 1995 as a possible blueprint for a new governmental arrangement in the province. The document contemplated cross-border administrative bodies, staffed jointly by Belfast and Dublin officials, with open-ended executive authority. While nationalists were pleased, outraged unionists saw it as leading inexorably to a united Ireland.

A long impasse ensued over the IRA's refusal to 'decommission' – surrender its arms – or expressly to forswear future violence. The International Body on Decommissioning was established in November 1995 to oversee the surrender of arms. An international committee, chaired by former US Senator George Mitchell, issued a report on 23 January 1996 recommending decommissioning in parallel with all-party negotiations, and a requirement (embodied in the so-called Mitchell Principles) that parties to the talks pledge to use exclusively peaceful means and bind themselves to any negotiated settlement. The IRA broke its ceasefire on 9 February 1996, by bombing the landmark Canary Wharf office building in

London. Tit-for-tat terrorist violence resumed, but at a substantially lower level than before the 1994 cease-fires. Multi-party peace talks, chaired by Mitchell, began on 10 June 1996. *Sinn Féin* was banned from talks due to the IRA's resumption of violence. Through a year of posturing, the talks went in circles.

On 20 July 1997, the IRA reinstated its cease-fire. *Sinn Féin* representatives were admitted to the talks on 9 September 1997 and signed up to the Mitchell Principles. Despite boycotts by Ian Paisley's Democratic Unionist Party (DUP) and the UK Unionist Party, and fractious splits by anti-Agreement dissidents from the Republican and Loyalist movements, the talks culminated in the popularly-named Good Friday Agreement (which was actually signed by most of the parties to the peace talks on Saturday, 10 April 1998 – the day after Good Friday – following all-night negotiations). Notwithstanding perilous friction and delay over the implementation of the Agreement, 1998 was a singularly salutary year for Northern Irish politics.

Snatching Victory from the Jaws of Defeat

As 1998 began, prospects for a peace accord looked dim. On 27 December 1997, two members of the Irish National Liberation Army (INLA), a savage Republican group not on cease-fire, murdered Billy Wright, a Loyalist inmate of the Maze Prison, using pistols smuggled inside. Wright was the founder and leader of the Loyalist Volunteer Force (LVF), a militant splinter group of the UVF that surfaced in July 1996, and Loyalism's most vehement voice against reconciliation on the constitutional question. During the six weeks following his death, terrorists committed ten sectarian murders and one major bombing.

Resisting the jaded pessimism that such bloodbaths had produced in the past, Northern Irish politicians (and their constituents) were determined to find a peaceful solution, as was the government of the Republic of Ireland. In particular, David Trimble, head of the Ulster Unionist Party (UUP), the province's largest unionist group, resisted fierce anti-reconciliation opposition, within his own party and from Paisley, and remained open to compromise. John Hume, head of the Social Democratic and Labour Party (SDLP), the largest Nationalist party, did not have to deal with a comparable degree of intramural dissent, and more than anyone relentlessly urged his constituents and fellow politicians to seize the opportunity for lasting peace. Trimble and Hume were awarded the Nobel Peace Prize for 1998.

As with the 1995 'framework document,' the principal sticking point in the negotiations was whether proposed cross-border bodies would have executive powers. Both the Irish Republic and the SDLP demanded these powers. The Unionists were just as strongly opposed to any joint bodies whose overarching powers smacked of an all-Ireland government.

Unionists were equally insistent that *Sinn Féin* commit the IRA to decommission its weapons. The IRA refused as it had in the past. UK Prime Minister Tony Blair finessed the problem by privately giving vague, informal assurances to David Trimble that decommissioning would be one of his personal priorities in arriving at any forthcoming settlement. These assurances were enough to satisfy Trimble.

Against prevailing expectations, and after further contentious compromises on early prisoner release and police reform, the Good Friday Agreement materialised. It contains no hard-and-fast decommissioning requirement, and the cross-border bodies it contemplates are subject to the mutual vetoes of the Belfast assembly and the Irish parliament and therefore do not possess truly 'executive' powers.

On 10 May 1998, 350 delegates to *Sinn Féin*'s party conference voted by an overwhelming 96% to support the Agreement and participate in a devolved assembly. This tally reflected a monumental change in Republican ideology. It effectively abrogated the Provisional IRA's rules and *Sinn Féin*'s constitution, under which the consent principle was invalid and any Northern Ireland assembly unlawfully 'partitionist'. On 22 May 1998, the Agreement was approved by 71% of the voters in Northern Ireland and 94% in the Irish Republic. There was euphoria in the province.

A Helping Hand

In its involvement in the Northern Ireland problem, Washington displayed shrewdness and patience that it has not always demonstrated in more momentous crises. After granting Gerry Adams a visa in February 1994, President Bill Clinton's administration was generally sensitive to the understandable Unionist perception that the US harboured a pro-nationalist bias. The administration came to appreciate the importance of entertaining the Unionist case, and established a cordial relationship with David Trimble.

At the same time, the administration took its political cue from a nationalist, John Hume. Despite the deflating IRA backsliding in 1996 and the sobering wave of sectarian killings in January and February 1998, the White House, through Senator Mitchell, continued to sponsor the process vigorously and thus helped keep it alive. After the Good Friday Agreement was signed, Hume, Trimble and Adams indicated that eleventh-hour telephone calls from President Clinton had focused minds and inspired success.

The Terms of the Good Friday Agreement

The central *quid pro quo* of the Agreement is the Irish Republic's repeal of the territorial claim on Northern Ireland (enshrined in articles 2 and 3 of its Constitution) which Unionists considered illegal and predatory. In exchange, it is to have an institutionalised voice in governing the province through 'cross-border bodies'. While Britain retains sovereign dominion over the province as long as its electoral majority wants it to do so, the Irish Republic has a permanent (and potentially expanding) influence in Northern Irish government through a North–South Ministerial Council. That includes the cross-border bodies composed of members of the Northern Ireland Assembly and the Irish parliament. Again, both bodies must approve Council action.

The 108-member Northern Ireland Assembly, elected by proportional representation, is to have full legislative and executive authority, devolved from Westminster. To ensure cross-community consensus, parallel consent (majorities of both Nationalists and Unionists) or a 60% weighted majority is required to pass key measures. All measures must comply with the European Convention on Human Rights and a new Northern Ireland Bill of Rights.

Problems of Implementation

Once the new Northern Ireland Assembly was elected on 25 June 1998, celebration gave way to hangover. The assembly consists of 58 unionists and 50 nationalists. All of the Nationalists favour the Agreement, but only a scant intramural majority of 30 Unionists do so. Since assembly action requires approval from both communities, a shift of one or two Unionists to the anti-Agreement side could effectively paralyse the new government. Ominously, a *Belfast Telegraph* survey, published in early February 1999, indicated that support for the Agreement has shrunk by 6% since the May 1998 referendum.

As a result, David Trimble, First Minister of the assembly, has had to take care not to let any of his flock stray. This has meant strident insistence on IRA disarmament. Superficially, such a demand appeared eminently reasonable in the wake of the bomb detonated on 15 August 1998 in Omagh by the 'Real' IRA – a new, explicitly anti-Agreement Republican splinter group – that killed 29 civilians. Yet the essential working parts of that bomb were a car and 500 pounds of fertiliser, so the confiscation of military weaponry would not have inhibited its construction. Moreover, the bomb bore none of the hallmarks of an IRA bomb-maker. As a practical matter, then, the terrorists most inclined to continue violence are not those of whom disarmament is requested. (Although the LVF turned in a small number of its weapons in December 1998, which were then destroyed in front of news cameras, this was widely seen as a ploy to win early releases for imprisoned LVF members who were not eligible when the Agreement was signed.)

According to the February 1999 *Belfast Telegraph* poll, 84% of Northern Irish voters (including 58% of *Sinn Féin* supporters) believe paramilitaries should start decommissioning. So do London, Washington, and, somewhat surprisingly, Dublin. Nevertheless, wholesale disarmament appears an unrealistic aspiration, and the decommissioning body has been ineffectual throughout its existence. By implicitly conceding the legitimacy of British rule in Northern Ireland, *Sinn Féin* and the IRA have cast aside a central tenet of Republicanism. Their compensation was the early release of their imprisoned supporters. If they would not humble themselves by disarming before signing the Agreement, they would be even less likely to do so now.

Due to the impasse over decommissioning, the UUP has delayed the formation of the Assembly's cabinet, or executive, which is required before power is devolved from Westminster. This was initially planned for February 1999, but was postponed by the British government to 10 March, then 2 April. Further delays are expected. At the end of March 1999, the stumbling block had not yet been removed.

Post-Implementation Perils

Even if the Unionists and Nationalists somehow fudge the decommissioning problem to facilitate devolution, Unionists are likely to continue to press for complete disarmament to take place eventually. The IRA will only be persuaded to give up weapons openly if what it holds to be the armed threat to the Nationalist community is removed. For Republicans, the main threat resides, both historically and currently, in the Royal Ulster Constabulary (RUC).

The Agreement calls for 'a police service, in constructive and inclusive partnerships with the community at all levels, and with the maximum delegation of authority possible'. This provision seems to augur the overhaul of the RUC, since 92% of its members are Protestant and therefore cannot, in Nationalists' opinion, forge 'constructive and inclusive partnerships' with the Nationalist community. Since over 300 RUC personnel have been killed during the troubles, the force remains primarily an anti-terrorist unit rather than a traditional community police force.

Some Nationalists further construe 'maximum delegation of authority' to require vesting police responsibility in Nationalist areas with local Catholics. But for most Unionists, radical change in the composition of the RUC would amount to a slap in the face to men and women who maintained law and order at considerable risk during the height of 'the troubles'. They also feel it to be particularly unfair in the light of the fast two-year track (running from July 1998) for the early release of IRA and Loyalist prisoners. An Agreement-mandated Commission for Policing, chaired by former Hong Kong Governor Chris Patten, has been formed. Its report on how to deal with the policing problem is due in July 1999.

The two Agreement requirements appear to be incompatible: the IRA will not decommission its weapons without massive police reform that it could reasonably equate with disarming the Unionist security machine, and Unionists will not accept the restructuring of the RUC unless it is marginal enough to ensure that incumbent police officers retain their jobs. However, the respective Nationalist and Unionist positions are subject to a degree of circumstantial influence that could break the apparent stalemate.

In recent years the security forces of the UK, Northern Ireland, and the Irish Republic have been increasingly successful in uncovering hidden weapons. If this rigorous anti-terrorist enforcement continues, Unionists could decide that they do not need to insist on voluntary Republican disarmament. Conversely, if the IRA cease-fire is sustained in conjunction with *Sinn Féin's* modest *détente* with Unionists, Catholic fears of Republican intimidation if they join the RUC is likely to decrease. This thawing of the 'chill factor' might lead to an increase in the police force's Catholic recruitment levels and soften Nationalist calls for the wholesale disbandment of the force.

Neither problem will go away easily. One central complication of police reform is the practical need to downsize the force in the face of declining terrorism. Thus, it may take an entire generation to make serious inroads into changing the RUC's sectarian makeup. But there is at least a reasonable chance that small movements from each side in turn will lead, in time, to workable compromises. Such convergence could eventually lead to Westminster's relaxation of the divisive Prevention of Terrorism Act and a more substantial withdrawal from the province of British troops, which, as of September 1998, numbered 16,000.

Related to the decommissioning and policing issues is the problem of punishment attacks. These range from minor beatings to execution, imposed by Republican paramilitaries on Catholics and Loyalist para-militaries on Protestants in their respective working-class communities. The paramilitaries have been administering punishments to their own side since the troubles began, and have rationalised them as a reluctant response to community demands to discourage 'anti-social' behaviour, such as drug-dealing, theft and sex offences. Yet the attacks are also carried out in support of the paramilitaries' own criminal enterprises – protection rackets and drug trafficking, for example – or simply to avenge insults.

The attacks have increased since the signing of the Good Friday Agreement. According to the Belfast community watchdog group Families Against Intimidation and Terror (FAIT), in the first months of 1998, before the Agreement, punishment beatings and shootings averaged 15 per month. For the remainder of the year, they rose to over 20 per month, and through February 1999 there was more than one attack each day. The likely explanation for the rise is that, with the cease-fires in place, ex-terrorists need a coercive *modus operandi* other than cross-community political violence to maintain their hold (whether political or merely illicit) over their communities. Weapon decommissioning would not eliminate this problem: while paramilitaries sometimes 'kneecap' victims by shooting them with handguns, their weapon of choice is just as often an iron bar, an electric drill or a baseball bat. Police reform, insofar as it might increase the neighbourhood presence of officers, may help diminish the problem.

Meanwhile, the annual strife over Protestant parades during 'the marching season' looms as a recurring destabilising influence in Northern Ireland. The parades, conducted mainly by the Orange Order and the Apprentice Boys of Derry, are considered triumphalist and inflammatory taunts by Nationalists and benign cultural celebrations by Unionists. For the past three years, the July march along the Garvaghy Road in Portadown has produced the greatest unrest. Whether the RUC allows it to proceed (as in 1996 and 1997) or blocks it (as in 1998), the parade has resulted in three consecutive sieges by defiant Protestants, violent clashes between police and protesters, a multitude of injuries and several deaths. Tensions over such marches could well impede, or even derail, political progress.

Can Peace in Northern Ireland Endure?

The Good Friday Agreement reflects the desire of the people of Northern Ireland and the British and Irish governments to move beyond claustrophobic ancient conflict. It is significant that, since the Agreement was signed, the constitutional question has become less prominent.

On the ground, the peace process itself has produced lasting and positive changes in Northern Ireland's political landscape. The process began with the IRA's 1994 ceasefire. Without the IRA as a foil, the principal loyalist groups also lost their *raison d'être*. Yet the Republican and Loyalist political movements have not disappeared; they have become more civilised. The process provisionally legitimised politicians like Gerry Adams and his deputy Martin McGuinness on the Republican side, and David Ervine of the Progressive Unionist Party (the UVF's political wing) and Gary McMichael of the Ulster Democratic Party (the UFF's political wing) on the Loyalist side.

There is thus grounds for cautious hope. The brutal murder of Catholic barrister Rosemary Nelson by a nascent Loyalist renegade group, the Red Hand Defenders, in Lurgan on 15 March 1999, is an example of the sporadic terrorism there will be from fringe groups for some time to come. But as long as the more prominent Loyalist and Republican politicians sustain the cease-fires already in place and continue to work hard for their constituencies within the Agreement framework, there appears to be a reasonably good chance that opposing forces will be contained. The economic benefits of peace may solidify it. Northern Ireland is now a more attractive destination for both tourists and foreign investment. European unity, a strong if subtle, force behind the Good Friday Agreement, will also help. The European Parliament and the EU's Committee of the Regions provide both communities with broadly based non-local forums that may reduce the antagonistic polarity that has plagued provincial bodies. EU economic policies will continue to benefit Ulster, as will the EU's pledge of direct aid for cross-community projects totalling over $500 million through 1999.

Northern Ireland still faces considerable challenges in reconciling two communities divided by generations of strife, and profoundly mistrustful of each other, and in rebuilding an economy that must be painfully weaned from Westminster's $5 billion annual subsidy and an inordinate reliance on security-related jobs. Moreover, the decommissioning dispute is an ongoing source of volatility. The Patten Report on policing, due in July 1999, is liable to produce even greater instability. And during the same month, the Orangemen's march in Portadown will further aggravate cross-community relations. In sum, sustained peace, while politically supportable, is far from an accomplished fact.

●

The Middle East

Despite the continued efforts of the United States throughout 1998 to nudge, encourage and then push and pull the peace process forward, the end result was dismal. Israeli Prime Minister Binyamin Netanyahu and Palestinian Authority Chairman Yasser Arafat did sign an agreement at the end of their talks at Wye Plantation in October, where US President Bill Clinton invested many hours of personal arm-twisting to produce yet another hollow compact. But implementation was frozen by both sides almost as soon as they returned home. Netanyahu's efforts to manoeuvre between those who felt he had not gone far enough and those who believed he had gone too far merely disappointed the left wing and infuriated the right. The subsequent vote of no confidence in his government froze any further action until after elections for a new government take place on 17 May 1999.

The Palestinians are hopeful that a change in the Israeli government will bring a change in the negotiating atmosphere. To avoid providing ammunition for the Israeli right, Arafat has withdrawn his threat to proclaim a Palestinian state unilaterally on 4 May. If there is not a significant change in the relations between the two sides after the Israeli elections, however, he can be expected to renew his efforts to construct a new state on his own. In that case, violence can be expected and the peace process, which is now moribund, will expire.

The Israeli–Palestinian impasse was not the only threat to peace in the Middle East. Saddam Hussein once again overstepped the bounds of acceptable behaviour, bringing down upon his country UN Security Council wrath, and a four-day bombing campaign by US and UK aircraft. Iraq's insistence on challenging US and UK patrols of the 'no-fly' zones led to almost daily attacks on Iraqi military targets. There were few signs, however, that this costly campaign could achieve its real political aim, Saddam's removal.

Threats of military action were more effective in two other showdowns in the Middle East. Turkey, angered by Syria's continued support for the Kurdish insurgents who had sought sanctuary in that country, deployed a large number of troops on their border and threatened to attack if Syria did not eject the leader of the Kurdistan Workers' Party (PKK), Abdallah Öcalan. Syria's acceptance of all Turkey's demands reflects its weakened, and somewhat isolated, position in the region, at the same time as Turkey has grown stronger. Iran had somewhat less success when it sent a massive number of troops to threaten the *Taleban* in Afghanistan, ostensibly to recover Iranian hostages that were being held there, but in reality to try to redress the loss of Iranian leverage among the competing regional powers. Although Iran was successful in retrieving its citizens, the episode did little to alter the new security arrangements that are now being created in the Middle East.

●

In a State of Suspended Animation

During most of 1998, two forces pulled the Israeli–Palestinian peace process in opposite directions. The first was the continual efforts of the international community, especially the US government, to cajole and prod the main decision-makers to implement outstanding obligations under the 1995 Interim Agreement and the 1997 Protocol on Redeployment in Hebron, and to move forward on permanent-status negotiations. The second factor was domestic politics, which constrained the ability or willingness of the Palestinian and, especially, Israeli leaderships to agree. For most of the year, the second force proved stronger than the first, and the result was stagnation.

In October 1998, the prospect of a unilateral Palestinian declaration of statehood when the interim period expired on 4 May 1999, coupled with intensive American intervention, did help to produce a new Israeli–Palestinian agreement – the Wye River Memorandum. However, any sense that momentum in the process had been revived was very short-lived. Implementation of the new agreement was quickly suspended as the two sides descended into yet another round of recriminations and accusations of bad faith. The Israeli government suspended further withdrawals stipulated in the Wye agreement in hopes of maintaining the support of its right-wing coalition partners. Nonetheless, it was abandoned by some of them and defeated in a no-confidence motion at the end of December. New elections were scheduled for 17 May 1999, and the peace process, now completely a hostage of domestic electoral politics, was once again placed in a state of suspended animation pending the verdict of Israeli voters.

There was even less movement on the other main track of the process, involving Israel and Syria. Violence in southern Lebanon periodically rekindled the perennial Israeli debate over withdrawal from the security zone along Israel's northern border, especially following a cabinet decision early in the year to endorse UN Security Council Resolution 425, calling for Israeli withdrawal from Lebanon. However, the conditions attached to this endorsement implied commitments which the Lebanese government could not give, at least in advance of progress in Israeli–Syrian negotiations. That was precluded by the gap between Syria's demand to resume negotiations

Map 3 The Middle East

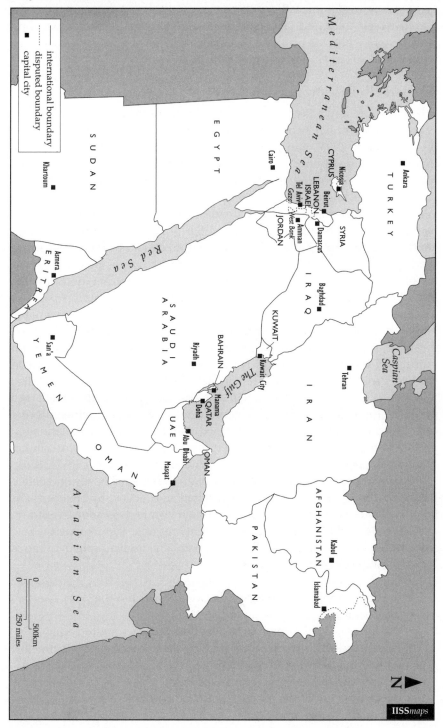

international boundary
disputed boundary
■ capital city

Mediterranean Sea

SUDAN
Khartoum ■

EGYPT
Cairo ■

CYPRUS
Nicosia ■
LEBANON
Beirut ■
ISRAEL
Tel Aviv ■
Gaza
West Bank
Amman ■
JORDAN
Damascus ■
SYRIA

TURKEY
Ankara ■

Red Sea

ERITREA
Asmera ■

IRAQ
Baghdad ■

Caspian Sea

SAUDI ARABIA
Riyadh ■

KUWAIT
Kuwait City ■

IRAN
Tehran ■

YEMEN
San'a ■

BAHRAIN
Manama ■
QATAR
Doha ■

The Gulf

UAE
Abu Dhabi ■

OMAN
Masqat ■

AFGHANISTAN
Kabul ■

PAKISTAN
Islamabad ■

Arabian Sea

0   500km
0   250 miles

N

IISS*maps*

at the point where they had broken off in March 1996, and Israel's insistence on resuming talks with no pre-conditions. As a result, both the Syrian–Israeli track and its Lebanese–Israeli spur-line remained well and truly frozen, with little prospect that even a change of government in Israel would produce any quick or significant thaw.

The Israeli–Palestinian Track

When the nine-day talks between Israeli Prime Minister Binyamin Netanyahu and Palestinian Authority (PA) Chairman Yasser Arafat concluded on 23 October 1998 with a memorandum of agreement, there was an immediate surge of optimism that the moribund peace process had been revived. This prognosis quickly proved premature. Even so, the suspension of the implementation of the Wye River Memorandum did not validate the undertone of most analysis before Wye: that the peace process had come to a complete end. Instead, the process had limped through another year of diplomatic activity without much real progress. Yet every time it seemed to have reached an impasse, it was somehow revived because its preservation, even in a state of suspended animation, was too important for any of the interested parties to allow it to expire.

The reasons for the persistent sense of pessimism and despair were not hard to find. Much of the previous year had been taken up with efforts by outsiders, especially Americans, to encourage continuing implementation of the 1995 Interim Agreement, reaffirmed by Israelis and Palestinians in the 1997 Protocol on Redeployment in Hebron. Implementation had stalled in March 1997, when the Palestinian side rejected as inadequate the Israeli proposal for a further redeployment (three such redeployments were called for in the Interim Agreement) and then suspended negotiations in protest at the Israeli decision to begin housing-construction work in the Har Homa/Jebel Abu Ghneim neighbourhood of Jerusalem.

Following several months of Palestinian–Israeli stalemate and outside passivity, the US administration was jolted into action by two terrorist bombings in Israel in summer 1997. During a visit to the region in autumn 1997, Secretary of State Madeleine Albright was able to persuade the two sides to resume negotiations. But the parties themselves failed to move forward on the outstanding issues:

- the opening of a 'safe passage' between Gaza and the West Bank;
- the opening of air and sea ports in Gaza;
- the release of Palestinian prisoners held in Israeli custody;
- Palestinian security measures and the dismantling of what Israel termed the 'terrorist infrastructure';
- the transfer to Israel of terrorist suspects;
- the completion of the process of amending the Palestinian National Charter; and

• the size of the further Israeli redeployments.

Given this lack of progress, the US administration decided on even higher-level intervention in the process. This intervention took the form of invitations to Netanyahu and Arafat to meet President Bill Clinton in Washington in January 1998. Whether or not intensive and persistent pressure by Clinton at that point would have elicited enough flexibility by either or both of the protagonists to permit an agreement must remain a hypothetical question. Arafat's visit coincided with the first revelations about the scandal involving former White House intern Monica Lewinsky, and while the president did succeed in securing some commitment from Arafat to annul the offensive clauses in the Palestinian National Charter, his focus, along with that of the US press, public and political system, quickly turned to other matters.

Events in the area, however, made ignoring the Middle East a luxury the US could not afford. In particular, the eruption the following month of a new crisis provoked by Iraqi restrictions on the activities of UN Special Commission (UNSCOM) inspectors confronted the administration with the unpleasant reality that many former regional partners were reluctant to associate themselves with American threats of force against Iraq, and justified their view by citing the absence of muscular American pressure on Israel. The administration itself denied that there was or should be any such linkage; it even refused to use the term. But its allies' obvious lack of solidarity with American objectives on Iraq forced the US to remain engaged in Israeli–Palestinian diplomacy.

For the most part, this involved continuous efforts to elicit an Israeli commitment on a 'significant' second redeployment (the first had never been carried out), and much of the dialogue was in fact reduced to discussing the percentages of the West Bank from which Israeli forces should withdraw. In public, the US took no specific stand, because it had confirmed in a side-letter to the Hebron Protocol that the extent of redeployment was to be decided unilaterally by Israel, though the term 'significant' was widely understood to mean a double-digit percentage. In private, the US was pressing Israel to withdraw from 13% of the territory, thereby bringing to 40% the total amount of the West Bank to be transferred to Palestinian jurisdiction in advance of permanent-status negotiations. Despite the urgings of the Israeli opposition, and even of some cabinet members, to move the process forward, the pressures of the settler movement and other right-wing elements in the cabinet and ruling coalition proved stronger. The Israeli government refused to cross the symbolically significant double-digit threshold, or even to undertake the 9–10% withdrawal it was willing to offer, except under conditions (such as cancellation of the third redeployment) that were unacceptable to the Palestinians.

What the government did do was to continue its ongoing and inconclusive debate about the contours of a permanent-status agreement, from which its position on interim redeployments presumably derived. American efforts to influence this debate were persistent. At one point, following an early May meeting in London, Albright even gave the parties (meaning Netanyahu) an ultimatum to accept American proposals and present themselves in Washington a week later; if they did not do so, the US would be forced to 'reevaluate and reexamine [its] role in the peace process'. But such threats failed to move Netanyahu, who resented Albright's peremptory tone and was in any event ambivalent about active American mediation. Thus, the 'deadline' passed without any perceptible effect on the pace of negotiations, and it was only towards the end of the summer that a sense of urgency was injected into the process.

There were several reasons for this. One was the growing spectre of 4 May 1999, the end of the interim period. Arafat had for some time been indicating that he would make a unilateral declaration of statehood on that date. In the absence of real progress on the Interim Agreement, this threat not only took on added credibility, but was also likely, at least according to the assessment of the Israeli security services, to be accompanied by violence. This would have potentially serious ramifications for the whole fabric of Israel's foreign relations, especially with Egypt and Jordan. These warnings could not be ignored, especially in light of the fact that the Israeli Defense Force (IDF) and the Palestinian Protective Security Service (PSS) had already clashed on more than one occasion, most recently in July, and violence involving Palestinian civilians had already broken out several times during the year.

A second reason had to do with the changing calculus of domestic politics. Despite his narrow parliamentary majority, Netanyahu had resisted the urgings of those of his coalition partners who had pushed for more flexibility, including former Deputy Prime Minister and Foreign Minister David Levy, who had resigned at the beginning of the year. But in August, an opposition motion to dissolve the Knesset passed its first reading. This did not necessarily mean that early elections were inevitable, only that they had become a distinct possibility. This forced Netanyahu to confront the unpleasant prospect of running for re-election without any real achievements in the 'peace' plank of his 'peace and security' platform.

As a result, American bridging proposals began to fall on more receptive ears. The most creative of these was an idea to pocket the Israeli offer of 10% and suggest that an additional 3% be designated a 'nature reserve', formally belonging to Area B (that is, under Palestinian civil jurisdiction), but with special restrictions on construction activity and Palestinian security presence. Israeli responsiveness to this idea made it possible for Clinton to risk what he had hitherto avoided: a summit meeting without an advance guarantee of a successful outcome. This willingness to gamble with presidential prestige may have been prompted by the sense that Clinton, now under the threat of an imminent impeachment process, had little to lose; with a different perspective, Egyptian President Hosni Mubarak declined an invitation to come.

For whatever reason, Clinton resolved to exploit the opportunity that had presented itself, and to move ahead. Arafat had little reason to hesitate. He had already endorsed the basic American ideas, though not without some misgivings, and stood to gain either from a successful outcome of what looked to be largely an American–Israeli negotiation, or from the political fallout if those negotiations failed. Netanyahu had more reason to be apprehensive, but it was impossible for him not to respond to the invitation. He therefore tried to shore up his right wing by appointing Ariel Sharon, up to then the most potent threat from the right inside the government, as Foreign Minister and a member of the negotiating team.

The summit was held in October at Wye Plantation in the US. Even with the territorial component of the package basically in place, a successful outcome was by no means a foregone conclusion. There was virtually no progress during the first few days of meetings, and only intensive, around-the-clock involvement by the president himself during the final 21 hours, and a last-minute decision by King Hussein of Jordan to leave his sick-bed in Minnesota and throw his influence on to the scales, ultimately produced agreement.

The problems were not only substantive, but also reflected the domestic political vulnerabilities of both main actors. Netanyahu had to navigate between the conflicting pressures of the 'moderates' (including his defence minister and at least one of the parties in the governing coalition), whose unrequited demands for progress were beginning to invite ridicule, and the 'rightists' (with their extra-parliamentary consti- tuency). Either of these could conceivably cause his government to collapse. To retain his parliamentary majority, he also had to satisfy the budgetary and legislative demands of ultra-Orthodox constituents, who otherwise might make common cause with the opposition. This left Netanyahu in the difficult position of having to secure an agreement at a territorial price – suitably disguised – that he had hitherto rejected, while insisting on non-territorial compensation – 'reciprocity' – that had either long been available, or had already been promised, and withheld, in the past.

For Arafat, the problem was slightly different. His domestic pressure came, not from both ends of the spectrum, but from only one. Free of any demands for greater flexibility, his only constraint was to yield nothing more (and perhaps even less) than what had already been worked out with the Americans. But it was a powerful constraint, because the legitimacy of his regime and the durability of his rule were under strain. Apart from general exposure to charges that his achievements in the peace process thus far had fallen short of his self-proclaimed objectives and that he had conceded too much to the Israelis on the road to an unconsummated agreement, Arafat was also vulnerable to criticism on grounds of human-rights violations. To some extent, this stemmed from the arbitrary measures by the security forces necessary to prevent any major terrorist attacks against Israelis, lest that provide Netanyahu with the pretext to avoid doing what he was clearly reluctant to do. But it was also a result of the response to grievances over the performance of the PA, particularly its perceived tolerance of widespread corruption while economic conditions for the majority of the population either deteriorated or at least failed to improve.

The corruption issue had already precipitated a crisis with the Palestinian Legislative Council (PLC) in 1997. Another erupted in June 1998, when the PLC demanded that Arafat reshuffle his cabinet and dismiss some of the worst offenders; his response, in August, was simply to add new members to the existing cabinet. The PLC resigned itself to this situation – it had also done nothing to protest against Arafat's refusal to sign the Basic Law regulating the constitutional division of power between executive and legislature – but two ministers resigned in protest. Such actions did not result in a marked strengthening of *Hamas* or other opposition elements; Arafat was able to place *Hamas* leader Sheikh Ahmad Yassin under house arrest at the end of the year without provoking any serious resistance. But they did perpetuate an undercurrent of discontent that constrained any room for manoeuvre he might otherwise have had on the diplomatic front.

As a result, an agreement was eventually reached that was so full of ambiguities that some critics described it as 'Swiss cheese'. In particular, the Wye River Memorandum made no reference to those issues that had complicated pre-Wye progress and lent urgency to the negotiations themselves: the size of the third redeployment and the question of a unilateral Palestinian declaration in May 1999. The Memorandum did, however, lay out the path for resumed implementation of the Interim Agreement.

Israel agreed to transfer 13% from Area C (1% to Area A and 12% to Area B). Just as significant, though given far less notice, was the commitment to transfer 14.2% from Area B to Area A, bringing the total area of the West Bank under full Palestinian civil and internal security control to just under 20% (see map, p. 268). Israel also agreed to accelerate negotiations about implementation of agreements on the Gaza air- and sea-ports, the Gaza industrial estate, the southern route of the safe passage, and various economic measures. But these commitments were firmly tied to a 12-week period, divided into three phases, during which the Palestinians were obliged to complete the process of amending the Charter, prevent hostile incitement, reduce the size of the Palestinian police force to agreed limits, and, especially, carry out a variety of security measures. These included presenting a detailed work plan for the registration of weapons, the confiscation of prohibited weapons, and the arrest and prosecution of suspected terrorists, and the rearrest of those already convicted, who had managed to escape or otherwise avoid the completion of their prison terms.

In an important departure, the agreement provided for a more intensive and intrusive American role than ever before in the continuing implementation of the process. Indeed, it stipulated that the US – that is, the Central Intelligence Agency (CIA) – through the mechanism of a trilateral security committee, would essentially act as monitor and arbiter on the security issues that lay at the heart of Netanyahu's claim that he had, for the first time, truly introduced reciprocity into the process and achieved tangible gains in exchange for Israel's territorial concessions.

The Wye River Memorandum drew criticism from both the Israeli right and Palestinian rejectionists, as much for its substantive achievements as for its lacunae and loopholes. Nevertheless, it was initially accepted by the general public on both sides. In Israel, Netanyahu's approval rating climbed to unprecedented levels, and he was able for a time to overcome opposition both in the cabinet and in the Knesset. The Palestinian leadership was able to argue not only that this was the best possible deal under the circumstances, but that the close working relations with the US and the personal bond that had developed between Arafat and Clinton at Wye were gains of strategic proportions. As a result, the first phase of the redeployment was carried out on schedule on 20 November, when Israel transferred 2% of Area C to Area B and 7.1% of Area B to Area A; the airport at Dahaniyya in Gaza was officially opened four days later. During the same period, the PA cracked down vigorously on the infrastructure of *Hamas* and made preparations to convene the Palestinian National Council (PNC) and other bodies in Gaza in order to rescind the offensive clauses of the Charter.

But any sense of optimism very quickly dissipated. The catalyst for the breakdown was the inclusion of common criminals in the first group of Palestinian prisoners released by Israel in early December. The prisoner issue had not been directly addressed in the Wye River Memorandum, but there was a separate understanding that Israel would release 750 prisoners in three phases. When it became apparent that the understanding was not confined to what the Palestinians called 'political prisoners' (and what Israel called terrorists with 'blood on their hands'), widespread disturbances erupted throughout the West Bank and Gaza. Israel insisted that these were instigated by the local *Fatah* organisation with Arafat's tacit blessing, if not active encouragement. The fact that the riots subsided just before Clinton's arrival at the 14 December PNC meeting in Gaza re-inforced these suspicions.

Simultaneously, the Israeli right recovered from its initial shock and, galvanised by the virtual isolation of several Jewish settlements following the first phase of the redeployment, began to organise parliamentary and extra-parliamentary opposition to Wye's continued implementation. On 16 December, Netanyahu, citing other alleged Palestinian violations, especially continuing threats to declare statehood the following May, announced a suspension of further redeployments until the Palestinians complied fully with their obligations. But this came too late to save his government and, on 21 December, those who condemned Wye joined with those who condemned the failure to implement it and passed a bill dissolving the Knesset and forcing new elections. These were eventually scheduled for 17 May 1999, with a run-off on 1 June in the event that no prime-ministerial candidate won a majority in the first round.

Although the Israeli government insisted that it remained committed to Wye and would resume implementation as soon as the Palestinians fulfilled their obligations, it was clear that the Israeli–Palestinian track was essentially on hold. Routine contacts were maintained during the first part of 1999, especially between the security organs of the two parties, but there was little prospect of renewed political momentum, and none at all of productive permanent-status negotiations, until after the Israeli elections.

Apart from that, what dominated the agenda was the question of Palestinian behaviour on 4 May. As that date approached, Arafat came under increasing pressure to defer the declaration of statehood that he had repeatedly promised. One argument advanced by third parties (other Arab actors, Europeans, and even the Israeli opposition) was that a declaration would have an 'adverse' impact on the elections in Israel – that is, strengthen Netanyahu. Indeed, some Palestinians suspected that the scheduling of the elections was intended to hamstring Palestinian decision-making on this issue. Another argument was that, without any prior assurances of recognition, even by those sympathetic, in principle, to the Palestinian cause, the declaration would amount to nothing more than a rhetorical gesture.

It was already clear from one of the Wye side-letters that the US – the most important international actor from the Palestinian perspective – was opposed to a unilateral action of this sort and would not recognise a Palestinian state. Nor was there any irresistible domestic pressure to move ahead; a Palestinian poll in January 1999 showed that only 40% of the public supported a unilateral declaration, while 50% opposed it and 10% were undecided. Nevertheless, though Palestinian pronouncements began to be shaded in some ambiguity, Arafat had invested considerable personal prestige in the issue. In addition, Palestinians continued to believe that the potentially disruptive consequences of a declaration constituted an effective bargaining tool that could be used to extract concessions from the various interlocutors. For most of early 1999, there was little evidence that such concessions would be forthcoming. Nevertheless, the outcome of this issue remained uncertain as the critical month of May loomed larger on the horizon.

The Israeli–Syrian Track

With most attention focused on Israeli–Palestinian matters, the direct Israeli–Syrian track remained dormant throughout 1998. Some perfunctory diplomatic intervention by Americans and Europeans produced reaffirmation of Syria's basic commitment to the peace process, and even some expressions of unease that its concerns were being neglected in favour of the Palestinians. But neither Syria nor Israel viewed the three-year moratorium on this track as dangerous enough to induce any changes in their basic positions. Syria was preoccupied either with domestic affairs (the economy, a shake-up in the army high command, the continued grooming of President Hafez al-Asad's son, Bashar, as successor) or with relations with other regional actors (especially ongoing tensions with Turkey). Israeli concern with Syria was primarily a function of periodic re-evaluations of Israel's presence in southern Lebanon.

The Lebanese 'spur' of the Syrian–Israeli track was the only real locus of activity. This began in January 1998 with a proposal by Israeli Defence Minister Yitzhak Mordechai that Israel accept UN Security Council Resolution 425 calling for Israeli withdrawal from Lebanon, on condition that measures be taken to ensure implementation of Paragraph 3 of the resolution calling for the return of the Lebanese government's effective authority in the south. This was an oblique and slightly tortured interpretation of the resolution in order to make Israeli withdrawal contingent on satisfactory security guarantees. Nonetheless, it did reflect Israel's desire to pull out of Lebanon without leaving the aftermath entirely to chance. This desire was confirmed by a formal cabinet decision in early April.

Unfortunately, the proposal encountered the same obstacle that confounded all previous Israeli ideas (including Netanyahu's 'Lebanon First' policy immediately after his election) to tie withdrawal to some sort of peace agreement or security understandings with the Lebanese government. Lebanon was not a free agent and could not, whatever its inclinations may have been, enter into any kind of arrangement with Israel without Syrian approval. As Syrian Chief-of-Staff Ali Aslan put it in early 1999, 'The Lebanese army has become the reserve units of the Syrian army'. Syria insisted on subordinating developments in Lebanon to an Israeli withdrawal from the Golan Heights and, in fact, had an interest in promoting low-intensity warfare along Israel's northern border in order to promote that outcome. As a result, Israel was left with few options other than those it had faced since 1985: conceding the Golan, risking the possible consequences of a unilateral withdrawal from southern Lebanon, or managing the status quo. The first was unacceptable, and the debate therefore continued to concentrate on the other two.

Many viewed this as a 'Hobson's choice' and looked for other alternatives. Indeed, some innovations during 1998 appeared, for a time, to offer modest relief from the burden of maintaining the security zone in southern Lebanon. While the number of recorded 'incidents' increased in 1998 and the number of IDF soldiers wounded in action rose to 105, compared to 93 in 1997, Israeli battle deaths actually fell from 39 (in addition to 73 killed in a helicopter crash) to 22. As a result, the domestic debate was somewhat less intense than in the previous year.

Nevertheless, the basic dilemma did not disappear. Periods of relative calm were punctuated by occasional outbursts of violence, sometimes involving the firing of rockets into northern Israel (as in August and again in late December) that revived questions about the basic rationale of the security zone. Moreover, there were worrying longer-term trends, including evidence of military cooperation between *Hizbollah* and *Amal*, alongside their ongoing political competition, and of demoralisation in the pro–Israeli South Lebanon Army, indicated by several defections and intelligence successes by *Hizbollah*. The latter was almost certainly prompted by the sense that Israeli public sentiment in favour of unilateral withdrawal was steadily mounting, notwithstanding the fluctuations in response to day-to-day developments, and that those Lebanese who had cooperated with Israel would do well to make their peace with the Lebanese resistance and/or authorities before it was too late.

Policy in Lebanon was not a political issue in Israel in the sense that it coincided with party or ideological divisions. Proponents of unilateral withdrawal, conditioned withdrawal, maintenance or even expansion of the security zone, different operational doctrines, and even accommo-dation of Syrian demands as a way of achieving stability in southern Lebanon were found in almost all parties and across the political spectrum, and had been for a long time. What changed in early 1999 was the injection of the Lebanon question into the Israeli election campaign.

Following a spate of battle casualties in early March, including that of a brigadier-general in command of the IDF Liaison Unit in Lebanon, prime-ministerial candidates, sensing that withdrawal had become a more salient issue in public opinion, began to compete for votes with promises of a quicker, safer or more balanced way to liquidate the security zone in Lebanon and end Israel's 20-year misadventure in the country. But none of them made a specific commitment to unilateral withdrawal, in the sense of withdrawal not tied to any conditions or arrangements. Moreover, the defence establishment remained firmly opposed to unilateral withdrawal. Unless conditions deteriorate to the point where a clear public consensus for unilateral withdrawal emerges, the opinion of the defence establish-ment will predominate and the chances that the long-standing pattern will change in any radical way will remain low.

The Implications of the Israeli Elections

Elections in Israel are not just, and perhaps not even primarily, about the Arab–Israeli peace process. In important respects, the declared policy differences between the major contenders in post-Hebron, post-Wye Israel are marginal. Instead, the elections provide a vehicle for the public to pass judgement on the style and character of the candidates or parties, and on the world-view they seem to embody in the peace and security debate, as well as on important issues not connected with the peace process, such as the role of religion in the state. In many ways, these judgements are actually an expression of sub-group identities, which are quite durable. Consequently, fluctuations in election results are usually quite small. Nevertheless, the fragmented character of the Israeli electorate, coupled with the nature of the Israeli electoral system (particularly following the institution of the direct election of the prime minister), means that small changes can have a decisive impact on the outcome.

Even if these changes are not directly attributable to voter concerns with peace-process policies, different outcomes will have different implications for the future course of the peace process. This is particularly applicable to the Israeli–Palestinian track. The assumption of power by a government more committed to the basic approach of the Rabin–Peres team – which led Israel between 1992 and 1996, and viewed the issues dividing the two sides as problems to be resolved rather than contests to be won or lost – would almost certainly lead to an improvement in the atmosphere of the relationship.

The elections of 1999 involve more candidates than ever before; for the first time three major political factions are involved: *Likud*, Labor and a centre group headed by former Defence Minister Mordechai, who had defected from the *Likud* camp. This set of candidates probably increased the possibility that a prime minister could come to power more willing to move on the Israeli–Palestinian track. That might result from a variety of electoral outcomes: a Labor-led coalition, a centre-left coalition led by either Labor's candidate Ehud Barak or by Mordechai, or even a National Unity Government including more moderate elements of the *Likud* and religious parties. Indeed, only a narrow coalition dependent for its survival on right-wing parties would preclude this possibility. Any other outcome, while it would not immediately lead to agreement on the major questions reserved for permanent-status negotiations (on which the major parties and candidates are, after all, not radically divided), nor even on the unfinished business of the Interim Agreements, might – barring some massive outbreak of terrorism – restore some of the mutual confidence lost in recent years and encourage a revival of the sense of momentum on this track.

It might also serve as a signal, or even a necessary condition, for renewal of Israeli–Syrian negotiations. But it would certainly not guarantee their success. None of the major candidates indicated a willingness to make the commitment that the Syrians insisted they had received from Rabin and Peres – to withdraw completely from the Golan Heights. And even if some of them might eventually do that, there was practically no possibility that any would settle for less than what Rabin and Peres had demanded in return: satisfactory Syrian undertakings with respect to normalisation of relations and security arrangements. Asad had been unwilling to concede these undertakings before 1996, or even to indulge either in the kind of public diplomacy needed to build support in Israel for the idea of withdrawal, or in the kind of informal contacts usually needed to inject some flexibility into the positions taken in formal negotiations. Thus, without some equally profound transformation in the policy or character of the Syrian regime, a change of government in Israel alone would not be sufficient to produce either a Syrian–Israeli agreement, or the political context for agreed Israeli withdrawal from Lebanon.

All in all, the developments of 1998 and early 1999 left the Arab–Israeli peace process in a semi-comatose state – clinically alive because none of the parties was willing to pronounce it dead in the absence of a more promising alternative, but still awaiting the kind of transformations needed to restore it to a semblance of health. Some of these might be provided by the Israeli elections; others would have to await significant changes elsewhere.

Force Projection and Changing Partnerships in the Middle East

In a departure from the careful policies that both Iran and Turkey have pursued in their foreign affairs, both countries resorted in 1998 to the threat of force against neighbours. Iran moved a large number of troops to its borders with Afghanistan, ostensibly in response to the seizure and murder by the *Taleban* of a number of Iranian diplomats, demanding their immediate return. Behind this public cause, however, lay a more basic problem: Iranian fear that the *Taleban* would consolidate its control over Afghanistan, thus tipping the balance of power in the area towards Pakistan and Saudi Arabia, and, through them, allowing an opening for US influence on Iran's eastern borders. Meanwhile, Turkey moved its troops to the Syrian border, threatening an attack if Syria continued to allow the separatist Kurdistan Workers' Party (PKK) to use Syrian territory to fight the government in Ankara. Although there were significant internal reasons for the new threats of the use of force in both cases, they also represented a new regional security configuration that has been slowly evolving in the Middle East.

The Turkish–Syrian Showdown

In late summer 1998, Turkey announced a new strategic plan under consideration by the National Security Council (NSC) that involved using military, political and diplomatic pressure to stop Syria from supporting the PKK, either in Syria or in the Syrian-controlled Bekaa Valley in Lebanon. This was followed by a Turkish parliamentary ultimatum in early October demanding the expulsion of the Kurdish leader Abdullah Öcalan from Syria – an ultimatum that was backed by 10,000 troops sent to the border with Syria. Turkish President Suleyman Demirel warned that Turkey reserved 'the right of retaliation' against Syria. The Turkish Chief of Staff, Ismail Hakki Karadayi, also stated that there was an 'undeclared war' with Syria, while boasting that 'the powers of Turkey and Syria cannot even be compared'.

Turkey's decision to use the military threat should be viewed in the context of changing internal and regional calculations. From 1984, Turkey had been trying to quell Kurdish resistance, primarily through military means. With the loss of more than 30,000 lives on both sides, and not even the glimmer of an end to Kurdish opposition, this policy can hardly have been considered successful. The government, therefore, changed course at the end of 1997, when it began openly to blame 'foreigners' for the failure to liquidate the PKK. Announcing that henceforth the Kurdish threat would be tackled at source, Turkey primarily blamed Syria for giving logistical support to the PKK, and the European Union for allowing it access to financial aid and propaganda outlets. As a prelude to its military initiative, in June 1998 Turkey proposed to negotiate a declaration of principles with Syria that would include non-interference in each other's internal affairs, and require cooperation against 'terrorist organisations', a term Turkey uses to refer to the PKK.

Another internal factor influencing the military showdown was that Turkey's weak and unstable civilian governments in the 1990s had brought the military more to the centre of decision-making. The military was less willing than civilian leaders to continue overlooking the external sources of the 'Kurdish problem', and it did not need to be concerned that the civilian government or the opposition parties in the Grand National Assembly would oppose its new Syrian policy. Caretaker Prime Minister Bulent Ecevit warned that Syria had adopted a hostile attitude for years by allowing PKK leader Öcalan to move his headquarters to Syria. Tansu Çiller, the leader of the opposition True Path Party (DYP), confirmed that her party would support any decision reached by the Assembly as an issue of national concern.

Changing external relationships were equally important in Turkey's decision to adopt a more assertive foreign policy. In seeking greater influence in Central Asia, Turkey's confidence was reinforced by its closer ties with Israel, a partnership that had US support. The EU's intransigence over Turkey's application for membership had angered the country, yet at the same time had helped to liberate Ankara from the need to present a constant peaceful outlook. Turkey was now also more willing to distance itself from Arab concerns and sensitivities.

The Turkish–Israeli strategic partnership, which is based on agreements signed in February and August 1996, carries considerable regional significance for both countries. Although the details remain secret, they are believed to include joint training, cooperation in counter-terrorism and border security, defence industrial cooperation and intelligence exchanges. While these elements affect the region as a whole, they have particular resonance for Syria. Syria's anxiety about the partnership reflects its recognition that it is squeezed between the two allies; that it is engaged in territorial conflict with both; and that it supports insurgencies and terrorism against each as an instrument of its foreign policy.

Syria has been using the PKK as a lever against Turkey in their two outstanding disputes. One is the Syrian claim to the Turkish province of Hatay. Far more important is the second, its claim over water flowing from Turkey. Syria insists that Turkey overuses the water of the Euphrates and Tigris rivers, in effect stealing from Syria's main water resources. The Turkish Southeast Anatolian dam project will, when it is completed in early 2000, give Turkey far more control over the water supply to Syria and the rest of the Fertile Crescent, thus further poisoning the atmosphere between the two countries. Syria believes that Turkey has been avoiding a peaceful discussion of these issues, using the excuse that the dam project is an internal affair.

Syria tried to present the massing of Turkish troops on its borders, not as a conflict between Turkey and Syria, but as one between Arabs/ Muslims and Israel, claiming that the Turkish–Israeli military-cooperation pact was being used by Israel to weaken the Arab/Muslim front. Turkey's military cooperation, according to Syria, was an endorsement of Israel's occupation of the 'Islamic and Christian holy shrines' and a design to divide the 'Muslims'. Both at the 1996 Cairo summit of Arab states, and during the 1997 Islamic summit in Tehran, Syria and Iran had tried to rouse Arab nationalist and Islamic sentiments against the Turkish–Israeli agreement, and to persuade others to put pressure on Turkey. But there was little support from other Arab countries for either criticising the Turkish–Israeli axis, or supporting Syria during the 1998 military showdown.

Turkey's show of force clearly paid off. President Hafez al-Asad was forced to agree to a memorandum of understanding, signed on 20 October 1998 in Adana, Turkey, that met Turkey's demands on the PKK. The memorandum was negotiated with Egyptian mediation, and was concluded in the presence of Egyptian and Iranian representatives (Iran took part as the head of the Organisation of the Islamic Conference (OIC)).

The key parts of the memorandum were that Turkey would remove the military threat in exchange for Syrian agreement to ban PKK activities on its territory; to refuse PKK members' entry into the country; to obstruct PKK trade activities; and to seize PKK camps and detain its members. In order to reassure Turkey, Syria agreed to allow Turkish officials to be based in Syria to ensure the implementation of the Adana agreement. To close the Lebanese loophole, Turkey insisted that both sides hold tripartite talks with Lebanon on the PKK, with Turkey reserving the right to intervene if the memorandum's conditions were not met.

Forcing Damascus to bow to its demands under military pressure added credibility to Turkey's assertive regional and domestic policy, and reinforced Turkey's military standing in the region. Pressure on Syria denies the PKK its main support base, and weakens its leadership. The showdown also provided Turkey with room to clamp down on domestic anti-government protests.

Although Turkey won this battle in its war against the PKK, and gained a victory for its more assertive regional policy, it neither resolved Turkey's Kurdish problem nor ensured Syria's implementation of the Adana memorandum. Turkey had reached a similar understanding in 1992 that Syria failed to implement, and Turkey can have little confidence that Syria will not try to find a way to finesse this agreement as well. Syria did deport Öcalan on 19 October 1998, leading to his capture by Turkish intelligence agents in Kenya and his jailing in Turkey on 14 February 1999 after 14 years of exile. But his forthcoming court trial will be only a first step in resolving the Kurdish problem.

The Iranian–*Taleban* Imbroglio

Although it fielded many more forces than Turkey had against Syria, Iran had less success in its effort to put pressure on the *Taleban* in Afghanistan. Afghanistan has been a fertile playground for competing regional and international interests since the nineteenth century. Its importance as an area within which great-power politics and regional actors mingled faded when the so-called 'Great Game' between Britain and Russia ended. But it regained its distinction when the Soviet Union intervened militarily in 1979 to ensure Soviet influence, and the US supported a proxy war against the Red Army. During the Soviet occupation, Pakistan played an active role in support of US aims, as well as its own, while Iran's influence diminished, partly as a result of its revolution in 1979. The US–Pakistan axis retained an important role both before and after the Red Army's withdrawal. The *Taleban*, one of the forces unleashed by Washington to fight the Red Army, continued to be backed by the Pakistan–Saudi Arabia axis and was tolerated by the US. The *Taleban* has no political project other than an extensive programme of Islamisation, and its extremism is a source of embarrassment for its partners.

The Afghan conflict has important long-term influence on the politics and economics of the region. The fall of the Soviet Union brought new elements – particularly those flowing from the oil-rich Central Asian and Caspian Sea region – affecting Iran, Pakistan, Russia and others both inside and outside the region. The US–Pakistan interest is to see a friendly and stable Afghanistan develop as a safe outlet for oil. A passage through Afghanistan controlled by pro-Pakistani groups like the *Taleban* would secure Pakistan's long-term economic interests and Afghanistan's continued strategic relevance. A southern route through Afghanistan is against Iran's interest, since the country is another contender for a similar access route to 'warm waters'. The rise of the Pakistan-backed *Taleban*, therefore, further undermines Iran's position in Central Asian energy development and, in Tehran's view, is designed by the American, Pakistani and Saudi Arabian 'triangle' to establish a foothold for the US on Iran's eastern borders.

Iran's decision to threaten force against the *Taleban* should be viewed in the context of these wider regional concerns. The *Taleban*'s 1996 defeat of the *Mujaheddin*, the force which had traditionally been seen as representing Iranian influence in Afghanistan, is a clear setback for Iran's regional policy. Forced out of the capital, Kabul, the *Mujaheddin* forces, led by deposed President Burhanuddin Rabbani, moved into Mazar-i-Sharif and turned the city into their stronghold. Iran was their main supporter, supplying economic, financial and military assistance. To facilitate this, Tehran established an air corridor between Meshad, a major city in Iran's north-east, and Mazar-i-Sharif. Iranian support had thus helped the *Mujaheddin* to remain a strong force among the opposition fighting to stop the advancing *Taleban*.

The *Taleban*'s consolidation of its grip on the country challenges Iran's position as the backer of the pro-Iranian *Hazaras*, an ethnic *Farsi*-speaking community which adheres to the *Shi'ite* Islamic beliefs. The *Taleban* is a complex ethnic and religious group, dominated by *Pashtuns*, who are *Sunni*-Muslim and non-*Farsi* speaking. *Farsi*-speakers feared that the *Taleban*, which is infamous for its extremism in pursuit of its own ethnic and religious orientation, planned to turn them into disfranchised communities. Some sense of *Taleban* extremism can be gleaned from its massacre of thousands of *Hazara* civilians during the seizure of Mazar-i-Sharif.

To make viable the threat that, if the *Taleban* did not free the captured Iranians, it would face a 'disaster', Iran embarked on an extensive military operation involving the deployment of 70,000 Revolutionary Guards, and later of 200,000 Army personnel, to the border. Despite the size of this operation, it is difficult to imagine that Iran was eager to carry out an all-out attack. The eight-year war with Iraq in the 1980s was still very much in Iranian minds. Entering a new war while the government still faced the colossal financial difficulties which were partially a result of the first one, would have been imprudent. President Mohammad Khatami's regime not only had economic problems to deal with, but was also struggling with political infighting. There was little enthusiasm to thrust itself into a civil conflict that the Soviet Union had been unable to master. Thus, while projecting force in large numbers, Tehran stressed the need for a diplomatic solution. Khatami is believed to have been against military confrontation and mainly interested in preventing the fanatical Revolutionary Guards from taking matters into their own hands. Nonetheless, he too followed the propaganda line of praise for the 'combatants of Islam' during his tour of the province where the troops were massed in October 1998.

The *Taleban* was no more interested than Iran in a military confrontation. Its success in expanding its rule in Afghanistan had more to do with the divisions and weaknesses of its opponents than with its own strength. Control over a country like Afghanistan requires a greater degree of homogeneity than the group has so far displayed. To avoid further confrontation with Iran, the *Taleban* denied being behind the capture and killing of the Iranian nationals. Instead, as the chief of *Taleban* forces Mullah Mohammad Omar put it, it accused Iran of 'crying foul' over the diplomats to hide its interference in Afghan affairs. The *Taleban* also hoped to gain US support by persuading Washington that the pressure on this question came from an Iranian–Russian alliance.

The crisis which began over the Iranian diplomats in August 1998 ended in mid-October through UN mediation. The *Taleban* released its prisoners with a promise to capture and punish those who had been responsible for their seizure. The two sides had kept channels of communication open, and Iranian officials and *Taleban* representatives had continued to meet, including during the twelfth summit of the Non-Aligned Movement (NAM) in September. By keeping up its military presence on the border under the cover of controlling drug trafficking across it, however, Iran could strengthen the *Mujaheddin* in relations with the *Taleban*.

Nevertheless, the defeat of pro-Iranian groups in summer 1998 underscored Iran's regional policy failure. As one Iranian journalist put it, Afghanistan has become 'the graveyard of Iran's foreign policy'. An ironic parallel is that the Islamic Republic found itself in the same position as the US when American diplomats were taken hostage in Iran in 1979. Then, Tehran supported the hostage-taking, while this time it adopted the US line, denouncing it as the failure of 'the host-state to meet its international obligations', thereby reserving 'the right to take any action to protect the lives of its diplomats'. Forcing the *Taleban* to return the Iranian prisoners was a victory, but it was a very small one when set against the long-term regional repercussions of Iran's Afghan debacle.

A Changing Balance

On the whole, the two military initiatives during 1998, beyond demonstrating a willingness on the part of Iran and Turkey to threaten force as part of their foreign policies, were built on a change in regional partnerships. Iran is not alone in its Afghan policy. Russia shares its views on Central Asia and Afghanistan. Both Iran and Russia are denied a role with regard to Caspian oil, and they agree that the US, with the help of its regional allies, is working to contain their influence. As a result, Russia and Iran have created an implicit alliance over Afghanistan, with Russia stepping up the supply of military aid and exports to the coalition forces fighting the *Taleban*. Iran's position on the *Taleban* also has the support of China and many of the Commonwealth of Independent States (CIS) countries sharing a border with Afghanistan. These countries are not eager to see the *Taleban* establish its type of Islamic fundamentalism on their doorsteps. China is particularly concerned over the potential impact on the Muslim separatist movements in its mineral-rich western province of Xinjiang, which discourage Western investors from helping to develop the oil resources of the province so desired by Beijing.

Turkey was far more successful in achieving its objectives, mainly because its threat was more viable, and was directed against a country which has been weakened and isolated by the shifts in Middle Eastern politics. Syria is still a significant player in developments concerning Lebanon, and to some extent Israel, but it can no longer play the role that Asad continues to assign it. Yet Turkey's successful use of a military showdown, and the concern that the Turkish–Israeli partnership can create throughout the region, may ultimately bring more uncertainty and competing partnerships to the Middle East, rather than a new and stable regional order.

Iraq: Still Desperately Defiant

All parties involved in the Iraqi impasse experienced mounting frustration during 1998. The Iraqi leadership, exasperated by the failure of the UN Security Council to end the punitive economic sanctions against it, became increasingly obstructive to the work of the weapons inspectors of the UN Special Commission on Disarmament (UNSCOM). This led to warnings, then threats and eventually to four days of air and missile attacks by US and UK forces in mid-December. Although Operation *Desert Fox* did much damage to selected targets in Iraq, it was not the answer to the problem of Iraq's refusal to cooperate with UNSCOM.

Equally frustrating for the US administration, *Desert Fox* did not seem to have shaken Saddam Hussein's regime. Overthrowing the Iraqi government had become a declared US policy objective, sometimes complicating its relations with allies and fellow members of the Security Council. Undeterred, the US devoted considerable energy to this task, bringing together the two main warring Kurdish factions in Iraq, and promising financial and military aid to a number of Iraqi opposition groups in the hope that they might help unseat Saddam.

As the year ended, this seemed unlikely. Secure as he ever can be in Baghdad, Saddam tried to capitalise on the international protests caused by Operation *Desert Fox* and by the repeated attacks on Iraqi air-defence systems by US and British aircraft in the first months of 1999. Growing disquiet in the UN Security Council and in the Middle East about these bombardments did not amount to support for lifting sanctions, but divided opinions at the Security Council and Iraq's refusal to cooperate with UNSCOM also prevented either the US or the UN from taking the weapons inspection regime any further.

Return to a Stalemate

In early March 1998, UN Security Council Resolution (UNSCR) 1154 endorsed the Memorandum of Understanding signed by UN Secretary-General Kofi Annan and Iraqi Deputy Premier Tariq Aziz, and threatened the 'severest consequences' if Iraq failed to comply with its provisions. These stipulated that the 'presidential sites' which had been declared off-limits by Iraq should now be open for inspection, and that UNSCOM should resume its work. In return, Iraq was allowed to increase its oil sales to roughly $10 billion per year under the 'oil for food' scheme. Apparently reading too much into Annan's personal intervention, the Iraqi government seemed to consider this a prelude to the imminent lifting of economic sanctions.

This was not to be the case and within months Iraq had begun once more to obstruct and denounce UNSCOM. By mid-April, the eight 'presidential sites' had been inspected by the 'Special Group', formed for this purpose from among UN officials and diplomats. Predictably, nothing incriminating was found. The Iraqi government then claimed that this was sufficient to justify the ending of sanctions, choosing to see the report on these sites as tantamount to UN certification that Iraq no longer held any weapons of mass destruction (WMD). If this was genuinely the belief of the Iraqi leader, he was soon to be disabused.

The UNSCOM Technical Evaluation Meeting, held in Vienna on 20–27 March 1998, at the request of Iraq itself, stated that Baghdad's reporting of its biological-weapon programme was 'incomplete and inadequate'. Additionally, Iraq's failure to account for thousands of tons of precursor chemicals for VX nerve agent was of concern to the Security Council.

Similarly, the International Atomic Energy Agency (IAEA) report to the UN Security Council, dated 22 April 1998, acknowledged that no new evidence of nuclear weapons had been found in Iraq during the preceding six months, but stated that the information on certain sites and processes was less than complete. This gave the US the grounds it needed to argue at the UN that Iraq's nuclear file should remain open, despite an attempt by Russia, France and China to make some concessions in this area. The renewal of the sanctions regime for a further six months swiftly followed, ending Iraq's hope that the February crisis had generated enough momentum to accelerate the ending of UNSCOM's mission and the lifting of sanctions.

Against this background, UNSCOM resumed its work in Iraq, coming under increasing criticism in the official Iraqi media which singled out its head, Richard Butler, for particular attack as an 'American agent'. By the end of April, Saddam was reminding the world that the Iraqi National Assembly had given UNSCOM a deadline of 20 May 1998 by which it must finish its work. He further stated that maintaining the economic sanctions after this date would 'lead to a new state of affairs' and to 'grave consequences', implying both the ending of cooperation with UNSCOM and intensification of Iraqi efforts to break the sanctions.

The deadline came and went without a significant crisis, although the diplomatic atmosphere deteriorated significantly. It was in these circumstances that, in June, Butler presented first to the UN Security Council and then to the Iraqi authorities, a 'road map' indicating what Iraq must do if the sanctions regime was finally to be lifted in October 1998. In particular, UNSCOM was demanding a more rigorous and detailed account of the biological and chemical weapon material that Iraq was known to have developed, but which had not yet been found. The 'map' also drew attention to the unknown scale of Iraq's continued clandestine missile production programme.

Iraq was thrown onto the defensive once again. This was compounded by the discovery in June that some of the missile components destroyed and buried by the Iraqi authorities in 1991 contained evidence of chemical weapons. Although vehemently denied by Iraq, the original findings were eventually supported by the independent experts who investigated these claims some months later. On 18 July, an UNSCOM team made an important discovery in an Iraqi Air Force headquarters of documents giving information about the holdings of chemical weapons. At this point, the Iraqis probably realised that, even under the more politicised regime introduced by the Annan–Aziz memorandum, they could not keep the inspectors from uncovering more of the hidden programmes.

These developments soured relations between UNSCOM and the Iraqi authorities, giving rise to a number of relatively minor incidents of obstruction and deception. Butler, who had initially been optimistic about

Baghdad's response to his 'road map', found himself in a series of tense negotiations with Iraqi officials in August. He tried both to gain their agreement to the programme he had set out, and to resolve the growing problems encountered by UNSCOM in its day-to-day operations.

Butler could make no headway, and, on 5 August, Iraq announced that it would no longer cooperate with UNSCOM's on-site inspections unless they were restructured and US influence within them reduced. In retaliation, the Security Council voted unanimously that the UN should suspend its periodic reviews of economic sanctions, to bring home to the Iraqi government the gravity not only of reducing its cooperation with UNSCOM but also of breaking its February 1998 agreement with the UN Secretary-General. At the same time, the Security Council promised Iraq a 'comprehensive review' of its relations with the UN if it resumed full cooperation. This was intended to entice Iraq by suggesting that its nuclear file might indeed be closed as a result. However, Baghdad made it clear that the only review of interest to it was one which would unequivocally recommend removing sanctions. Anything less was unacceptable.

Frustrated by Iraq's inability to exploit differences among Security Council members to achieve this goal, Saddam took the confrontation one step further when, at the end of October, he announced the end of all cooperation with UNSCOM until sanctions were lifted and Butler removed as UNSCOM's head. Despite concern within the Security Council about the immediate threat to use US military force, and unease within the UN about the intimacy between some US government agencies and UNSCOM officials, no move could have been better calculated to create Security Council solidarity. Even Russia and France, often sympathetic to Iraq's case, condemned its leadership for violating the agreement with Annan. They were joined by the Gulf Cooperation Council, and by Egypt and Syria, all denouncing Baghdad's action and stating that, if force were used, it would be the fault of the Iraqi government.

Apparently acknowledging that he had made a strategic mistake, and faced by the unanimous hostility of the Security Council, Saddam backed down in mid-November and eventually agreed to resume cooperation with UNSCOM. During the stand-off period, as in the crises of November 1997 and February 1998, the US, backed by the UK, made no secret of its willingness to use military force to compel Iraqi cooperation with UNSCOM. As before, the US made clear that such an attack would come unannounced and would be of a scale not seen since the Gulf War of 1991. Indeed, in November the US let it be known that its aircraft were on their way to bomb Iraqi targets when they were recalled because of Baghdad's sudden climb-down.

As in previous crises, each side drew rather different lessons from these events. For the US and the UK there was little doubt that the scale of the threatened military attack made Saddam reconsider his position. For

Saddam, the solidarity of the UN Security Council was probably more important. He was willing to risk a military attack if that held out the prospect of dividing the Security Council and isolating the US, and the possibility of real movement towards a resolution premised on the lifting of sanctions. This was clearly not going to happen. It was more advantageous, therefore, to give ground in the hope that the full implications of a possible US military attack would create the basis for dissent and impel some Security Council members to concentrate on finding a course of action they considered more acceptable.

Back to the Use of Force

These attitudes and priorities set the scene for the violent confrontation of December 1998, when Operation *Desert Fox* made the long-threatened use of military force a reality. In the month-long period from mid-November to mid-December during which UNSCOM resumed its work, the inspectors found that the Iraqi authorities cooperated in some areas, but generally did their best to prevent further enquiries into the details of chemical, biological or missile programmes. Butler's report to Annan on 15 December made it clear that UNSCOM was unable to fulfil its mandate under these circumstances. For the US, it was not simply the UN's authority, but also the credibility of American deterrence – and to some extent, therefore, the authority of the US President himself – that seemed to be at stake. This combination of factors led to the decision to launch *Desert Fox*.

During four nights, from 17–21 December, American and British planes carried out over 600 missions, and around 400 cruise missiles were launched at targets in Iraq. These included the headquarters of Iraq's military intelligence, *Ba'ath* party buildings and Republican Guard barracks, as well as command-and-control centres, airfields and sites associated with Iraq's missile development programme. It seems clear that two different kinds of target were in the sights of the US and UK planners. The first were associated with Iraq's arms programmes and therefore linked to the ostensible reason for the attack – the obstruction of UNSCOM. The second, however, seemed related more to a goal of weakening Iraqi power structures.

During 1998, overthrowing Saddam's regime had become an ever-more public aspect of US policy, which was echoed by the UK. Since 1996, when various US-sponsored opposition groups had met with disaster at the hands of Saddam's security services, the US had downplayed this strategy. The crises of November 1997 and spring 1998 changed that. The US administration was increasingly sensitive to the charge that, by failing to use the oft-threatened military force, it had 'gone soft' on Saddam. This was a theme taken up by a group of US Senators who were determined to make the US take a more interventionist role in undermining the Iraqi leader.

The establishment of Radio Free Iraq in autumn 1998, which trans-mitted anti-regime propaganda into the country, was one consequence. This followed a decision by the US administration in May to dedicate several million dollars to the 'Iraqi democratic opposition'. The stakes were dramatically raised in October, when the US Senate passed the Iraq Liberation Act, authorising President Bill Clinton to give financial and military assistance to the Iraqi opposition to the value of $97 million, and urging him to set up an international criminal tribunal to prosecute Saddam and his henchmen. This was initially regarded with some apprehension by the administration and its military planners because of the apparent implications for open-ended US military commitment on behalf of the fragmented Iraqi opposition. Speaking to the US Senate Armed Services Committee on 28 January 1999, General Anthony Zinni, the US commander in the Persian Gulf, criticised the plan to overthrow Saddam, arguing that support for Iraqi opposition groups was ill-conceived and might further destabilise the region.

However, frustration with Saddam's regime grew, and, as the possibility of using serious military force loomed larger, the US began to incorporate sponsorship of the opposition into its strategy. It had already been deeply engaged in attempts to broker an agreement between the two main Kurdish parties, whose mutual hostility had led to thousands of deaths since 1994 and had allowed both Baghdad and Tehran to reassert powerful influences in the Kurdish areas of Iraq. US efforts were rewarded in September 1998 when the leaders of these parties, Masoud Barzani of the Kurdistan Democratic Party (KDP) and Jalal Talabani of the Patriotic Union of Kurdistan (PUK), were persuaded to sign a peace agreement under US auspices in Washington. This committed them to a truce, a more equitable division of the revenues of the region and general elections for a new Kurdish assembly in summer 1999. The Iraq Liberation Act provided the US administration with the means of channelling substantial assistance to the two Kurdish parties, as well as to the smaller but strategically important Islamic Movement of Iraqi Kurdistan.

Figure 4 Iraqi Opposition Groups designated for US support

- Iraqi National Congress (INC)
- Iraqi National Accord (INA)
- Movement for a Constitutional Monarchy
- Kurdistan Democratic Party (KDP)
- Patriotic Union of Kurdistan (PUK)
- Islamic Movement of Iraqi Kurdistan
- Supreme Council for Islamic Revolution in Iraq (SCIRI) [rejected US support]

These three groups were among the seven designated recipients of US aid under the Act, forming part of a policy that was now labelled 'containment plus', the added element being active encouragement of Saddam's overthrow. Another part of this strategy, which the administration believed was more likely to succeed in changing Iraq's regime, was encouraging a coup from within the military. Organising such an attempt was obviously going to be difficult for any outside power. However, the US thought it might be able to create the conditions that might both goad a determined group of officers into action and provide them with the opportunity to act. This seems to have been the rationale behind the attack on key power points of the regime during Operation *Desert Fox*.

This mixture of motives, and concern that the US and its allies were using the UN as a cover for pursuing a unilateral policy to overthrow Saddam's regime, a policy that could have no UN mandate, sharpened some of the international protests about the bombardment of Iraq. Yet it was noticeable that, within the region itself (with the possible exception of Syria), the official reaction to the December air strikes seemed muted. The protest demonstrations in the streets of many Arab capitals were of a local and short-lived kind. Although many people reacted with understandable shock to the use of military force, the repeated warnings to Iraq and fear in the region about the implications of Iraq's clandestine arms programmes may have helped to mute the response, at least at government level. Nor would many of the neighbouring states have objected had the bombardments demonstrably succeeded in debilitating Sadam's regime, paving the way for his overthrow.

Operation *Desert Fox* could not be judged a great success in either sphere. Iraq, adopting a characteristically defiant stand, made clear it would no longer submit to UNSCOM's intrusive inspections and ceased even minimal cooperation with the inspectors, expelling them from the country. This led to much activity at the UN, as, no doubt, Iraq had calculated. Eventually, three panels were set up in February 1999, each charged with investigating different aspects of the Iraqi case. The first would examine the issues relating to Iraq's WMD development. The second would monitor the humanitarian situation in the country, while the third would look at issues resulting from Iraq's occupation of Kuwait in 1990. The panels would then report to the UN Security Council. A number of UNSCOM members were included in the panel studying Iraq's WMD, and the comprehensive UNSCOM report of 25 January 1999, detailing Iraq's arms programme, served as a primary source for the investigations. But, with Russian and some other members of the UN Security Council pronouncing it dead before the investigations were really underway, UNSCOM's future and that of its mandate were in considerable doubt. The revelations of former inspector Scott Ritter, and allegations that the US used UNSCOM as a front for intelligence operations in Iraq, did not help the Commission.

Faced with Baghdad's obduracy, the US and the UK resumed their overflights of Iraqi territory, patrolling the 'no-fly' zones in the north and south which had been established in 1991 and 1992. Inevitably, this provided Saddam with another opportunity to express his continuing defiance, not simply through his rhetorical rejection of this infringement of Iraq's sovereignty, but also by ordering his air defence systems to engage American and British warplanes. Given the technological superiority of the allied planes, the Iraqi air defences paid a high price, with some 20% of their capacity destroyed by the end of February 1999, according to US government sources. However, as always with Saddam, this was less important than the political capital he hoped to gain from the prolonged engagement.

Baghdad tried to capitalise on the generally adverse international reactions to Operation *Desert Fox*, but had little or only transitory success. Iraq considered the apparent lack of solidarity and active support from the Arab world unforgivable, and during January 1999 Saddam and mouthpieces of the regime launched a series of bitter verbal attacks on Egypt, Saudi Arabia and Kuwait. These attacks went so far as to hint that Iraq might withdraw its 1994 public recognition of Kuwait's independence and sovereignty. This was poor preparation for the Arab League meeting in Cairo on 24 January 1999, where Iraq had apparently hoped for unanimous support. Needless to say, this was not forthcoming, and the Iraqi representative left the meeting in fury. In February, Baghdad tried to cultivate Turkey, whose Incirlik air base was being used to launch overflights of Iraq. However, when the Turkish government refused to comply with its demand that all US flights from the base should be stopped, Iraq reverted to threats of military retaliation.

Nevertheless, the continuing allied bombardment was causing disquiet at the UN. Some countries had always disputed whether the concept of the no-fly zones had a UN mandate. These concerns were sharpened when it appeared that the US and UK had extended their pilots' rules of engagement, allowing them to attack not simply the anti-aircraft batteries that locked onto them, but also command-and-control centres and other military targets. In Turkey and in the Security Council, fears were expressed about the escalation of the conflict, and about its use to serve the specifically US and UK determination to undermine Saddam's regime. Whether or not their goal would eventually be achieved, it was doing little to ensure peace and security in the region in the short term, nor would it allow for the incorporation of Iraq into an effective weapons monitoring system in the longer term.

Searching for a Compromise

The continuing impasse during 1998 over arms-monitoring on the one hand, and over the lifting of economic sanctions on the other, led to thoughts about the need for a new approach that would at least be minimally acceptable to all parties. Unless there is a sudden change of regime in Iraq, Saddam's agreement is obviously needed, difficult as such a situation may be for some to accept. The past 18 months have demonstrated that agreement would only be forthcoming if the Iraqi government felt that progress was being made towards removing the various mechanisms presently limiting Iraqi sovereignty. It is also clear by now that Iraq is determined to retain some capacity for manufacturing WMD.

The challenge for Saddam, apart from the basic one of political survival, is to retain his WMD capacity while complying with any new system of monitoring that may be devised. For the international community, the challenge is how to monitor Iraq's WMD and missile programmes without plunging headlong into confrontation with the Iraqi government, or, at least, to try to deter any possible use of these weapons. For the US, the UK and a number of other states, another large question is how to bring about the transition to a more compliant regime in Baghdad while not over-committing their own resources or troops to the process. These preoccupations were evident in the events of 1998 and early 1999, and are unlikely to change in the near future. Nor does it seem likely that a formula can easily be devised that would reconcile these differing objectives.

Asia

For the average Asian, this has been the worst year in a generation. This was the year when the most calamitous economic crisis since 1945 devastated East Asian economies that had gown used to nothing but turbo-charged advances in their economies. The crash in financial markets was akin to that suffered by the developed world in the Great Depression, while the crash in expectations will leave scars for at least a generation. In South Asia, economies also suffered, but particularly in Pakistan, primarily because of reactions to the other highly depressing event in Asia – the nuclear tests by India and Pakistan.

For all the suffering that the year entailed, it was also a year remarkable for what did not happen. Despite the glib assertion before the Asian crash that economic prosperity kept the dogs of war at bay, in fact a massive economic crisis made no appreciable difference to regional security. Even in Indonesia, where casualties from the May 1998 events were highest, the dire predictions of racial bloodbaths, mass migration and military rule were not fulfilled. By and large East Asians demonstrated astounding maturity in blaming their own rascals for their woes. The three most badly hit economies – Indonesia, Thailand and South Korea – actually made important progress towards more political pluralism. Even in South Asia, where the prophets of doom forecast nuclear war, this was a year of remarkable political maturity and, if anything, a warming in Indo-Pakistan relations.

But it is certainly too early for too much optimism. The events of the past year also demonstrated the fragility of these encouraging trends. East Asians still had major challenges of political and social reform ahead and China seemed to teeter on the brink of its own economic crisis. Japan, the vital engine of growth that accounts for two-thirds of Asian economic wealth, was still stuck in neutral and slipping backwards down the hill of reform. In South Asia, India and Pakistan have restored calm to their relationship, but weak domestic coalitions and still simmering bilateral disputes ensured that no one could be a confident optimist.

Map 4 Asia

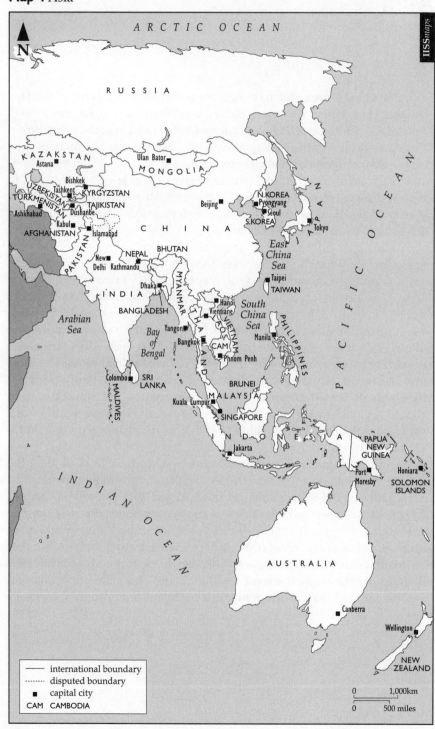

ARCTIC OCEAN

RUSSIA

KAZAKSTAN
Astana

Ulan Bator

MONGOLIA

Bishkek
UZBEKISTAN Tashkent KYRGYZSTAN
TURKMENISTAN
TAJIKISTAN
Ashkhabad Dushanbe
Kabul
Islamabad
AFGHANISTAN

Beijing

N.KOREA
Pyongyang
Seoul
S.KOREA

Tokyo

CHINA

PAKISTAN

New NEPAL BHUTAN
Delhi Kathmandu

Dhaka

INDIA

East
China
Sea

Taipei
TAIWAN

MYANMAR

BANGLADESH

Hanoi
Vientiane

Arabian
Sea

Bay
of
Bengal

Yangon

Bangkok

THAILAND

LAOS

VIETNAM

South
China
Sea

CAM
Phnom Penh

Manila

PHILIPPINES

Colombo
MALDIVES

SRI
LANKA

BRUNEI

MALAYSIA

Kuala Lumpur

SINGAPORE

INDONESIA

Jakarta

PAPUA
NEW
GUINEA

Honiara

Port
Moresby

SOLOMON
ISLANDS

PACIFIC OCEAN

JAPAN

INDIAN OCEAN

AUSTRALIA

Canberra

Wellington

NEW
ZEALAND

— international boundary
······· disputed boundary
■ capital city
CAM CAMBODIA

0   1,000km

0   500 miles

IISSmaps

China: Problems Increase as Economy Slows

By the end of 1998, China's leaders were forced to recognise that it had been a most troublesome year. The country's much praised economy had begun to show serious fault lines and relations with the US had slipped from the high-water mark reached in the summer. Yet, at the beginning of the year, Chinese authorities, basking in the afterglow of President Jiang Zemin's successful US visit in October and November 1997, and looking forward to a return visit by President Bill Clinton in the summer, must have thought the coming year would be a favourable one.

Nonetheless, China pressed ahead with its reform agenda as the newly established Prime Minister Zhu Rongji confirmed, at the National People's Congress in March, the policy of restructuring the state-owned enterprises (SOEs) that had been announced at the Communist Party Congress six months earlier. In fact, he went further, pledging to shed four million from the workforces of the overmanned central bureaucracies, thus cutting them by half, and promising to complete restructuring the SOEs within three years. Internationally, the country was being praised for the responsible way it had responded to the Asian economic crisis and for the way it had kept its word in allowing Hong Kong a high degree of autonomy following its return to Chinese sovereignty on 1 July 1997. China was also seen as an increasingly effective participant in key international institutions involving non-proliferation, arms-control and economic cooperation. Indeed, China even appeared to be moving towards adherence to international norms in the practice of human rights. It signed the UN Covenant on Economic, Social and Cultural Rights on 27 October 1997 and the Covenant on Civil and Political Rights on 5 October 1998.

Ironically, it was just as American Secretary for the Treasury Robert Rubin praised China for being an 'island of stability' in Asia's stormy economic waters, that it became evident, in the summer of 1998, that China, too, was not immune from Asia's economic crisis. As economic growth slowed, Beijing became increasingly concerned about the impact on unemployment and social stability. Accordingly, the programme for rapid economic reform, announced in March, was quietly modified and elements of it put aside as banks were instructed once again to renew non-performing loans to the ailing SOEs. As sporadic signs of social discontent appeared, the regime began to take a tougher line on open expressions of political dissent. Relations with the US and the European Union also took a turn for the worse as the Chinese sought to increase exports to those markets. They needed to do so to make up for the fall in sales to Asian countries, which used to take 25% of Chinese exports. The EU and the US then complained that their growing trade deficit with China was partly due to unfair trade practices. Relations with South-east Asian neighbours also began to cloud over later in the year as the Chinese were seen to be taking advantage of their neighbours' economic difficulties and new political uncertainties to establish yet more structures on a disputed island reef near the Philippines. Even the glow of the June summit with President Clinton had lost its lustre as the year drew to an end, with the Chinese Minister of Defence Chi Haotian openly casting doubt on the regional security benefits provided by the American alliances in Asia.

The Economic Downturn

China's official claim to have achieved economic growth of 7.8% in 1998 was universally greeted with scepticism. Domestic demand was known to be flat and electricity use had increased by only 2.8%. Factory inventories were full to overflowing and it seemed as if output was simply registered as growth. Indeed, one of the reasons for the decisions in October 1997 and March 1998, to address the problem of SOE reform at last, was that their losses had risen so much (twenty-fold since the reform era began in 1978) that, far from contributing to state revenue as before, they had become net liabilities.

These economic considerations appeared to have persuaded the regime finally to tackle SOE restructuring despite its fear of unemployment. But, as some of the 100,000 smaller Soviet-style SOEs began to be amalgamated, restructured or closed altogether, the emerging evidence of sporadic unrest being generated by the resultant unemployment seemed to unnerve Beijing. By instructing the banks in June to resume lending to the SOEs, the central government indicated that it was more concerned to preserve social stability than to carry out the reforms that all agreed were necessary to overcome China's deepening economic difficulties.

Beijing did tighten up on the profligate use of capital, but it balked at making fundamental reforms of the financial system for fear of knock-on effects on the state sector as a whole. Nevertheless, it was recognised that the country's finances were in great trouble. The four key banks were laden with debts and non-performing loans that elsewhere would have forced them into bankruptcy. Precise figures are unavailable, but the best Western estimates put the Chinese banks' bad loans at $270–$360 billion in 1998, equivalent to 30–40% of gross domestic product (GDP). Meltdown has been avoided so far because of the high rate of household savings, at around 40% of GDP, which account for more than half of all bank deposits.

The earlier policy of 'grasping the big and letting go of the small', which sought to hold onto the 500–1,000 huge SOEs and to allow the 100,000 small and medium-sized ones to be restructured, was substantively curtailed in the summer. Not only had it resulted in rising unemployment, but, as in Russia, it had provided golden opportunities for state managers and their associates in local government to seize control of public assets. This led to what has been called the 'privatisation of profits and socialisation of losses'. It also unleashed social discontent and rioting by cheated workers and pensioners, especially in the interior where economic development was not repeating the successes achieved in the coastal regions.

Conscious of the growing discontent, China's leaders, in the second half of 1998, began to crack down hard on political dissidents and especially on those who were trying to register formally the new Chinese Democratic Party. Fearing lest they might provide a focal point for the surging discontent, the leaders caused activists in various cities to be summarily tried and sentenced to long prison terms. Beijing also saw the crackdown as necessary to pre-empt potential trouble on key anniversaries due in 1999. (These include the fortieth anniversary of the Tibetan uprising and the flight of the Dalai Lama; the eightieth birthday of the May 4th Movement; ten years since the Tiananmen Square massacre; and even the fiftieth anniversary of the establishment of the People's Republic of China.)

China also finally felt the pain of the Asian economic turmoil as its export markets in the region melted away, investment flows slowed and the much vaunted economic success of the coastal provinces began to falter. Some of the slack was filled by increasing exports to the US and the EU through various export promotion and import restriction measures. The government also sought short-term relief through huge state infrastructure investment in the interior, which largely benefited the inefficient, but favoured, SOEs.

By the end of the year, however, it had become apparent that many of the new infrastructure projects were dangerously flawed because corrupt officials had used inferior construction materials. In key cities, such as Chongqing in the interior or Ningbo on the coast, lives were lost as new bridges collapsed within weeks of opening. Even the prestigious Three Gorges Dam was set back by what has come to be called 'tofu construction'. The increasingly angry Zhu Rongji tried to address the problem by introducing a new responsibility system.

The government also struck hard at smuggling, which was depriving the state of tens of millions of dollars a year in revenue. For the same reason, the government also moved to rein in the business operations of the military, many of whose units were deeply implicated in smuggling and even piracy. Meanwhile, foreign investors also began to feel the pinch as the much vaunted provincial investment trusts suddenly found themselves without government backing. The Guangdong International Trust and Investment Corporation (GITIC), in the southern province of Guangdong, was the first and most prominent casualty. It was declared bankrupt on 6 October 1998, with debts of over $4bn. To their dismay, foreign banks found that they had to settle for tenth place in the order of priority for repayment, and China suddenly lost its much prized status as a favoured destination for foreign capital.

By the year's end, China's establishment economists were admitting that the country's true rate of unemployment was around 10% and would stay at that level for at least a decade. Such gloomy forecasts were unlikely to encourage the leadership to open up their economy to foreign competition. One result was that prospects for negotiating China's entry to the World Trade Organisation (WTO) faded.

The Partnership with the United States

President Bill Clinton and his team tended to ignore China's deepening economic troubles during their visit from 25 June to 3 July 1998. Clinton appeared far more occupied by the opportunity which Jiang Zemin gave him to address the Chinese on the subject of human rights live on state television, and by a similar live broadcast of his question-and-answer session with Beijing University students. More formally, the American side expressed pleasure at China's signing of the two UN conventions on human rights, especially that on civil and political liberties. The Americans also praised renewed Chinese commitments on arms control in general, and its stand against nuclear proliferation to Iran in particular. Presidents Clinton and Jiang agreed that they would work towards establishing a 'constructive strategic partnership'.

For their part, the Chinese were pleased by the US adopting in Beijing a common stance with them in condemning mainly India, but also Pakistan, for conducting nuclear tests. The Chinese felt that this implied the US recognised China's entitlement to be the dominant power in Asia and did not recognise India's claim to a right to defend itself against Chinese nuclear weapons. But, as the Americans began to negotiate with India on nuclear matters, they distanced themselves somewhat from these implications and focused instead on nuclear proliferation.

The Chinese also chose to believe that, because Clinton did not include America's closest Asian ally, Japan, or any other Asian country, on the itinerary of his summer visit to China, there was an implied rebuke to Tokyo. They were pleased by what could be considered the elevation of China's status at Japan's expense when the President and his aides praised the Chinese for their behaviour in the course of the Asian economic crisis, while sharply criticising the Japanese for their allegedly unhelpful approach. Yet Japan had contributed $30–$40bn to the International Monetary Fund (IMF) and other international bodies to address the crisis, and had had its offer to establish a substantial regional fund turned down by the US. The Chinese, on the other hand, were being highly praised for having contributed less than $2.5bn in total and for not devaluing their currency, a strategy very much in China's interest.

But what pleased the Chinese most of all was that President Clinton, on Chinese soil, made a statement reiterating what has become known as the 'three noes', saying: 'We don't support independence for Taiwan; or two Chinas, or one Taiwan–one China. And we don't believe that Taiwan should be a member in any organisation for which statehood is a requirement'.

The Americans softened the blow to Taiwan by pointing out that this did not amount to a change of policy as this had been placed on the record by an administration official in testimony before a congressional committee in Washington. It was further argued that Clinton had resisted Jiang Zemin's insistence that a communiqué including the 'three noes' be signed in Beijing, and that Clinton made the statement in the course of an informal radio broadcast in Shanghai. Nevertheless, the Chinese still felt that Clinton's statement had improved their position on Taiwan.

There was little progress, however, in giving substance to the proclamation, in the aftermath of the summit, that a US–China partnership would be developed. In fact, the relationship may be said to have regressed rather quickly as the US repaired some of the damage to relations with Japan and Taiwan and as it began to negotiate separately with India on nuclear issues. Meanwhile, the American trade deficit with China grew to $56bn – smaller only than that with Japan – amid complaints within the US about China's unfair trade practices. The Chinese crackdown on political dissidents and various religious groups, and a renewed harshness in its treatment of Tibet, also evoked growing criticism in the US. This culminated in the US Department of State *Annual Country Reports on Human Rights Practices*, released on 26 February 1999, in which China was severely criticised. The US Senate voted 99 to nil to recommend that the administration once again condemn China at the UN Commission on Human Rights in Geneva. The Chinese contribution to the backsliding was to profess alarm at American interest in working with Japan, and possibly Taiwan, to develop a theatre missile defence (TMD) system.

By the time the US Secretary of State, Madeleine Albright, went to Beijing in early March 1999, the difficulties in US–China relations had grown. In addition to the problem around TMD, there was a report in late January 1999 that a bipartisan Congressional investigation had found that Chinese legitimate and illegitimate acquisition of particular kinds of advanced technology (mainly in connection with miniaturisation of nuclear weapons) over a twenty-year period had endangered American security. By March 1999, Republican senators were accusing the Clinton administration of having been lax about what they called the most serious security breach ever, and China was angrily denying that it had engaged in any espionage of this kind. Additionally, towards the end of February 1999, the Departments of State and Defense turned down, on security grounds, the export of satellite-related technology to a Singaporean company that was formally linked to Chinese military interests, even though the Department of Commerce had already authorised the $450 million deal.

Despite differing sharply in public with her hosts on human rights questions, Albright sought to prepare the ground for negotiating on trade issues as a means of trying to get China into the WTO later in 1999. It was argued that, as WTO rules were due to be tightened towards the end of the year, it was essential to try and negotiate entry terms before then, since otherwise it might be another five years before this would become feasible again. It was hoped that significant progress could be made before Premier Zhu Rongji's visit to the US, scheduled for April 1999. Cynical observers suggested that the main reason for the haste was that the Clinton administration wanted to register a distinctive mark in history, for, given China's current economic problems, it was difficult to think of a less propitious time for the exercise.

Talks Begin with Taiwan

Talks between the senior envoys of Taipei and Beijing had been suspended by Beijing in 1995 in response to Taiwanese President Lee Teng-hui's visit to the US. They were restarted during a five-day visit to the mainland in October 1998 by Koo Chen-fu, head of Taiwan's Straits Exchange Foundation. He held discussions with his counterpart Wang Daohan, head of the Association for Relations Across the Taiwan Straits, and with Vice Premier Qian Qichen in Shanghai before going to Beijing to be received by Jiang Zemin. No new breakthrough appears to have been made and, if Beijing had seen this as an opportunity to test whether Clinton's visit had strengthened its hand with Taipei, it must have been disappointed.

Beijing at first seemed to look favourably on the Kuomintang (KMT)'s success in the December 1997 parliamentary elections when the KMT for the first time gained seats at the expense of the independent-minded Democratic Progressive Party (DPP). In particular, Beijing seemed pleased with the success of the KMT candidate in unseating the DPP incumbent Mayor of Taipei. A senior member of one of the Chinese institutes dealing with Taiwan expressed a favourable view of Lee Teng-hui's concept of the 'New Taiwanese' (which suggested an accommodation between mainlanders and Taiwanese).

But by the end of January 1999, Beijing's mood had soured. Qian Qichen dismissed the slogan of the 'New Taiwanese' and called upon the KMT to accept the political condition of 'One China'. Beijing was undoubtedly upset that Taiwan had engineered its recognition by Macedonia, and that it was acquiring more advanced weapons and military technology from the US. Beijing, which was increasing the number and quality of missiles aimed at Taiwan, protested angrily at the suggestion that Taiwan might benefit from a TMD system centred on Japan, and reacted even more strongly to the possibility that Taiwan might acquire *Aegis* destroyers from the US as part of an anti-missile defence shield. To express its anger, it also made clear that Wang Daohan, who had been expected to visit the island in March 1999 in return for the Koo Chen-fu visit in October 1998, would not do so.

Beijing Advocates Cooperative Security

As relations with the US stumbled after Clinton's visit, Beijing began to renew its professed interest in cooperative security as an alternative approach in Asia to the US-dominated series of alliances that had recently been enhanced. Calling them leftovers from the Cold War, Chi Haotian lectured a meeting in Singapore in November 1998 about the greater suitability of mutual consultative arrangements and cooperative approaches for contemporary regional security needs. Interestingly, the lecture was delivered less than a week after American Secretary of Defense William Cohen had presented a report proclaiming the virtues of US security commitments in the region and affirming American determination to remain militarily engaged there. Like the previous official Chinese support of the cooperative approach, in a March 1997 meeting of the Regional Forum of the Association of South East Asian Nations (ASEAN) held in Beijing, the target audience of Chi's lecture was again South-east Asian.

The audience might have been more impressed by the Chinese stance had it not been preceded by yet another instance of the stealthy way in which Chinese forces were asserting their presence in the Spratly Islands in the South China Sea. In October 1998, the Philippines vigorously protested about additional construction work on the suitably named Mischief Reef. The Chinese claimed that the fortified concrete buildings were merely for the convenience of their fishermen, but they looked very much like new military structures. With ASEAN preoccupied with other matters, the Filipinos were left to cope by themselves with the establishment of a Chinese military presence less than 200 miles from their coast and more than 1,000 miles from any Chinese territory with a resident population.

For good measure, the new Chinese approach was incorporated in a joint communiqué issued by the Russian and Chinese presidents during Jiang Zemin's visit to Moscow in November. As seen by the Chinese leaders, (who privately assure the US of their satisfaction with the current American military deployments in the region), adherence to the new approach serves a number of useful purposes. These include making smaller neighbours feel uncomfortable about supporting the US military presence, encouraging American uncertainty about the wisdom of maintaining these deployments in the long term, and helping to gain support for Chinese advocacy of a multipolar world in which the American capacity for unilateral manoeuvre would be sharply curtailed.

Relations with Japan, however, proved to be difficult to accommodate within this new approach. Nothing in it suggested that the Chinese recognised Japan's legitimate security interests. In the course of a five-day visit to Japan in late November 1998, Jiang Zemin did not conceal his irritation at his failure to extract the same kind of apology from the Japanese government for Second World War atrocities that his South

Korean counterpart, Kim Dae Jung, had obtained when he visited Tokyo on 7–10 October. This was partly due to the entry of a more conservative party into the Japanese ruling coalition. But it also reflected the difficulty Beijing and Tokyo had in placing their political and strategic relations on as firm a footing as their economic ties.

Patience, but Firmness, is Required

The past year has clearly demonstrated that China, a potentially great country, is still beset by social and economic difficulties at home, and has not yet found what its proper role in the world should be. The country and its leaders gravitate between a sense of their own superiority and a realistic appraisal of their present weakness. As a result, flashes of arrogance mix uneasily with periods of self-doubt. Foreign statesmen can best help China's transition to maturity by firmly opposing its sometimes aggressive and illegitimate behaviour, while simultaneously recognising and exhibiting understanding for its enormous difficulties. A China that is comfortable with itself and its place in the world can be an asset; a prickly country, undeterred, can become a menace.

●

China's Party and Army: New Complexities

The relationship between China's armed forces and the Communist Party, static for most of the 50 years since the establishment of the communist regime, has recently been undergoing gradual but momentous change. Already discernible in the twilight of the Deng Xiaoping era, the new pattern has become much clearer under his successor, Jiang Zemin. It amounts to nothing less than a replacement of the military's hitherto unconditional subordination to the party and leader by a much less certain commitment to either.

While the situation is still evolving, two central trends have become clear. Both point to a declining military presence in politics, but also, paradoxically, to an increase in its potential capacity for political intervention. These trends reflect changes in two elements of what is now a much more complex party–army relationship than before – how the army relates to its leader and how its leadership relates to the political hierarchy generally.

The Leader and The Army

The relationship between the armed forces and the leader remains central. When Jiang was thrust to national power by Deng Xiaoping in 1987, many thought that he would not remain in power long after Deng's death. In striking contrast to the godfathers of the revolution, Mao Zedong and Deng, Jiang had little personal authority on the national scene and no personal standing in the military. His power derived from his institutional positions at the top of China's power structure, and those were wholly a gift of Deng's patronage.

This was particularly apparent where the armed forces were concerned. Without any military experience or connections, and no particular knowledge of military affairs, he was, by his own admission, not equipped to lead the armed forces. He was accepted by their chiefs only because Deng had requested it.

But Jiang quickly proved that he had been underrated, particularly after Deng's death in February 1997. Obviously endowed with considerable political skills, he has not simply managed to survive as Deng's successor in the jungle of Chinese politics, but has consolidated his position as leader. In achieving this, he has made full use of his institutional posts – as General Secretary of the Communist Party, Chairman of its Central Military Commission, and President of the Republic – which give him much power and symbolic prestige. Beyond the symbolism, these posts have given Jiang the supreme advantage of being able to place trusted officials in key posts in the bureaucracy.

In the armed forces, Jiang has replaced the top 20–30 military commanders. These include the commanders, deputy commanders, and political commissars in:

- The General Staff, Logistics, and Political Departments which make up the General Staff of the People's Liberation Army (PLA).

- The seven Military Region Commands which blanket China.

- The two top armed forces educational institutions and think-tanks: the National Defence University and the Academy of Military Sciences.

- The Commission on Science, Technology and Industry and its newly-established successor organ, the Armaments Department of the General Staff.

In the Central Military Commission, China's top military body, more than half the members have been appointed in the past few years. In addition, Jiang has made major efforts to consolidate armed forces' support by adopting exceptionally pro-military policies, especially by increasing allocations for new weapons.

Jiang's performance in the political and military arenas has narrowed the gap between his symbolic and real power as leader. It has also strengthened his position among army leaders, which is already buttressed by their professionalism and ingrained inclination to support the incumbent leader. His position was also enhanced by the long-delayed retirement, at the 15th Party Congress in September 1997, of the two senior armed forces commanders, Liu Huaqing and Zhang Zhen. As revolutionary veterans, Liu and Zhang had towered over Jiang in military stature and owed him no political debts. The new army chiefs, Zhang Wannian and Chi Haotian, are from Jiang's generation and owe their appointments to him. No other military leader has the personal stature to stand up to Jiang.

However, where armed forces' support for Mao and Deng, given their unique authority in the army, was axiomatic and immutable, it is not automatically assured for Jiang. But this does not mean that the military are constantly looking over his shoulder. On the contrary, as long as things are going well from their point of view, they will support him and stay out of politics. The army, of course, has never spelled out publicly what it will take to keep it happy, but this presumably includes at least the following: reasonable economic progress which ensures social stability; wide autonomy for the military backed by appropriate allocations; and influence in policy areas of vital military concern.

If these conditions are not met over a prolonged period, Jiang might lose the army's support, and he cannot assume that support would be forthcoming in adverse circumstances. For example, military leaders might refuse to intervene on his behalf in a power struggle, or they might even intervene in support of a rival.

The Changing Leaderships

The possibility of military support ebbing away in difficult times is strengthened by the accession to power of a younger generation of leaders. This has been under way for several years, with implications for the second element of the party–army relationship – relations between the military and political hierarchies. In the armed forces, this generational change has elevated to the highest ranks professional commanders whose primary concern is to oversee the long-term transformation of the Chinese army into a modern force. Most have risen through the ranks of the ground forces with, at best, only limited combat experience; are gradually becoming familiar with the imperatives of modern warfare; and have focused on military rather than political careers.

These officers are the products of the professionalisation of China's armed forces, which has been increasing steadily in the past two years and has important implications for the officers' political role. On the one hand, it has strengthened internal cohesion in the armed forces, sharpened the institutional separation between them and other bureaucracies, and distanced them from the political arena. On the other hand, a unified military, animated by a strong institutional identity, and increasingly separated from other bureaucracies, will find it easier to move into politics on its own account.

This possibility could be reinforced by changes in the party and the government, where leaders with similar characteristics have entered the top echelons. Most are university-educated technocrats who have worked their way up in specialised bureaucracies. The result is that both military and civilian leaders are increasingly oriented towards their professional pursuits. In contrast to the founding fathers of the party, who, as national figures, did not respect institutional boundaries and blurred the distinction between the military and political spheres, the new leaders tend to stick to their bureaucratic bailiwicks and emphasise their separation.

New Organisational Roles

This separation is reflected in changes in the third relationship axis, that between party and army organisations. This is partly the result of the Communist Party's decline as the epicentre of the Chinese political system and its concurrent weakening in the armed forces, and, more importantly, by the modernisation of the armed forces and the flowering of military professionalism at the expense of political intrusion. As a result, the traditional organisational grip of the party over the army has considerably loosened. While the ultimate subordination of the army to the party is intact, the army has become much more autonomous.

The net result of these changes has been the emergence of a new party–army relationship, based on a variety of common interests between increasingly separate organisations, rather than on unconditional compliance of the army to the party. The overriding interest of the party leader and his colleagues is to maintain the support of the armed forces, while distancing them from politics and civilian administration. This interest coincides with the military chiefs' inclination to concentrate on military modernisation and to avoid bruising political entanglement. This balance of interests began to take shape at the end of the Deng period and has been fully in force under Jiang.

Its first manifestation was the military chiefs' steady support for Jiang during the transition period. This has continued since Deng's death, as Jiang has carefully pursued economic development. The army leaders frequently praise Jiang and his policies, as do the military media. They also show him symbolic respect, for example, by according him a central place in manoeuvres, and they make public efforts to educate the troops to be loyal. Most importantly, they avoid any action that might undermine Jiang's position, such as publicly criticising his policies.

In return, Jiang has granted the army unprecedented freedom to manage its own affairs. Mao and Deng were active commanders of the armed forces who intervened in the details of military life. Jiang does not, except in the critical area of high-level appointments, and here he probably consults top army commanders. Of the seven most important members of the Central Military Commission, which directs China's military estab- lishment, Jiang is chairman by virtue of his paramount position, but he is the only civilian, and, being completely devoid of army experience, is unlikely to oppose the professionals.

On the contrary, Jiang has gone out his way to cultivate their support. He shows great respect to the armed forces and their leaders, has strength- ened personal ties with high-ranking officers and has been unusually generous with promotions. He makes frequent and well-publicised visits to military units and pays homage to military traditions.

Most importantly, Jiang has ardently advocated modernisation of the armed forces and has underwritten it with increased allocations. The military budget has risen steadily for a decade under his aegis, by about 5% per year when adjusted for inflation. In part, this should be attributed to the relative neglect of the armed forces in budgetary allocations during the first decade of economic reform. In part, it stems from the upsurge in the economy during the 1990s and the obligation of the leaders to make good on their promise that the forces would also benefit from the greater prosperity. But an important reason has doubtless been Jiang's desire to show his goodwill towards the armed forces by providing funds for new weapons. As a result, since the early 1990s, the Chinese military has step- ped up arms purchases and joint production agreements which, though limited and selective, have given China some state-of-the-art weapons, such as the Russian SU-27 ground-attack fighter.

Whether Jiang took these steps to ingratiate himself with the forces' chiefs, or whether he responded to pressure from them, cannot be known. What is known is that neither Mao nor Deng had to take similar steps. In the new relationship, the military participates, as never before, in select policy areas outside the armed forces. At the top level, this is via their two representatives in the party's Politburo (three if Jiang also counts as their nominal head outside the armed forces), but military views are also expressed through other channels; for example, research institutes. Exactly how they exert their influence is, of course, secret, but the impression is that the armed forces do not intrude into civilian areas, such as the economy, but limit themselves to defence and foreign policy issues that directly impinge on their institutional interests.

Foremost among these are policy towards Taiwan and relations with the United States. During the Taiwan crisis of 1995–96, which began with the visit of Taiwan's president, Lee Teng-hui, to the US in June 1995, and escalated into attempted intimidation of Taiwan by China, the military leaders played a central policy-making and operational role. However, there is no evidence that they took a harder line than Jiang, or strayed beyond the national consensus on the need to thwart Taiwanese moves towards an independent international stance. In relations with the US, the military has loudly decried supposed US efforts to block China's rise, but, like Jiang, it has welcomed cooperation with America. It has also been vocal on related issues such as US–Japan relations, potential US development of theatre missile defence, and India's nuclear tests, which suggests that its voice carries important weight.

A Healthier Relationship – for the Moment

Nowhere has the convergence of interests between Jiang and the military been more remarkable than in Jiang's sudden and surprising order, in July 1998, which required the forces to divest their myriad business activities. After more than a decade of commercial pursuits, the military has created a massive economic empire which supplements the military budget, but which also involves enormous corruption and undermines profession-alism. Although the number of military enterprises has not been divulged, it is estimated that the armed forces run some 15,000 industrial, production and service companies, from huge pharmaceutical conglomerates through resorts and hotels to karaoke bars.

The wide-ranging order to divest could not have been issued, and would not have had the faintest chance of implementation, without close cooperation between Jiang and the military leaders, for their different reasons. Jiang and the leaders of the economic bureaucracies want to further distance the army from non-military pursuits and sources of in-come which have led to much corruption. The armed forces, for their part, want to stop the erosion of their professional standards and concentrate resources on military activities. They are apparently prepared to give up numerous profitable enterprises and Jiang and the civilians are prepared to compensate them for their lost income. Despite the immense difficulties involved, the process is under way.

Although all elements of the new party–army relationship seem to be functioning smoothly now, this will last only so long as the two sides have common interests. If they cease to do so, there are two possible outcomes. One is that, because of their new autonomy, the army will simply fail to intervene to back Jiang in a power struggle, or to put down unrest, even if called upon to do so. The other is that, for the same reason, the military might decide it is necessary for it to intervene in politics, even against Jiang's wishes. If this happens, Chinese party–army relations will enter uncharted territory.

Another Year of Leadership Failure in Japan

There was little sign during 1998 of light at the end of the long, dark tunnel through which Japan has been travelling for too long. The economy – which has been in the doldrums since the collapse of the 'bubble economy' in the early 1990s, with only a partial and temporary resuscitation in 1996 – showed no real signs of life and the economic indicators only grew worse as the year wore on. The government, repeating well-tried responses such as introducing stimulation packages and switching prime ministers, continued to prove ineffective and unenterprising. Even a hectic round of high-level exchanges amongst regional and international leaders and the floating of a financial rescue plan for Japan's equally-troubled Asian neighbours in the later months of the year did little either to enhance Japan's international reputation or to impress its own citizens.

Many of Japan's problems boiled down to leadership failure and a reluctance to take hard decisions about economic reform. Then Prime Minister Ryutaro Hashimoto accepted responsibility for the setback suffered by the ruling Liberal Democratic Party (LDP) in the Upper House elections of July 1998 and resigned. This marked a disappointing end for a politician who had promised much on coming to power two-and-a-half years earlier, but who in the end delivered too little, too late. He is not the only one. Indeed, the 1990s are set to be the lost decade for Japanese political leadership.

The new Prime Minister Keizo Obuchi is straight out of the postwar Japanese tradition of uninspiring politicians who have generally been better as party managers than men of vision. In the past five decades, only four prime ministers have made any deep impact on Japanese life in terms of significant policy initiatives and changes. Shigeru Yoshida in the late 1940s and early 1950s restored Japan's international position after its defeat in the Second World War. Eisaku Sato set the country onto an ambitious, and successful, economic growth path in the 1960s, and Kakuei Tanaka in the 1970s had plans for remodelling the Japanese archipelago, but achieved a more lasting impact by institutionalising 'money politics'. The last forceful premier was Yasuhiro Nakasone, who, in the mid-1980s, pushed Japan towards a much higher profile in international affairs as well as carrying out large-scale privatisation policies at home.

Since then, prime ministers have come and gone rapidly and, as German Chancellor Helmut Kohl once famously remarked when introduced to the third new Japanese premier in as many months, it has been difficult for foreign leaders even to remember their names, let alone recall what policies they have pursued. Hashimoto looked like being the man for the 1990s, but he failed to deliver. His tough-talking style, which earlier made his reputation during trade negotiations with the US, and his 'macho' public image as a martial arts enthusiast seemed to dissolve once he was in office.

The blame must partly lie with the post-war party system, in which promotion to top jobs depends more on length of service, avoiding risks, and the ability to cultivate loyalty within the faction and outside contacts with wealthy business backers than on competence and initiative. But it is more than just politics. Japanese society in general prefers to operate through a process of consensus in which individuals' thoughts and feelings are subordinated to the group of which they are a member. Charismatic and powerful individuals do exist, and some of them became notable entrepreneurs in the Japanese economy's boom years, but only someone of exceptional perseverance and drive can break out of the mould. The Japanese saying that 'the nail which sticks out is hammered down' applies as much to politics as to society in general.

Politics: The Prodigal Returns

One of the few individuals who do stand out in Japanese society, Ichiro Ozawa, demonstrated his almost Houdini-like ability to escape from disaster and managed to revive his political career in 1998. While still a rising star in the LDP he had taken a political gamble by walking out of the party and into opposition in 1993. He masterminded several anti-LDP coalition governments in succeeding years, but never came close to the premiership himself. His ego, intelligence and drive won him as many enemies as it did friends. But, despite having started 1998 by effectively destroying his own opposition party, the New Frontier Party (NFP), by the end of the year Ozawa was being courted by former LDP colleagues intent on creating yet another of the political marriages of convenience that have typified much of the post-1993 political scene in Japan.

As Ozawa's stature grew, one of his chief rivals among his contemporaries, Hashimoto, demonstrated how to throw away a strong position and disappoint high popular expectations. Although he managed to earn himself a place in the record books in the spring of 1998 by becoming the sixth longest-serving post-war prime minister, his position was not as secure as he would have liked. Grumbling about his leadership continued within the LDP and the continuing bad news about the economy, and the apparent inability of his administration to do anything about it, battered his popularity-rating which sank to less than half what it had been when he took over.

Constitutionally required to hold elections for the Upper House in July 1998, Hashimoto had tried to talk up the LDP's chances of gaining seats and even regaining a majority. Half the Upper House is re-elected every three years; if the LDP had done no more than retain its existing seats and gain an extra handful it would have been able to claw back the majority which it had lost in 1989. But it was not to be.

Public disillusionment with Hashimoto's economic policies was not alleviated by a last-minute electioneering ploy of announcing possible tax-cuts. Instead, one of the largest election turnouts for more than a decade resulted in ground being lost to the new gaggle of opposition parties. Several small groups from the shattered NFP had joined the revamped Democratic Party (DP), led by Naoto Kan, a former health minister who had become well-known nationally for revealing a scandal about the use of blood products infected with the HIV virus. The LDP lost rather than gained seats, falling to an overall total of 103, while DP seats rose to 55 and Ozawa's Liberal Party (LP), the rump of the NFP, achieved a marginal gain to 12 seats.

The LDP still held control of the more important Lower House, but clearly was in need of new partners to help get legislation through the Upper House. For the previous two years, the party had cooperated with its long-time ideological and political rival, the Social Democratic Party of Japan (DSPJ), and a tiny LDP splinter party, *Sakigake*. This alliance, a hang-over from the coalition politics of 1994–96, had caused much resentment within the LDP, some of whose members felt that they were being held hostage to the particular sensitivities of the pacifist DSPJ. The Upper House elections ended any possibility of those parties being effective coali-tion partners. (The DSPJ sunk to 13 seats and *Sakigake* all but disappeared.) The hunt was on for a new prime minister and new coalition partners.

The head of the LDP's largest faction, the mild and amiable Obuchi, won the intra-party election and was duly installed as prime minister. For the next few months, his administration muddled through, but in the process it was forced to make painful concessions to opposition parties to ensure that its banking reform plans, so essential to economic restructuring and recovery, were passed. Anticipating that even more controversial bills, relating to the new guidelines for Japan–US cooperation, would have to be put before the Diet in early 1999, Obuchi and his senior LDP colleagues therefore decided to turn to Ozawa and the LP to try to gain allies for the next round of parliamentary battles.

Some of the ambitious younger LDP politicians, especially the so-called YKK trio of rising stars, Taku Yamazaki, Koichi Kato, and Junichi Koizumi, were unhappy about reunion with Ozawa, who had, after all, deserted the party and precipitated its loss of power in 1993. But, after difficult negotiations stretching over nearly two months, the LDP and LP agreed to form a new coalition government in January 1999, with the LP taking one of the cabinet posts. Significantly, however, the post was not filled by Ozawa who said he wanted to continue to manage his party affairs.

The coalition is likely to be an unstable one. The YKK trio and others who initially opposed it remain suspicious of Ozawa's intentions and his potential for political manoeuvring from outside the cabinet. A formal merger between the two parties, a distinct possibility during 1999, would give Ozawa the platform he wants to achieve the premiership. But it might also force some LDP members to resign in protest. Moreover, the coalition with the LP does not give the LDP a majority in the Upper House; it still needs other 'allies' at least on a case-by-case basis. Another round of intra-party and inter-party struggle is set to begin.

Economy: Going Nowhere Slowly

While the politicians were busy playing their political games, for most ordinary Japanese the key issue was the moribund state of the economy. Neither Hashimoto nor Obuchi, who brought back veteran politician and former prime minister Kiichi Miyazawa to be his Finance Minister, looked as if they knew how to turn the economy round. Indeed, one of Obuchi's first policy pronouncements after taking up his new post was to appeal to 'businessmen, scholars or anyone else with a good idea' for economic recovery.

Good ideas were certainly needed. Although recession seemed to be a word that government economic agencies and their spokesmen would go to almost any length to avoid using, it was clear that the economy was deeply mired in a prolonged slump. Obuchi finally admitted the worst in the autumn. Miyazawa went further, and was even quoted as describing the economy as 'a shambles and a mess'.

By September 1998, the economy had suffered its fourth consecutive quarter of shrinkage, a record unparalleled since Japan's postwar economy began to take off more than 40 years earlier. The fiscal year April 1998–March 1999 was expected to show a decrease in gross domestic product (GDP) of 2.5%, the worst since the oil shock of 1973–74. Spending by consumers and corporate investment in plant and equipment continued to slow. The flagship corporations of the Japanese economy, such as Toshiba, NEC, Mitsubishi and Hitachi, all reported losses for the first time in the postwar era. Many companies in the retail and services sector wobbled on the edge of bankruptcy; some fell over. Faced with oceans of red ink, com-panies began to think the unthinkable – not only closing down overseas operations, but even laying-off workers at home. Resistance to adopting harsh 'Western-style' hiring-and-firing practices remained strong, but by the end of the year the Japanese unemployment rate had reached an official record high of 4.4% (if calculated in the same way as in most Western countries, it was more like 7%) and had overtaken that of the US for the first time ever.

The government twice tried the usual remedy of a stimulation pack-age: one in April for 17 trillion *yen* and another, the ninth since 1992 and the largest ever, for ¥4tr, in November. Both packages were based on tax cuts (temporary in April and more permanent in November) and the traditional mainstay of public works spending. More innovative, though smacking rather of desperation, were the plans to distribute free shopping coupons to the elderly and families with children in an attempt to bolster consumer spending. But even the government's chief economic planner admitted that these various measures would at best do no more than hold the line and prevent the economy deteriorating further. Time, and probably luck, would be needed before the economy turned up.

Japan's biggest weakness remains the banking system and the mountain of accumulated bad debts. Some estimates suggest that Japanese banks are as much as $1tr in debt. Much of the year was spent discussing how to resolve their situation. Ministry of Finance officials argued that recapitalising the banks was the first, and essential, step towards restoring economic health. But how to do it? The answer was to let Japanese taxpayers foot part of the bill in a massive ¥60tr bail-out plan launched by the government in October 1998. This included recapitalising weak banks and the 'temporary nationalisation' of banks on the verge of collapse. It was just in time to save the substantial Long Term Credit Bank, which had trillions of *yen* in bad loans. Others followed.

At the same time, Japan tried to revitalise its financial system through deregulation and liberalisation, specifically through its own version of the 'Big Bang' financial liberalisation that London had undertaken 12 years earlier. Launched in April 1998 under the slogan of 'free, fair and global', which somehow implied that the Tokyo financial market had been none of these previously, the aim was to shake up one of the most conservative sectors of Japan's economy. However, the weak state of the economy and the stock market have meant that the full and positive impact of these reform measures has been delayed and Japan's Big Bang looked in danger of ending in a whimper. Undoubtedly, the whole process has been overshadowed by the problem of dealing with the banks' bad loans. As Japanese government officials reluctantly admitted, the lack of a system for writing off the massive irrecoverable debt, something that Japan had never needed to do before, has seriously delayed economic recovery. Predictions that it could take up to three years to deal with the problem do not inspire confidence.

Asia's Saviour ?

Speaking in May 1998, Tung Chee-hwa, the Chief Executive of the Hong Kong Special Administrative Region, called on Japan to 'come out to bat for everyone' in Asia. His comments were not untypical of those made elsewhere in Asia, and, indeed, in North America and Europe too, on a common theme: that action by Japan was crucial to the recovery of the battered Asian economies. The implication was not only that Japan should contribute to international aid packages, but that it could also help regional recovery by getting its own economy back into shape.

Where revitalising the Japanese economy is concerned there was not much of a case for the defence: there has been plenty of talk, some limited action, but no signs of improvement. However, as frustrated Japanese officials have been at pains to point out, Japan has done more than its fair share of providing financial aid to its suffering Asian neighbours. By the end of 1998, Japan had announced assistance to Asia, through the International Monetary Fund (IMF) and other international organisations, amounting to $44 billion, the largest amount contributed by any single country. Additionally, in October 1998, Japan announced its own $30bn rescue package, which has become popularly known as the Miyazawa Initiative, in honour of the Finance Minister who first proposed it. Half this amount was to be in medium- and long-term funds for business expansion and debt restructuring, made available through traditional channels such as the Export-Import Bank, with the other half being *yen* loans for short-term capital requirements, drawn directly from Japan's foreign reserves. While disbursement will take some time (and Malaysian Prime Minister Mahathir Mohamad openly criticised Japanese 'slowness and excessive red tape' in early 1999), there was no shortage of takers among the five worst affected Asian nations at which it was primarily aimed.

In November, at the Asia-Pacific Economic Conference (APEC) summit in Kuala Lumpur, Japan agreed to work with the US on a separate $10bn joint aid package, to which Japan would contribute $3bn for bank and corporate restructuring and trade-finance insurance in APEC nations. This more modest initiative was not conceived without some difficulties. Japan had itself proposed, at the end of 1997, establishing some form of Asian Monetary Fund, only to find the idea shot down by the Americans and Europeans who feared it might eventually usurp IMF supremacy. Yet, one year later, the Americans were pushing for an APEC-related fund and twisting the arms of the Japanese to contribute. Some Japanese finance officials felt that this was simply a blatant US attempt to hijack a Japanese plan and dictate how Japan should spend its money; and there were strong echoes of the US aid programme in the 1980s, known as the Brady Plan, which closely resembled an earlier Japanese initiative vetoed by Washington. Consequently, the Japanese decided to resurrect their aborted idea. Miyazawa publicly returned to the theme of creating a separate Asian Monetary Fund in December 1998, but other Asian states remained sceptical about its feasibility without hearing further details. Nonetheless, some – however tentative – signs of Japanese activism in financial diplomacy, at least towards the suffering economies of South-east Asia, were needed to compensate for the frustrations of summitry in North-east Asia.

Awkward Visitors

The APEC summit was just one example of increasing friction in the Japan–US relationship as 1998 drew to a close. Not only was the funding for the Asian financial crisis an irritant, but the Japanese also resented being criticised for their failure to agree an APEC deal on opening up the forestry and fishery products markets. They also felt uncomfortable with

US Vice-President Al Gore's outspoken calls for democracy in the host nation, Malaysia. But worse was to come when US President Bill Clinton visited Tokyo later in November.

Following an invitation to Obuchi to visit Washington in September, the Clinton visit was the second sop to compensate the Japanese for their unhappiness with the US President's failure to visit them on the way either to or from his June visit to China. But even the November visit gave an impression of being merely a stopover on the way to Seoul to discuss the pressing North Korean missile issue. Clinton reiterated the calls being made by his officials for some months previously that Japan should act quickly to revive its economy and he cast doubt on whether the latest stimulation package, announced on the eve of his visit, could achieve that. The Japanese resented being lectured yet again on the state of their economy.

Although the large – and still growing – US trade deficit with Japan has engaged less attention than usual from the US Congress (which has instead been more focused on the more rapidly rising trade deficit with China), the Clinton administration continued to harp on specific trade problems, especially the sudden doubling of Japanese steel exports during the year and a perceived failure to implement agreements on opening up the Japanese insurance market. The US Treasury also seemed to adopt an increasingly hard line on the need for Japanese financial reforms.

In contrast to the sullen mood on economic relations, the Japan–US security relationship began to show signs of improvement in the second half of 1998, but this was less due to US policies *per se* than to North Korea's ability to reinforce the arguments of those LDP and LP politicians in favour of a strong defence posture. Japan had watched developments on the Korean peninsula with interest, though with little real inclination to go back to the negotiating table with Pyongyang. However, the launch, on 31 August 1998, of a North Korean rocket which flew over part of Japan and landed in the Pacific Ocean drastically altered the wait-and-see mood. The Japanese were embarrassed by their failure to spot and intercept the rocket and by their inability to make an early assessment of whether it was a satellite launch (as the North Koreans maintained) or a ballistic missile. (In part, of course, this was due to Japanese dependence on US intelligence and the US was initially just as uncertain as the Japanese.) The Japanese Defense Agency ultimately concluded that it was a test of a long-range missile.

This galvanised Tokyo into finally agreeing to cooperate with the US in developing a ballistic missile defence (BMD) system, about which it had been non-committal for some time, and to announce its own plan to develop intelligence satellites. Less than a week after the North Korean missile launch, a joint meeting between Japanese and US security ministers agreed to begin joint research during 1999 into creating a BMD system, which would use satellites, radar and sea-based missiles to pinpoint, intercept and destroy incoming enemy ballistic missiles. The initial technical studies are expected to take at least five years, with Japan taking the lead on the detection systems and lightweight materials, while the US will focus on the shape and construction materials. Given the technical problems likely to be encountered, it could well be up to 15 years before a theatre missile defence (TMD) system can be deployed in Japan. The Japanese will also undertake initial planning projects during 1999 for having four reconnaissance satellites in operation by the year 2002. Seeking to answer Asian neighbours' objections to both these projects, Obuchi explained that TMD was purely for defensive purposes and that the satellites were only for collecting information to help with crisis management. This did not, however, prevent China, in particular, protesting about what it claimed were the aggressive intentions behind the new Japanese commitments, which, they warned, could provoke a new arms race in the region.

The bilateral security relationship was also helped by the victory of the pro-LDP candidate in the Okinawan prefectural elections in November. The previous governor had been an outspoken opponent of the US bases in Okinawa and had exploited popular outrage over a rape case in 1996 to impel US agreement to closing some of them down. The Japanese and US governments had devised a plan to construct a heliport to replace one of the largest bases due for closure, but local residents had voted against it in a referendum in February 1998. However, the new governor favours a new air base, rather than the heliport plan which has now been quietly dropped, provided that the base is turned over to Japanese control after 15 years. This compromise position is likely to be acceptable to both the Japanese and US governments.

Both governments regard the Okinawan bases as indispensable to the new Japanese commitments to provide rear support and participate in joint defence operations under guidelines agreed in September 1997. Legislation to formalise these guidelines will be introduced by the LDP in early 1999, and is certain to be a focal point of controversy. Not only will the bills come under attack from the opposition, but the LDP will find the LP an awkward ally. Ozawa has made clear that he would like the legislation to be categorical about the geographical extent of Japan–US cooperation, as well as its exact nature. The LDP prefers to live with a degree of ambiguity.

Clinton was not the only Tokyo visitor to cause problems for Obuchi in 1998. Given the long history of friction in Japan–South Korean relations, the October 1998 visit by new South Korean President Kim Dae Jung went better than expected. Kim seemed prepared to look forward and the Japanese finally agreed to put into writing their apology for past misdeeds. This, however, set a precedent which was to cause problems when the Japanese refused to do the same during Chinese President Jiang Zemin's visit in November. Intended to celebrate the twentieth anniversary of the Sino-Japanese peace treaty, the visit did produce a list of bilateral agreements on economic and social issues, but this could not make up for Jiang's refusal to sign a joint statement pledging friendly and cooperative partnership. The Chinese were unhappy that Obuchi would only state verbally, rather than in writing, both his apology for past actions in China and the Japanese position on Taiwan. Jiang spent the rest of his tour around Japan making constant reference to the need for a 'correct attitude' to the past. Hair-splitting explanations from Japanese officials of the legal differences between the South Korean and Chinese situations remained unconvincing, and, overall, Jiang's visit failed to advance the relationship.

Some of the bloom also went off Japan's relations with Russia, the other important player in North-east Asia. Obuchi was unable to carry on the close personal relationship which Hashimoto seemed to have cultivated with Russian President Boris Yeltsin, and the deterioration of the Russian economy destroyed any Japanese business interest in the Russian market. Rising expectations of a peace treaty (theoretically to be achieved by the year 2000) and a solution to the 'northern territories' problem were in danger of becoming bogged down in slow moving negotiations.

These were unhappy tidings. But the year's biggest shock for Japanese policy makers came from Europe. They were slow to realise that the member countries of the European Union were finally going to succeed in introducing a unified currency as scheduled in January 1999. Although several of the larger Japanese corporations had been studying the problem for some time, distractions at home and a deep-seated scepticism about European coherence and convergence led many Japanese to underestimate the euro's potential impact. After talking for more than a decade about the internationalisation of the *yen*, but doing little practical to achieve it, Japan found that the euro was suddenly emerging as a real force in international financial markets, threatening to rival the dollar and leave the *yen* as a very poor third. Obuchi quickly arranged a trip to Europe in early January 1999 and once there argued for three-sided, euro–*yen*–dollar cooperation on monetary and currency policies. He could not avoid giving the impression, however, that Japan, and the *yen*, had been left behind.

Even while he was trying to persuade the Europeans to take him, and the *yen*, seriously, Obuchi was looking over his shoulder at what was happening back in Tokyo. The parliamentary deal with Ozawa and the LP, completed almost immediately after his return to Tokyo, boosted Obuchi's popularity, but he still faced two major problems: getting the controversial security guidelines legislation through the Diet and reviving the economy. Of these two, the economy is the most challenging task. Obuchi has staked his political future on achieving positive growth in the 1999–2000 fiscal year, a promise he may yet come to regret. Passing a few banking reform laws and a pump-priming budget will not be enough. Japan has been putting off the difficult decisions and muddling through for most of the 1990s. Many in Japan are coming to accept that broad structural change is indeed necessary, but there is still a strong body of opinion which says that the economic fundamentals are sound and that fine-tuning the system should be sufficient. Yet, as more time passes, the need for wide ranging change is becoming ever more imperative. If Obuchi does not have the necessary boldness, then Japan must wait for a new leader. In the meantime, the economy will continue to limp along. And without an economic revival, Japanese efforts to step onto the international stage are also going to remain uncertain and unconvincing.

●

The Korean Peninsula: Dealing with Adversity

Koreans on both sides of the divided peninsula can probably agree on at least one thing: the Year of the Tiger, known traditionally for its ferociousness and volatility, fully lived up to its reputation. Acute hunger and economic decay prompted some shuffling of the political deck in the North and new bellicosity towards the outside world. Failing banks and financial turmoil in the South precipitated widespread hardship, mass layoffs, and major political, economic and social change. Although the nature and extent of economic deterioration differed greatly between the two countries, the resulting challenges tested both severely. How each responded tells much about both the underlying fundamentals of the two systems and the prospects for security on the peninsula.

North Korea: Still Treading Water, But More Furiously

North Korean leaders set the overall tone for the year's developments at the outset. A joint New Year's Day editorial in three official publications, emphasised the main themes for the coming year: guaranteeing Kim Jong Il's absolute authority; preserving the ideology of *juche* (self-reliance); building up the military; and maintaining the country's unique economic system ('socialism of our own style'). While the editorial alluded to North Korea's 'arduous' situation, little was said about the economy, which had shrunk by another 7% in 1997, let alone about the need for fundamental change in the system. The clear message was that Pyongyang did not intend to initiate major, systemic changes in the foreseeable future.

North Korea did, however, have something to celebrate in 1998: the country's fiftieth anniversary on 9 September. The principal political aspect of the celebrations was a decision to convene a session of the Supreme People's Assembly (SPA), North Korea's rubber-stamp parliament, on 5 September, just before the anniversary. Contrary to widespread expectations, Kim Jong Il did not use the occasion to assume the position of State President. Nor did he give a speech drawing lessons from the country's past experience and charting new courses. But he did use the session to reconstitute government institutions which had been suspended since Kim Il Sung's death in July 1994, and to formalise a new power structure under his personal control. There were three main changes:

- Abolition of the post of State President, with the embalmed Kim Il Sung designated the country's 'eternal' President and a new position, Head of the SPA Presidium, created to represent North Korea in its relations with foreign countries.

- Upgrading the National Defense Commission (NDC) to be the highest state organ, with its Chairman (Kim Jong Il) defined as holding the top position in the state and granted wide authority over all national decisions.

- Further institutionalisation of the military's influence, with seven of the ten NDC members (apart from Kim Jong Il, who also retains his title of Supreme Commander of the Armed Forces) being senior military officers, and all ranked within the top 20 in the North Korean hierarchy.

While such changes in communist dictatorships often simply provide a façade of 'constitutionality' to legitimise the raw exercise of power, some inferences can still be drawn. First, North Korea now has a political structure that reflects Kim Jong Il's own preferences and priorities. Whatever his reasons for not assuming the presidency, the effect is to create a government structure that maximises his direct control over all facets of government policy, and minimises the large group meetings and official public activities he finds distasteful. By dividing up responsibility for executive management, moreover, Kim can insulate himself from blame for North Korea's dire economic conditions and focus on the ideological and military matters closest to his heart.

Second, the military's enhanced role is now formalised. This was heralded in a new ideological slogan, introduced on 22 August 1998, which called on the country to build a 'strong and prosperous nation' (*kangsong taeguk*) and urged the maintenance of a 'military-first' policy that would turn North Korea into a 'big' power. While the military has always had a central position in North Korea, and conspicuously so in recent years, the expansion and upgrading of the NDC represents a further institutionalisation of its central role. Indeed, its membership and authority give the impression of a wartime crisis-management committee or military junta.

This may not be inappropriate given the magnitude of the crisis North Korea faces, but the NDC can not be described as a 'normal' ruling body, even for a communist country.

Characterising the new structure as a 'military' dictatorship is probably misleading. For one thing, the party remains important, as its formal role in submitting Kim Jong Il's nomination to head the NDC suggests. Although Kim did not take the opportunity to revitalise the party – most probably because of his inability to come up with a coherent economic plan to announce at a party congress – its authority over ideology and elaborate control mechanisms within the military suggest that it will remain an important organisation. More to the point, however, Kim Jong Il controls the key levers of power not the armed forces. By formally identifying the NDC as the nation's highest military organ and re-designating himself its chairman, Kim bypassed the party and contributed to the perception of the military's primacy. But the effect was formally to ensure his personal and direct control over all military matters. In this sense, the chief result of 1998 appears not to be increased military influence over Kim, but his increased control over the military.

Nevertheless, the increased status and role of the armed forces is significant. On the one hand, it suggests the perceived need to send a signal of strength and determination to the outside world. On the other hand, it implies that North Korean leaders define the internal challenge as being more procedural – getting the people to work harder and implement the leadership's decisions more thoroughly – than systemic. While Kim may or may not reconstitute party organs in the coming year, the importance of the military in achieving both these goals is likely to ensure its continuing primacy in North Korean politics.

A final inference is that radical change remains, at best, a distant prospect. Kim's refusal to assume the post of State President is itself a discouraging sign, since it suggests a lack of will to tackle North Korea's pressing problems aggressively. This sense is reinforced by his decision not to give a major speech at the SPA session. Instead, past fantasies took the place of current reality, and delegates were forced to listen to a taped recording of the late Kim Il Sung's speech at the last SPA session in 1990. Although it would have been truly noteworthy had the dearly departed leader shared his analysis of current conditions, listening to his economic plan for 1987–94 – a plan that had not been realised even in 1998 – can hardly be seen as a sign of new directions; nor can the other main theme of the speech: the need to achieve reunification by the end of the 1990s. Together with the constitutional revalidation of *juche* ideology as the basis of North Korea's economic policy, these developments suggest that the leadership sees reshuffling the government and tinkering with the management system as sufficient to deal with the country's economic crisis.

Several clauses of the revised constitution do imply somewhat greater room for economic experimentation. However, many of the newly sanctioned activities, such as farmers' markets and participation by social entities in foreign trade, have been taking place for some time. In any event, none of the constitutional clauses addresses the fundamental issues involved in moving from a centrally planned to a market economy. Similarly, the advent of a 'new', younger leadership and appointment of certain allegedly 'reformist' figures to important government positions do stimulate hopes for increased flexibility.

But these hopes must be tempered by reality: the North Korean system does not allow truly 'new' leaders to rise, only loyal followers of the 'Great Leader.' And several of the 'old' leaders purged or recently executed, such as Suh Gwan Hee, Kim Dal Hyon, Kim Hwan, and Kim Jung Woo had been regarded as leading North Korean proponents of reform and opening. The most striking aspect of personnel moves in 1998 was not a search for 'new thinking' but the regime's extreme sensitivity to even hints of ideological weakening. Advocating moves towards a 'Chinese model' of development appeared a particular career hazard.

In short, while economic reform may come to North Korea, it is hard to see it following from last year's political developments. What is most conspicuous is the absence of any clear vision for the North's economic future, let alone a coherent plan for overcoming its pressing difficulties.

Digging the Hole Deeper

Economically, 1998 ended as it began: with continued deterioration. Statistics North Korea itself provided to the UN Development Programme (UNDP) in May suggest that gross domestic product (GDP) declined by almost half (from $20.8 billion to $10.6bn) between 1992 and 1996 – a significantly larger fall than even that posited by South Korean agencies. While these statistics were undoubtedly designed to ensure the maximum international assistance, outside estimates for North Korean GDP in 1997 and 1998 confirm the general trend. By the end of 1998, there were widespread reports that North Korean industrial plants were being cannibalised and machinery scrapped to exchange for food or hard currency. This continued decline was exacerbated by a sharp drop in trade between North Korea and its principal trading partners. In the first half of 1998, for example, North Korean trade with China, Japan, and South Korea fell by 30%, with trade between the two Koreas alone declining by almost 50% over the same period. For the year as a whole, North–South trade fell by 28% – a figure that would have been much larger but for the inclusion of non-commercial items like food aid in South Korea's export statistics. This decline reflects both the recession in the South and further deterioration in the North's productive and extractive capacity.

The food situation was more complex. On the one hand, both outside relief agencies and the North Korean government itself declared there were enormous grain deficits. In January, the UN's World Food Programme (WFP) launched the 'biggest emergency operation in WFP history', appealing for 658,000 tons of food. Pyongyang's central news agency joined the begging queue in mid-March, warning that its grain stocks would run out 'within two weeks' even if daily rations were reduced to 100 grams per person. This did not happen, despite a tepid response to the WFP appeal, and, by the end of the year, most outside observers concluded that the food situation had at least marginally improved over 1997. A significant deficit was expected to continue into 1999, however, with the cumulative effects of chronic malnutrition becoming increasingly apparent. There have been reliable reports that, since the mid-1990s, up to two million people have died of starvation. In February 1999, there were reports of young Korean women whose families could no longer feed themselves being sold to Chinese farmers as brides.

North Korea's response to its economic crisis focused on enticing, cajoling or extorting resources from the international community. Pyongyang fared poorly in its efforts to attract foreign investment in the Rajin-Sonbong free-trade zone. Plagued by continuing infrastructure inadequacies, political constraints (a UN-sponsored investment fair on 24–26 September 1998 was undermined when Pyongyang unexpectedly excluded more than 60 South Korean firms), and spillover from Asia's financial crisis, external investment was only a fraction of that sought by North Korea. Pyongyang also gained little from its decision to allow foreign cargo planes to transit its airspace, because of the continuing restrictions on the routes allowed.

Even North Korea's relative success in securing international food and medical assistance has to be qualified. As the year progressed, there were signs of increasing donor fatigue, along with demands for North Korea to take more fundamental steps to solve its problems. Similarly, as reflected in the withdrawal of the medical aid organisation *Médicins Sans Frontières* from North Korea in September 1998, international aid agencies grew increasingly resistant to the lack of transparency in Pyongyang and continued official constraints on their activities. Meanwhile, North Korea's 'demands' for huge monetary compensation for restraints on its missile sales or other destabilising activities were fruitless.

On the military front, North Korea's economic difficulties began to affect its conventional capabilities. Shortages of fuel and spare parts cut into Pyongyang's ability to field and reinforce mobile forces. Readiness declined significantly in the face of cutbacks on training exercises. Inadequate supplies of food and other resources raised problems of sustaining troops and maintaining morale. There have been reliable reports of soldiers robbing market traders at gun-point to get food. Even arms procurement was affected. The decline of some 10% in 1998 resulted from resource constraints, not central policy decisions, but it contributed to the army's increasing problem of antiquated or obsolete weapons. The deterioration in North Korean conventional military capabilities increasingly called into question Pyongyang's strategy of rapidly overrunning South Korea and achieving unification on North Korean terms before US reinforcements arrive.

Being Offensive in Defence

Perhaps linked to this deteriorating situation, the belligerence of North Korean rhetoric increased significantly. The New Year's Day joint editorial, for example, urged that the army be built-up into 'death-defying ranks' and 'accomplish the historic cause' of national unification if 'the US war maniacs and the South Korean puppets dare to provoke us'. On 20 April 1998, the party's Central Committee and Central Military Commission issued a joint statement calling on the people to 'become heroic human bombs and suicide squads' and 'mercilessly annihilate the enemies'. On 8 December, a senior North Korean general, with almost biblical wrath, warned that Pyongyang 'will let loose its pent-up anger and shower thunderbolts of revenge upon the enemies like an angry tiger'.

Worrisome rhetoric aside, three military developments dominated events on the ground. The first was Pyongyang's repeated attempts at armed infiltration and other paramilitary operations in South Korea. On 22 June, for example, a North Korean submarine with nine dead crew and espionage agents aboard was caught off the South Korean coast. On 12 July, the remains of an armed North Korean agent were found on an east-coast beach. On 20 November, another North Korean boat, capable of carrying four or five agents, intruded into the Kanghwa-do area of South Korea, but eluded capture. On 17 December, the South Korean navy discovered – and this time sank – yet another North Korean spy vessel trying to infiltrate the southern coastal region. Even more striking than the frequency of these actions was their audacity, if not stupidity. For example, less than three weeks separated the 22 June and 12 July incidents, which were both along the same route. The 20 November event took place when South Korean forces had been placed on alert due to US President Bill Clinton's visit to Seoul.

The second important military development in 1998 was North Korea's unannounced launch of a long-range ballistic missile on 31 August. Pyongyang later claimed this had 'successfully' put a satellite into orbit, but it was widely believed to be a test of North Korea's new *Taepodong* 1 missile. Either way, the launch demonstrated greater North Korean capability to develop the solid fuel required for propelling a multi-staged rocket than had generally been appreciated. It constituted a significant step towards the development of an intercontinental ballistic missile. This highlighted the vulnerability of Japan, and even parts of the US, to future North Korean missile attacks and set off alarms in both countries. Reports at the end of the year that North Korea was building at least two new launch facilities for this missile indicate the high priority Pyongyang attaches to its missile programme, not only as a hard currency earner (mainly from its shorter-range missiles) but also as a political lever, particularly after the strong international reaction to the August test.

The third military development of the year was emerging evidence that North Korea was still actively involved in a hidden nuclear weapon programme in contravention of the 1994 'Agreed Framework' between North Korea and the US. The evidence, made public following a classified Ccngressional briefing with US Secretary of State Madeleine Albright on 4 August 1998, focused on a huge underground facility north-east of Yongbyon, that Western analysts believe is intended to house a reactor capable of making weapon-grade plutonium. But a number of other underground sites have also been identified as components of an ongoing nuclear weapon programme, including facilities that have tested high-explosive lenses used to detonate nuclear devices. Despite repeated US efforts, North Korea refused throughout 1998 to allow unconditional inspections of these underground complexes; it first asked for $300m to allow inspection. Further negotiations in early 1999, however, have apparently focused on an undeclared deal in which Pyongyang would allow inspection in exchange for some 400,000 tons of food from the US, but the two would not be publicly linked. In early March, it was reported that the two countries had finally reached an agreement. The US would supply more than 500,000 tons of food aid through the WFP, as it had in 1998, and Pyongyang dropped its insistence on linkage while allowing US inspection of the underground site.

Two additional developments deepened Western concerns about these nuclear activities. One was North Korea's continuing refusal to cooperate with the International Atomic Energy Agency (IAEA) to resolve doubts about its past plutonium production. As the IAEA made clear in a public report on 14 November 1998, the North Korean regime refused to accept radiological monitoring and other measurements at the Yongbyon reprocessing plant that would help determine its past plutonium production. North Korea also refused to guarantee the preservation of information vital to confirming North Korea's compliance with its obligations to the IAEA and under the Nuclear Non-Proliferation Treaty. The other development was a continuing North Korean effort to produce and deploy chemical weapons. The country not only has factories capable of producing an estimated 1,500 tons of chemical agents; but has also formed chemical warfare platoons at each regiment level and trained them to use these weapons in wartime. The decline in North Korea's conventional capabilities may lead Pyongyang to believe that weapons of mass destruction (WMD) should play a greater role in its military strategy.

South Korea: Making the Most of the 'IMF Era'

Kim Dae Jung's inauguration as president in February 1998 was a historic event for South Korea. Not only did it represent the first transfer of power to the political opposition in the country's history, but it also brought to the top of the power structure a man who had struggled and campaigned against South Korea's authoritarian system for more than a quarter of a century. Unfortunately, Kim captured his long-sought prize at a time when Asia's financial crisis had just exploded in South Korea. With a run on the currency and most financial institutions on the verge of bankruptcy, the government was forced to turn to the International Monetary Fund (IMF) for a $57bn bailout package only two weeks before the presidential elections on 18 December 1997. Severe economic conditions thereafter ensured that Kim's primary preoccupation in his first year in office would be the state of the economy.

The legitimacy of this preoccupation was unassailable. In the first six months of 1998, South Korea's real GDP declined by 5.3% compared with the same period in 1997 (real GDP for the year as a whole declined by over 6%). The Korean *won* sank from around 800 to the dollar in the autumn of 1997 to around 1,700 by the beginning of 1998. Unemployment, which had averaged only 3.2% from 1980 to 1997, shot up to 5.9% by February 1998 as more than 10,000 companies became insolvent. By the end of the year, banks alone had dismissed some 39,000 people – roughly 10% of South Korea's entire pool of bankers – with the country's total unemployment rate reaching 6.8% and still rising. All this reflected a range of fundamental problems, including enormous over-capacity, a near-bankrupt banking sector, and mountains of private sector debt.

Honouring his commitment as president-elect to implement the IMF-sponsored programme, Kim moved systematically after his inauguration on 24 February 1998 to reform and restructure the South Korean economy. In April the government formed the Financial Supervisory Commission (FSC) to regulate and oversee this process. By the end of the year, the FSC had shut down roughly 100 financial institutions and more than 50 non-competitive corporations. Among the financial institutions forcibly closed were five commercial banks, 16 merchant banks and five securities houses. Other major banks were either merged or sold off to foreigners. Among the corporations liquidated were 20 subsidiaries of South Korea's five large business conglomerates (*chaebol*), with most of the rest associated with second-tier business groups known to be in trouble. 'Workout plans' were approved for more than 30 other companies, designed to reduce their heavy debt leverage and improve standards of corporate governance.

Reforming and restructuring the *chaebol* themselves proved to be much more difficult. A number of the smaller conglomerates like Doosan moved to maintain liquidity by selling off both core and non-core businesses. But the 'Big Five' (Hyundai, Samsung, Daewoo, LG and SK) strongly resisted reform pressures. This was particularly true of the government's so-called 'Big Deal', a plan requiring the five largest *chaebol* to swap businesses in such a way that each would end up with its own clearly defined core competence. While all of the 'Big Five' accepted the need for some rationalisation, they resisted both the jettisoning of what they considered to be critical business areas and the motivating rationale that each sector should have its own clear leader.

Nevertheless, progress was made. In January 1998, most of the large *chaebol* agreed on a set of changes – including banning new cross-debt guarantees, adopting consolidated financial systems and appointing outside directors – designed to improve transparency, accountability, and corporate governance. In September, the 'Big Five' agreed to pool their weaker companies in seven industries, ranging from petrochemicals and oil refining to aerospace and semiconductors, into new joint ventures. In early December, they announced their creditor bank-approved reform programmes.

These involve a sweeping reorganisation of each group around three to five core companies; lowering their debt-to-equity ratios to under 200% by the end of 1999; and a substantial reduction (of about 40%) in the number of their subsidiaries. This progress will not transform the *chaebol* overnight – indeed, there are still substantial hurdles to overcome, raised by both big business, which remains resistant to reform, and labour, which will bear much of the fallout, before even the first package of measures is fully implemented. Nevertheless, the reform programmes reflect the sea change that has taken place in South Korea and provide a start towards making the *chaebol* a more streamlined, competitive force in the economy.

South Korea also took important steps to liberalise its capital markets, eliminating ceilings on foreign portfolio investment in the equity, bond and money markets, liberalising regulations on hostile takeovers and foreign ownership of land and opening most industries to foreign direct investment. Foreign-exchange transactions and investment flows were fully liberalised. The government bolstered these measures with vigorous encouragement of overseas investors and introduced new tax incentives and subsidies to attract them. These efforts paid off. Whereas foreign investment decreased by 73% in the first quarter of 1998, it rapidly revived from May onwards. By the end of the year, new foreign investment totalled $8.9bn – accounting for 36% of total direct foreign investment in South Korea between 1962 and 1997. In December 1998 alone, some $2bn was invested in the country, the highest monthly figure on record.

Few believe that South Korea is out of the woods. Economic hardship is pervasive as unemployment continues to climb to potentially explosive levels, while the country remains vulnerable to external economic forces beyond its control. A complete economic restructuring that establishes a new foundation for long-term growth will take years to accomplish. However, Seoul has come a long way. By the end of the year, foreign currency reserves had reached a record level. The exchange rate had stabilised. Industrial output resumed growth, with a 4.7% rise in December, although there was a 7% decline over the year as a whole. Many economists predict a return to growth – albeit a relatively low 1–2% – in 1999. Symbolising this progress, South Korea repaid its $2.8bn debt to the IMF in December. In short, as 1999 dawned, there were grounds for hope.

Politics Bubbling on a Back Burner

Political change during the year was far less dramatic, despite the historic transfer of power from the traditional conservative élite to the opposition. The government's preoccupation with the economy, coupled with the minority status of Kim's ruling party, the National Congress for New Politics (NCNP), largely kept political reform off the policy agenda. Instead, there was political stalemate for much of the year – symbolised by the refusal of the Grand National Party (GNP), now in opposition, to approve Kim's appointment of his Prime Minister Kim Jong Pil for over six months – and bitter confrontation between the parties.

Bad relations between the rival parties were inflamed by a number of issues: Kim's open effort to secure a governing majority in the National Assembly by inducing members of the GNP to join the NCNP; an investigation launched by the government into charges that the GNP had illegally raised money from big business concerns in the December election; and arrests of several GNP supporters on charges of plotting to influence the election by staging a border shoot-out with North Korea. Policy disagreements between the ruling coalition partners, the NCNP and United Liberal Democrats (ULD), further hindered progress on a reform agenda.

The significant development during the year was, therefore, not political reform but a shift in the ruling élite's social and ideological centre of gravity. With the inauguration of President Kim, new Korean leaders came to the fore with far more liberal ideas about national policy than their predecessors. Many were either former dissidents themselves or liberal scholars long isolated in academia. Others hail from the Cholla area, Kim's home territory, and have long perceived themselves to be the target of official discrimination. These new leaders now occupy important positions in almost all parts of the South Korean establishment, including both government and media. Their prominence has implications not only for internal reform but also for South Korean foreign policies, as could be seen in the government's decision to lift the ban on Japanese cultural imports, a step long resisted by the traditional conservative élite.

Pyongyang has Trouble Taking 'Yes' for an Answer

As in most things involving North Korea in 1998, there was no fundamental change in relations between the two Koreas, but there were a number of important developments. Not surprisingly, most were the result of new policies in Seoul. Kim Dae Jung had long proposed increased efforts at North–South reconciliation. In the face of South Korea's severe economic crisis, he made clear that achieving peaceful coexistence and cooperation – rather than achieving unification – would be his top priority.

Accordingly, he dropped all reference to 'unification policy' and talked instead of a more general 'policy towards the North'. More importantly, he explicitly ruled out 'absorbing' North Korea as a goal of South Korean policy. The administration dubbed the new efforts to engage North Korea in expanded interaction its 'sunshine' policy, with equal emphasis on the principles of 'separating economics from politics' and 'flexible reciprocity'. By the beginning of 1999, engaging the North had become a central plank of South Korea's foreign policy.

Whether it was Seoul's new policy, or the pressure of malnutrition and economic collapse on Pyongyang, there has been some small progress towards greater interaction between the two governments. During 1998, there was a formal bilateral meeting between the two sides – the first in four years. The talks, held in Beijing on 11–14 April 1998, were to discuss fertiliser aid to Pyongyang (the North Korean goal) and more broadly based improvement in relations (the South Korean objective). However, Pyongyang rejected Seoul's insistence that North Korea reciprocate South Korean 'humanitarian' fertiliser aid by allowing equally 'humanitarian' visits of families separated since the Korean War. The talks collapsed without an agreement on either objective. So much for reciprocity.

Despite this failure, North Korea proposed on 3 February 1999 that high-level North–South political talks be held during the latter part of the year. Although it attached, as always, preconditions which South Korea will not accept, its proposed agenda contained such items as drafting measures to implement the North–South Basic Agreement, North–South exchange and cooperation and the issue of separated families. These issues are also part of the new administration's hope that the North will agree to exchange official envoys to discuss a broader improvement in North–South relations, an item also on Seoul's agenda, so South Korea will try hard to get the talks going while not agreeing to the North's preconditions.

Although relations between the two governments fared poorly in 1998, non-government interaction improved. The most dramatic development was the initiation of a regular cruise trip taking South Korean tourists to North Korea's Mount Kumgang, an area famous for its scenic beauty. The first of these, on 18 November 1998, was highly restricted but nonetheless successful, providing South Koreans with their first chance to visit North Korea legally as tourists since the two governments were established on the peninsula in 1948. Estimates that North Korea might earn up to $1.5bn from this highly controlled tourist project – nearly twice its total export earnings in 1997 – did little to diminish the sense of astonishment provoked by pictures of South Korean tourists climbing North Korean mountains.

South Korean businessmen also continued actively to explore new investments in North Korea, spurred by the government's emphasis on separating economics from politics and loosening restrictions on inter-Korean contacts. Although there were no major breakthroughs in 1998, South Korea's private sector remains interested in exploiting North Korea's cheap labour and abundant mineral resources and is developing a range of plans for future joint ventures. On the North Korean side, Kim Jong Il's surprise meeting with Chung Ju Yung, the founder of South Korea's Hyundai conglomerate, on 30 October 1998, made clear Kim's personal support for the Mount Kumgang project. It also signalled the regime's new openness towards private ventures with South Korean businessmen as a way to alleviate its economic crisis. The question is whether Pyongyang's reluctance to deal with the South Korean government and continued efforts to infiltrate and subvert South Korean society will undermine this development before it can bear fruit.

Despite the series of provocative North Korean military incursions, South Korea adhered to its 'sunshine' policy throughout the year. Indeed, on 15 August 1998, Kim publicly stressed his determination to pursue inter-Korean exchanges despite the June and July infiltration incidents. He reiterated this commitment on 21 November, the day after another submarine incursion, during his summit talks with Clinton.

From the beginning , however, there has been strong opposition to the government's policy from South Korean conservatives who consider it both 'weak' and ineffectual. Repeated North Korean military provocation only strengthened the opposition, as did the North Korean missile test and apparently ongoing nuclear development. Government leaders responded by increasing their declaratory emphasis on national security, but they did not alter their commitment to engagement. On the contrary, they emphasised that reacting to each and every North Korean action by changing course would simply produce an inconsistent policy, and held up the Mount Kumgang trips as evidence that their policy was working. Whether they can continue to maintain this position in the face of continued North Korean belligerence and militancy remains to be seen.

The two principal multilateral fora involving direct North–South interactions, the Korean Peninsula Energy Development Organisation (KEDO) and the so-called 'Four Party Talks', also struggled during the year. KEDO, the international consortium formed to construct light-water reactors for North Korea in exchange for Pyongyang freezing its nuclear programme under the 1994 Agreed Framework, ran into protracted difficulties with funding in 1998. Consortium members – South Korea, Japan, the European Union and the US – did not reach formal agreement on cost sharing until 9 November 1998, mainly because Japan refused to commit itself following the August 1998 North Korean missile test. Although the US does not contribute financially to the light-water reactor project, KEDO was also plagued by the Clinton administration's difficulty in securing congressional funding for the 500,000 tons of heavy oil the US is committed to provide each year until the reactors are built. The host of restrictions attached to the ultimate congressional approval on 15 October 1998 makes future disbursement of this funding contingent on satisfactory resolution of the underground site and missile issues. Not surprisingly, North Korea's reaction to these developments was to threaten to abrogate the Agreed Framework and overtly resume its nuclear programme.

Such North Korean bombast makes it more difficult to gain US congressional support for the present US policy on North Korea and its approval for necessary future funding. In an effort to buttress the administration's position, Clinton appointed the highly respected former Defense Secretary William Perry as his North Korean policy coordinator on 12 November 1998. Perry has been reviewing past policies and is expected to produce a report, which may appear in early summer, offering alternatives to overall US policy towards North Korea.

The Four Party Talks also laboured for little return. First proposed by South Korea and the US in 1996 as a possible means of reaching a peace settlement, and also involving China, the talks were finally agreed to by North Korea in a preliminary meeting in December 1997. The first round of substantive talks was finally held on 16–20 March 1998 in Geneva. After nearly collapsing over North Korean objections to the seating arrangements, the long-awaited talks ultimately broke down over North Korea's insistence that the principal agenda items should be withdrawal of US troops from South Korea and a separate bilateral treaty between North Korea and the US.

The second round of substantive talks on 21 October 1998 was marginally more successful. While none of the fundamental issues was resolved, the four sides reached procedural agreement on setting up two sub-committees, one dealing with reducing tension and the other with establishing a peaceful regime, to explore these issues further. North Korea's continued insistence on US troop withdrawal and a bilateral peace treaty, coupled with the unresolved issue of North Korea's underground facilities, clearly indicated that the third round of substantive talks, scheduled for January 1999, had little chance of success, and they duly proved a damp squib.

The Active and the Passive

Rarely has a single year presented such sharply contrasting performances by rival countries under stress. South Korea opted for comprehensive reform and restructuring to deal with its economic crisis, instituting radical internal change and opening itself further to outside interactions. It had a busy diplomatic year, whose overarching goals were to attract foreign investors, secure support for the new policy of engaging the North, and position South Korea as one of the leading democracies in Asia. Nevertheless, reflecting its awareness that the fundamental answers to South Korea's problems are at home, the government changed not only structures and processes but South Korean attitudes as well.

The North Korean regime, on the other hand, made clear it could not risk the political consequences of major economic change. It contented itself instead with rearranging government institutions and personnel in an effort to guarantee the existing system's preservation. With a further increase in the military's role and policy options dwindling rapidly, the regime increasingly relied on threats and outright extortion to ensure its political survival. Its efforts to engage with the wider world were conspicuous by their absence. Thus, as the gap widened between North and South Korea, it became ever more certain that reunification, when it comes, will be on the South's terms.

●

The Year It Came Unstuck in South-east Asia

After the financial implosion came the economic, social and political fall-out. The frenzy that gripped currency and stock markets in South-east Asia in the second half of 1997 and the first quarter of 1998 has abated. Currencies have stabilised, at least in comparison with the wild oscillations they suffered for months after Thailand devalued its currency, the *baht*, in July 1997. Stock markets, while still valued at a fraction of their capitalisation when the long regional boom reached its zenith in 1994–96, have rebounded from their floors. Indeed, in some months, their indices have been among the world's best-performing.

Crisis-watchers have moved to other emerging markets: to Russia, which, in effect, defaulted on its domestic government debt in August 1998; and to Brazil, the world's ninth-largest economy, which, in January 1999, was forced to follow Thailand, Indonesia, the Philippines, South Korea and Russia and allow its currency, the *real*, to float, and sink. Many spoke, rather glibly, of South-east Asia having 'hit bottom', and of its showing 'signs of recovery'.

But this represents a very narrow view of 'recovery' – that of the international investor rather than the resident citizen. The effects of the financial crises are still rippling through the 'real' economies, where people work – or try to – and make their livings, or, in the case of a growing number of people, do not. A corollary of this is that the domestic social and political implications of the economic downturn have not been fully worked through. In a number of countries – Thailand, the Philippines, Indonesia and, in North-east Asia, South Korea – financial collapse has been accompanied by, and has partly caused, political change. But in all of them, change has been confined to a shuffle of the ruling élite. The perceived rottenness of those élites as a whole, and of the systems which sustained them, has not yet led to the broader upheaval that might be expected. Similarly, the diplomatic and strategic consequences of the crash have only been in evidence in embryo. They may well grow into far stronger forces for change than at present seems imaginable.

Suharto's Long Shadow

In one sense, they have confounded expectations of continuity. On 11 March 1998, when President Suharto of Indonesia was 're-elected' by a tame assembly to his seventh term of office, it seemed inconceivable that he would be forced to resign just two months later. But the end of his rule, in a hastily arranged television broadcast on 21 May, marked the end of an era for more than just his own country, which he had ruled for 32 years. First, it showed the extent to which economic crisis could unravel even the most enduring of political arrangements. Second, it significantly diminished Indonesia's ability to exercise an effective, if discreet, leadership role in the region. Third, the potential changes it unleashed in Indonesia itself threatened to challenge regional cohesion and the ideological underpinnings of a dominant authoritarian culture – legitimised as so-called 'Asian values'. Even more fundamentally, Suharto's downfall marked the latest stage of regional adaptation to the post-Cold War age. Suharto was the last national leader to survive from the mid-1960s, when, at the height of the American war in Vietnam, the present regional order was put in place.

Unease at the first stirring of plural political life after the long slumber of Suharto's rule was felt across the region. Indonesia's sheer size – 200 million people spread across more than 17,000 islands – dwarfs its neighbours. Just as smoke from Indonesia's forest fires has periodically smothered and poisoned huge tracts of neighbouring states, so the country's hazy political future and economic collapse cast a pall far beyond its borders. The Suharto dictatorship was for so long a defining feature of the political and strategic landscape, that without it there are no trustworthy maps.

There had been nightmares about the transition from Suharto for years. The worst fears – that his rule might end, as it began, in a bloodbath costing hundreds of thousands of lives – have so far not been realised, though that is not to ignore the terrible violence endured by the ethnic Chinese minority in 1998. There are still worries that the region might become again the volatile, dangerous place it was in the early 1960s, when Suharto's predecessor, Sukarno, engaged in 'confrontation' with his neighbours. The regional club, the Association of South East Asian Nations (ASEAN), was founded in Bangkok in August 1967 precisely in order to enmesh Indonesia in a web of peaceful, cooperative links with the region. The comparison with the European Union's role in containing Germany is often made. With respect to Indonesia, it has worked. But like Gulliver, waking up to find himself bound in Lilliputian threads, Indonesia still has the potential to wreck the neighbourhood.

For the time being, the giant is forced into introversion by economic devastation and political uncertainty. After growing at an average of more than 6% a year for three decades, gross domestic product (GDP) shrank by 14% in 1998. Currency 'stability' for the Indonesian *rupiah* came in the range of 7,000–9,000 against the US dollar, a devaluation of roughly 65–75% from pre-crisis levels. The prices of many imported goods have moved beyond the reach of many, and it turned out that a large number of basic necessities were, ultimately, imported, despite Suharto's boasts of having achieved self-sufficiency in food. Not only did the damage to harvests in 1998 caused by the *el Niño* effect invalidate that boast in respect of its key element, rice, but also millions of chickens were slaughtered because of the cost of imported feed; *tempe*, a staple for many, became a luxury because it was often made from imported soybeans. Based on inadequate statistics, the government calculated that the number of people living in poverty had risen to 79m, nearly 40% of the population.

In a country where mob violence is something of a tradition, such distress is a dangerous ingredient to add to an already explosive mixture of religious and ethnic tension and political confusion. Throughout the country, but most visibly in Jakarta in May and again in November 1998, ugly outbreaks of vandalism, arson, looting, pillage, rape and murder have shattered the confidence of many ethnic Chinese business-people. The Chinese, who make up only about 4% of the population, dominate not just the thin ranks of the super-rich tycoons, but the distribution network for many commodities. By the middle of 1998, for example, it was said that more than half Indonesia's lorries were off the road because of the difficulty of securing spare parts.

The political transition remains a fragile process. Multi-party elections are planned for June 1999, followed in November by voting for a President in a rejuvenated version of the assembly which for years voted Suharto back into office because that was what he told it to do. The odds in such a process still seem stacked in favour of the present incumbent, Baharuddin Yusuf Habibie, should he, as seems likely, decide to try to stay on. *Golkar*, the party of the bureaucracy and, until 1998, Suharto's political vehicle, still has a nationwide network. So does an even more important national institution, ABRI, the armed forces. However, if the elections approach even a modicum of 'freedom and fairness', then the opposition stands a good chance of taking office. As during Indonesia's last brush with pluralism, in the 1950s, it is splintered into a plethora of tiny parties (more than 130 had registered by January 1999). Of these, however, three have particular significance, because, unlike the others, they command some-thing approaching a national constituency. One, the National Mandate Party is led by Amien Rais, the most vocal critic of Suharto's rule in its dying days, and formerly the head of *Muhammadiyah*, a Muslim social organisation. The head of an even bigger, 34m-strong, Muslim group, *Nahdlatul Ulama*, Abdurrahman Wahid, may also harbour presidential ambitions. Certainly, Megawati Sukarnoputri, Sukarno's daughter, who heads the Indonesian National Party, does. Her old friendship with Wahid could create an alliance that might even be capable of winning an overall majority.

What sort of polity any of these leaders might run is unknowable. As in so many other political systems in transition, politics is still defined by hostility to the old regime, with which Habibie, despite his many breaks with the past, is still identified. (He was a lifelong protégé of Suharto, who installed him as vice-president in March 1998, partly, it appeared, because he did not believe he was a credible successor.) But in the region there are three main concerns about the turbulent period before, during and after the elections.

First, the country might descend into chaos, and even break up. One of Suharto's greatest achievements was to persuade large numbers of people that Indonesia was ungovernable by anybody else. Without his firm hand, according to the Suharto myth, the huge young country would disintegrate in a maelstrom of communal violence. Anarchy would spill out from Indonesia's borders in a tide of boat people fleeing for Malaysia, Singapore and Australia. Pirates would take to the high seas, jeopardising sea-lanes vital to Japan, Taiwan and South Korea, as well as to Indonesia's immediate neighbours.

Parts of Indonesia might secede. In East Timor, which was invaded by Indonesia in December 1975, Portugal, the former colonial ruler, is still recognised by the UN as the administering power. The independence movement there took heart from Suharto's downfall, and won from Habibie a promise of greater autonomy, but at first no concession on what had become its central demand – a referendum on East Timor's future. However, on 27 January 1999, members of Habibie's cabinet made an astonishing about-turn, saying that, after the elections, if East Timorese were not satisfied with autonomy, they could 'separate' from Indonesia. The brutal Indonesian record in the territory has left so deep a legacy of distrust that many were reluctant to take the promise at face value. In particular, it seemed to conflict with the escalating violence on the ground, between pro-independence and 'pro-integration' Timorese, armed and incited by the Indonesian army. The suspicion was that the army was looking for a pretext to thwart autonomy and secession (just as, in 1975, an incipient civil war provided part of the justification for invasion). Equally likely, however, was that the army, locally, was fighting its own war, while the central government had decided that the diplomatic and military costs of suppressing low-level rebellion were no longer justified.

That, in turn, implies that one of the main arguments for clinging on to East Timor – that it might start a secessionist chain reaction across the archipelago – was no longer believed. Certainly, East Timor's different history has always made it unique. But there is no shortage elsewhere of resentment at what is seen as domination from the most populous island, Java. There are armed movements in both Irian Jaya and Aceh, in Northern Sumatra. Just as alarming are the grumbles of resource-rich provinces about the disproportionate share of regional wealth taken by the central government. Should the economy continue to languish, and disorder reach anarchic proportions, there will be calls for, at the least, a more federal structure of government from, for instance, Riau, in Sumatra, East Kalimantan, the Christian spice islands of the Moluccas, and even parts of Habibie's home island of Sulawesi. Despite the considerable achievements made in forging a sense of national identity, Indonesia is a new and to some extent artificial country, overlaid on a wide range of diverse cultural and ethnic traditions.

A second possibility that causes regional concern is the emergence of a more stridently Islamic form of government. Many of the new political parties appeal directly to religious and ethnic sensibilities. Islam is officially the religion of some 88% of the population, but many of the Chinese, for example, are Buddhists or Christians. Much mob violence has been directed at churches as well as at shops and store-houses. The danger is mitigated by the diversity of Indonesian Islam, by its traditional tolerance and absorption of other local belief systems, and by the ideas of the two most important Muslim leaders, Rais and Wahid. Rais worries many non-Muslims because of his past writings about the 'Islamic brotherhood', but he resigned from the leadership of *Muhammadiyah* to form his own political party which has a secular platform. For his part, Wahid has made it his life's work to halt a perceived drift towards sectarian politics, and chaired a 'democracy forum' set up partly to work towards precisely that end. This worries, in particular, Indonesia's ethnically and religiously diverse neighbours, Singapore and Malaysia. But, even in the (largely Christian) Philippines and (Buddhist) Thailand, there are concerns about the impact on Muslim minorities.

Either of the above outcomes might alarm the army, which is factionalised and demoralised by the opprobrium it has attracted as past atrocities in Aceh have come to light, and as more is learned about the shameful role some units played in the unrest of 1998. But its commander, General Wiranto, belongs to a tradition which saw ABRI as the guardian of both national unity, and of *'pancasila'* – the set of principles enunciated by Sukarno, and including a tolerance of minority religions. Just as Suharto intervened in 1965–66, with the support of even some liberal students, so might chaos again prove the midwife of military rule. That, however, is also unlikely; Indonesia is dependent on foreign aid, and particularly the International Monetary Fund and its largest shareholders, the United States and Europe, which are unlikely to welcome a military putsch.

The Bright Side

But it is at least possible that Indonesia will manage to avoid anarchy, Islamisation or a renewed military dictatorship, and that the elections will be held and result in a government with at least a plausible claim to popular legitimacy. The process could be, at best, messy, and at worst extremely violent, but it does hold out some hope of a more participatory style of government. For ASEAN, that too would be unsettling. Although his diplomatic style was never to lead from the front, Suharto in many ways set the tone for ASEAN. Other leaders – Mahathir Mohamad of Malaysia and Lee Kuan Yew, now 'senior minister' of Singapore – were more articulate spokesmen for 'Asian values'. But Suharto's success in delivering political stability and high rates of economic growth for so long was the greatest advertisement for the alleged benefits of 'discipline' over 'democracy'. The two ASEAN countries which have adopted the most raucous and unruly forms of electoral democracy – Thailand and the Philippines – were regarded as aberrations. Indeed, the Philippines was seen as a hopeless case, its economic potential throttled by its perverse pursuit of pluralism. This bias towards strong, intolerant government has grown as ASEAN expanded, from its original 'core' membership of five to include five authoritarian states (Brunei in January 1984, Vietnam in July 1995, Myanmar and Laos in July 1997, and, to join in 1999, Cambodia).

Now that trend is in reverse. The 'stability' of Suharto's Indonesia has proved illusory, but the Philippines is withstanding the slump better than most. In 1998, there was even a relatively peaceful transfer of power from one democratically elected Filipino president to another. The newcomer, Joseph Estrada, is a walking model of the perceived evils of populism – he owes his electoral majority to his past as a film-star more than to any technocratic expertise. But he easily won the election held on 11 May, winning 46.4% of the vote to 17.1% for José de Venecia, former President Fidel Ramos' anointed candidate. The Filipino élite, once aghast at the prospect of an Estrada presidency, was quick to jump on the bandwagon of a man who at least has a popular mandate. Meanwhile Thailand, while hardly a model of chastened economic rectitude and political liberalism (though, *pour encourager les autres,* it is often advertised as such by the international financial community), has also shown a certain political solidity. Rumours of impending military coups, which used to circulate monthly, are now rarely heard.

A more liberal Indonesia would mark a decisive shift in ASEAN's centre of political gravity. Opposition politicians and activists are delighted by the possibilities. 'Asian values', which were claimed to place a higher price on family ties, social stability and deference to authority than does decadent Western liberalism, have been made to seem mythical. In truth, they always were: invented in Singapore precisely because it was the most westernised country in the region. Vietnamese, Thais, Indonesians and Filipinos, more securely rooted in their own cultural traditions, were less bothered about the search for a regional identity.

The other great international advocate of 'Asian values', Malaysian Prime Minister Mahathir Mohamad, has succeeded Suharto as ASEAN's longest-serving leader, with 17 years in power behind him. His repeated attacks on the 'new colonialists' whom he blames for the region's financial woes, make him seem a dinosaur to some outside observers. He has also lost much middle-class and grass-roots support at home through the bizarre legal persecution of Anwar Ibrahim, who, until 20 September 1998, when he was sacked and arrested, was Mahathir's deputy, finance minister and presumed heir. Anwar, accused of sodomy (charges which were set aside in January) and of tampering with the legal system to cover-up his alleged sexual misdemeanours, which would be crimes under Malaysian law, had disagreed with Mahathir over economic policy. He had also appeared poised to challenge him for leadership of the dominant political party, the United Malays National Organisation. So whatever the merits of the charges against him, many see his legal travails as a punishment for political ambition.

The ASEAN Way Under Threat

The outcome of the Malaysian political drama has regional dimensions. Alone in the region, Malaysia has not responded to financial turmoil by embracing the 'Washington orthodoxy' of neo-liberal economic reform. Rather, at the same time as he sacked Anwar, Mahathir imposed strict exchange controls, to insulate Malaysia from the tidal flows of global capital, which he blamed for destabilising an otherwise sound economy. If Mahathir wins through, and recovery remains elusive elsewhere, the many people in Thailand, Indonesia and the Philippines who are sceptical about the benefits of unfettered 'globalisation' will be encouraged. Politicians will be increasingly tempted to appeal to the nerve of anti-Western nationalism that has been touched by recent economic hardship.

But also, while Mahathir remains in power, the old ways of doing things in ASEAN are likely to survive recent threats. These centre on its 'core principle' of 'non-interference' in fellow members' internal affairs. This came under threat from two events in particular. The accession of Myanmar, with its thuggish, intolerant regime, caused strains between ASEAN on the one hand and Europe and the US on the other. And the aftermath of the bloody coup in Cambodia in July 1997 also raised questions about whether ASEAN, given its principles, could apply any minimum criteria for the behaviour of member governments. Cambodia's accession to ASEAN in 1997 was delayed. Even the election held on 26 July 1998, which was easily won by the perpetrator of the coup, Hun Sen (as was predictable given his party's dominance of the machinery of govern-ment, the media and official intimidation), did not lead to immediate accession. This was despite the fact that, following the death on 15 April 1998 of their genocidal leader Pol Pot, and a series of subsequent defections, the *Khmers Rouges* seemed finally to have lost their long jungle campaign against annihilation.

At ASEAN's annual foreign ministers' meeting in Manila from 20–29 July 1998, there was unprecedented debate about the principle of non-interference. Thai Foreign Minister, Surin Pitsuwan, whose country has to bear the burden of refugees from tyranny in Myanmar and sporadic internal strife in Cambodia, led the assault on the old orthodoxy, with the support of his Filipino counterpart, Domingo Siazon. They found them-selves in an isolated minority. Since then, however, even Indonesia has expressed unease about, for example, the treatment of Anwar Ibrahim. Singapore, for its part, does not want to see ASEAN's image reduced to that of a group of dictators and their apologists. Should Mahathir be succeeded by a less virulent nationalist, it is conceivable that all five of ASEAN's founder members might soon support a more robust diplomatic style.

Already, intra-regional relations have been characterised by a new tetchiness. Malaysia and Singapore have squabbled over everything from the interest paid by Singaporean banks on deposits to the location of a Malaysian customs and immigration post. Estrada has complained about Malaysia's treatment of 'my friend Anwar'. So, privately, has Habibie. Vietnam's loyalty to Cambodia's Hun Sen and his desire for accession to ASEAN led to an embarrassing muddle at the group's summit in Hanoi on 15–16 December 1998, when different countries gave different interpreta-tions of Cambodia's membership status. Exasperation with Myanmar's intransigence towards its domestic opposition was widely felt, and more loudly voiced.

None of this amounts to a serious challenge to ASEAN's existence. Its greatest achievement – that war between its member countries seems inconceivable – still holds. But 1998 was perhaps the first year since the organisation's founding when the ASEAN project seemed to have gone into reverse. While never harbouring dreams so ambitious as those of the

European Union, ASEAN has nevertheless worked towards a steady enhancement of lower-level integration, the habit of dialogue and the building of institutional processes that, at a glacial pace, foster a regional identity. That process has stuttered badly. The strategic worry this poses for the architects of regional cooperation is that it leaves South-east Asia vulnerable to attempts by other powers to exert greater influence. When, in November 1998 and again in January 1999, tension flared up between the Philippines and China over Mischief Reef, part of the disputed chain of Spratly Islands (where Brunei, Malaysia, Taiwan and Vietnam also have claims), it seemed to some a foretaste of struggles to come. China has seemed happy not to pursue its claims in what it calls the South China Sea in more than a piecemeal and pragmatic way, by sending its ships, sailors and oil-rigs into disputed waters; but nor have ASEAN countries found China sincere in seeking a negotiated settlement. Rather, it has seemed to be biding its time until it became feasible to adopt a tougher approach to a jurisdictional ambition which would give it control over waters surrounded by South-east Asian countries and used by a quarter of the world's shipping. The strategic danger of economic collapse, political upheaval and intra-regional bickering in South-east Asia is the invitation they provided to opportunistic efforts to profit from the disarray.

●

South Asia: An Explosive Mixture?

The nuclear weapon tests conducted by India and Pakistan in the spring of 1998 changed their status from nuclear-threshold to declared nuclear weapons states, and sent a shiver of nuclear fear through the international community. The perennial antagonists have fought three wars since they gained independence in 1947. Their disagreements over Kashmir, in particular, have kept tensions in the region at a constant boil. The tests, which actually changed little because it has been recognised for some time that both countries had the capability, nevertheless sharpened concern that the unresolved antagonism between them could get out of hand. Since the tests, there has been a concerted effort, led by the US, to minimise the effects of the development on the non-proliferation regime. Without showing the least inclination to return to non-nuclear weapons status, both countries are willing to meet this effort half-way, believing that this is the best way to exploit their new status for positive gain.

While both countries have sought to manage the international consequences of their tests, within each country, public discussion has focused primarily on domestic issues. In India, these revolved around the chronic instability of the governing coalition. The government which emerged after the February–March 1998 elections was constantly undermined by its own partners and by Hindu nationalist factions within and outside the coalition. India had already undergone two short-lived experiments in coalition rule during the previous 22 months when the left-leaning United Front (UF) was in power, but the new government had additional handicaps arising from tensions within the dominant *Bharatiya Janata* Party (BJP). Atal Behari Vajpayee, the new prime minister, was perceived as weak and indecisive, and in poor health. A relative moderate within the conservative, Hindu-nationalist BJP, he appeared at odds with party hard-liners, including the Home Minister L. K. Advani. The compromises necessary to keep the governing coalition together were unpopular with more extremist Hindu organisations operating outside parliamentary politics, to which the BJP owed much of its support. Vajpayee's government proved unable to control violence against the Christian community or to buoy up a flagging economy, failings which helped benefit the ailing Congress Party.

In Pakistan, the main preoccupation was concern about the economy, although there was also alarm at Prime Minister Nawaz Sharif's confrontational style, and his undermining of democratic institutions. The prime minister was seen increasingly to favour his own fellow Punjabis over the country's other ethnic groups, especially the *Mohajirs* – Urdu-speakers who migrated to Pakistan after the partition of the subcontinent in 1947. As in 1997, when he was engaged in a series of confrontations with the supreme court and the president, Sharif moved to eliminate potential restraints on his power, confronting the army and the press, and undermining the judiciary by introducing two parallel systems: the *Sharia*, or Islamic legal code, and military courts. Sectarian killings by armed *Shi'ite* and *Sunni* groups continued in Punjab, while the violence worsened dramatically in Karachi, leading to the dismissal of the state government in October.

By virtue of its support for the *Taleban* Islamist militia in Afghanistan, and militants in the Kashmir Valley, Pakistan also came under international scrutiny for its links to Islamic extremist movements, and to international terrorism. The folly of Islamabad's support for Islamic militants like the *Taleban* was already apparent in Punjab, where armed *Sunni* extremist groups have actively targeted Pakistani *Shi'ites* and Iranian diplomats. But the direct influence of the *Taleban* – whose rigid doctrines emerged from *deeni medrassas* (Islamic seminaries) in Karachi and the North-West Frontier Province (NWFP) – also spread. Pakistani disciples of the *Taleban* took control of pockets of the NWFP, imposing their version of Islamic justice.

Pakistan's connections to extremist groups was underscored again on 20 August 1998 when US cruise missiles pounded tented camps near the town of Khost in eastern Afghanistan. Although Washington was targeting the bases of the Saudi renegade, Osama bin Laden, indicted in the US for the bombing of its embassies in East Africa, most of the 30 casualties were Pakistani. Recruited by the *Sunni* extremist groups active in Punjab, they were in Afghanistan to receive military training before being sent to the Kashmir Valley, a network that Pakistan has always tried to conceal. After the failed attempt to eliminate bin Laden, Pakistan faced steady pressure from Washington to persuade the *Taleban* to hand over the Saudi for trial.

Breaking the Taboo

India and Pakistan became the world's newest declared nuclear weapon states in May 1998. On 11 May, less than two months after the installation of the coalition government led by the avowedly pro-nuclear BJP, India carried out three underground nuclear explosions at Pokhran, in the western deserts of Rajasthan – its first since 1974. Two days later, Indian scientists conducted two more test explosions. India was motivated less by feeling threatened by Pakistan than by the perceived threat from Chinese nuclear weapons and missiles; the continuing Chinese support for Pakistan's missile (and perhaps nuclear) programme; and the pressure created by the September 1999 deadline for signing the Comprehensive Test Ban Treaty (CTBT).

Despite intense diplomatic pressure, led by the US and Japan, which sent envoys to Pakistan to plead for restraint, Islamabad conducted its own tests on 28 and 30 May, the culmination of the covert nuclear programme it had been pursuing for two decades at heavily guarded laboratories at Kahuta, near Rawalpindi. Nawaz Sharif's government argued that national security interests obliged Pakistan to match the Indian tests. From Pakistan's point of view, once India led the way, Pakistan had no choice but to follow. But Sharif admitted that comprehensive mandatory US sanctions under the Glenn Amendment would extract a heavy toll on a treasury already struggling to meet repayments on a $32 billion foreign debt.

The tests were almost universally condemned by the international community, and particularly by China. (India had singled out China as the particular source of the threat it was seeking to counter with its nuclear weapons.) The Foreign Ministries of the five permanent members of the UN Security Council drew up a list of specific steps that India and Pakistan must take in the interests of international security, which were adopted and reinforced by the Security Council as a whole in UN Security Council Resolution (UNSCR) 1172. Concerns expressed by the summit of the Non-Aligned Movement and the Association of South-East Asian Nations Regional Forum (ARF) demonstrated a North–South unity of approach. Some countries imposed sanctions on India and Pakistan, mainly in the field of development aid, while the US was obliged by the Glenn Amendment to take firmer action.

After the tests, both countries sunk into a state of wilful denial about the dangers of the changed security scenario, and what it was costing them. In India, politicians insisted that US and Japanese sanctions would have a minimal effect. That fiction was more difficult to maintain in Pakistan, which came close to defaulting on its foreign debt, until the international community relented and the International Monetary Fund (IMF) agreed to a bail out.

Within a month of the tests, however, the Group of Eight (G8) industrial countries recognised that humanitarian aid to both countries should be exempted from sanctions. Further relaxation of the sanction regime followed for Pakistan because of its foreign debt problem. In November, US President Bill Clinton lifted more sanctions, citing 'concrete steps' taken to reduce subcontinental tensions. Domestic debate on the nuclear question in India and Pakistan then focused on the countries' success in rolling back the sanctions.

In the months following the tests, US Deputy Secretary of State Strobe Talbott opened a dialogue with India and Pakistan on moving ahead with the agenda set out in UNSCR 1172. His mission was aimed particularly at securing commitment to sign the CTBT before the September 1999 deadline and to take part in negotiations for the Fissile Material Cut-off Treaty; to cap nuclear weaponisation and missile programmes; and to enter into a meaningful dialogue on South Asian security. New Delhi had parallel discussions with Russia, France and Britain.

These encounters have been conducted quietly and, by late March 1999, had yielded few concrete commitments. However, there were some sketchy indications of what had been happening behind the scenes. India has adopted a nuclear policy which would lead it to maintain a 'minimum deterrent' force while proceeding with a missile development programme that got increased funding in the March 1999 budget. There has been considerable speculation that India planned to test-fire its intermediate-range *Agni* missile, an extended range version of the *Agni*, and *Dhanush*, a 350-km naval missile. All were intended to be armed with nuclear weapons. Other elements of restraint have been an assurance that India would not be the first to use nuclear weapons in conflict; a volunteer moratorium on further testing; and an indication of possible signature of the CTBT.

Conscious of international pressures and no doubt recognising their own interests, Indian and Pakistani diplomats did meet in Islamabad to set out a programme for talks on the Kashmir issue and seven other, less intractable, questions, such as the Siachen Glacier and water resources. Although a further round of talks in New Delhi a month later yielded no apparent progress on any front, the two neighbours appeared committed to continuing the dialogue. The lack of substantive progress was camouflaged by a breakthrough that was almost entirely symbolic: the support by both prime ministers for a bus link between Lahore and New Delhi, the first road link between the two countries. Indian and Pakistani officials carried out trial runs of the bus route in late 1998, and on 20 February 1999 Prime Minister Vajpayee travelled the new route into Pakistan on the first bus, painted in gold. The symbolic meeting between Vajpayee and Nawaz Sharif on that occasion led to agreement in principle on a range of possible confidence building measures, but made little at all, concrete progress. It was far more important for the fact that it took place than for anything that it accomplished.

Desperation Politics

India is believed to have considered a nuclear test in 1995, and then abandoned it, after then Prime Minister P.V. Narasimha Rao was confronted with satellite pictures of preparations at Pokhran by an angry US ambassador. In 1996, the subsequent coalition government reversed India's long-held position and opposed the CTBT. When the BJP came to power, India's nuclear policy was seen as an area of consensus: New Delhi retained its right to 'exercise its nuclear option' in strategic planning against China and Pakistan. It continued to oppose the CTBT and the Nuclear Non-Proliferation Treaty (NPT) as part of a 'nuclear apartheid' regime imposed by the declared nuclear weapon states. Vajpayee promised to set up a national security council to review nuclear and other defence issues.

When that ambiguous posture was destroyed by the tests, the small minority opposed to India's nuclear programme accused Vajpayee of exploiting nationalist sentiment to boost support for his rackety coalition from the urban middle classes. Conducting the tests was the only aspect of the *Hindutva*, or Hindu nationalism, policies, promised by the BJP before the election, which might find wide acceptance. All the others had already been dropped. Affluent Indians, who have gravitated increasingly towards the BJP during the last decade, have seen the nuclear weapons programme as a means of gaining more influence for India on the global stage. In the days immediately following the Pokhran tests, public approval for them was 80% according to some opinion polls, and the dancing crowds that gathered daily outside the prime minister's home in New Delhi gave a temporary boost to a government that had been seen as weak, ineffectual and extremely unlikely to last its full five-year term.

The euphoria which followed the explosions soon vanished, however, and the first months of the first BJP-led government since independence – barring a 13-day attempt by Vajpayee in 1996 – were marked by unremitting pressure from its coalition partners. The BJP-led coalition was even more disparate than the UF coalition governments that preceded it. The largest coalition partner, the All India *Anna Dravida Munnetra Kazhagan* (AIADMK) of Tamil Nadu, was driven by the priorities of its leader, M. J. Jayalalitha, who openly linked support for the coalition to her campaign to extricate herself from a series of corruption cases. Building on pre- and post-election agreements, regional parties used their leverage within the fragile coalition to push for concessions for their own states.

Such machinations contributed to the paralysis that prevented the government from responding to early warning signals of an unexpected monsoon and poor harvests. Food prices soared, propelled by the government's failure to check hoarding by the merchant class, which is the BJP's traditional support base and source of funds. The price rises – particularly of such staples as onions and potatoes which rose eight-fold – proved ruinous for the BJP in elections to four state assemblies on 25 November 1998.

The party lost the western state of Rajasthan, where there was a 10% swing against it, and its stronghold, New Delhi, where there was a 17% swing. Meanwhile, the opposing Congress Party also defied earlier poll predictions to hang on to the central state of Madhya Pradesh. The debacle left the BJP even more exposed to the wiles of its allies, who sought to disassociate themselves from the price rises by being seen to put pressure on the coalition leader.

The elections were an important rite of passage for the Congress leader, Italian-born Sonia Gandhi. Her campaign appearances had helped stave off disaster for Congress during the February–March 1998 elections, and she had become the Congress Party's president in March. She was able to claim the state election victories as evidence of the enduring popularity of the Nehru–Gandhi dynasty, and of her successful efforts to breath new life into the party. With its regional party satraps becoming weaker, Congress is turning its attention to state elections due in southern Andhra Pradesh and Karnataka in the autumn of 1999. Those polls, which, early in the year, Congress appeared well-positioned to win, will influence Gandhi's decision on whether to seek early national elections. Although she has faced pressure from within her own party and the remnants of the UF coalition to replace the BJP-led coalition with a differently structured grouping, she appeared disinclined to seek power other than through elections. While support from regional groups would still be needed, Gandhi appeared to believe she could return the Congress to its status as a national party.

Apart from prices, there was growing concern about the attempts of the BJP's extremist allies, within and outside the coalition, to replace India's official ideology of secularism with *Hindutva* – a notion of Indian character, with roots in Hinduism, that is purposely left vague. Such a programme would have to be enacted by stealth. The BJP dropped the most contentious aspects of the creed to attract voters in the 1998 election and to win over regional parties during the process of coalition building. These were:

- a pledge to build a temple on the site of the *Babri Masjid*, the medieval mosque at Ayodhya, Uttar Pradesh, that was destroyed by Hindu extremists in December 1992;

• revocation of special constitutional status for Kashmir;

• abolition of 'personal laws' on marriage, divorce and property for India's 120 million Muslims.

The 'national agenda for governance' adopted by the coalition made no mention of the BJP's defining issues, an omission that reassured Indian Muslims that the party's rise to power would have a moderating effect. Since 1993, when thousands were killed in violence that followed the destruction of the *Babri Masjid*, there has been no significant Hindu–Muslim violence, and the first months of the BJP government brought no change in that regard. However, a series of running battles over education, cultural events and the activities of the Christian churches were to expose the tensions between the BJP and more extremist forces, and even within competing factions of the ruling party itself. In June, the *Vishwa Hindu Parishad* (VHP) – world council of Hindus –threatened to revive the passions that had been unleashed at Ayodhya by announcing it would build a temple on the ruins of the mosque. Vajpayee was forced to offer public reassurances that the government would block such a move. Such episodes were repeatedly to embarrass the prime minister.

One regularly visited battleground was education, a traditional area of concern for the *Rashtriya Swayamsevak Sangh* (RSS), the secretive and quasi-military organisation that has been the self-appointed guardian of Hinduism since 1925. The RSS is a militant wing of the BJP, as well as of the VHP. When the Vajpayee government took office, the RSS adopted a more public posture than ever before. Most senior BJP leaders, including Vajpayee, are members of both organisations, and the organised workers of the RSS are crucial to the BJP during elections, so it is difficult to gauge the sincerity or feasibility of the BJP's claim to have temporarily abandoned *Hindutva*.

The Education Ministry was entrusted to a BJP hard-liner, Murli Manohar Joshi, and there were moves early on to install BJP loyalists in the civil service, police, diplomatic corps, universities and cultural institutions. The Indian Council of Historical Research, which had been instrumental in creating a secular nationalist and Marxist orthodoxy among scholars during the past 25 years, was the first casualty in June 1998. In October, Joshi called on state education ministers to introduce the teaching of Hindu scriptures and to devote more time to Sanskrit. The BJP government in the state of Uttar Pradesh moved to introduce compulsory school prayer, and the recital of a hymn *Vande Mataram* (Hail to the Mother) which has become a symbol of cultural tyranny for India's Muslims.

The BJP faced an even more extreme brand of militancy from the *Shiv Sena*, the creation of a charismatic Maharashtrian leader from outside the RSS tradition. In December, the group attacked cinemas screening a film which contained lesbian love scenes. *Shiv Sena* activists also threatened the first Pakistani cricket test tour of India in more than a decade, which proved very unpopular with the general public.

Of more immediate concern was the government's inaction in the face of rising violence against India's 23m Christians. Church leaders registered more than 100 incidents in 1998 – burning of churches, raping of nuns and attacks on schools. Hindu extremists claimed that the attacks were spontaneous reactions to aggressive conversions by Christian missionaries. This claim was unfortunately lent some credence when Vajpayee called for a national debate on conversions. Although the violence was initially concentrated in the western state of Gujarat, a stronghold of the VHP and *Bajrang Dal*, the government's inaction was seen as acquiescence. Amid protests from Advani that the attacks on Christians were isolated incidents, they spread to Uttar Pradesh, Haryana and Karnataka and in January 1999 claimed their first victims when an Australian missionary and his two young sons were burnt to death in eastern Orissa. Again, Advani publicly absolved the *Bajrang Dal* of the killings, which did little to discourage continued violence. However, the situation led to the resignation of one BJP cabinet minister, and threats from at least four allies to leave the coalition. The violence against the Christians threatened to become the breaking point for Vajpayee's government.

Unhappy Economic News

While the anti-Christian attacks showed up the vulnerabilities of the Vajpayee government, the prime minister did succeed in pushing through one key measure in the series of economic reforms underway since 1991: the qualified opening of the insurance industry to foreign firms. Elsewhere on the economic front, however, he did little to reduce the food and other subsidies that had helped drive the fiscal deficit up to 6.1% of gross domestic product (GDP).

The sanctions which followed the nuclear tests affected some $2.8bn in World Bank and Asian Development Bank loans for infrastructure, but, even before then, economic growth had been declining for several years. Growth slipped below 5% in 1998, approaching the levels prevailing before the economic reforms began. Agricultural and industrial production fell, as did exports and foreign investment. Within days of the nuclear tests, India's currency dropped below 40 *rupees* to the dollar – a symbolic new low. Its slide continued throughout the year, with some recovery following the announcement of the budget.

Pakistan: Moving to the Right

A deepening debt crisis, compounded by the international sanctions imposed after the nuclear tests, continued to preoccupy Pakistan's government. At the time of the tests, debt servicing accounted for 37% of public spending. With defence expenditure absorbing another 26%, the government was crippled when it contemplated spending on development. The immediate effect of the tests, and the anticipated sanctions, was capital flight, and a 30% devaluation of the *rupee*. In late July, when foreign exchange reserves fell to $450m – less than three weeks' worth of imports – Islamabad stopped repayment on commercial and institutional debt.

Although it won a reprieve at the end of the year, when the IMF agreed to reschedule some $3bn of debt, it was uncertain whether Sharif had the political strength to take the tough measures demanded by lenders. The fall of the *rupee*, and a 25% rise in petrol prices and utility tariffs, already threatened further social discontent. The country has so far proved unwilling to cut government spending, or to impose a tax on agricultural income. Instead, Sharif has revived a $9bn project to build a dam on the Indus river. Though directed by lenders to settle a row with independent power producers, Sharif scrapped agreements reached under former Prime Minister Benazir Bhutto, and charged foreign electricity company executives with corruption.

Amid looming economic disaster, Sharif, who had come to power in February 1997 with a nearly two-thirds majority, was determined to neutralise any potential checks on his authority. On 28 August 1998, he unveiled a proposal to make *Sharia* the supreme law of Pakistan. The country has had a version of Islamic law in the federal *Sharia* courts since the military dictatorship of the 1980s. Sharif, however, claimed his Islamisation project would lead to a wholesale reform of the police and administration, and free Pakistan of corruption, crime and poverty.

Few were convinced by Sharif's vision of 'instant justice'. His parallel justice system was seen as a ruse to grant the prime minister the powers to over-ride existing legal and constitutional safeguards, and overturn legislation passed by the four provincial assemblies. Opponents of the bill – virtually all political parties bar Sharif's Pakistan Muslim League (PML), human rights activists and the military – also feared it would lead to growing intolerance in a society riven by sectarian violence and general lawlessness. There was even a fluttering of revolt against the *Sharia* bill from within Sharif's party before it was passed, with a few amendments, by 151 to 16 in the National Assembly on 10 October. By the end of 1998, Sharif had yet to present the law for approval by the upper house, or Senate, where his PML did not enjoy such a strong majority.

Two days before the passage of the *Sharia* bill, Sharif managed to get rid of his most formidable critic: Pakistan's military chief, General Jehangir Karamat, who retired four months before he was due to do so. His exit was precipitated by his public criticism of the government's attempts to manage Pakistan's economic crisis, and his proposal of a National Security Council to 'institutionalise' decision-making and rid the country of 'polarisation, vendetta and insecurity-driven politics'.

While Karamat's dramatic gesture appeared to reflect the military's continued respect for civilian rule, ten years after the restoration of democracy in Pakistan, it also raised questions about Sharif's long-term relationship with the army. General Pervez Musharraf, Karamat's successor, is also a Mohajir and is believed to share his predecessor's concern about the economy and political violence.

Meanwhile, Sharif moved against the *Muttahida Quami* Movement (MQM), which represents the Mohajir community, dominant in urban areas of Sind province especially Karachi. In November, following the murder of a leading philanthropist and former governor of Sind, Hakim Mohammed Said, the prime minister dismissed the provincial government, which was a coalition of his own PML and the MQM. Although violence had been rising in Karachi, with more than 1,000 murders in 1998, MQM leaders saw the dismissal of the government as retribution for their refusal to support Sharif's *Sharia* bill.

As part of the crackdown in Karachi, Sharif replaced the provincial police chief with a trusted officer from Punjab, adding to the resentment of Pakistan's largest and most politically dominant province, and introduced military courts to try serious crimes involving activists in the MQM and its splinter group, the MQM *Haqiqi*. Initially, Sharif ordered the military courts to deliver verdicts within three days. However, even the army was disturbed at his haste, and, in January 1999, the Supreme Court stayed the first death sentences to be handed down by the courts. Undeterred, Sharif announced he would introduce military courts throughout Pakistan, resorting again to the claim that such a measure would deliver 'instant justice'. Meanwhile, a dispute that had been simmering for several months between the country's largest newspaper group, the Jang Group, and the prime minister reached a crisis point. In February, Sharif defied the Supreme Court to order police vans to stop the delivery of newsprint to the group's publications by force. Sharif is clearly moving towards authoritarian rule.

By following India in becoming a declared nuclear state, Pakistan may have developed a deterrent to attack by Indian armoured divisions or nuclear bombs. But this does little to offset the true threat to the security of the Pakistani people, which is contained in the massive deterioration in public law and order. Everyday life in Pakistan must contend with political, sectarian and criminal violence at a level never seen before. It is taking an increasing toll on human life, destroying popular trust in the government's ability to control it, and undermining economic growth, both by inhibiting foreign investment and weakening local business. Against this dismal background of failure of existing institutions and tensions involving the military and Islamic authoritarians there is a risk that the vestiges of parliamentary democracy will be undermined. Nuclear weapons are of no use against this threat.

Troubles Ahead

The nuclear tests by India and Pakistan have further upset the stability of an already unsettled region suffering from acute poverty. They have challenged global efforts on arms control and non-proliferation and have provoked international condemnation. Whatever may have been the supposed rationale for the tests in terms of national security and domestic opinion, such consequences are in no country's interests. The economic and political costs for India and Pakistan could prove devastating.

Both countries are showing some awareness of these effects. The resumption of bilateral dialogue, the agreement on a way forward, presided over by the two prime ministers in Lahore in February 1999, and the possibility of adherence to the CTBT offer some promise of progress. But much more remains to be done. There is a desperate need for substantive confidence- and security-building measures in the region as a whole, extending beyond the subcontinent to take in China. Arms control regimes need to be reinforced. All this will call for restraint and responsibility in economic and political governance in the countries concerned and measured stimulation from the international community. The challenge, and the dangers arising from failure to meet it, are very great.

Africa

During 1998 there was a return to the larger scale wars not seen since the 1960s, engulfing many states in sub-Saharan Africa in bloody turmoil. Of the 45 countries in the region, over 20 are involved in conflict, or directly affected by it. One of the most critical and worrying developments has been the escalation of Africa's wars from internal conflicts to regional wars as states abandoned any reluctance to cross borders. The most significant of these is the war in the Democratic Republic of Congo (DROC), which erupted in August 1998 and has dragged in seven other African nations. DROC's size – equivalent to that of Western Europe – and its strategic position, bordering nine other states, puts it in a pivotal position where Africa's north–south and east–west axes cross. Its future, which seems to defy attempts at negotiation, will determine the stability of Central Africa.

In West Africa, Sierra Leone's war has directly involved the Nigerian-led regional peacekeeping force, the Economic Community of West African States Cease-fire Monitoring Group (ECOMOG), in bitter fighting against a rebel force that is receiving backing from Liberia and Burkina Faso. The situation has the potential to destabilise other neighbouring states such as Guinea. Other long-standing hot spots have continued to smoulder. Member states of the Inter-Governmental Authority on Agriculture Development (IGAAD) have been frustrated in their efforts to resolve Sudan's war between the northern Islamic government and the Sudan People's Liberation Army (SPLA). The see-sawing of some rapacious southern factions undermined the slender threads of survival to which the population clings and resulted in a famine in the south-west that was partially, but belatedly, eased by an international humanitarian response. And Somalia's clan-based factions are still unable to reach agreement on the future of the state.

But even those countries once believed to be stable have become embroiled in new fighting. Most alarming is the war between former allies, Eritrea and Ethiopia, over a disputed part of their mutual border. Should this conflict escalate, the large military capability of these two states, including aircraft capable of hitting each other's capitals, could have devastating consequences, not only for themselves but for their neighbours as well. Historically peaceful Lesotho erupted into violence that brought South Africa and Botswana in as reluctant peacekeepers, and a stand-off between the military and the leadership in Guinea Bissau has suddenly also surfaced. Angola threatened Zambia with war after finding evidence of support for the rebel group *União Nacional para a Indêpendencia Total de*

Map 5 Africa

Angola (UNITA) within the Zambian government. Botswana and Namibia seemed determined to fight a war over an island in the Cunene river. Both countries have increased their military capabilities.

This propensity for conflict has dismayed the West. It has withdrawn further from involvement in the resolution of conflicts, underscoring Africa's strategic insignificance in its eyes. Traditional leverage has had little effect; peacekeeping ideas such as the vaunted African Crisis Response Initiative (ACRI) proposed by the US some years ago are increasingly viewed as moribund, while actual missions like the one in Angola have been terminated. Had such violence featured in any other part of the world, the international response would inevitably have been very different, as it has been in reaction to the relatively low-level conflict in Kosovo. But the lack of international response is also partially due to a growing propensity by African states – or at least their leaders – to insist on sorting out their own problems, even if this means with a military solution. In DROC, for example, the warring parties have largely abjured outside assistance, and in Sierra Leone it is the regional ECOMOG forces that have taken the lead in the fighting.

●

Africa's Regional Wars

The war in DROC has perhaps the most serious implications for the continent. Seven different states have been dragged into the war. In the east, Rwanda and Uganda have supported local rebels, the *Rallye pour le Congo Democratique* (RCD), who are attempting to overthrow DROC President, Laurent Kabila. A southern grouping of states, Zimbabwe, Angola and Namibia, has come to Kabila's aid. Chad and Sudan on DROC's northern border have also provided support to Kabila.

DROC's new descent into war was a result of Kabila's neglect of Rwandan and Ugandan security concerns. The two countries had helped propel Kabila to head the rebellion of the Alliance of Democratic Forces for the Liberation of Congo-Zaire (ADFL), which in May 1997 toppled Mobutu Sese Seko's 32-year-long dictatorship. The main reason why Rwanda and Uganda supported Kabila had been to block insurgent attacks into the border areas of Rwanda and Uganda by *Hutu* ex-members of the *Forces Armeés de Rwanda* (FAR) and *Interahamwe* militias from DROC. These groups, which were guilty of the 1994 genocide in Rwanda, had sought sanctuary in DROC and continued to harass the government from there. From Rwanda's and Uganda's point of view, Kabila had a regional obligation to fulfil its security agenda.

Once in power, however, Kabila failed to act decisively to deal with the rebels in the east. He gradually distanced himself from his patrons, increasingly placing his own people from his home province of Katanga in positions of power. Kabila's leadership style is at best erratic. His 1960s Marxist rhetoric, replete with frequent attacks against the West, also poisoned his relations with the US, Belgium and France. But his deteriorating relations with the Rwandans and Ugandans were more dangerous to his position.

For his part, Kabila had been concerned at the degree of influence wielded by the Rwandans, particularly their role in reshaping Kabila's army. A Rwandan, James Kabarebe, was Kabila's chief of staff charged with the task of uniting the army after the war. The armed forces were a disparate group, taking in around 3,000 original members of the ADFL, mainly from eastern DROC, around 15,000 new recruits, nearly 70,000 of Mobutu's former forces and approximately 5,000 Katangese *gendarmerie* who had been based in neighbouring Angola, but who joined Kabila midway through the rebellion.

Finding themselves increasingly marginalised, and convinced that Kabila was not prepared to serve their interests, the Rwandans left Kinshasa in July 1998. Kabila's reaction was to replace with his own men many senior army officers whom he felt could threaten him. The result was a mutiny by some parts of the army, notably the Tenth Brigade based in Goma in eastern DROC. As forces rebelled in the east, quickly taking the Kivu provinces, an audacious offensive with Rwandan support was launched from Matadi in the west against the capital Kinshasa. It faltered on the outskirts of the city when Angola joined the war in support of Kabila. Zimbabwe and Namibia had already pledged assistance.

Attempts at resolution of the war have failed. South Africa has tried to mediate, but Kabila suspects it of being too close to US interests as well as to Uganda and Rwanda. Zambia is a more acceptable mediator but its independence could be compromised by its interest in maintaining relations with its more powerful neighbour, Angola. The US, France and the UN all have tried to push the warring parties to the table but with no success. Instead, Rwandan and Ugandan forces have consolidated their positions in the south-east and north-east respectively and have been making slow gains against Zimbabwean and DROC troops. The key reason why a negotiated agreement is unlikely is that Rwanda sees the war as essential to its own security, or – in the eyes of the ruling minority *Tutsi* group – its survival. Kabila, they believe, committed the gravest of sins when he gave military assistance to the ex-FAR forces that had taken refuge in DROC and were willing to back him. That, noted one senior Rwandan official, condemns him to being a 'permanent enemy'.

Yet Rwanda may have taken on more than it can handle. Its most critical problem is convincing the local DROC citizens that this second rebellion is in their best interests. Most Congolese have railed against the Rwandans whom they feel want to extend a *Tutsi* hegemony across DROC. Kabila has exploited this fear, encouraging his citizens, in September 1998, to kill the *Tutsi* invaders. This has unfortunately been extended to include those *Tutsis* who have been long-term residents in the country. Kabila's tactic has earned him short-term popularity, but threatens to awaken longer-term tribal hatred. In the latter part of 1998 anyone who had the stereotypical tall, thin *Tutsi* physique was hunted down and killed. Rwanda also appears to be having problems agreeing with its ally Uganda over whom to support within DROC as an eventual replacement for Kabila.

While Rwanda may appear to be facing problems in DROC, compared with the states arrayed against it, it may hold the advantage of time. Zimbabwe's entry into the war on Kabila's side is not merely altruistic support for a threatened ally. It is also linked to commercial considerations, and the opportunity it presents to raise the prestige of Zimbabwean President Robert Mugabe. Also, most importantly, Angola appears to be running into problems. Without these two allies, it is unlikely that Kabila could survive.

Angola's Agenda

How the war will develop will hinge chiefly on how long Angola can continue its participation. It reluctantly backed Kabila, sending troops to his aid, because it was concerned that a Rwandan-orchestrated alternative might prove sympathetic to its long-standing enemy, UNITA. Although Angola also wished to express loyalty to the southern African alliance, its key motive for intervening was to keep UNITA from growing stronger through an alliance with Rwanda. But since then UNITA forces have inflicted a series of military setbacks on Angolan forces inside Angola.

Under the 1994 Lusaka Accords, UNITA was supposed to give up its territory in the central highlands, demobilise its armed forces and enter the political process. But UNITA has consistently refused to demobilise, infuriating Western states, especially the US, Portugal and Russia which have taken the lead in the peace process. There are clear indications that UNITA has been rearming and strengthening its military position rather than relinquishing it.

UNITA's leader, Jonas Savimbi, has never given up his clear designs on achieving the presidency of Angola. The fighting that has drawn Angolan forces into DROC has given him a strategic opportunity to gain militarily, and ultimately to re-negotiate the Lusaka Accords which he has always felt amounted to little more than a surrender. At the very least, his latest offensives have retaken the diamond-rich Lunda Sul and Lunda Norte provinces, so that he will once again be able to finance his war effort. His forces have also threatened the hugely lucrative prize of the Soyo Oilfields in the north of the country.

Neither side can achieve an ultimate military victory. UNITA's forces are estimated at around 25,000 men, although in real terms they probably total closer to 15,000. They are ranged against a theoretical Angolan government force of 85,000, but many of these are young conscripts who have been hastily called-up to fight and whose effectiveness is doubtful. The government forces have advantages in weapons and equipment, and can count on the continuing support of the West, for the most part linked to Angola's oil wealth. The country's off-shore reserves currently produce around 750,000 barrels a day, but exploration suggests that the fields could be among the most productive in the world. The French company Elf Aquitaine was recently awarded a concession estimated to be equal in size to the Brent oilfield in the North Sea. In 1998, Angolan oil accounted for around 7% of US oil imports, mainly through US companies such as Chevron.

As the fighting moves closer to the Soyo and Cabinda oil installations, international attention is likely to intensify. These two centres lie adjacent to the large Elf-dominated oil capital, Point Noire in neighbouring Congo-Brazzaville. France has good reason to keep this area stable. Angola still maintains troops in Congo-Brazzaville in support of President Denis Sassou Nguesso, following its invasion in October and November 1997, that ousted then President Pascal Lissouba in favour of Nguesso. Luanda engineered this coup because Lissouba had allowed UNITA to use Congo-Brazzaville as a base, and Angola's government was concerned about the effects of instability on its nearby Cabinda oil plant. The move drew little international censure. In fact, because of its concern about Elf's investments, France gave the operation its blessing; not only did it halt the war between the two rivals, but Nguesso had been a staunch French ally. Fighting, however, has not ended and there is now pressure for Angolan troops to stay longer to support Nguesso, at a time when Luanda would prefer to devote its resources to dealing with domestic problems caused by UNITA.

Meanwhile, Angola's economic prospects look bleak. It has traded on its future riches – from the exploitation of new oilfields – but this has not helped its current balance-of-payment problems. The slump in oil prices has hit Angola hard, and the possibility of its repaying its debts during a war is unlikely. Oil companies are also concerned that UNITA has acquired new weaponry that might be used to target oil installations, or to enable it to engage in economic sabotage. Unlike the government, UNITA appears to have retained sufficient resources to enable it to rearm. Diamond dealers are still reported flying into UNITA-occupied highland areas to buy stones. Savimbi is also reported to be receiving assistance from Zambian businessmen. The Angolan government has threatened Zambia with reprisals unless it cracks down on UNITA's activities there.

Zimbabwe Spirals Downwards

Zimbabwe too, can ill-afford to continue its war in DROC. Kabila has claimed he has paid Zimbabwe's troop bills to retain its support – although reports indicate that Libya has been funding the Zimbabwean intervention forces. This assistance is necessary as Zimbabwe faces severe economic and political crises. Economic decline has been a constant in the country; World Bank figures show that its per capita wealth has fallen since independence, and that in the last ten years there has been no economic growth. That unremitting decline has shown itself in the steady deterioration of roads, schools and medical services. In 1998 it resulted in a financial crisis, with the Zimbabwean dollar collapsing from 15.2 to the US dollar at the beginning of the year to 37 at the end.

Life is hard, particularly for the low-waged and unemployed in urban areas who mounted a series of weekly strikes towards the end of the year. The government responded by banning strikes and cracking down on dissent, trying to blame the economic problems on whites. It tried to solve its economic problems by reverting to a command economy, imposing import duties and promising to reinstate subsidies on fuel and food. It also tried to bolster its support in rural areas by encouraging squatters to move on to farms owned by whites, and threatening to seize such farmland for redistribution without compensation. For a while the government spoke with several voices on this issue. President Robert Mugabe said the seizure would go ahead while officials said it would not. The threat to seize land owned by whites, and Zimbabwe's intervention in DROC, led the International Monetary Fund (IMF) to threaten to suspend a $176 million loan which would have unlocked a further $800m in grants and aid. By the end of the year, however, the IMF seemed to have relented, not because Zimbabwe was pursuing what the IMF would consider the right policies, but because the country was facing disaster.

Although there is no election in Zimbabwe until next year and no presidential election until 2002, the race for the succession is already on. Given the present economic climate, it is uncertain whether Mugabe can hold on to power until the election, and he may even be forced from office by elements within the ruling party. At the end of 1998 there were rumours of a coup. Two journalists who reported the story were imprisoned and tortured. Judges who demanded that the men be released were dismissed by the Defence Ministry for interfering in state affairs.

The Unravelling of West Africa

Natural resources are also the major factor behind the continuing chaos in Sierra Leone – another conflict that looks likely to spread regionally. Diamond mining has fuelled the war, paying for arms for the Revolutionary United Front (RUF) rebels and attracting the attention of outside fighters, particularly from Liberia and Burkina Faso. Fighting escalated sharply at the end of 1998, hitting a peak in January 1999 when the RUF rebels infiltrated and captured parts of Freetown, the capital. The 15,000-strong, Nigerian dominated, West African peacekeeping force, ECOMOG, was hit badly. Unofficial reports put the Nigerian death-toll as high as 700. Over 3,000 civilians died in the street fighting. Many others, at least 1000, had their hands and other limbs amputated by machete, a rebel method of intimidation. Although ECOMOG regained control of Freetown by 17 January, further rebel offensives are expected. In the meantime, ECOMOG has brought in reinforcements, including special forces from Ghana.

ECOMOG had originally retaken Freetown in January 1998, over-throwing an alliance between the RUF and former members of the Sierra Leonean army. This group, the Armed Forces Revolutionary Council (AFRC), had seized power in May 1997, toppling President Ahmed Tejan Kabbah. ECOMOG had driven out the rebels, and then consolidated its own gains by capturing other towns in Sierra Leone's interior. But during the latter part of 1998, there was a sudden increase in rebel strength, and the government began to suffer losses. Behind their change of fortunes is Liberia's President, Charles Taylor, who came to power following an overwhelming victory in the Liberian elections of July 1997. Although he denies any participation, Taylor is clearly implicated: the RUF commander, Sam 'Mosquito' Bockarie, for example, has a house in Liberia and enjoys the protection of Liberian security when in town.

Taylor's motives for supporting the RUF are linked to his dislike for Nigerian involvement in West Africa. The Nigerians were also dominant in ECOMOG when it intervened in Liberia in 1989, preventing Taylor's National Patriotic Front of Liberia (NPFL) from taking Monrovia after President Samuel Doe had been killed. An eight-year war followed. Although now officially reconciled with the Nigerians, Taylor has opposed their military presence in the area. During the Liberian conflict, he supported the RUF, especially its leader, Foday Sankoh, now imprisoned in Freetown. The Sierra Leonean government's support for ECOMOG in Liberia provides a motive for revenge. But the current Sierra Leonean conflict also gives Taylor the possibility of stronger regional influence should the RUF succeed. It also distracts attention from his disastrous attempts to move the country to civilian rule, a transition that has made little progress. Taylor still continues to run the country as he did his NPFL faction that had once battled against ECOMOG forces. He has also mounted systematic attacks against factions dominated by the *Krahn* ethnic group that once dominated the Liberian military.

Suspicions of Liberian involvement against the Sierra Leonean government have been further promoted by the sighting of up to 3,000 Liberian 'mercenaries' who have been reported fighting on the side of the RUF. In addition, possibly up to 200 Ukrainian mercenaries have been involved. The large quantities of weaponry that have been flown into the country are thought to have come from Burkina Faso and Libya. A number of Western companies have also obtained and supplied ex-Soviet arms and military equipment, and a South African military adviser is reported to be training RUF rebels and Liberians in small-unit insurgency warfare. These tactics have been particularly successful against the more orthodox Nigerian force which lacks counter-insurgency training.

The war in Sierra Leone demonstrates how quickly a civil conflict can explode into regional war. It has also highlighted the difficulty of resolving such a wider conflict. Aside from its goal of overthrowing what they perceive as the corrupt political élite, the RUF has no political philosophy and limited popular support. During its period in power, civilians refused to recognise it, with many choosing not to work. Acts of brutality have further isolated it. Although to negotiate with such a group is not an attractive option, there may be no choice, as outside support for opposition is faltering. ECOMOG, and the Nigerians in particular, are not keen to stay there, a reluctance which may increase following the election of a civilian regime in Nigeria in February 1999.

Just before the elections, Nigeria's interim military leader, General Abubakar, had hinted that the government could not continue its role in ECOMOG past May 1999. This announcement caused panic in Sierra Leone. Behind such posturing lay the hope that the West would supply much-needed financial support. So far there has been very little, although the UK recently announced a $25m package. ECOMOG has received praise from Western capitals, but little financial aid. Given the mounting death-toll as a result of insurgent action, and the consequent need to maintain a military presence, the West's reluctance to engage with Africa in any meaningful way, even when Nigeria acts as a proxy for Western interest, is amply demonstrated in Sierra Leone.

Nigeria's Winds of Change

The death on 8 June 1998 of Nigeria's military leader, General Sani Abacha may signal some positive change in the region. The officially reported cause of death was a heart attack, but the exact circumstances are mysterious. Abacha's place was taken by former Chief of Staff, General Abdusalam Abubakar, who immediately took a reformist line. Political parties were permitted to operate freely, and many political prisoners were released. The dual exchange rate – a notorious mechanism of corruption that enabled ruling élite to profit from an ability to buy foreign exchange at 25% of the international rate – was also removed. The changes have encouraged open political debate, public meetings and a much freer press.

As a result, the February 1999 presidential election was won by General Olusegun Obasanjo of the People's Democratic Party (PDP).

Obasanjo, a former military officer who was president from 1976–79, was the only military leader in Nigeria who had stepped down and handed power back to civilian rule. Well respected internationally, he was regarded as a threat to the later rule of Sani Abacha and imprisoned in 1995 for allegedly plotting a coup. Following his release after Abacha's death he was nominated to head the PDP. The February presidential election was far from perfect, however, with Obasanjo's main rival, Chief Falae, claiming that there was massive vote rigging. International observers, while acknowledging irregularities and inconsistencies, have generally accepted that Obasanjo's 63% portion of the vote left the result beyond doubt.

Suspicions linger, however, about Obasanjo's true allegiances. A southerner from the *Yoruba* ethnic group, Obansanjo has less support from his home territory than from the north, which has dominated Nigerian politics and the army since independence. His most significant financial supporter was former military ruler, General Ibrahim Babangida, which has raised concern that the military is still ultimately in control. Yet the reality is that someone more radical than Obasanjo might have not been acceptable to the military hierarchy.

Within Nigeria, there are high expectations. The real question, however, is whether Obasabjo will be able – and permitted – to weed out the more corrupt members of the military hierarchy and to establish fairer and democratic rule. One neglected issue relates to the Niger Delta area of Ogoniland. Although the area contains some of the world's highest quality crude oil, very few of the attendant benefits have reached the region's population. Local uprisings, including the sabotage of pipelines, have been the inevitable result. Shell, the company that dominates the area, has been under pressure to provide schools and medical facilities directly to the local inhabitants, in areas where government funding is invariably siphoned off by corrupt officials.

If democracy is allowed to develop in West Africa's giant, it will send a positive message to other states in the region. While it may be too much to believe that such a situation will inspire good government in its neighbours, it will, at the very least, attract more international support to Nigeria than was previously possible. But Nigeria is also hamstrung by its poor economy: the World Bank estimates its debt at $31bn. As oil constitutes 95% of Nigeria's export earnings, the expected continued low price will seriously impede Nigeria's growth in 1999. Although the government confidently anticipates a 3% growth in the economy, most international analysts have projected a contraction.

Eritrea and Ethiopia Go to War

The war between Ethiopia and Eritrea that erupted in May 1998 has been the biggest surprise to observers. The immediate cause was a disputed border between the two states. Behind that, however, linger old animosities between the Eritreans and the Tigrayans who now dominate the Ethiopian government. On 21 May 1991 the combined Eritrean and Tigrayan forces had ousted the Ethiopian dictator Mengistu Haile Mariam and, shortly thereafter, Eritrea achieved independence. It took with it the ports that gave Ethiopia access to the outside world. Although Ethiopia could not in reality have denied independence to Eritrea, it continues to chafe under the high taxes demanded for access to the ports and it has continued to look for a way to avoid this impasse.

With Mengistu overthrown, the interests that had kept the countries together have diverged. Unfortunately, the borders that divide the states have never been officially agreed. The province of Tigray lies adjacent to Eritrea and it provided the spark that ignited nationalist pride which has enflamed the conflict. Ethiopian Prime Minister Meles Zenawi, a Tigrayan, and Eritrean President Issayas Afeworki have traded personal insults, making settlement of the dispute even more difficult. In mid-1998 both sides agreed to a cease-fire following a combined US–Rwandan mediation initiative. But they used the intervening time to rearm, and on 7 February 1999, vicious fighting resumed.

Although Ethiopia statistically has the upper hand in military equipment, especially armour and air power, the Eritreans retain the tight organisation successfully used in their war of independence. They are unlikely to be beaten; indeed in mid-March 1999 they apparently repelled an Ethiopian attack and inflicted serious losses, which they claim amounted to 10,000 men. The Eritreans have also acquired MiG-29 aircraft, which gives them the capability to hit the Ethiopian capital, Addis Ababa – a step they took after Ethiopian jets bombed the Eritrean capital Asmara in earlier fighting. Ethiopia has bolstered its forces with the purchase of *Sukhoi* 27 fighters. As neither country reportedly has pilots or maintenance crew for these aircraft, east European technicians have been employed. (Ethiopian Airlines, as a precautionary move, have shifted their aircraft fleet to Nairobi.)

Both states have attempted to rally the support of other states and factions. Somali warlord, Hussein Mohamed Aideed, has been wooed by both and has apparently been accepting arms from both sides. More significantly, the war has distracted Asmara and Addis Ababa from their opposition to the Sudan Government. Both had allowed the combined Sudanese opposition group, the National Democratic Alliance – which is an umbrella alliance of both the northern Muslim factions and the South Sudan People's Liberation Army – to use their territory to launch attacks on Sudan. Eritrea has now tried to encourage them to take a stance against Ethiopia. So far it has refused, but unless the war between Ethiopia and Eritrea can be settled soon it can be expected to suck in neighbouring forces, as has the war in DROC.

Western Influence Takes a Back Seat

The Ethiopia–Eritrea war has been a major setback for the US, as it has distracted the two countries from supporting one of the key US policies: isolating and removing the Sudanese regime which the US believes has supported terrorism. The US is also in the uncomfortable position of supporting both Rwanda and Angola, countries now on opposite sides of the war in DROC. Washington now firmly backs the Kigali administration. It has also chosen to support Eduardo Dos Santos, the Angolan President elected in 1992, on the grounds of supporting democratic processes; but US oil interests also play a part. A further casualty has been the US-supported African Crisis Response Initiative (ACRI). This organisation had envisaged the training of African armies to provide regional peacekeeping forces that could intervene in local crises. However, with so many countries currently at war, it seems to have outlived its usefulness before it even started.

France, the country which has played a central role in this region of Africa in the past, has also become more careful about its involvement. DROC President Laurent Kabila visited Paris in December 1998 in an effort to enlist support against the Rwandan- and Ugandan-supported offensives – which he characterised as an Anglophone invasion. It is unclear how far France would be prepared to back Kabila, whom they view as erratic and opportunistic. Just months earlier Kabila had denounced the French, particularly for their support of President Mobutu Sese Seku whom he had overthrown in May 1997. However, the possibility of unilateral French intervention on the continent has receded, and the release of an investigation into the French role in the Rwandan genocide has forced it to look at intervention with greater care. In cases where there is no direct French interest, its response is likely to be muted, although Paris still harbours the view that the US has a greater strategic plan to extend influence throughout Africa. As attempts to involve Western powers wane, more interest has been focused on the role of African players, most notably South Africa.

Crisis of Leadership

At the end of 1997, Africa was touted as 'coming of age', a view founded to a large extent on the new leadership style that had emerged in many countries. But the same leaders President Clinton had applauded during his trip to Africa in March 1998 have each in turn taken their countries to war. Uganda's President Yoweri Museveni, Rwanda's Vice President, Paul Kagame, and the Eritrean and Ethiopian heads of state are all directly involved in fighting. Far from being a swathe of positive influence that extended from the Red Sea to the Atlantic – a prospect when Laurent Kabila first took office – the continent is in turmoil and US policies have been derailed.

That Zimbabwe, with the highest literacy rate in Africa, should be in such dire straits, is an indication of the quality of leadership of the continent's rulers. Although many countries in southern Africa have strong institutions and well respected officials, there are signs that some rulers are turning from national presidents into predatory warlords. The suspicion that many are primarily interested in gathering revenue for personal gain and accumulating fortunes to maintain their political position is becoming a certainty. If war is a necessary element in achieving this, they are prepared to plunge into war whatever the cost to their country. Wars can be extremely profitable for the rulers and their families and cronies. Within weeks of its intervention in DROC, for example, Angola had set up a joint oil company with DROC, and a businessman close to Mugabe – Billy Rautenbach, a white Zimbabwean – secured a deal with the DROC state mining company, Gecamines. Other Zimbabwean companies with links to Mugabe, or owned by relatives of Zimbabwe's army commanders, have also obtained lucrative contracts to supply the armies, or have obtained concessions inside DROC. General Salim Saleh, Uganda's army chief of staff, and brother of President Yoweri Museveni, was accused of having mining interests in northern DROC, and Rwanda is believed to be subsidising the costs of its war through taxes and royalties levied on mines and timber milling inside DROC.

What these developments also illustrate is an abiding African reality. In countries such as Namibia, Zimbabwe, Zambia and Angola, power was concentrated in the hands of one man who had no need to consult almost anyone before taking his country to war. Zimbabwe's President Mugabe announced the intervention in DROC without a cabinet meeting, and in Angola President José Eduardo dos Santos dispensed with his technocratic prime minister to pursue the war with UNITA. Such actions have shattered any illusions that the democratic procedures that Clinton professed to see are even beginning to develop in Africa.

Little Hope in Sight

It has sometimes been suggested that 1998 was a year of transition in Africa – that in retrospect, it might be seen as a time when long-standing disputes were resolved. However, the current bout of African wars differ from their predecessors. They are being fought with African agendas to the fore, free of earlier colonial or Cold War pretexts. International opinion appears to count for very little. The wars are increasingly fought over economic issues, in many cases over access to minerals.

The conflict in West Africa and, to a certain degree, the involvement of outside states in DROC reflect this trend. But for some of these states, particularly Rwanda, Uganda and Angola, the prime motivation is one of maintaining internal security. These countries have become involved in the DROC because its vast expanse makes it ideal for factions that oppose their governments, allowing them to seek sanctuary and launch attacks. Such a situation is untenable for neighbouring states. The battle for control of DROC, therefore, is one to ensure that a sympathetic government is installed in Kinshasa which can secure its own borders, thereby preventing threats to its neighbours' security interests. Given the range and scale of its conflicts, Africa is unlikely to return to peace easily and its economic development, already lagging far behind the rest of the world, will once again be retarded.

South Africa and its Place in the Region

It is now clear that expectations laid upon South Africa following the end of apartheid have been far too great. In 1994 there was hope that a free, democratic South Africa, at peace with itself, would transform southern Africa, if not the whole continent. Thabo Mbeki, the Deputy President and President-in-waiting, spoke of an African renaissance. The South African economy, free from sanctions and open to the rest of Africa, would, it was hoped, develop in leaps and bounds, providing the economic stimulus necessary to lift the region out of poverty.

As long as Nelson Mandela was president, these dreams have remained alive. They were his dreams. When he retires after the elections scheduled for 2 June 1999, the verdict will be that the man was remarkable, and his greatest achievement was to see through the transition from apartheid and avert catastrophe. But under his presidency, South Africa – state, economy and society – has not moved as far and as fast as it needed to.

A Shaky Society

The South African economy registered no growth in 1997, and 1998 figures are expected to show growth of only 1.5%. The *rand* lost 25% of its value between April and August, and real investment was estimated at one-third of its target set in 1997. The government is unwilling to raise interest rates, fearing an immediate effect on unemployment, but a failure of economic growth in the longer term will create more serious political problems if the government is unable to provide a better life for the vast majority of black South Africans.

The 1996 Growth, Employment and Redistribution (GEAR) programme aimed at a growth rate of 6% and the creation of 400,000 new jobs, with higher savings and investment. These targets now look wildly optimistic. When it was launched, GEAR presented a more market-orientated plan than its predecessor, the 1994 Reconstruction and

Development Programme. But neither had been implemented in such a way as to encourage greater investment and thereby to meet their targets.

The causes of South Africa's decline have been both internal and external. The global economic slowdown has particularly affected demand for South Africa's products, and has caused undiscriminating capital flight from all emerging markets. Internally South Africa's rigid labour laws and high labour costs have continued to discourage investors, while the world-wide image of crime-ridden South Africa has also been off-putting.

Turn-out in the June general election is expected to be low. That can be seen either as an expectation that the ANC will win without question, or as a lack of confidence in the ANC government. In 1998, there was a resurgence of political violence in KwaZulu and a mixture of gang warfare and militant fundamentalism in the Western Cape, making the two provinces not ruled by the ANC vulnerable to disruption in the lead-up to the election. Elsewhere, most people do not feel that the election will do much to affect their well-being.

Ironically the only serious opposition at a national level to the ANC's policies comes from its allies, the South African Communist Party, and the Congress of South African Trade Unions. For the moment, however, they remain in alliance. In the longer term, it is hard to see why they would be willing to be identified with free-market policies which, they would say, are not delivering better lives for the people. None of the other parties provides a threat to ANC rule. The National Democratic Alliance, formed by politicians who had been pushed out of the National Party (NP) and the ANC, has made inroads in NP support in some areas, but it is a long way from being able to challenge the government. Although trying to reinvent itself, if anything, the NP seems to be also losing ground to the Democratic Party which is becoming, at least intellectually, the most effective critic of the government. In KwaZulu, the *Inkatha* Freedom Party was deemed victor in the province in 1994 after the election there proved too chaotic, but it is not yet clear who will emerge the winner in 1999. It seems likely that with the *Inkatha* leader, Mangosuthu Buthelezi, happy in government, the party may wish to continue or even deepen its alliance with the ANC.

After the euphoria that accompanied the change of government in 1994, the country seems to have settled into a deep depression. It is as if the political transfer of power was finessed brilliantly and smoothly but the social and economic changes following the end of apartheid are only now beginning to affect the lives of ordinary South Africans. For those with a stake in the country, both black and white, the biggest worry is crime. In the first half of the 1990s as apartheid was finally consigned to history, every white person seemed to have a tale of violent robbery to tell, either experienced personally or by an acquaintance. Now the whites are almost used to the level of crime and have reinforced their homes, bought more guns and organised patrols in their traditional areas. Currently it is the black middle class who tell the tales and, despite the impression given by the white newspapers, the typical victim of crime is not white and female, but young, black and male. Crime has not only become more widespread, it has become more organised as international syndicates have targeted South Africa to steal cars, smuggle drugs and launder money. If, as has happened elsewhere in Africa, these international crime syndicates establish links with senior members of the government, the rule of law will degenerate rapidly in South Africa. The failure of the police to stem the rise in crime is at present due to a poorly trained and low-paid police force originally designed as a paramilitary force to prevent black political activity. It is trying slowly to become a more citizen-friendly institution designed to protect society. The South African National Defence Force (SANDF) has had to take over some of the responsibilities for border security from the over-stretched police. The SANDF, throughout 1998 and into 1999, has been undergoing major reorganisation – a challenging task in a time when funds are short. This only adds to the crisis in confidence over security generally.

The crime wave has helped to fuel an increase in 'white flight' as well as discouraging foreign investment. There is also a feeling among young whites that they do not have a future in South Africa because, however good they may be at a job, they will be discriminated against in favour of blacks. In the longer term 'white flight' may or may not have an adverse effect on South Africa's economy, but in the short term it represents a set-back for the racial harmony that Mandela has tried to promote.

The First Succession

The big political question of 1999 is what happens when Mandela goes. Some believe that the handover has already been achieved because Mbeki has been running the country for the past few years anyway and everyone has got used to him at the helm. Yet there will be some differences. The international perception of South Africa will change without Mandela. He has represented black liberation but also racial reconciliation with whites during the transition period. Mbeki, on the other hand, will be anxious to deliver the fruits of liberation to his constituency. This is not a question of personal preference: he has to do this in order to survive politically. His problem is that, with a stagnant economy, he is unable to give to blacks without taking from whites. In a period of economic contraction, everyone will be looking for scapegoats.

What may be more important in the longer term is that Mbeki will run the South African government in a manner which resembles that of other African leaders. That is to say he will personalise it. Mandela had great faith in institutions. He gave his full support even to the judiciary, which had been tainted by the apartheid years, agreeing to attend a court to give evidence when summoned by a judge. Mbeki, in contrast, is a network man. In dealing with ministries he is more likely to telephone one of his close contacts to make his wishes known rather than work through the official structures. This may seem arcane but it reveals how Mbeki as president will see himself in relation to the state. With the retirement, forced or otherwise, of several ministers who are only slightly younger than Mandela, Mbeki will have a good deal of leeway in appointing his own supporters to top jobs.

While Mandela has taken criticism seriously and tried to answer it, Mbeki has shown himself to be more sensitive. This suggests that he will probably rule more according to whim. He is already notorious for breaking appointments and will, like many African leaders, probably follow closely whatever he thinks is important rather than keep to a schedule.

Unhappy Relations

South Africa's relations with its neighbours (and with Africa as a whole) have been very disappointing despite hosting a successful, if largely irrelevant, meeting of the Non-Aligned Movement in Durban in October. The meeting established South Africa as symbolically committed to the poorer southern hemisphere, but failed to commit members to any practical action which might add substance or affect the decisions of the international heavyweights.

South Africa's foreign policy, both in the region and internationally, has been a series of embarrassing failures. Since Foreign Minister Alfred Nzo, his deputy, Aziz Pahad and Mbeki himself were responsible for links between the ANC and the rest of the world from the mid 1980s onwards, one might have expected better results. The first setback last year was the failure to dissuade Angola, Zimbabwe and Namibia from sending troops to DROC. The original mistake was to let DROC, ungoverned and vast, into the Southern African Development Community (SADC). Under an agreement between members of the SADC, members are obliged to come to the aid of any member which requests help when attacked by external forces. When Uganda and Rwanda helped launch a rebellion in DROC, Zimbabwe, Namibia and Angola sent troops. Having failed to dissuade them from this action, South Africa felt it necessary to sign up to a SADC statement which appeared to agree to the troops being there.

The dispute revealed a deeper split within Southern Africa. Far from being perceived as an engine of growth for the region, South Africa is perceived as a domineering bully whose huge companies will gobble up their neighbouring economies, and whose manufacturing industries will crush all others in the region. For this reason Mandela's standing among his immediate neighbours is far lower than it is in the rest of Africa and the world. Relations with Zimbabwe's Robert Mugabe have been particularly bad. In 1996 SADC set up the Organ on Politics, Defence and Security to replace the Frontline states military committee which Mugabe used to chair. South Africa insisted that the new committee should be responsible to Mandela, the Chairman of SADC as a whole. Despite several meetings, there has been no agreement. Mugabe seemed to take great pleasure in scoring points off Mandela and, at the Non-Aligned meeting in Durban, publicly snubbed Mbeki.

Further humiliation was in store for South Africa when, in October, it sent 600 troops to Lesotho to quell a suspected officers' revolt using the SADC agreement to justify its action. (Only Botswana was prepared to send troops and they arrived after the fighting was over.) The Basutu soldiers fought back, casualties were relatively heavy on both sides, and much of the centre of the capital, Maseru, was burned out. Although South African forces finally took control, they did so at such a price that the whole exercise was an embarrassment for its new army. Unflattering comparisons were made with the apartheid regime which had controlled Lesotho politics for many years by political manipulation and the occasional blockade.

Without Mandela

Mandela's glittering personal prestige has blinded many to the fact that South Africa has gradually become a more normal African state. It is hovering between the economic success that once marked it as different, and a slide into crime, poverty and chaotic conditions. Its economy is suffering from the effects of the worldwide slowdown, with overseas markets shrinking and much-needed investment finance at a premium. If South Africa continues on the path it is now treading, it will almost certainly become a failed state. Mandela's legacy as the man who engineered the transition from apartheid to democracy is secure. To prevent his achievement from being the last, rather than the first step towards a happier future, his successors will need to do more than simply trade on his reputation.

Prospectives

As the second millennium of the Christian Era limps to a close, the world's nations find themselves no closer to peace than they ever were. There is little chance that the two world wars that wracked the twentieth century will be repeated, but the foreseeable future holds little promise that brutal conflicts of the kind that raged through much of the world in 1998–99 will become a memory of the past. Each will have consequences that were unforeseen by those who began the wars. The massive air assault that NATO launched against Serbia at the end of March 1999 will not prove an exception.

The avowed aims of the action, in US President Bill Clinton's formulation, were to demonstrate NATO's determination to oppose aggression, to deter Yugoslav President Slobodan Milosevic from continuing and escalating his attacks in Kosovo, and to damage Serbia's capacity to wage war. The first and third of these objectives were more easily obtainable than the second. Once determination itself was set as a policy goal, it could be achieved, if only because it lay within the power of NATO to stay engaged once engagement itself was put forward as a primary objective.

Indeed, the fact that NATO's credibility was put forward so prominently raised the stakes for the Alliance. It would no longer be relevant to argue that Kosovo, in itself, was not an issue for which Westerners should die, since the conflict was being presented, in part, as a vindication of the relevance of the NATO alliance. Begun just a few weeks before its fiftieth anniversary celebrations, the operation against Serbia, the first attack by NATO on a sovereign country, confirmed that the Alliance's purpose had been subtly transformed from one primarily of collective defence to one largely for collective security. The prospects of further instability in Europe being strong, NATO will be entering its fifty-first year assuming the role of policeman for security in a still potentially unstable central and eastern Europe.

While the operation against Serbia could clearly damage Serbian military power, the value of air power as an instrument to force diplomatic compliance was shown to be limited. Just as use of air power alone could hardly induce Saddam Hussein to allow the reintroduction of the United Nations Special Commission (UNSCOM) to Iraq, so dropping bombs on Milosevic could hardly inspire him to sign the Rambouillet Accords when the facts of war might produce other, more useful, options. For Milosevic, any outcome other than agreement to Rambouillet as drafted could appear better.

The experience of using air power against Saddam and Milosevic will force Western strategists to think in a more sophisticated way about the vaunted relationship between force and diplomacy. It is not enough to say that diplomacy is more effective when backed up by the threat of force. The force contemplated, if used, must be capable, although at greater pain, of bringing about results unachievable by diplomacy alone. If the use of force cannot bring about the same results as diplomacy, its threatened use cannot force the unrepentant into compliance with Western wishes.

Moreover, unless the threat of force is coupled with a promise to deliver a less attractive political outcome than that promised by diplomacy alone, dictators will often prefer to play poker with the West's military machine. Had diplomats told Milosevic that force would be used to assure Kosovo's independence, and managed to convince him that the West had both the will and capacity to do this, he might have preferred the softer diplomatic outcome offered at Rambouillet. In an era when force is increasingly being used for limited political objectives, Western strategists will have to find better formulas for tailoring their diplomacy to the threat of force, instead of merely attaching the threat of force to their diplomatic effort.

The Uncertain Hegemon

In any case, the fate of the NATO attack on Serbia became inextricably intertwined with US constitutional and electoral politics. Because many American states have brought forward to early in 2000 their party primary elections, at which the candidates who will run for president are chosen, campaigning started to intensify before spring 1999. The Republican Party's popularity among US voters had dropped steeply by the time the year-long effort to impeach President Clinton sputtered to a close. Since they were losing the battle on the domestic front, would-be presidential candidates and Republican Senators were poised to raise foreign policy as the club with which to beat the president.

His policies in the Balkans could become an obvious target. But this is hardly the only convenient issue. Clinton was an early, heavy and continuing supporter of President Boris Yeltsin and reforms in Russia. Now that both are clinging to the ropes, Clinton's, and the West's, policies seemed more unsure than ever. Then there is China. Every administration finds dealing with this important, but sensitive, country difficult. In his first campaign against former President George Bush Sr., Clinton made much of what he insisted was too 'soft' a policy towards China. Once in power, he adopted engagement as the only sensible approach, and pursued a similar line to his predecessor. Ironically, he may find that George Bush Jr. will run for President against the Democratic candidate, probably Vice-President Al Gore, parroting the clever words he used in 1992. And policy towards the erratic, and strangely aggressive, North Korea will enliven the critical debates.

Russian Roulette

Frustrated by its growing impotence, Russia lashed out at Western action in Yugoslavia. Although Moscow had few assets beyond rhetoric to throw into the balance, there was the risk that it might ignore the arms embargo, supply the Serbs with needed weaponry, and perhaps allow, if not encourage, 'volunteers' to fight on the Serbian side. At the same time, Russia was trawling for further funds from the International Monetary Fund (IMF) and the West, for its financial state was so dire that without new money, or permission to postpone payment of its debts, it would be forced to default. Although the IMF offered to make a further loan at the end of March 1999, Russia is still wrestling with incompatible goals. Should Moscow decide that its national pride requires it regularly to oppose Western diplomacy, it will find that the possibility of raising more needed Western money in the future might fade.

Russia will find itself torn between trying to maintain its tattered nationalist pride and its need to shore up its chaotic finances through continued infusions of Western cash. This is a sure formula for a recrudescence of nationalist fervour. Prime Minister Yevgeny Primakov heard the news about the strikes against Serbia when he was on his way to the US to talk to the head of the IMF; he turned his aeroplane around and headed back to Moscow. There could be no stronger suggestion that he is planning to become a candidate for president. With an increase in nationalist feeling, Russia's relations with the West are sure to decay; that will ensure that, for Russia, the coming year is grimmer than the one just past.

For the West, the diplomatic and economic experience with Russia will, here too, mean facing strategic questions. Ever since the arrival of apparently reforming spirits in the Kremlin, Western strategists have asked themselves what they should do 'to help the reform process'. Typically, the answer has been to continue providing economic aid to demonstrate that there are rewards for dealing with the West. Increasingly that economic aid has been disconnected from any credible reform process, and has taken on a largely political character. Since it has become nearly automatic, some could begin to doubt the quality of the leverage such assistance provides over Russian political or economic policies. An open-ended commitment to provide economic support to Russia is unlikely to survive political, and especially Congressional, scrutiny.

The Chinese Yo-Yo

Even more delicately poised are US–Chinese relations. These have swung widely from euphoria to gloom ever since the two countries opened diplomatic relations on 1 January 1979. The relationship is now headed for one of its periods of gloom, with developments in both countries contributing to the almost guaranteed head-on clash. In the US, allegations of

China's attempt to steal nuclear warhead secrets and to gain influence over the Clinton administration through illegal political contributions fill the air, as do attacks on Beijing's human rights record. In China, the significant slowdown in the economy will increase the already growing number of incidents of social unrest, frightening the insecure leaders in Beijing into clamping down yet tighter on anyone they can characterise as a dissenter.

Differing military views on the two sides of the Pacific will contribute to the mistrust. Pentagon revelations of Chinese plans to increase the quantity and improve the quality of the missile threat opposite Taiwan are met by shrill Chinese opposition to US plans to construct a theatre missile defence (TMD) system across the Pacific area. That both nations' plans are for well in the future and may not even come into being, cuts no ice. Clear differences over TMD and Taiwan, coupled with US concerns over Chinese military developments, and charges in 1999 concerning alleged Chinese spying, demonstrated that the declaration of a US–Chinese 'strategic partnership' in summer 1998 was empty rhetoric. China is not a strategic partner of the US. Good diplomacy could ensure that it becomes neither a rival nor a serious hindrance. But it adds nothing to diplomacy to invent a partnership when the communality of strategic interest does not yet support such high-sounding language. The ups and downs of 1998–99, in the best conditions, might allow for a more sober appreciation of the limits to a US–Chinese relationship.

Bluff or Reality

Hopes that China would help convince North Korea to remove its threats to develop a long-range missile, and perhaps even a nuclear weapon, capability has faded with the souring of the atmosphere. The loss of any help from China has produced greater uncertainty about future security prospects on the Korean peninsula. The big issue is the Agreed Framework – the nuclear agreement with North Korea which is the foundation for Western interactions with Pyongyang.

Both sides were disenchanted with the fruits of the Agreed Framework process in 1998. North Korea appears to feel it has received neither the economic nor diplomatic pay-offs it anticipated from its commitment to 'freeze' its overt nuclear programme, while it is no closer to achieving its fundamental goal of securing a withdrawal of US troops from the Korean Peninsula. For their part, both Washington and Tokyo are increasingly frustrated by their inability either to constrain North Korean weapons of mass destruction and missile programmes, or to encourage concrete steps by Pyongyang to reduce tensions on the Peninsula. Failure to resolve the nuclear and missile issues satisfactorily could unravel the Agreed Framework completely and precipitate a major crisis in North-east Asia.

More fundamentally, however, the events of 1998 have raised questions about the basic assumptions and goals underlying Western policies in North-east Asia. Do North Korea's military programmes represent mere 'chips' to be bargained away in exchange for diplomatic relations with the US and increased economic assistance, as many Western policymakers have long assumed? Or is Pyonyang's negotiating strategy simply to attempt to buy time to achieve a strategic breakthrough on the Korean Peninsula and fundamentally alter the balance of power in the region? North Korea has long served as a kind of international Rorschach test, in the sense that different observers could look at the country and reach very different conclusions about what they were seeing. What the world concludes in 1999 on this key question will probably determine both short-term developments on the Korean Peninsula and longer-term prospects for regional security.

A Questionable Leader

For better or for worse, the US has led the search for security all around the world. However, despite the hyperactivity of US diplomacy at key times, the impetus for any activity has usually been a shock from abroad, rather than any home-grown strategy to shape political and military actions abroad in the US or world interest. In reacting to Iraq's dismissal of UN inspectors, Milosevic's burning of Kosovo villages, Israel's reluctance to implement the Oslo Accords, and many other crises, the US has shown admirable concentration of effort. But the attempt to solve a particular crisis has all too seldom been linked to a clearly defined, overtly strategic objective.

In the lull between crises, it is difficult to discern the consistent pursuit of a strategic goal. And the reason for this may be disarmingly simple: the principle threats to the US from abroad are more to its credibility than to its interests. Assaults on that credibility inspire strong responses. But American national security interests do not mean that the country must risk massive amounts of treasure or blood to reshape political situations abroad. The paradox is that, in a unipolar world, the incentives for a truly hegemonic role are low. The opportunity therefore exists for European and Asian friends of the US to help shape strategies for their regions. Europe, however, is not yet sufficiently united on an agreed security policy to provide firm direction while conflict engulfs its southern flank, nor is there a candidate in Asia to handle strategic thinking on growing problems in that region. The US is thus doomed to play the role of crisis manager, without always developing clear strategic goals. That remains a recipe for uncertainty. And perhaps that is the note on which the millennium is bound to begin.

——	international boundaries	*Dar El Beida* ⊕	international airport
—·—	province or state boundaries	*Al Kharj* ⊕	air base
SONORA	province or state	*Tengiz* ▨	oilfield
----	disputed and other boundaries	⌒	rivers
▣	capital cities	⌒⋯	seasonal or intermittent rivers
●	cities/towns	⬭	lakes
◢	built-up areas	▲	mountain peaks

Europe *Security organisations and groupings*

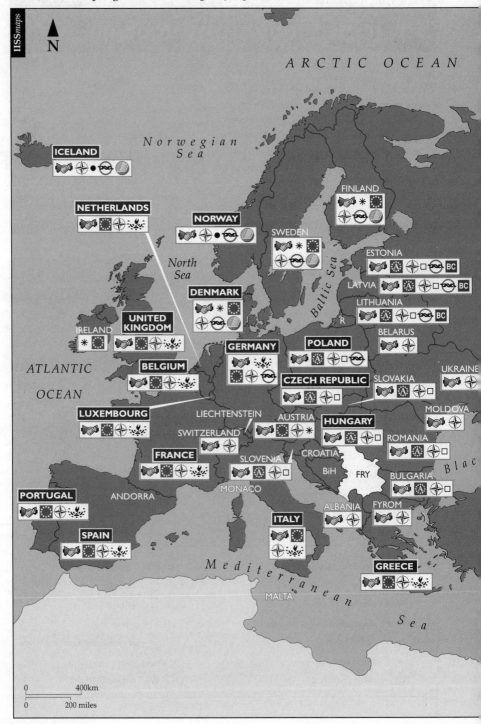

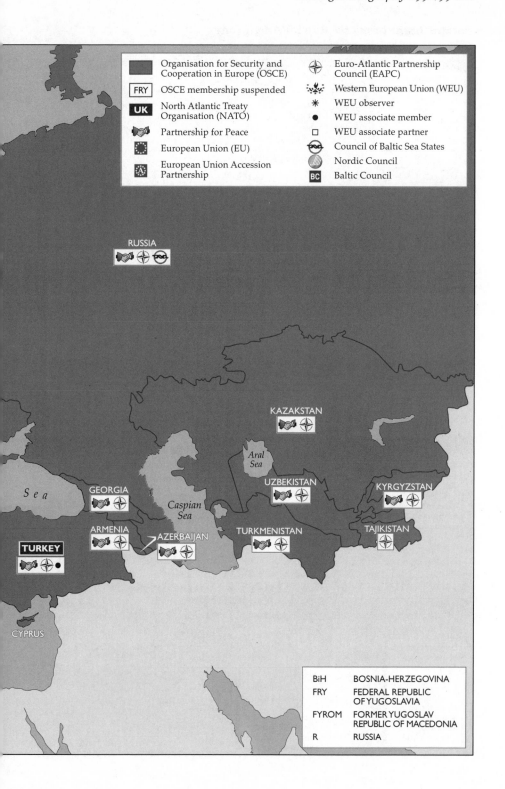

Organisation for Security and Cooperation in Europe (OSCE)

FRY OSCE membership suspended

UK North Atlantic Treaty Organisation (NATO)

Partnership for Peace

European Union (EU)

European Union Accession Partnership

Euro-Atlantic Partnership Council (EAPC)

Western European Union (WEU)

WEU observer

WEU associate member

WEU associate partner

Council of Baltic Sea States

Nordic Council

BC Baltic Council

RUSSIA

KAZAKSTAN

Aral Sea

UZBEKISTAN

KYRGYZSTAN

S e a

GEORGIA

Caspian Sea

TAJIKISTAN

ARMENIA

AZERBAIJAN

TURKMENISTAN

TURKEY

CYPRUS

BiH	BOSNIA-HERZEGOVINA
FRY	FEDERAL REPUBLIC OF YUGOSLAVIA
FYROM	FORMER YUGOSLAV REPUBLIC OF MACEDONIA
R	RUSSIA

Europe *Restructuring the Russian Armed Forces*

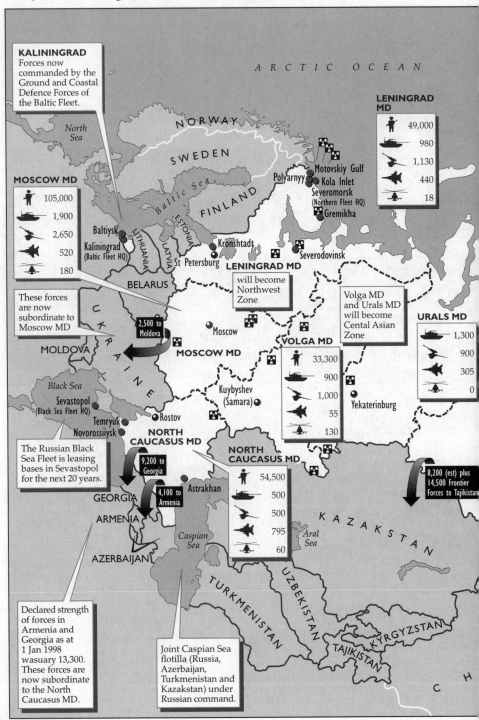

KALININGRAD
Forces now commanded by the Ground and Coastal Defence Forces of the Baltic Fleet.

LENINGRAD MD

49,000	
980	
1,130	
440	
18	

MOSCOW MD

105,000	
1,900	
2,650	
520	
180	

These forces are now subordinate to Moscow MD

LENINGRAD MD will become Northwest Zone

Volga MD and Urals MD will become Cental Asian Zone

URALS MD

1,300	
900	
305	
0	

VOLGA MD

33,300	
900	
1,000	
55	
130	

2,500 to Moldova

The Russian Black Sea Fleet is leasing bases in Sevastopol for the next 20 years.

9,200 to Georgia

4,100 to Armenia

8,200 (est) plus 14,500 Frontier Forces to Tajikistan

NORTH CAUCASUS MD

54,500	
500	
500	
795	
60	

Declared strength of forces in Armenia and Georgia as at 1 Jan 1998 wasuary 13,300. These forces are now subordinate to the North Caucasus MD.

Joint Caspian Sea flotilla (Russia, Azerbaijan, Turkmenistan and Kazakstan) under Russian command.

North Sea · NORWAY · SWEDEN · FINLAND · Baltic Sea · ESTONIA · LATVIA · LITHUANIA · BELARUS · UKRAINE · MOLDOVA · Black Sea · GEORGIA · ARMENIA · AZERBAIJAN · Caspian Sea · KAZAKSTAN · Aral Sea · TURKMENISTAN · UZBEKISTAN · TAJIKISTAN · KYRGYZSTAN

ARCTIC OCEAN

Motovskiy Gulf · Polyarnyy · Kola Inlet · Severomorsk (Northern Fleet HQ) · Gremikha · Baltiysk · Kaliningrad (Baltic Fleet HQ) · Kronshtadt · St Petersburg · Severodvinsk · Moscow · Kuybyshev (Samara) · Yekaterinburg · Sevastopol (Black Sea Fleet HQ) · Temryuk · Novorossiiysk · Rostov · Astrakhan

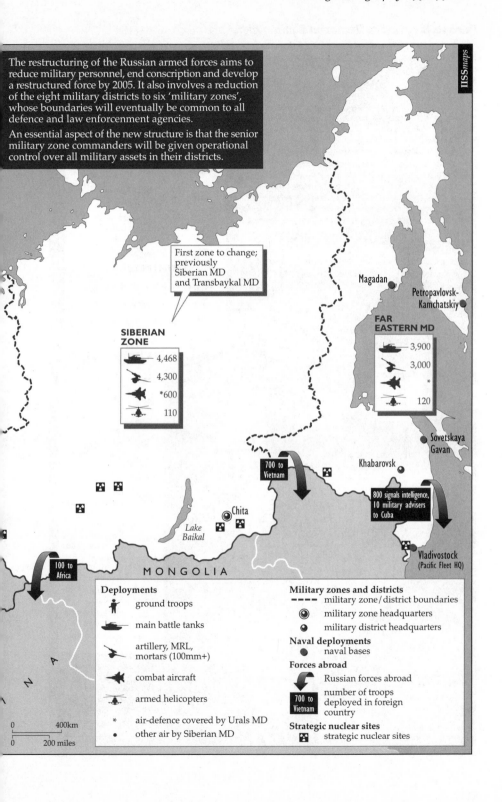

IISSmaps

The restructuring of the Russian armed forces aims to reduce military personnel, end conscription and develop a restructured force by 2005. It also involves a reduction of the eight military districts to six 'military zones', whose boundaries will eventually be common to all defence and law enforcement agencies.

An essential aspect of the new structure is that the senior military zone commanders will be given operational control over all military assets in their districts.

First zone to change; previously Siberian MD and Transbaykal MD

Magadan

Petropavlovsk-Kamchatskiy

SIBERIAN ZONE
4,468
4,300
*600
110

FAR EASTERN MD
3,900
3,000
*
120

Sovetskaya Gavan

700 to Vietnam

Khabarovsk

800 signals intelligence, 10 military advisers to Cuba

Chita

Lake Baikal

100 to Africa

MONGOLIA

Vladivostock (Pacific Fleet HQ)

Deployments

👤 ground troops

🚂 main battle tanks

artillery, MRL, mortars (100mm+)

combat aircraft

armed helicopters

* air-defence covered by Urals MD

• other air by Siberian MD

Military zones and districts

- - - - military zone/district boundaries

◉ military zone headquarters

◕ military district headquarters

Naval deployments

● naval bases

Forces abroad

Russian forces abroad

700 to Vietnam number of troops deployed in foreign country

Strategic nuclear sites

☢ strategic nuclear sites

0   400km

0   200 miles

Europe *Bosnia: The 'Train and Equip' Programme*

'Train and Equip' Programme

The US-sponsored programme for the Bosnian–Croat Federation was set up in early 1996 to strengthen and modernise the armed forces of the Federation within the framework of the force levels agreed under the Dayton Peace Accord. The programme, condsidered ill-advised and potentially destabilising by the European members of the Contact Group, is organised and administered by a US civilian contractor: Military Professional Resources Inc (MPRI). The table shows deliveries to the Federation as of late 1998. Because relations between the two halves of the Federation remain tense, much of the equipment has yet to be deployed with regular units.

In addition to heavy equipment, some 1,000 machine guns and 45,000 M16A1 rifles (with ammunition) have been delivered. To improve combat performance and mobility of military units, 'Train and Equip' has also included the delivery of Hughes–Magnavox AN/PRC-126 handheld radios, NAPCO AN/PRC-77 manpack radios, more than 4,000 tactical telephones as well as trucks and transport vehicles.

Distribution of equipment

15 x UH-1H
6 x MI-24 (*Hind*) (still in Germany as of January 1999)

MND SOUTHWEST MND (SW)

840 x AT-4 *Spigot* (*Fagot*)

MND SOUTHEAST MND (SE)

45 x M60-A3
50 x AMX-30
80 x M-113 A2
10 x M-3 'Panhard'
36 x 105mm *Howitzer*
12 x 122mm D30
12 x 130mm M46
31 x AML-90

MND NORTH MND (N)

10 x T-55 (Egypt)
126 x 155mm *Howitzer*
6 x MLRS APRA 40 (Romania)
18 x ZU-23 (Egypt)

The current strength of the NATO-led Stabilisation Force (SFOR) is 29,000. It is composed of contingents from 29 countries.

Europe *Ethnic Albanians in the Southern Balkans*

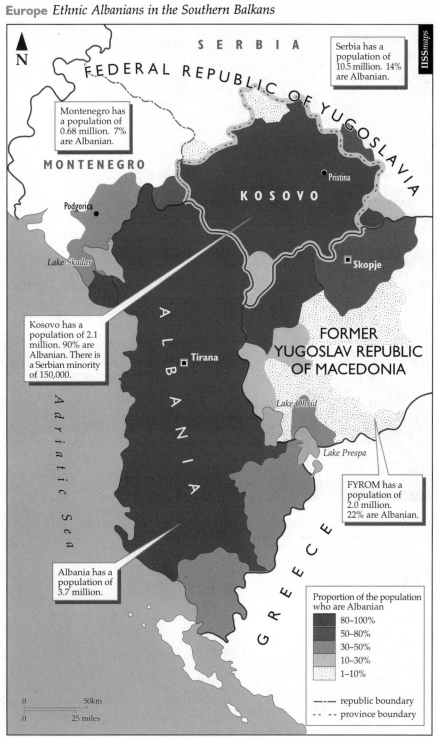

Serbia has a population of 10.5 million. 14% are Albanian.

Montenegro has a population of 0.68 million. 7% are Albanian.

Kosovo has a population of 2.1 million. 90% are Albanian. There is a Serbian minority of 150,000.

FYROM has a population of 2.0 million. 22% are Albanian.

Albania has a population of 3.7 million.

Proportion of the population who are Albanian

- 80–100%
- 50–80%
- 30–50%
- 10–30%
- 1–10%

—·— republic boundary
- - - province boundary

0   50km
0   25 miles

Europe *The conflict in Kosovo*

Holbrooke Agreement 12 October 1998:

● Serbian forces in Kosovo to be reduced to pre-conflict levels (around 10,000 police and 11,000 army troops compared to more than 50,000 before the agreement).

● Refugees allowed to return to their homes.

● Up to 2,000 international 'compliance verifiers' from the OSCE to be deployed to monitor the situation on the ground.

OSCE Kosovo Verification Mission
The mission was set up in November 1998.

Central HQ	Pristina
Regional HQs	5
field offices	25
'compliance verifiers'	up to 2,000*

* less than half were deployed by January 1999

Refugees and Internally Displaced Persons
Kosovo has a population of 2.1million. It is estimated that over 200,000 have been displaced or badly affected by the conflict. The majority of these fled within the province, however 65,000 sought refuge in Montenegro and Serbia and a further 35,000 became refugees in other countries like Albania and Bosnia-Herzegovina.

Main elements of the proposed Interim Peace Agreement, March 1999:

● extensive autonomy granted to Kosovo.

● phased withdrawal of Serb military and police forces from Kosovo.

● the disarming and disbanding of the KLA and the creation of an ethnically-mixed police force.

● deployment of NATO-led force to oversee implementation.

● future status of Kosovo to be reviewed after 3 years.

● elections to be held within 9 months. To be overseen by the OSCE.

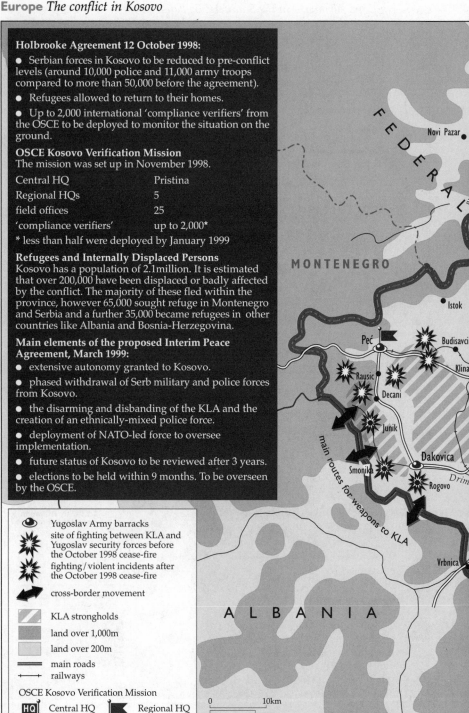

Yugoslav Army barracks

site of fighting between KLA and Yugoslav security forces before the October 1998 cease-fire

fighting/violent incidents after the October 1998 cease-fire

cross-border movement

KLA strongholds

land over 1,000m

land over 200m

main roads

railways

OSCE Kosovo Verification Mission

HQ Central HQ   Regional HQ

0   10km
0   5 miles

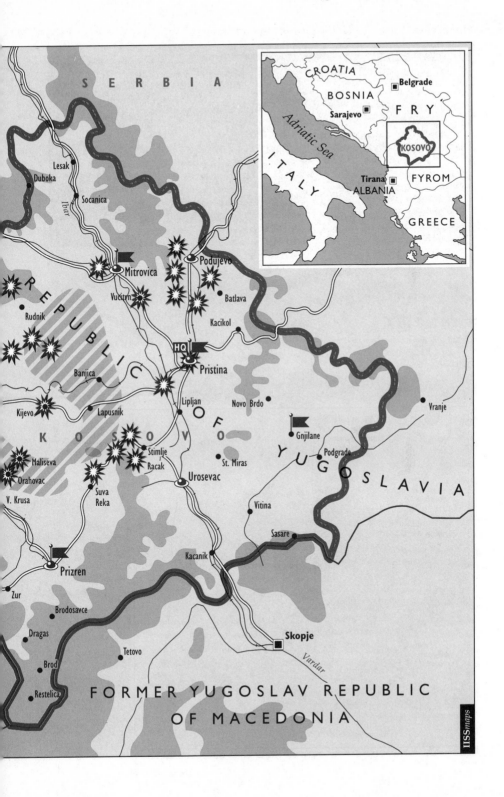

The Middle East *The UNSCOM inspection crisis*

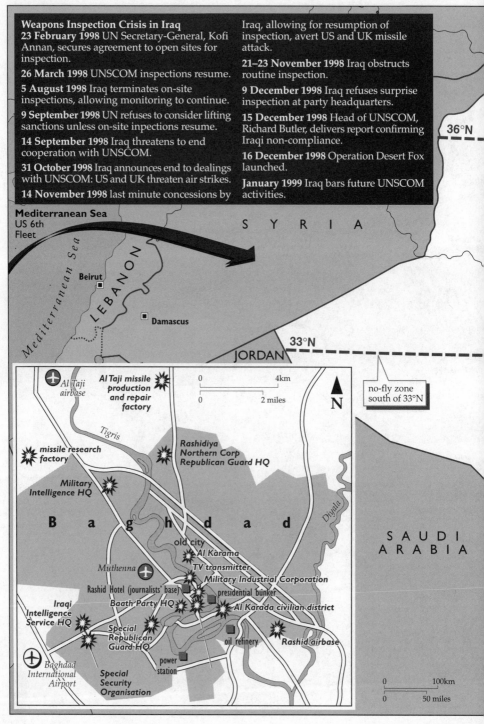

Weapons Inspection Crisis in Iraq

23 February 1998 UN Secretary-General, Kofi Annan, secures agreement to open sites for inspection.

26 March 1998 UNSCOM inspections resume.

5 August 1998 Iraq terminates on-site inspections, allowing monitoring to continue.

9 September 1998 UN refuses to consider lifting sanctions unless on-site inpections resume.

14 September 1998 Iraq threatens to end cooperation with UNSCOM.

31 October 1998 Iraq announces end to dealings with UNSCOM: US and UK threaten air strikes.

14 November 1998 last minute concessions by Iraq, allowing for resumption of inspection, avert US and UK missile attack.

21–23 November 1998 Iraq obstructs routine inspection.

9 December 1998 Iraq refuses surprise inspection at party headquarters.

15 December 1998 Head of UNSCOM, Richard Butler, delivers report confirming Iraqi non-compliance.

16 December 1998 Operation Desert Fox launched.

January 1999 Iraq bars future UNSCOM activities.

36°N

Mediterranean Sea
US 6th Fleet

S Y R I A

Mediterranean Sea

Beirut

L E B A N O N

Damascus

33°N

JORDAN

Al Taji airbase

Al Taji missile production and repair factory

no-fly zone south of 33°N

0   4km
0   2 miles

N

Tigris

missile research factory

Rashidiya Northern Corp Republican Guard HQ

Military Intelligence HQ

B a g h d a d

Dijala

old city
Al Karama
TV transmitter
Military Industrial Corporation

Muthenna

Rashid Hotel (journalists' base)
presidential bunker

Iraqi Intelligence Service HQ

Baath Party HQ
Al Karada civilian district

SAUDI ARABIA

Special Republican Guard HQ

oil refinery
Rashid airbase

power station

Baghdad International Airport

Special Security Organisation

0   100km
0   50 miles

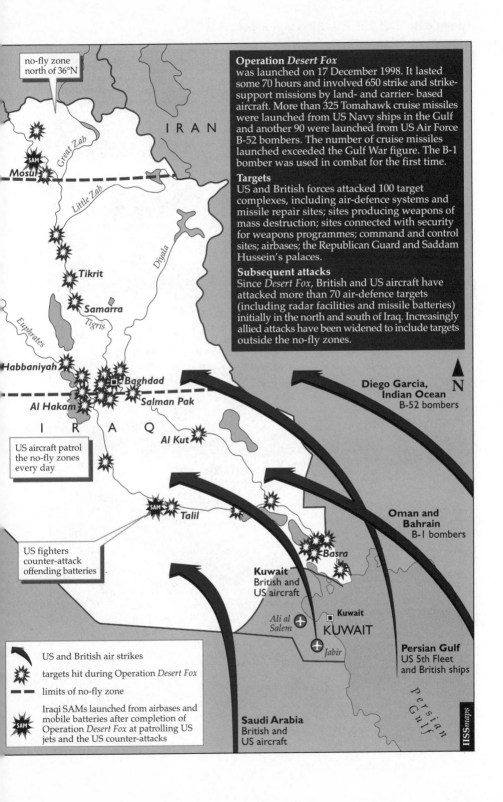

no-fly zone
north of 36°N

Operation *Desert Fox*
was launched on 17 December 1998. It lasted
some 70 hours and involved 650 strike and strike-
support missions by land- and carrier- based
aircraft. More than 325 Tomahawk cruise missiles
were launched from US Navy ships in the Gulf
and another 90 were launched from US Air Force
B-52 bombers. The number of cruise missiles
launched exceeded the Gulf War figure. The B-1
bomber was used in combat for the first time.

Targets
US and British forces attacked 100 target
complexes, including air-defence systems and
missile repair sites; sites producing weapons of
mass destruction; sites connected with security
for weapons programmes; command and control
sites; airbases; the Republican Guard and Saddam
Hussein's palaces.

Subsequent attacks
Since *Desert Fox*, British and US aircraft have
attacked more than 70 air-defence targets
(including radar facilities and missile batteries)
initially in the north and south of Iraq. Increasingly
allied attacks have been widened to include targets
outside the no-fly zones.

IRAN

Great Zab
Little Zab
Mosul
SAM
Tikrit
Diyala
Samarra
Tigris
Euphrates
Habbaniyah
Baghdad
Al Hakam
Salman Pak
I R A Q
Al Kut

US aircraft patrol
the no-fly zones
every day

SAM
Talil

US fighters
counter-attack
offending batteries

Basra
Kuwait
British and
US aircraft

Ali al
Salem
Jabir
Kuwait
KUWAIT

Diego Garcia,
Indian Ocean
B-52 bombers
N

Oman and
Bahrain
B-1 bombers

Persian Gulf
US 5th Fleet
and British ships

Saudi Arabia
British and
US aircraft

Persian Gulf

US and British air strikes

targets hit during Operation *Desert Fox*

limits of no-fly zone

Iraqi SAMs launched from airbases and
mobile batteries after completion of
Operation *Desert Fox* at patrolling US
jets and the US counter-attacks

IISSmaps

The Middle East *The Wye River Agreement*

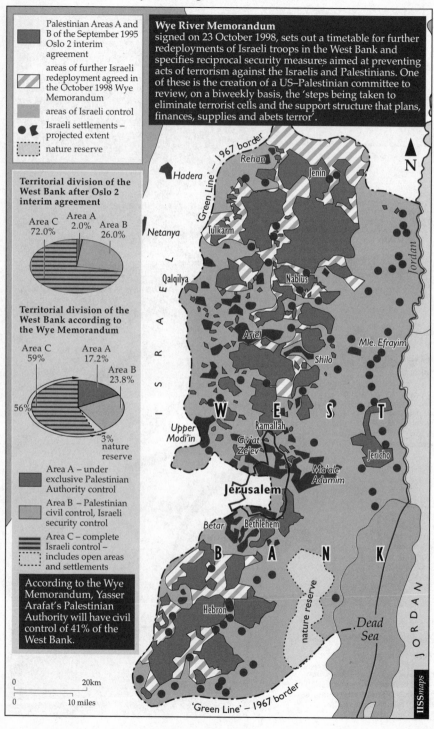

Palestinian Areas A and B of the September 1995 Oslo 2 interim agreement

areas of further Israeli redeployment agreed in the October 1998 Wye Memorandum

areas of Israeli control

Israeli settlements – projected extent

nature reserve

Wye River Memorandum
signed on 23 October 1998, sets out a timetable for further redeployments of Israeli troops in the West Bank and specifies reciprocal security measures aimed at preventing acts of terrorism against the Israelis and Palestinians. One of these is the creation of a US–Palestinian committee to review, on a biweekly basis, the 'steps being taken to eliminate terrorist cells and the support structure that plans, finances, supplies and abets terror'.

Territorial division of the West Bank after Oslo 2 interim agreement

Area C 72.0% Area A 2.0% Area B 26.0%

Territorial division of the West Bank according to the Wye Memorandum

Area C 59% Area A 17.2% Area B 23.8%

56% 3% nature reserve

Area A – under exclusive Palestinian Authority control

Area B – Palestinian civil control, Israeli security control

Area C – complete Israeli control – includes open areas and settlements

According to the Wye Memorandum, Yasser Arafat's Palestinian Authority will have civil control of 41% of the West Bank.

0 — 20km
0 — 10 miles

IISSmaps

The Middle East *Kurdish populations in the Middle East*

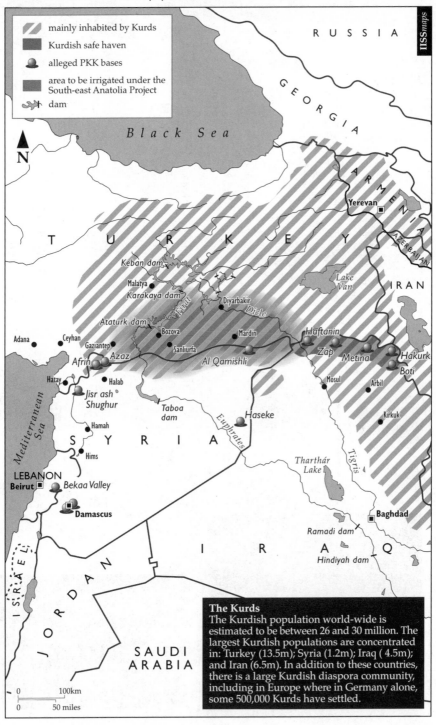

mainly inhabited by Kurds

Kurdish safe haven

alleged PKK bases

area to be irrigated under the South-east Anatolia Project

dam

IISSmaps

RUSSIA

GEORGIA

Black Sea

N

T U R K E Y

ARMENIA

Yerevan

AZERBAIJAN

IRAN

Keban dam

Malatya
Karakaya dam

Firat

Diyarbakir

Dicle

Lake Van

Ataturk dam

Bozova

Mardin

Haftanin

Zap

Metina

Hakurk

Adana

Ceyhan
Gaziantep

Sanliurfa

Boti

Afrin

Azaz

Al Qamishli

Mosul

Arbil

Hatay

Halab

Kirkuk

Mediterranean Sea

Jisr ash Shughur

Taboa dam

Haseke

Euphrates

Tigris

Hamah

S Y R I A

Hims

Tharthár Lake

LEBANON
Beirut

Bekaa Valley

Damascus

Baghdad

Ramadi dam

I R A Q

Hindiyah dam

I S R A E L

J O R D A N

SAUDI ARABIA

0   100km
0   50 miles

The Kurds
The Kurdish population world-wide is estimated to be between 26 and 30 million. The largest Kurdish populations are concentrated in: Turkey (13.5m); Syria (1.2m); Iraq (4.5m); and Iran (6.5m). In addition to these countries, there is a large Kurdish diaspora community, including in Europe where in Germany alone, some 500,000 Kurds have settled.

The Middle East *Water and conflict in the Middle East*

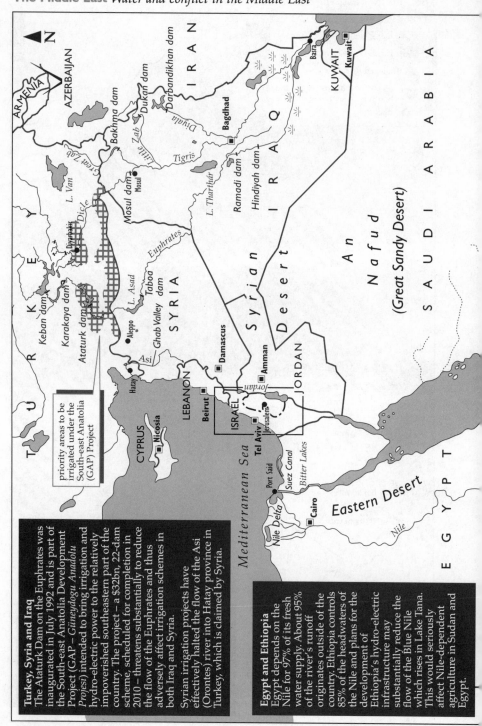

priority areas to be irrigated under the South-east Anatolia (GAP) Project

Turkey, Syria and Iraq
The Ataturk Dam on the Euphrates was inaugurated in July 1992 and is part of the South-east Anatolia Development Project (GAP – *Güneydoğu Anadolu Projesi*) intended to bring irrigation and hydro-electric power to the relatively impoverished southeastern part of the country. The project – a $32bn, 22-dam scheme, scheduled for completion in 2010 – threatens substantially to reduce the flow of the Euphrates and thus adversely affect irrigation schemes in both Iraq and Syria.

Syrian irrigation projects have effectively halted the flow of the Asi (Orontes) river into Hatay province in Turkey, which is claimed by Syria.

Egypt and Ethiopia
Egypt depends on the Nile for 97% of its fresh water supply. About 95% of the river's runoff originates outside of the country. Ethiopia controls 85% of the headwaters of the Nile and plans for the development of Ethiopia's hydro-electric infrastructure may substantially reduce the flow of the Blue Nile which rises in Lake Tana. This would seriously affect Nile-dependent agriculture in Sudan and Egypt.

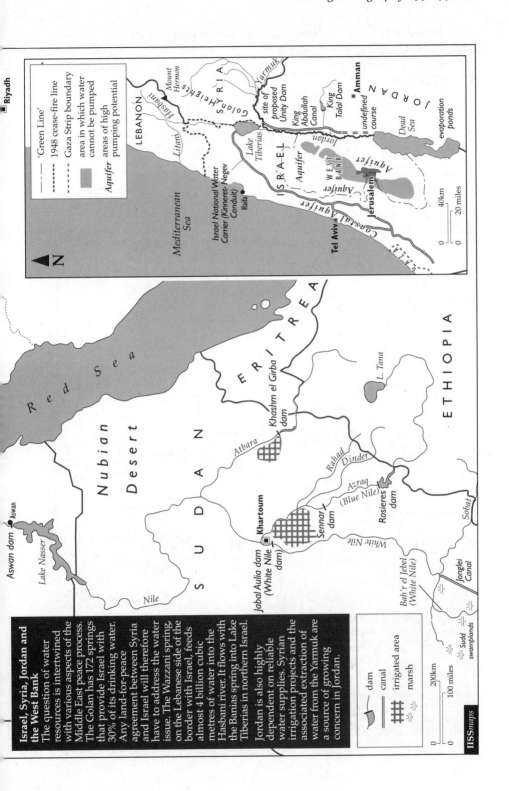

Israel, Syria, Jordan and the West Bank

The question of water resources is intertwined with various aspects of the Middle East peace process. The Golan has 172 springs that provide Israel with 30% of its drinking water. Any land-for-peace agreement between Syria and Israel will therefore have to address the water issue. The Wazzani spring, on the Lebanese side of the border with Israel, feeds almost 4 billion cubic metres of water into the Hasbani river. It flows with the Banias spring into Lake Tiberias in northern Israel.

Jordan is also highly dependent on reliable water supplies. Syrian irrigation projects and the associated extraction of water from the Yarmuk are a source of growing concern in Jordan.

IISS*maps*

Asia *India and Pakistan: nuclear tests and weapons programmes*

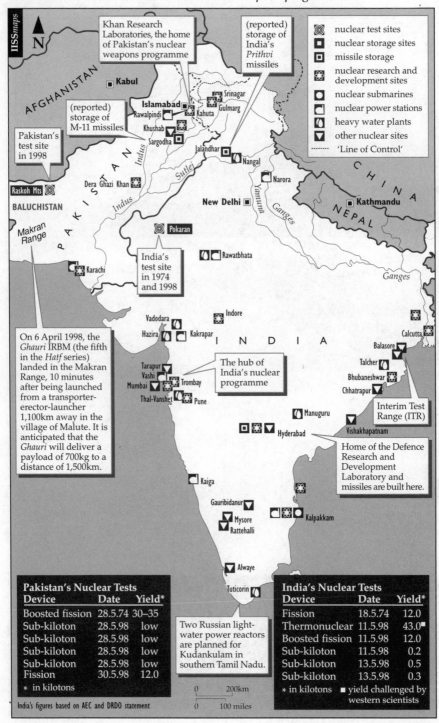

Khan Research Laboratories, the home of Pakistan's nuclear weapons programme

(reported) storage of India's *Prithvi* missiles

	nuclear test sites
	nuclear storage sites
	missile storage
	nuclear research and development sites
	nuclear submarines
	nuclear power stations
	heavy water plants
	other nuclear sites
-------	'Line of Control'

Kabul

AFGHANISTAN

(reported) storage of M-11 missiles

Srinagar

Islamabad
Rawalpindi
Kahuta
Gulmarg

Pakistan's test site in 1998

Khushab
Sargodha

Jalandhar
Nangal

C H I N A

Raskoh Mts

Dera Ghazi Khan

Narora

BALUCHISTAN

Indus

Sutlej

Yamuna

New Delhi

Kathmandu

NEPAL

Makran Range

Pokaran

Ganges

India's test site in 1974 and 1998

Rawatbhata

Karachi

Ganges

Vadodara
Indore

Hazira
Kakrapar

On 6 April 1998, the *Ghauri* IRBM (the fifth in the *Hatf* series) landed in the Makran Range, 10 minutes after being launched from a transporter-erector-launcher 1,100km away in the village of Malute. It is anticipated that the *Ghauri* will deliver a payload of 700kg to a distance of 1,500km.

I N D I A

Calcutta

Balasore

Tarapur
Vashi
Mumbai
Trombay
Thal-Vanshet
Pune

The hub of India's nuclear programme

Talcher

Bhubaneshwar

Chhatrapur

Interim Test Range (ITR)

Manuguru

Hyderabad

Vishakhapatnam

Home of the Defence Research and Development Laboratory and missiles are built here.

Kaiga

Gauribidanur

Mysore
Rattehalli

Kalpakkam

Alwaye

Tuticorin

Pakistan's Nuclear Tests

Device	Date	Yield*
Boosted fission	28.5.74	30–35
Sub-kiloton	28.5.98	low
Sub-kiloton	28.5.98	low
Sub-kiloton	28.5.98	low
Sub-kiloton	28.5.98	low
Fission	30.5.98	12.0
* in kilotons		

India's figures based on AEC and DRDO statement

Two Russian light-water power reactors are planned for Kudankulam in southern Tamil Nadu.

India's Nuclear Tests

Device	Date	Yield*
Fission	18.5.74	12.0
Thermonuclear	11.5.98	43.0■
Boosted fission	11.5.98	12.0
Sub-kiloton	11.5.98	0.2
Sub-kiloton	13.5.98	0.5
Sub-kiloton	13.5.98	0.3
* in kilotons	■ yield challenged by western scientists	

0   200km

0   100 miles

IISS*maps*

Asia *The Kashmir conflict*

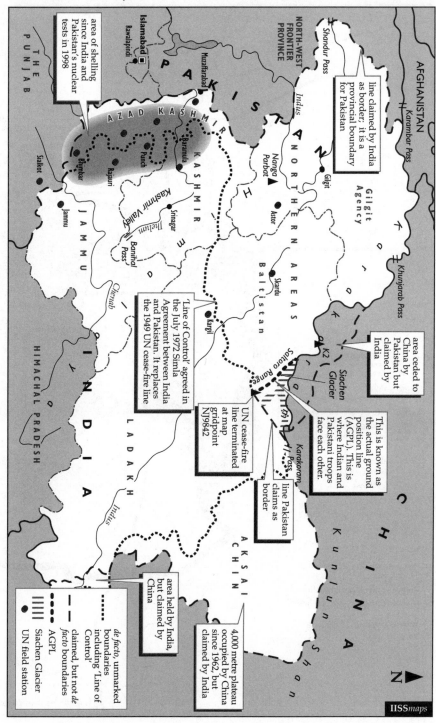

area of shelling since India and Pakistan's nuclear tests in 1998

THE PUNJAB

Islamabad

Rawalpindi

Muzaffarabad

PAKISTAN

AZAD KASHMIR

Baramula

Bhimbar

Rajauri

Punch

Sialkot

Jammu

JAMMU

Kashmir Valley

Srinagar

Jhelum

Banihal Pass

Chenab

HIMACHAL PRADESH

INDIA

Indus

Kargil

LADAKH

NORTH-WEST FRONTIER PROVINCE

Shandur Pass

line claimed by India as border; it is a provincial boundary for Pakistan

Indus

Nanga Parbat ▲

Gilgit Agency

Gilgit

NORTHERN AREAS

Astor

Baltistan

Skardu

AFGHANISTAN

Karambar Pass

Khunjerab Pass

'Line of Control' agreed in the July 1972 Simla Agreement between India and Pakistan. It replaces the 1949 UN cease-fire line

UN cease-fire line terminated at map gridpoint NJ9842

Saltoro Range

Siachen Glacier

K2

area ceded to China by Pakistan but claimed by India

This is known as the actual ground position line (AGPL). This is where Indian and Pakistani troops face each other.

line Pakistan claims as border

Karakoram Pass

AKSAI CHIN

Kunlun Shan

CHINA

area held by India, but claimed by China

4,000 metre plateau occupied by China since 1962, but claimed by India

de facto, unmarked boundaries
claimed, but not *de facto* boundaries
de facto boundaries including 'Line of Control'
AGPL
Siachen Glacier
UN field station

N ▶

IISS*maps*

Asia Taleban *control in Afghanistan*

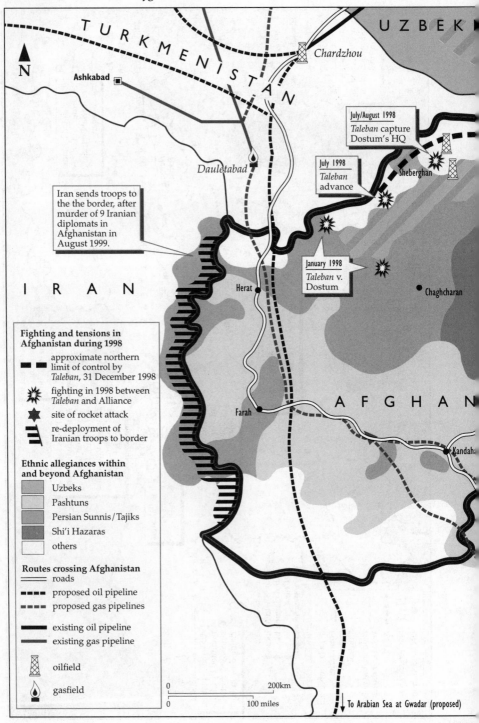

Chardzhou

Ashkabad

July/August 1998
Taleban capture
Dostum's HQ

July 1998
Taleban
advance

Sheberghan

Dauletabad

Iran sends troops to
the the border, after
murder of 9 Iranian
diplomats in
Afghanistan in
August 1999.

January 1998
Taleban v.
Dostum

I R A N

Herat

Chaghcharan

A F G H A N

**Fighting and tensions in
Afghanistan during 1998**

approximate northern
limit of control by
Taleban, 31 December 1998

fighting in 1998 between
Taleban and Alliance

site of rocket attack

re-deployment of
Iranian troops to border

Farah

Kandaha

**Ethnic allegiances within
and beyond Afghanistan**

Uzbeks

Pashtuns

Persian Sunnis/Tajiks

Shi'i Hazaras

others

Routes crossing Afghanistan
roads

proposed oil pipeline

proposed gas pipelines

existing oil pipeline

existing gas pipeline

oilfield

gasfield

0   200km

0   100 miles

To Arabian Sea at Gwadar (proposed)

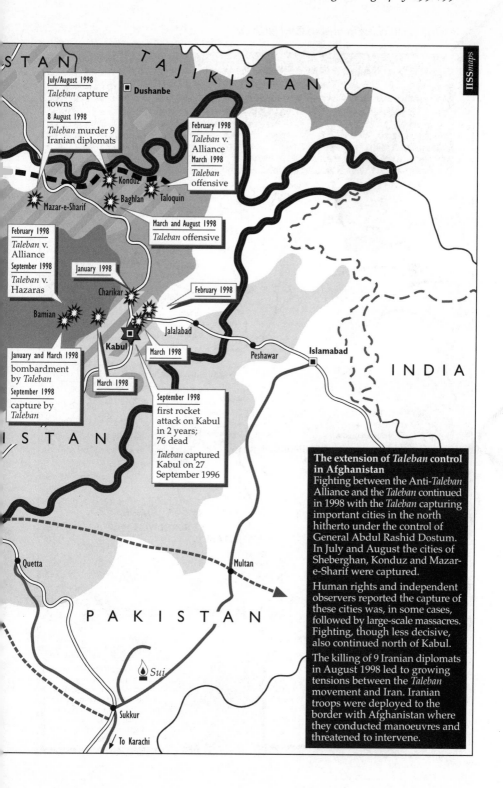

July/August 1998
Taleban capture towns
8 August 1998
Taleban murder 9 Iranian diplomats

February 1998
Taleban v. Alliance
March 1998
Taleban offensive

March and August 1998
Taleban offensive

February 1998
Taleban v. Alliance
September 1998
Taleban v. Hazaras

January 1998

February 1998

January and March 1998
bombardment by *Taleban*
September 1998
capture by *Taleban*

March 1998

March 1998

September 1998
first rocket attack on Kabul in 2 years; 76 dead
Taleban captured Kabul on 27 September 1996

Dushanbe, Konduz, Baghlan, Taloquin, Mazar-e-Sharif, Charikar, Bamian, Kabul, Jalalabad, Peshawar, Islamabad, Quetta, Multan, Sui, Sukkur, To Karachi

TAJIKISTAN, INDIA, PAKISTAN

IISS*maps*

The extension of *Taleban* control in Afghanistan

Fighting between the Anti-*Taleban* Alliance and the *Taleban* continued in 1998 with the *Taleban* capturing important cities in the north hitherto under the control of General Abdul Rashid Dostum. In July and August the cities of Sheberghan, Konduz and Mazar-e-Sharif were captured.

Human rights and independent observers reported the capture of these cities was, in some cases, followed by large-scale massacres. Fighting, though less decisive, also continued north of Kabul.

The killing of 9 Iranian diplomats in August 1998 led to growing tensions between the *Taleban* movement and Iran. Iranian troops were deployed to the border with Afghanistan where they conducted manoeuvres and threatened to intervene.

Asia *Drug trafficking routes in Central Asia*

Although the Central Asian states are not classified as major producers of opium, their significance as an easy and profitable transit route for international traffickers is increasing.

Afghanistan is now the world's second largest producer of opium. Production continues to rise and it is estimated that as much as 2,800 tonnes may have been producd in 1997.

Governments in Russia and Central Asia lack the resources to enforce drug control effectively along their borders. Poorly equipped and trained law enforcement agencies and inadequate border controls allow Russian and Central Asian traffickers to move heroin from Afghanistan and Pakistan through Uzbekistan, Tajikistan and Kyrgyzstan to the Baltic States and so to European markets.

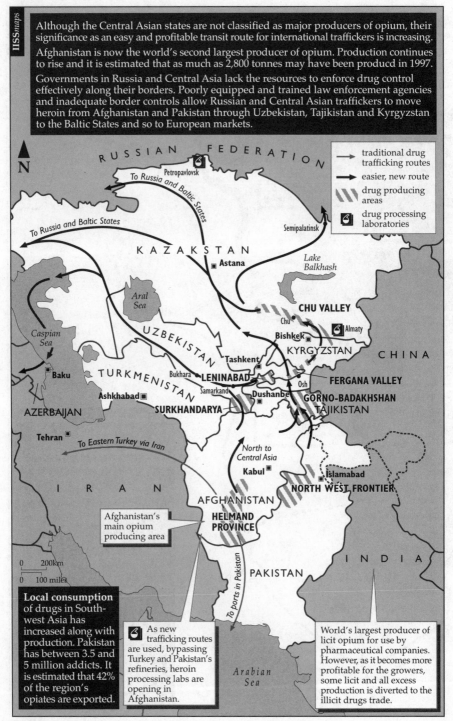

Legend:
- → traditional drug trafficking routes
- → easier, new route
- drug producing areas
- drug processing laboratories

Local consumption of drugs in South-west Asia has increased along with production. Pakistan has between 3.5 and 5 million addicts. It is estimated that 42% of the region's opiates are exported.

As new trafficking routes are used, bypassing Turkey and Pakistan's refineries, heroin processing labs are opening in Afghanistan.

World's largest producer of licit opium for use by pharmaceutical companies. However, as it becomes more profitable for the growers, some licit and all excess production is diverted to the illicit drugs trade.

Afghanistan's main opium producing area

Africa *Regional and sub-regional groupings in Africa*

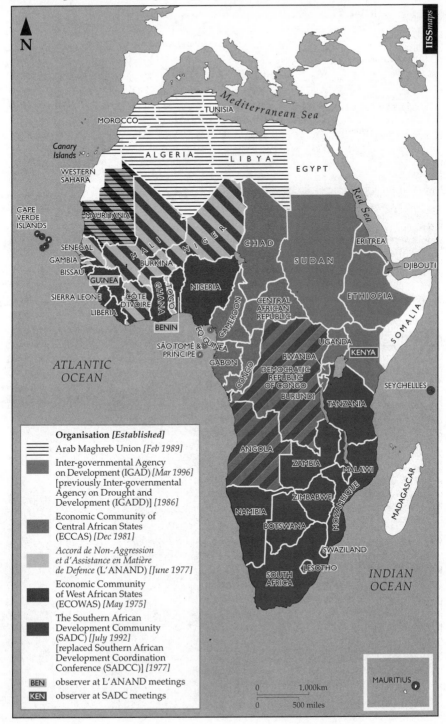

Organisation *[Established]*

Arab Maghreb Union *[Feb 1989]*

Inter-governmental Agency on Development (IGAD) *[Mar 1996]* [previously Inter-governmental Agency on Drought and Development (IGADD)] *[1986]*

Economic Community of Central African States (ECCAS) *[Dec 1981]*

Accord de Non-Aggression et d'Assistance en Matière de Défense (L'ANAND) *[June 1977]*

Economic Community of West African States (ECOWAS) *[May 1975]*

The Southern African Development Community (SADC) *[July 1992]* [replaced Southern African Development Coordination Conference (SADCC)] *[1977]*

BEN observer at L'ANAND meetings

KEN observer at SADC meetings

Africa *Mineral resources in Sub-Saharan Africa*

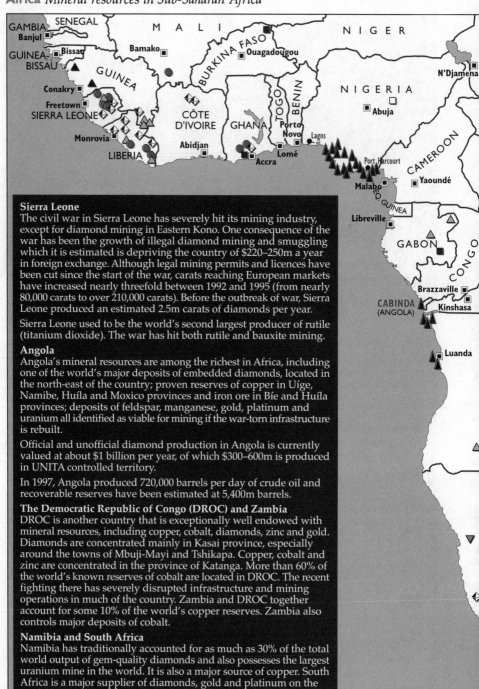

Sierra Leone
The civil war in Sierra Leone has severely hit its mining industry, except for diamond mining in Eastern Kono. One consequence of the war has been the growth of illegal diamond mining and smuggling which it is estimated is depriving the country of $220–250m a year in foreign exchange. Although legal mining permits and licences have been cut since the start of the war, carats reaching European markets have increased nearly threefold between 1992 and 1995 (from nearly 80,000 carats to over 210,000 carats). Before the outbreak of war, Sierra Leone produced an estimated 2.5m carats of diamonds per year.

Sierra Leone used to be the world's second largest producer of rutile (titanium dioxide). The war has hit both rutile and bauxite mining.

Angola
Angola's mineral resources are among the richest in Africa, including one of the world's major deposits of embedded diamonds, located in the north-east of the country; proven reserves of copper in Uíge, Namibe, Huíla and Moxico provinces and iron ore in Bíe and Huíla provinces; deposits of feldspar, manganese, gold, platinum and uranium all identified as viable for mining if the war-torn infrastructure is rebuilt.

Official and unofficial diamond production in Angola is currently valued at about $1 billion per year, of which $300–600m is produced in UNITA controlled territory.

In 1997, Angola produced 720,000 barrels per day of crude oil and recoverable reserves have been estimated at 5,400m barrels.

The Democratic Republic of Congo (DROC) and Zambia
DROC is another country that is exceptionally well endowed with mineral resources, including copper, cobalt, diamonds, zinc and gold. Diamonds are concentrated mainly in Kasai province, especially around the towns of Mbuji-Mayi and Tshikapa. Copper, cobalt and zinc are concentrated in the province of Katanga. More than 60% of the world's known reserves of cobalt are located in DROC. The recent fighting there has severely disrupted infrastructure and mining operations in much of the country. Zambia and DROC together account for some 10% of the world's copper reserves. Zambia also controls major deposits of cobalt.

Namibia and South Africa
Namibia has traditionally accounted for as much as 30% of the total world output of gem-quality diamonds and also possesses the largest uranium mine in the world. It is also a major source of copper. South Africa is a major supplier of diamonds, gold and platinum on the world market. More than 20% of the world supply of gold and nearly 70% of platinum originate in South Africa.

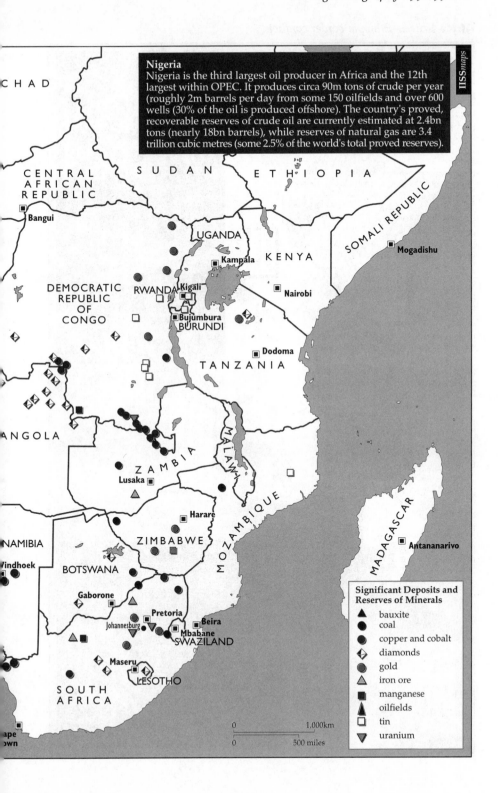

Nigeria
Nigeria is the third largest oil producer in Africa and the 12th largest within OPEC. It produces circa 90m tons of crude per year (roughly 2m barrels per day from some 150 oilfields and over 600 wells (30% of the oil is produced offshore). The country's proved, recoverable reserves of crude oil are currently estimated at 2.4bn tons (nearly 18bn barrels), while reserves of natural gas are 3.4 trillion cubic metres (some 2.5% of the world's total proved reserves).

CHAD

CENTRAL
AFRICAN
REPUBLIC

■ Bangui

SUDAN

ETHIOPIA

SOMALI REPUBLIC

■ Mogadishu

UGANDA

■ Kampala

KENYA

DEMOCRATIC
REPUBLIC
OF
CONGO

RWANDA Kigali

Bujumbura
BURUNDI

■ Nairobi

■ Dodoma

TANZANIA

ANGOLA

ZAMBIA

Lusaka ■

MALAWI

MOZAMBIQUE

MADAGASCAR

■ Antananarivo

NAMIBIA

Windhoek

BOTSWANA

Harare ■

ZIMBABWE

Gaborone

Johannesburg

Pretoria

■ Beira

Mbabane
SWAZILAND

Maseru

LESOTHO

SOUTH
AFRICA

ape
own

**Significant Deposits and
Reserves of Minerals**

▲ bauxite
● coal
◕ copper and cobalt
◈ diamonds
◓ gold
△ iron ore
■ manganese
▲ oilfields
☐ tin
▽ uranium

0   1,000km

0   500 miles

IISS*maps*

Africa *Eritrea–Ethiopia border conflict*

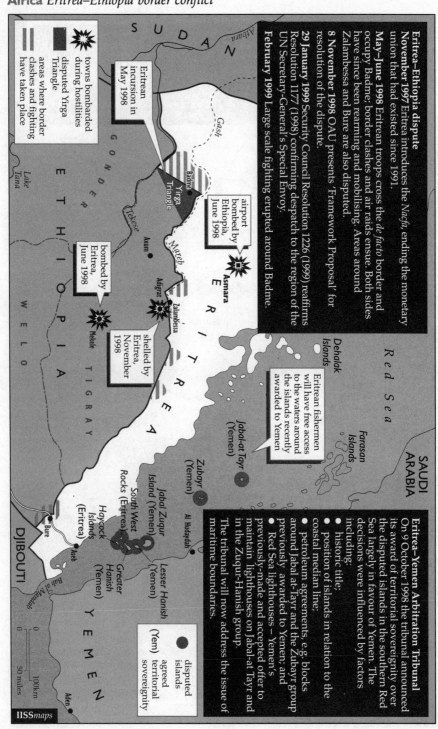

Eritrea–Ethiopia dispute

November 1997 Eritrea introduces the *Nacfa*, ending the monetary union that had existed since 1991.

May–June 1998 Eritrean troops cross the *de facto* border and occupy Badme; border clashes and air raids ensue. Both sides have since been rearming and mobilising. Areas around Zalambessa and Bure are also disputed.

8 November 1998 OAU presents 'Framework Proposal' for resolution of the dispute.

29 January 1999 Security Council Resolution 1226 (1999) reaffirms Resolution 1177 (1998), confirming despatch to the region of the UN Secretary-General's Special Envoy.

February 1999 Large scale fighting erupted around Badme.

towns bombarded during hostilities

disputed Yirga Triangle

areas where border clashes and fighting have taken place

Eritrean incursion in May 1998

airport bombed by Ethiopia, June 1998

bombed by Eritrea, June 1998

shelled by Eritrea, November 1998

Eritrean fishermen will have free access to the waters around the islands recently awarded to Yemen

Eritrea–Yemen Arbitration Tribunal

On 9 October 1998 the tribunal announced its award of territorial sovereignty over the disputed islands in the southern Red Sea largely in favour of Yemen. The decisions were influenced by factors including:

- historic title;
- position of islands in relation to the coastal median line;
- petroleum agreements, e.g. blocks around Jabal at Tayr and the Zubayr group previously awarded to Yemen; and
- Red Sea lighthouses – Yemen's previously-made and accepted offer to maintain lighthouses on Jabal-at Tayr and in the Zuqur-Hanish group.

The tribunal will now address the issue of maritime boundaries.

disputed islands

agreed (Yem) territorial sovereignty

SUDAN

Atbara

Gash

Tekeze

Mareb

ETHIOPIA

GONDER

WELO

TIGRAY

ERITREA

Red Sea

SAUDI ARABIA

YEMEN

DJIBOUTI

Lake Tana

Badme

Yirga Triangle

Asmara

Axum

Adigrat

Zalambessa

Mekele

Dehalak Islands

Farasan Islands

Jabal-at Tayr (Yemen)

Zubayr (Yemen)

Jabal Zuqur Island (Yemen)

South West Rocks (Eritrea)

Hanish Islands (Eritrea)

Haycock Islands (Eritrea)

Lesser Hanish (Yemen)

Greater Hanish (Yemen)

Al Hudaydah

Bure

Aseb

Bab al Mandab

Aden

0   50 miles
0   100km

IISS*maps*

Africa *The US African Crisis Response Initiative (ACRI)*

The US African Crisis Response Initiative (ACRI)
is a five-year initiative to build-up capacity at battalion and brigade level and consists of
six phases: Initial Battalion Training is a 60-day programme which provides basic soldiering
skills to troops at the battalion level. Five 'Follow-on Training' (FT) programmes, previously
known as 'Sustainment Training' (ST), are scheduled every six months after initial training.
FTs are computer-assisted or 'table-top' exercises run by US computer contractors.

A total of 4,426 soldiers have received initial training.

Equipment
is all non-lethal, primarily communications hardware, e.g. radio equipment, water
purification systems, night vision patrol devices and uniforms.

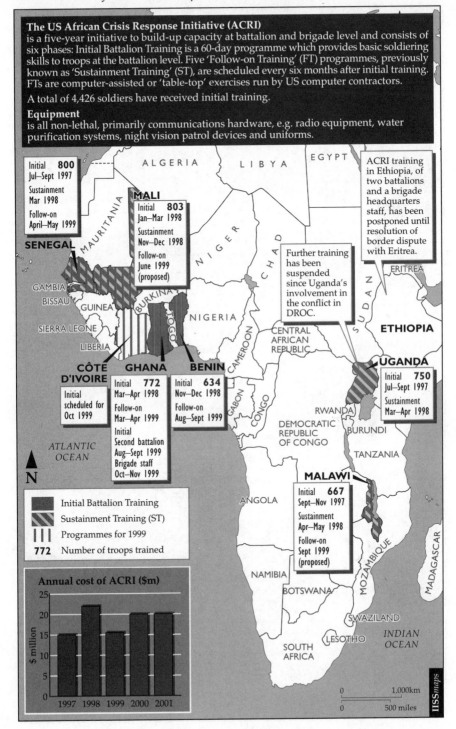

SENEGAL
Initial **800**
Jul–Sept 1997
Sustainment
Mar 1998
Follow-on
April–May 1999

MALI
Initial **803**
Jan–Mar 1998
Sustainment
Nov–Dec 1998
Follow-on
June 1999
(proposed)

ACRI training
in Ethiopia, of
two battalions
and a brigade
headquarters
staff, has been
postponed until
resolution of
border dispute
with Eritrea.

Further training
has been
suspended
since Uganda's
involvement in
the conflict in
DROC.

CÔTE
D'IVOIRE
Initial
scheduled for
Oct 1999

GHANA
Initial **772**
Mar–Apr 1998
Follow-on
Mar–Apr 1999
Initial
Second battalion
Aug–Sept 1999
Brigade staff
Oct–Nov 1999

BENIN
Initial **634**
Nov–Dec 1998
Follow-on
Aug–Sept 1999

UGANDA
Initial **750**
Jul–Sept 1997
Sustainment
Mar–Apr 1998

MALAWI
Initial **667**
Sept–Nov 1997
Sustainment
Apr–May 1998
Follow-on
Sept 1999
(proposed)

ATLANTIC
OCEAN

N

Initial Battalion Training
Sustainment Training (ST)
Programmes for 1999
772 Number of troops trained

Annual cost of ACRI ($m)
$ million
25
20
15
10
5
0
1997 1998 1999 2000 2001

0   1,000km
0   500 miles

IISS*maps*

Africa *War in the Democratic Republic of Congo*

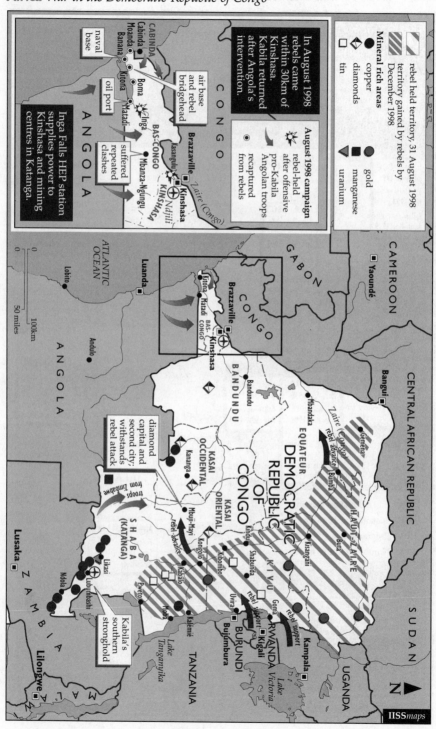

In August 1998 rebels came within 30km of Kinshasa. Kabila returned after Angola's intervention.

Mineral rich areas
- copper
- diamonds
- tin
- gold
- manganese
- uranium

rebel held territory, 31 August 1998
territory gained by rebels by December 1998

August 1998 campaign
- rebel-held after offensive
- rebel-held pro-Kabila
- Angolan troops recaptured from rebels

naval base

air base and rebel bridgehead

oil port

suffered repeated clashes

Inga Falls HEP station supplies power to Kinshasa and mining centres in Katanga.

diamond capital and second city: withstands rebel attack

Kabila's southern stronghold

troops from Zimbabwe

IISSmaps

Africa *Internationalisation of war in Central Africa*

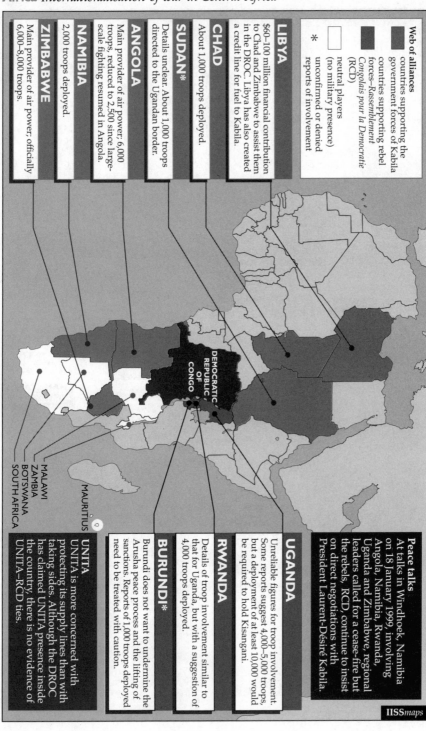

Web of alliances

- countries supporting the government forces of Kabila
- countries supporting rebel forces–*Rassemblement Congolais pour la Democratie* (RCD)
- neutral players (no military presence)
- unconfirmed or denied reports of involvement
- *

LIBYA
$60–100 million financial contribution to Chad and Zimbabwe to assist them in the DRROC. Libya has also created a credit line for fuel to Kabila.

CHAD
About 1,000 troops deployed.

SUDAN*
Details unclear. About 1,000 troops directed to the Ugandan border.

ANGOLA
Main provider of air power; 6,000 troops, reduced to 2,500 since large-scale fighting resumed in Angola.

NAMIBIA
2,000 troops deployed.

ZIMBABWE
Main provider of air power; officially 6,000–8,000 troops.

MALAWI
ZAMBIA
BOTSWANA
SOUTH AFRICA

MAURITIUS

Peace talks
At talks in Windhoek, Namibia on 18 January 1999, involving Angola, Namibia, Rwanda, Uganda and Zimbabwe, regional leaders called for a cease-fire but the rebels, RCD, continue to insist on direct negotiations with President Laurent-Désiré Kabila.

UGANDA
Unreliable figures for troop involvement. Some reports suggest 4,000–5,000 troops, but a deployment of at least 10,000 would be required to hold Kisangani.

RWANDA
Details of troop involvement similar to that for Uganda, but with a suggestion of 4,000 troops deployed.

BURUNDI*
Burundi does not want to undermine the Arusha peace process and the lifting of sanctions. Reports of 1,000 troops deployed need to be treated with caution.

UNITA
UNITA is more concerned with protecting its supply lines than with taking sides. Although the DROC has claimed UNITA presence inside the country, there is no evidence of UNITA–RCD ties.

DEMOCRATIC REPUBLIC OF CONGO

IISSmaps

World-wide *The proliferation of ballistic missiles*

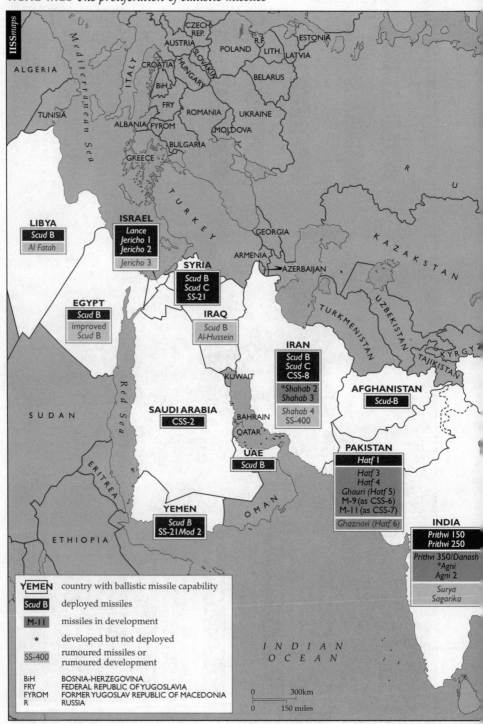

IISS*maps*

LIBYA
Scud B
Al Fatah

ISRAEL
Lance
Jericho 1
Jericho 2
Jericho 3

SYRIA
Scud B
Scud C
SS-21

EGYPT
Scud B
improved
Scud B

IRAQ
Scud B
Al-Hussein

IRAN
Scud B
Scud C
CSS-8
*Shahab 2
Shahab 3
Shahab 4
SS-400

AFGHANISTAN
Scud-B

SAUDI ARABIA
CSS-2

UAE
Scud B

PAKISTAN
Hatf 1
Hatf 3
Hatf 4
Ghauri (Hatf 5)
M-9 (as CSS-6)
M-11 (as CSS-7)
Ghaznavi (Hatf 6)

INDIA
Prithvi 150
Prithvi 250
Prithvi 350/Danosh
*Agni
Agni 2
Surya
Sagarika

YEMEN
Scud B
SS-21 Mod 2

YEMEN	country with ballistic missile capability
Scud B	deployed missiles
M-11	missiles in development
*	developed but not deployed
SS-400	rumoured missiles or rumoured development

BiH	BOSNIA-HERZEGOVINA
FRY	FEDERAL REPUBLIC OF YUGOSLAVIA
FYROM	FORMER YUGOSLAV REPUBLIC OF MACEDONIA
R	RUSSIA

INDIAN
OCEAN

0   300km
0   150 miles

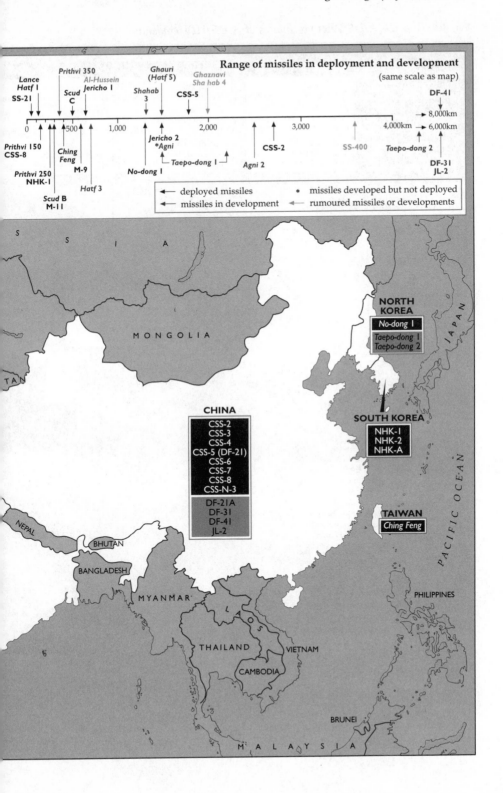

Range of missiles in deployment and development
(same scale as map)

Lance
Hatf I
SS-21

Prithvi 350
Scud
C
Jericho 1
Al-Hussein

Ghauri
(Hatf 5)
Shahab
3
Ghaznavi
Sha hab 4
CSS-5

DF-41

0   500   1,000   2,000   3,000   4,000km

→ 8,000km
→ 6,000km

Prithvi 150
CSS-8

Ching
Feng
M-9

Jericho 2
*Agni
Taepo-dong I
No-dong I
Agni 2
CSS-2
SS-400
Taepo-dong 2
DF-31
JL-2

Prithvi 250
NHK-1

Hatf 3

Scud B
M-11

←— deployed missiles   * missiles developed but not deployed
←—— missiles in development   ←— rumoured missiles or developments

NORTH KOREA
No-dong I
Taepo-dong I
Taepo-dong 2

CHINA
CSS-2
CSS-3
CSS-4
CSS-5 (DF-21)
CSS-6
CSS-7
CSS-8
CSS-N-3

DF-21A
DF-31
DF-41
JL-2

SOUTH KOREA
NHK-1
NHK-2
NHK-A

TAIWAN
Ching Feng

MONGOLIA

S S I A

TAN

NEPAL

BHUTAN

BANGLADESH

MYANMAR

LAOS

THAILAND   VIETNAM

CAMBODIA

PHILIPPINES

BRUNEI

M A L A Y S I A

JAPAN

PACIFIC OCEAN

World-wide *UNAIDS/WHO estimates of AIDS/HIV epidemic*

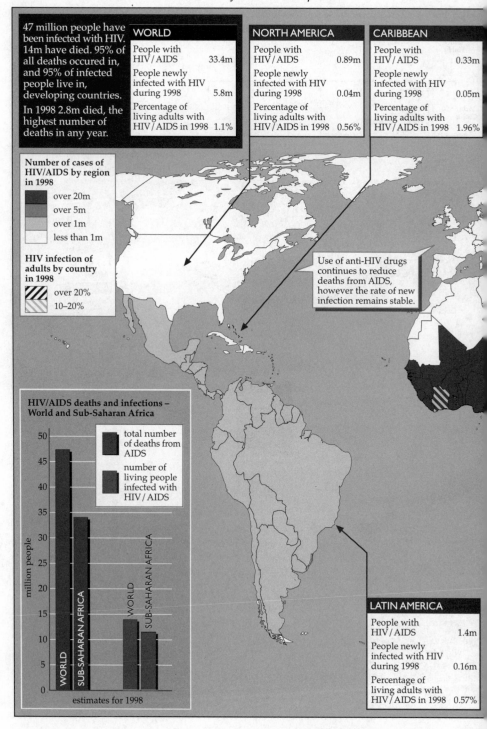

47 million people have been infected with HIV. 14m have died. 95% of all deaths occured in, and 95% of infected people live in, developing countries.
In 1998 2.8m died, the highest number of deaths in any year.

WORLD

People with HIV / AIDS	33.4m
People newly infected with HIV during 1998	5.8m
Percentage of living adults with HIV / AIDS in 1998	1.1%

NORTH AMERICA

People with HIV / AIDS	0.89m
People newly infected with HIV during 1998	0.04m
Percentage of living adults with HIV / AIDS in 1998	0.56%

CARIBBEAN

People with HIV / AIDS	0.33m
People newly infected with HIV during 1998	0.05m
Percentage of living adults with HIV / AIDS in 1998	1.96%

Number of cases of HIV/AIDS by region in 1998

- over 20m
- over 5m
- over 1m
- less than 1m

HIV infection of adults by country in 1998

- over 20%
- 10–20%

Use of anti-HIV drugs continues to reduce deaths from AIDS, however the rate of new infection remains stable.

HIV/AIDS deaths and infections – World and Sub-Saharan Africa

- total number of deaths from AIDS
- number of living people infected with HIV / AIDS

million people

estimates for 1998

WORLD
SUB-SAHARAN AFRICA
WORLD
SUB-SAHARAN AFRICA

LATIN AMERICA

People with HIV / AIDS	1.4m
People newly infected with HIV during 1998	0.16m
Percentage of living adults with HIV / AIDS in 1998	0.57%

WESTERN EUROPE

People with
HIV/AIDS   0.5m

People newly
infected with HIV
during 1998   0.03m

Percentage of
living adults with
HIV/AIDS in 1998   0.25%

NORTH AFRICA and MIDDLE EAST

People with
HIV/AIDS   0.21m

People newly
infected with HIV
during 1998   0.02m

Percentage of
living adults with
HIV/AIDS in 1998   0.13%

CENTRAL ASIA and EASTERN EUROPE

People with
HIV/AIDS   0.27m

People newly
infected with HIV
during 1998   0.08m

Percentage of
living adults with
HIV/AIDS in 1998   0.14%

AUSTRALIA and NEW ZEALAND

People with
HIV/AIDS   0.01m

People newly
infected with HIV
during 1998   0.00m

Percentage of
living adults with
HIV/AIDS in 1998   0.1%

Spread of HIV/AIDS through drug-injecting communites continues.

Although infection rates are low in some areas of Asia, more than 7 million are already infected.

Only 10% of the world's population live in Sub-Saharan Africa, yet 83% of all AIDS deaths, 95% of AIDS orphans and 90% of 1998's new infections have been in the region.

SUB-SAHARAN AFRICA

People with
HIV/AIDS   22.5m

People newly
infected with HIV
during 1998   4.0m

Percentage of
living adults with
HIV/AIDS in 1998   8.0%

SOUTH and SOUTH-EAST ASIA

People with
HIV/AIDS   6.7m

People newly
infected with HIV
during 1998   1.2m

Percentage of
living adults with
HIV/AIDS in 1998   0.69%

EAST ASIA and PACIFIC

People with
HIV/AIDS   0.56m

People newly
infected with HIV
during 1998   0.2m

Percentage of
living adults with
HIV/AIDS in 1998   0.06%

IISS*maps*

The Americas *Ecuador–Peru border dispute*

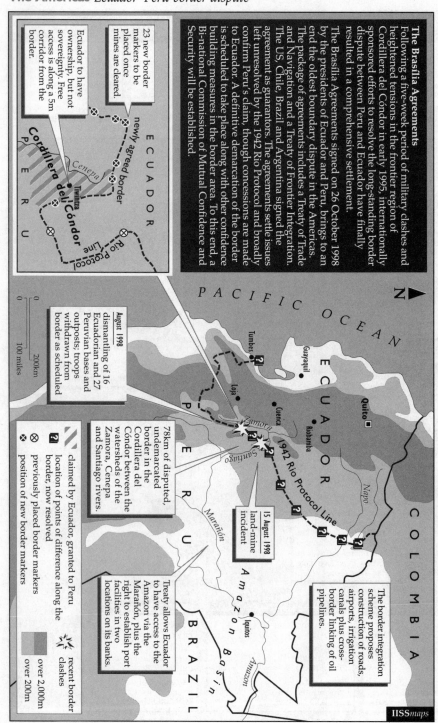

The Brasília Agreements

Following a five-week period of military clashes and heightened tensions in the frontier region of Cordillera del Cóndor in early 1995, internationally sponsored efforts to resolve the long-standing border dispute between Peru and Ecuador have finally resulted in a comprehensive settlement.

The Brasília Agreements signed on 26 October 1998 by the presidents of Ecuador and Peru, brings to an end the oldest boundary dispute in the Americas. The package of agreements includes a Treaty of Trade and Navigation and a Treaty of Frontier Integration. The US, Chile, Brazil and Argentina signed the agreement as guarantors. The agreements settle issues left unresolved by the 1942 Rio Protocol and broadly confirm Peru's claim, though concessions are made to Ecuador. A definitive demarcation of the border is scheduled to take place along with other confidence building measures in the border area. To this end, a Bi-national Commission of Mutual Confidence and Security will be established.

23 new border markers to be placed once mines are cleared.

Ecuador to have ownership, but not sovereignty. Free access is along a 5m corridor from the border.

ECUADOR

Cenepa

Tiwintza

Cordillera del Cóndor

PERU

newly agreed border

Rio Protocol Line

August 1998 dismantling of 16 Ecuadorian and 27 Peruvian bases and outposts; troops withdrawn from border as scheduled

78km of disputed, undemarcated border in the Cordillera del Cóndor between the watersheds of the Zamora, Cenepa and Santiago rivers.

15 August 1998 land-mine incident

The border integration scheme proposes construction of roads, airports, irrigation canals plus cross-border linking of oil pipelines.

Treaty allows Ecuador to have access to the Amazon via the Marañón, plus the right to establish port facilities in two locations on its banks.

claimed by Ecuador, granted to Peru

location of points of difference along the border, now resolved

previously placed border markers

position of new border markers

recent border clashes

over 2,000m

over 200m

PACIFIC OCEAN

Tumbes

Guayaquil

Loja

Cuenca

Quito

Riobamba

ECUADOR

Zamora

Santiago

Napo

1942 Rio Protocol Line

COLOMBIA

PERU

Marañón

Amazon Basin

Iquitos

Amazon

BRAZIL

N

0   100 miles
0   200km

IISSmaps